# STUDEBAKER CARS

**James H. Moloney**

*Motorbooks International*
Publishers & Wholesalers ®

First published in 1994 by Motorbooks International
Publishers & Wholesalers, PO Box 2, 729 Prospect Avenue,
Osceola, WI 54020 USA

© James H. Moloney, 1994

Motorbooks International books are also available at
discounts in bulk quantity for industrial or sales-
promotional use. For details write to Special Sales
Manager at the Publisher's address

Library of Congress Cataloging-in-Publication Data
Available

ISBN 0-87938-884-6

Printed and bound in the United States of America

# Many Thanks

To all who really gave me a big hand in getting this book completed on the deadline date, I want to give you a special THANK YOU!

First off, is my wife, Mary, who never once complained about all the clutter I created in various little packs and stacks that only I could identify and which mostly took over the dining area. For months, we ate our dinner on TV trays in our den. Then there is "Mr. Studebaker," himself . . . none other than the well-known Studebaker authority, Bill Cannon. Without Bill's help, we wouldn't have moved out of neutral. Thanks, Bill, for everything. I really appreciated all the days you sat there always ready to assist me. Then there is the party right here in Santa Barbara who put everything into her computer and, in no time, got things wound up to send off to Motorbooks International. This is the very accomplished Beverley Best who did a terrific job in putting everything in letter-perfect order. Finally, my good friend, George Dammann, who patiently worked with me for several years while I did the Encyclopedia of American Cars 1930-1942 and the Encyclopedia of American Cars 1946-1959. His help made this book much easier to complete. Thanks, Mary, Bill, Beverley and George!

Note: Prices quoted for the various models are according to factory pricing policy changes. Basic car price was the rule until 1937, when federal tax and more standard equipment was included in the "advertised delivered price". For 1948-57 cars, dealer car-conditioning cost was added. In all cases, they were factory prices at the point of manufacturer. As a general guide, dealer retail prices varied from 10% to 20% more. All weights quoted are factory shipping weight, excluding fuel, oil, and coolants. Individual prices and weights are for vehicles with standard equipment only, and all figures are quoted from authentic original sources.

# FOREWORD

Studebaker, the world's oldest manufacturer of highway vehicles, began in 1852. It was founded by two brothers of the Studebaker family — Henry and Clem. Their father, John Studebaker, of German descent, had been a blacksmith and wagon maker near Gettysburg, Pennsylvania, a place that later was destined to become a famous battleground.

In his shop, John heard much talk among men who had the "Western Fever" (then, the West was any place between the Alleghenies and the Mississippi River). Soon he caught the fever too, and decided to move Westward. He built three wagons, one of them of Conestoga Wagon style, and set out with his family for Ashland, Ohio. This was in 1835. But the family didn't prosper in Ashland in spite of hard work, so, in 1849, John Studebaker saddled a horse and rode out to look for a place farther west where opportunities might be a little better. He kept traveling until he came to South Bend, Indiana. There, the country seemed just about right for a new start in the wagon business.

In the vicinity of South Bend, there were forests of magnificent oak, hickory, ash, cherry and other woods suitable for wagon making. Nearby, small iron works could produce the iron that was needed. The surrounding rural districts were rich and productive. They would furnish the staples of life at low rates, while providing a market for Studebaker's wagons. New railroads were just being built which would provide a means for shipping in necessary raw material, and possibly carrying out the finished goods from the scene of production. And of great importance was the St. Joe River which would later furnish power for a flour mill and a hydraulic works. Yes, it would be a good place to start a new business, thought John Studebaker.

He returned to his family and reported what he had found. They decided to move gain. This time one of the young boys in the family, Clem, who was then 19, decided that he would go first to set up the new home. Upon his arrival, he did odd jobs and was given an opportunity to teach school because he knew how to read, write and calculate. Clem had already made a good beginning by the time the rest of the family reached South Bend.

Henry, Clem's oldest brother, quickly got work blacksmithing. These two brothers were ambitious and soon decided that they could get ahead faster by going into business together. They worked hard and managed to save $68. With this capital and two forges, they set up their own blacksmith shop in 1852. Henry was the woodworker and Clem the blacksmith. The first year's business included the construction of three new wagons plus wagon repairing, horseshoeing, and all the other usual activities of a country wagon and blacksmith shop.

Their father's motto was "labor omni vincit" (work overcomes all things) and it served his family well. An old newspaper clipping describes Henry and Clem thus, "They had clear heads, strong arms and honest hearts. They knew their business thoroughly. They put into their work the best of material and the best of skill."

Another brother, who was named John after his father, joined the gold rush and travelled out to California. When he found that he couldn't get rich by mining, he began to build wheelbarrows and other mining equipment. In 1858, he was persuaded by Henry and Clem to return to South Bend. He bought out Henry's share of the business upon his return, and was called Manager of Production because, in his travels throughout the country, he had learned the needs of the people who were pushing their way from the East to the West. He had foreseen that transportation would be the link that would join the vast sections of this country into one big unit. Here was the opportunity for expansion that his father had been seeking when he brought his family Westward. By now the Studebakers had a fairly substantial wagon plant in operation.

In 1863, Peter joined his brothers. He had had experience selling, so he became Sales Manager. At about this time, the Civil War came along and the Government needed supply wagons and gun carriages. The Studebaker brothers were asked if they would be able to provide such vehicles. "Yes," they said, and expanded their factory to build the military wagons. These wagons quickly gained a reputation for craftsmanship and durability, and as a result, there was a scattered demand throughout the country for Studebaker products after the war.

The business began to flourish and a few years later (1868) the Studebaker Bros. Mfg. Co. was formally organized under the statues of Indiana with a capital of $75,000, which was a substantial amount in that era. At this point, the company had a payroll of 190 men. Now, the youngest brother, redheaded Jacob, was taken into the firm as the head of the Carriage factory. As the factory grew, dealers and distributors were appointed throughout the United States. Before the turn of the century, Studebaker also had a representation in many foreign countries.

While the business of the brothers was expanding and pressing beyond the boundaries of America, a strange little carriage, which would run about the streets under its own power, was coming into existence. Obviously, there were many discussions about these mechanical vehicles. Some people even persisted in the view that human beings could not travel at speeds above 25 miles per hour and live, despite the fact that rapid advances in the railroad industry had pushed express train speeds upward of 60 MPH. There was both enthusiasm and much condemnation of the new horseless carriage invention.

Studebaker first gave serious consideration to this new vehicle at a director's meeting held on May 12, 1897. In the same year it built an experimental horseless carriage of its own. Engineering experiments continued during the next five years while the company was making bodies for electric runabouts produced by other companies. These bodies were very much like those previously built for horse-drawn carriages.

The first automobile show ever to be held in America

took place in Madison Square Garden in 1900, but Studebaker was not represented. Another show was held in Chicago in 1901. By this time, Studebaker was convinced that it should enter the automobile field and, in 1902, the first company-built electrics rolled out of the home factory. It was soon found that the range and power available from electric vehicles was fine for city usage, but could not satisfy the demands of early country roads and the relatively long distances between rural areas. Within a short time, these vehicles were confined largely to city use only, while the gasoline engine was being adapted for more general highway transportation service.

Beginning in 1904, the company sold the Studebaker-Garford gasoline car, the bodies being built by Studebaker and the chassis supplied on contract by the Garford Company.

By 1910, the company had combined with the Everett-Metzger-Flanders organization, and was manufacturing cars under the trade name of E-M-F. While this was a good car for its time, some people called it the "every morning fix."

In subsequent years, improved models of automobiles were sold under the name of Studebaker, and after the first World War, the company's manufacture of horse-drawn vehicles was discontinued.

This was the Ashland, Ohio blacksmith shop which the Studebaker Bros. used from 1835 until 1850, when they moved to South Bend. Note the rough-hewn construction of hand squared logs chinked with mud and rocks. This was true "log cabin" style.

This was the H. and C. Studebaker Factory. It was the first plant built in 1852 at Michigan and Jefferson Avenues in South Bend. Here the brothers both built and repaired Studebaker wagons. Of interest is the bell on the roof, which was an early fire alarm, and might also have been used to call workers to their job, since most craftsmen lived within earshot of their workplaces.

This facility was one of the original Ford plants in Detroit. Known as the Piquette Ave. Plant by Ford, it eventually became the main E.M.F. factory after Ford outgrew its confines. E.M.F. stood for the company's founders, Everitt, Metzger, and Flanders, though owners often referred to the initials as meaning "Every Morning Fix!"

This is the original Conestoga wagon now displayed in the Studebaker Museum. It was built in Pennsylvania by John Studebaker. He used the vehicle to move his family to Ohio.

# FOREWORD

In Pontiac, Michigan, this four-story building saw the manufacture of E.M.F. vehicles. Only car bodies were built here, and were then shipped to other plants for final assembly. At this time, E.M.F. was one of the major contenders in the automobile business.

This Studebaker manufacturing unit was referred to as Plant #3. Note the inscription on the building stating: Studebaker Corporation - Manufacturers of Automobiles. The smaller sign denotes the axle department for E.M.F. vehicles. Of interest are the two long wheelbase trucks, shown entering and along side the building. These sure don't look like Studebakers.

This building was referred to as Plant #4. The company apparently reserved the top floor for the Top Factory, which probably also included the upholstery department. The plant also included certain areas for the manufacture of Flanders cars.

The administration building for Studebaker was constructed in approximately 1910. Note the famous light fixtures which are at the front of the building, on the far left of the photo. This is where people posed with their new cars. The lights are seen many times in this book.

A Studebaker military vehicle used in the 1860s provided for the transportation of supplies. It differed very little from the freight or farm wagons also in production. The large lever above the front wheel is for the brakes, which acted on the rear wheels only.

The Studebaker Freight Wagon was built for heavy hauling. The photo caption states "Patent Steel Skeins will be put on all Thimble Skein Wagons when desired, and the height of the wheels will be made to suit all purchases." Prices varied accordingly. The "skeins" or top bows were removable, and in good weather could be taken down or left in the uncovered position as shown.

An early Studebaker wagon is carrying a family across the states. We've come a long way from here to the modern motorhome. Stop and think how hard travel must have been in those days. We get annoyed when a fanbelt breaks and the engine heats up on a freeway, or we are kept waiting a half hour on a turnpike due to a "fender bender."

Another military vehicle from the 1860s is waiting for the carriage department to install the canopy. Note the U.S. lettering on the front panel and the slanted side boards. These slanted boards allowed cargo to be loaded outside of the top bows, and also acted as mud splatter shields.

This is a typical Studebaker farm wagon. It was used for carrying grain, tools and even the family, if necessary. Be sure and notice the name on the side of the wagon. Of course, it's a Studebaker! Note that unlike the military version, the brakes on this wagon are foot operated.

8

# FOREWORD

The Police Patrol of the 1870s transported its "clients" in the rear compartment of the patrol unit. Of interest is the little item just behind the "C" cut of the driver's area. It looks like an electric spotlight, but in the 1870s there were no such things. Also interesting are the brake drums on the rear wheels. It appears that the patrol used solid rubber tires, which could not stand the pressure of standard brakes. Thus, these drums would have replaced the regular brake shoes that normally would have rubbed on the iron tires.

An aluminum wagon was tried in the 1870s. Note the hand-painted lettering in gold leaf on the sides of the wagon. It states, "Studebaker Brothers". It used a rosewood box, ash pole and steel tires. Little is known about aluminum wagons in this era, and this unit may have been an experimental model, a show vehicle for county fairs, or part of a small but expensive run. In this era, aluminum was a relatively expensive metal, and not generally thought of as suitable for farm wagons.

The Studebaker Bros. Mfg. Co. of South Bend catalogued this light bobsled with a body 6 feet, 6 inches to 7 feet long. The sled was fitted with two lazy-back cushioned seats and a pole or shaft for a 2-horse team. It, too, is on display at the South Bend museum.

This is General Grant's carriage in front of the Studebaker administration building on a day of South Bend celebration. Since no date was included with the photo, it is not known if the real General/President Grant is seated in the back, or if the bearded man is a look-alike appearing for the festivities.

This piece of equipment is a Studebaker Cutter for snow riding. It's on display in the Studebaker museum in South Bend. The 2-passenger sled lacks its upholstered seat and its harness. This was probably a one-horse vehicle.

This elegant piece of equipment is well liveried for President William Henry Harrison. Called a "Hansom" or a "Brougham," this piece of equipment is part of the memorabilia in the Studebaker museum. It is not known if Studebaker built pretentious coaches of this type as a general rule or only on special order. For that matter, it is not certain if they even did the total construction on such units, or if they farmed the coach part out to other builders. However, the company did list such expensive "city coaches" in their general catalog.

This wagon won the Gold Medal and First Award of Merit at the Centennial International World Exposition held in Philadelphia in 1876. It was exhibited also at the New Orleans Exposition with the note: "To Old Hickory, the Hero of New Orleans, Studebaker Brothers sends this "Young Hickory" from Indiana."

This example proved to be one of Studebaker's best products in its age of buggy manufacturing. The model was called the "Izzer" buggy. It was produced from the 1850s to 1919. The Izzer name was given by farmers who were tired of has-beens. "I don't want a Wuzzer, I want an Izzer" was said by a farmer one day and the name stuck for this type of buggy. During the years of production, approximately 10,000 a year were manufactured.

The Standard Oil Co. used this type of transporting wagon during the 1870s to 1900, primarily to carry 30 and 50 gallon barrels of kerosene to local vendors. The wheels were made of steel. Note the height of the driver's seat.

Studebaker Bros. of South Bend, Indiana produced this style of buggy, from 1885 until they started with electric vehicles at the turn of the century. The company advertised Light Buggies, Heavy Buggies, Top and Open Buggies in their catalogs, and all received a guarantee of "work done with satisfaction."

# FOREWORD

The familiar slogan of the Borax Twenty Mule Team of popular soaps and cleaning powders is seen here in a recreation of one of their early day events. The scene is taking place in South Bend, at the Studebaker factory with the Studebaker-built wagons. The wagons are advertising that Borax was used for toilet, laundry, household, and medicinal use. What percentage of the wagons and harnesses of these huge teams was actually built by Studebaker is unknown, but at least here the company seems to be taking full credit for the entire rig.

A heavy duty freight wagon of this type was mainly used to transport items such as furniture from store to customers home, or machinery from the freight depot to a local mill. This was not a vehicle for a light team of horses. Working with equipment such as this gave the teamsters their reputation for strength and toughness.

Delivery wagons of this type were used by the Grand Union Tea Co. in South Bend. This type of vehicle was well constructed and served all kinds of merchants in the latter 19th Century. But, they were probably best known for their roles in house-to-house milk delivery.

Here we see the Studebaker canopy surrey in front of the Studebaker mansion at Tippecanoe. This surrey was in production from 1907 to 1911. The equipment sold for $500 including the fancy fringed top. Oil lamps on the sides provided some illumination for rare night usage.

# FOREWORD

A view of the Studebaker carriage line shows the craftsmanship and rigid inspection of carriages being completed. The Studebaker Brothers motto was "Always give a little more than you promise."

John Studebaker...the all important one. He was the father of the Studebaker boys that eventually created the South Bend corporation. John Studebaker lived from 1799 to 1887. His five sons were: Henry, Clement, John Mohler, Peter, and Jacob.

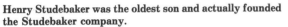

Henry Studebaker was the oldest son and actually founded the Studebaker company.

Clement Studebaker became the president of the Studebaker Brothers Corporation. He lived from 1831-1901.

Rebecca Mohler Studebaker was the mother of the five brothers. She lived from 1801 to 1887. Of old stock German heritage, she was probably well versed in using that spinning wheel.

# FOREWORD

Peter Studebaker was the sales manager for the firm, and later became the treasurer. He lived from 1836 to 1897.

The third Studebaker brother was John Mohler. He was basically in charge of wagon production in the early years. He also became a great promoter of industrial history in Indiana.

Jacob Studebaker was the treasurer of the company. He lived from 1844 to 1887. Upon his death, his office was taken over by brother Peter.

A familiar photo shows the five Studebaker brothers. In the background is a painting of where all five boys grew up in the early years. It shows a log cabin which was located on Pleasant Ridge, in Ashland, Ohio. Sadly, none of the five brothers lived to see Studebaker automobile production or the vast empire which proudly bore their name through the middle of the 20th Century.

# FOREWORD

Harold S. Vance helped pick up the sales of the corporation in the early 1930s and went on to be one Studebaker's top executives.

Paul G. Hoffman was known as "Mr. Studebaker" from the 1930s, until his resignation in April, 1948. At that time, he became director of the Marshall Plan, which is credited with being the financial salvation of post-war Europe.

Albert Russell Erskine joined Studebaker in 1911 and rose to the head of the firm, remaining there until his untimely death in 1933. The Erskine car was named in his honor, but sadly, the car was a failure.

Harold Churchill was one of the best liked people among the top executives at Studebaker. He worked his way up the ladder to chief engineer and later president of the corporation. He resigned when heavy clouds were hanging over the management at Studebaker.

Sherwood Egbert came in at a bad time at Studebaker. Trying to put the company back on its feet once again, he was often thought of as a real promoter. Unfortunately, with the many pressures put upon him, he didn't remain at Studebaker as long as he should have. Cancer took him in 1969 at the early age of 48.

# 1902

Shown here is what is credited as being a 1902 Studebaker Electric out for a test spin on the original proving ground . . . which was a board track. If the photo is correctly identified, this is the first prototype of what would become the 1902 Studebaker Electric Runabout. However, the true 1902 models all seem to have been equipped with wire spoke wheels rather than the wood spokes seen here.

Supposedly this was the second Studebaker Electric to leave the factory in 1902. The vehicle was purchased by Thomas Edison. Allegedly, this photo was sent by Charles Edison, son of Thomas, to A. R. Erskine in 1930. The photo shows Thomas Edison and his business associate, George Meister, in the chain-driven electric vehicle. The car is of Stanhope design, with the squared frontal area, which indicates that it was probably a 4-passenger model. Well outfitted for any type of driving, it has top, coach lamps, and interesting headlight that could be either propane or electric.

John Mohler Studebaker is shown sitting next to an unidentified man holding the tiller. He's probably reflecting on the vehicles he and his brothers have produced from the days of their first horse-drawn wagons. Or maybe he is thinking of the amazing horseless vehicles still to come. This electric was preferred by Studebaker over the noisy gasoline vehicles. In fact, it might be the same 1902 prototype shown here, or it may be an early 1902 production model, as the leather rear fenders of this car are different than those on the other model.

The 1902-1904 Studebaker Electric Runabout claimed to be noiseless and easy running. The motor was suspended in the body, above the springs, to avoid all jarring. The company claimed that superior spring suspension excelled that of all other makes when it came to the pleasure and comfort of its occupants, and also prolonged the life of the car, and reduced the cost of repairs. All the Studebaker electrics of these years were capable of traveling 40 miles without a recharge. Shown here are the various styles of electric models available during this period. Prices were only available to the customer, upon request.

The Stanhope offered far more elaborate coachwork than did the Runabout. It was priced at about $1,100 if built in 2-passenger form, or about $50 more if a 4-passenger. All Studebaker electrics used Westinghouse motors of approximately 1.7 horsepower, which would give the cars a top speed ranging from 13 to 16 mph.

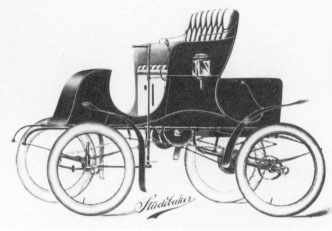

The Trap was essentially another form of Runabout, but with slightly fancier body work. It could be fitted with a leather top, if desired. As can be seen, all of these early Studebakers evolved directly from their horse-drawn counterparts. Lever steering was used on all models. The foot-operated brake worked on a drum on the rear axle.

The Stanhope is shown here without its optional leather top. Probably most buyers felt that they would never take their vehicles out in inclement weather in the first place, and thus did not need a top. Therefore, these units were made an option for many years. Coach lights meant that the vehicle could be seen at night, but gave scant light for the driver to see by. But again, it is doubtful if many vehicles were ever operated after dark in these early days of motoring.

A photo taken from the Studebaker archives shows this 1902-05 chassis for the light electric automobile. The view illustrates the fore and aft distribution of the battery weight, the spring suspension, the motor suspended from two horseshoe-shaped braces which would be hidden by the seat, and the rheostat control lever. The steering tiller and brake pedal are missing.

An example of a 1904 Studebaker Electric has the special leather top in the up position to help protect its two passengers. John Mohler Studebaker preferred these electric models until his death, rather than the gasoline powered cars which came about in 1904. This model was called the Victoria or Victoria Phaeton. It was a longer and much more elaborate version of the Stanhope, with its leather fenders running in a sweeping curve from front to rear and its body in the high-styled "French curves" so popular in this ear. With the top, and fitted with Exide batteries, it cost $1,600. However, when fitted with the optional Edison batteries, it went up $175 to a total of $1,775.

This example was referred to as the 1902-1907 Studebaker No. 13A Special High Speed Electric Stanhope. Essentially a variation of the 2-passenger Stanhope, it had higher gearing and an extra rheostat speed to allow faster travel. Of course, the higher speed greatly reduced the overall range of the car. All regular models used a rheostat with four speeds. On this type of electric car, there was no way to smoothly accelerate up to cruising speed.

# 1904-1907

Even though this book is basically dealing with Studebaker passenger cars, some of the early examples of rare Studebaker trucks are worth mentioning. Here is a 3-ton electric truck for 1906, referred to as No.2010-A. Besides building gasoline and electric passenger vehicles, the company also built delivery wagons and trucks that ranged from 1,000 pounds to 5-ton capacity. Top speed was about 15 mph for this unit. It used twin Westinghouse electric motors, one for each rear wheel.

Studebaker's first gasoline-powered car appeared in 1904. It was a 2-cylinder unit and was called Model 202 or Model C. The wheelbase measured 82 inches, which was 20 inches longer than the electric Runabout. The engine developed 16-horsepower. In 1905, the same car was offered, but the model designation was changed to 9502. The company had supposedly built two other models starting in late 1903, but these were not promoted, and are usually considered prototype vehicles. Chassis of these cars were built by the Garford Co. of Elyria, Ohio, and shipped to South Bend, where Studebaker installed the bodies. The cars were marketed under both the "Studebaker" and "Studebaker-Garford' names.

In 1906 Studebaker came out with its first closed car. It was the Electric Model 22-F Coupe, which delivered for $1,800. It was catalogued as "A Remarkable Car at a Remarkable Price." Of 4-passenger design, it featured a regular bench seat, plus two fold-down auxiliary seats by the dash. It offered a 15 mph top speed and a 35 mile driving range.

Studebaker's Suburban for 1905 was referred to as "the adaptable car." It was available as a Runabout; Combination Passenger Car, and/or Baggage Car (with the removal of the rear passenger seat), and as a Light Four-Passenger Car. These models were gas powered by a new 4-cylinder engine of 212 cubic inches that developed 20 horsepower. The engine was located under the hood.

In 1906, this Studebaker-Garford was produced in limited quantities, selling for $3,000. This was Model F-28 which offered a seating capacity for 5-passengers. Its 4-cylinder engine offered 30 horsepower from a 280 cubic-inch displacement.

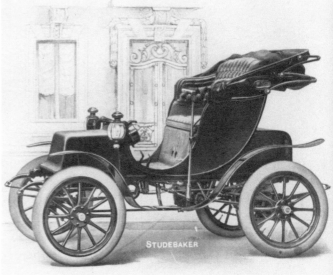

A slightly different example of the Studebaker Electric for 1907 is this version, which was referred to as Model 16-A and came with a different top mechanism. It is classed as an Electric Victoria Phaeton.

This 1906 Studebaker-Garford Runabout photo was taken in the mid-1930s. Notice near new 1934 and 1936 Chevrolets in the background. I wonder if the Garford was speeding through town and the citation is being accepted graciously? As a Studebaker-Garford, this car fell into the G-30 series, but after 1908 it was also sold as the Garford Model A.

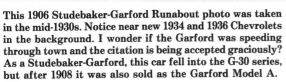

This 1906 Studebaker-Garford F-28 is basically the same car as described earlier, but small changes were made during the model run, even in those days. Note the example is not equipped with a side-mounted spare, which would have been an extra-cost accessory. It's not certain if the carbide headlamps and generator were standard items, or were written in at a cost above the base $3,000.

This 1906 example of the F-28 Side Entrance Tourer has an early DeVille-style top, which at least protected the rear-seat passengers. This was a 30 horsepower vehicle coming on a 104-inch wheelbase. It delivered for $3,000 and weighed 2,700 pounds.

This is a Model G-30 1907 Studebaker-Garford. This 30-horsepower vehicle came on a 104-inch wheelbase. Also available was a Model G-28, a 28-horsepower unit coming on the same wheelbase. Studebaker-Garfords played an important spot with the Washington D.C. political celebrities. President Taft had them for his entourage of cabinet members, and a few senators drove them, too. Not cheap, these cars were priced at about $3,700 without the top.

# 1907

This 1907 Studebaker Electric 14-Passenger Omnibus carried the model designation of 2006-E. It continued to be produced through 1909. The vertical steering wheel kept the driver in an erect position while transporting his customers. Of 14-passenger capacity, vehicles of this type were used most often as hotel buses, transporting guests between rail stations and resort or upscale hotels. Due to their limited range, they were seldom used on traditional bus routes.

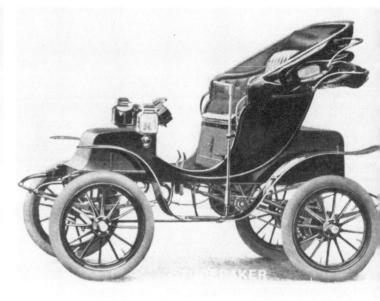

Also known as the Electric Victoria Phaeton, but with a different model designation, this example was called Model 16-D for 1907. This version was carried over for more than just a one-year model run. The main differences between the two Victorias seems to be in the design of the forward battery box, in the coach lights, and in the type of upholstery.

Offered for 1907 was this Model 2000 Electric Omnibus. The 14-passenger vehicle had a load capacity of 2,500 pounds and came on a 111-inch wheelbase. The roof rack gave added space for the passengers' luggage. The large box suspended beneath the body contained the banks of batteries necessary to move the heavy vehicle. Notice that on this bus, unlike on the first example, the motors are located to the rear of the back wheels.

This 1907 Electric truck was classed as Model 2009-A. With a load capacity of 2 tons, this vehicle had a top speed of 8 mph and could travel 30 miles before a charge was required. The wheelbase was 116 inches and empty it tipped the scale at 6,800 pounds. The wheel measurement was 36 inches, with solid rubber tires that were 5 inches.

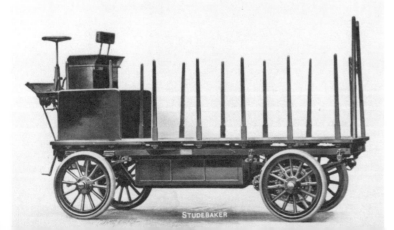

Here is a 3-1/2 ton Studebaker Electric Truck Model 2010-A. The vehicle had a weight capacity of 8,400 pounds. Its speed limit was 7 mph and it could travel 30 miles between charges. The front tires measured 5 inches diameter while the rears were 6 inches, both of solid rubber.

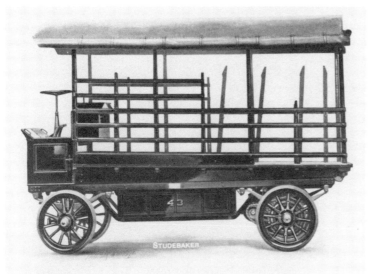

An Electric Model 2010-B for 1907 with a canopy top. This vehicle weighed 8,500 pounds and came on a 127-inch wheelbase. It, like its other brother leviathans, travelled approximately 7 mph and could go about 30 miles before needing a charge. Trucks of this type were virtually indestructible, and some were even in use in industrial and warehouse districts right up to W.W. II.

The Electric Delivery Van for 1907 was called the Model 2011-A. Its load capacity was 500 pounds. The vehicle weighed 2,900 pounds and, with its lightness, could get up to 40 miles before a charge was required. Its top speed was 12 mph. The wheels measured 30 inches and tires were 2 -inch  diameter, made of solid rubber.

This 1907 Model 2012-A Electric truck had a load capacity of 5 tons. This unit weighed 9,700 pounds and had a wheelbase of 126 inches. Its wheels measured 36 inches and tires were 7 inches across, made of solid rubber. Not designed for long hauls, when loaded it travelled no more than 25 miles before a charge was needed. And this was within a speed range of 1-to-6 mph. Judging by the size of that steering wheel, some brute force was needed to turn corners with this baby.

Since Studebaker was already producing horse-drawn ambulances, it was natural that it would soon offer its new electrics in a similar role. This rear view illustrates the Studebaker Electric Ambulance interior. This example was called Model 2004-A for 1907. The wicker stretcher and space for the attendant are neatly displayed. However, medical or first aid equipment is totally lacking. The rear door windows would slide down to sill level, being regulated by straps and notches.

Seen here is the 1907-1908 Studebaker Electric Model 17-B Coupe. It is fitted with drop windows especially adapted to all kinds of weather, and a solid coupe body of the "Telephone booth" school of design. Studebaker referred to this model as essentially an "all-year around" car. It became a favorite of wealthy and mature women and professional people, both because of its comfort, and its ease of operation.

This 1907-1908 Studebaker Electric is the Model 17-E Landaulet with what the factory termed a "Standing Front". This example sold for $2,300. In effect, it was the company's first true "convertible" model, featuring a total weather-tight interior combined with the option of putting the top down in nice weather. The roof portion above the doors and windshield was solid, and the top butted up against this header.

The 1907-1908 Studebaker Electric Model 17-C Landaulet was also catalogued as the "Folding Front Model." It was available for the same $2,300 price as the Standing Front model. On this car, the windshield dropped into the dash panel, while the solid roof portion can be seen resting on and attached to the folded top.

The 1907-08 Studebaker-Garford 7-passenger Touring Car saw a slight increase in the cubic-inch displacement of its 4-cylinder engine. For the two-year run, it now offered a 285 cubic-inch displacement. Known as the Model H, this example delivered, minus windshield and top, for approximately $3500.

Here is the 1907-1908 Studebaker Electric, Model 17-D Victoria Phaeton. This example came equipped with a gypsy quartered full hand-buffed leather top, with removable side curtains. It was the most expensive model of this group of 1907-1908 vehicles, delivering for $2,400. Owners of electrics, many who were women and elderly men, preferred them to gas vehicles because they did not have to be cranked, could run in freezing weather, and did not require the skills of manipulating what was considered a complicated arrangement of clutch and transmission controls.

A 1907-1908 Studebaker-Garford Model "H" had its tool box right by the right rear door, which also helped make it easy for exiting from the car. Studebaker used a high quality of leather for its seat material on these models, and the cars were noted for their excellent body work.

The 1908 Studebaker-Garford, as described before, was a popular car for those in high political positions. Here is Charles Evans Hughes, then Governor of New York, and his military staff riding in the Studebaker Garford Model A. The vehicle was a 5-passenger model with a 4-cylinder engine that developed 30 horsepower. It delivered for $3,500 in base form. With a windshield and top, an additional $160 was added to the price.

Looking virtually the same as the 1907 Garford 30 is this example known as a 1908 Garford Model "B". It developed 40 horsepower from the 4-cylinder engine. It sold for $4,000 or $4,150 if a top was ordered. The body was by Studebaker, but the car was marketed from Garford's plant at Elyria, Ohio, as an independent make, without the Studebaker name.

A couple of 1908 Studebaker-Garfords are shown parked in front of the Studebaker mansion at Tippecanoe. This event took place in October, 1908. In the cars are government people and various members of the Studebaker family. Both cars are fitted with aftermarket windshields, with the top portion folded down. These units were available at extra cost from most Studebaker dealers.

This is a 1908 Studebaker-Garford Limousine or Town Car in the Model "H" Series of Cars. It was the largest of the "H" models, coming on a 107-inch wheelbase. It sold for $4,200. One-half of the partition between the tonneau and the front could be slid open, to allow passengers to talk or give directions to the driver.

Here is a 1908 Model 16-D Electric Victoria Phaeton. The electrics were now capable of doing about 20 m.p.h at top speed. Built on a wheelbase of 69 inches, these were the most plush of the open electric models. It is not known if the fold-down third seat by the dash board was an option or a standard item on this model.

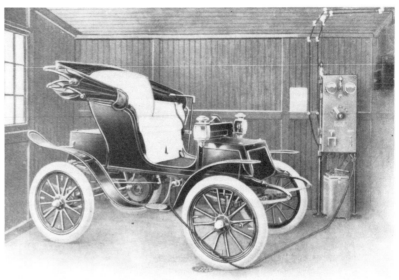

This is a 1908 Electric Stanhope Coupe known as the Model 22-C. The vehicle's total simplicity made it one owners enjoyed traveling in for short about-town sojourns. It was priced at $1,500, but the folding leather top was a $25 option.

This is the Model 22-C Stanhope Phaeton for 2-passengers. This tiller-driven vehicle is being recharged in the owners garage with a deluxe piece of charging equipment. Such rectifiers were necessary for owners of electrics, and were usually sold by the dealer in conjunction with the car sale. Because few rural areas of this time had electricity, these electric cars were virtually restricted to city streets. This model delivered for $1,500.

This three-quarter rear view of a 1908 Model "16" Electric Victoria Phaeton gives a close up look at how the top folded. The soft leather top wore well on these vehicles if a preservative like early Neats Foot Oil was applied at regular intervals. Probably in deference to the timid driving habits of electric car buyers, almost all such vehicles retained tiller steering, as opposed to the steering wheels common on virtually all gas-powered cars.

This Model "A" Studebaker-Garford was actually a 1907 model carried over into the 1908-09 years. This 5-passenger Touring Car used the early 280 cubic-inch displacement engine developing 30 horsepower. It like most other Garfords ranged in the $4,000 price bracket. In 1908 it was sold as both a Garford and a Studebaker-Garford, with absolutely no change in the vehicle except on the nameplate.

Another style for the 1907-1909 years is this Model "H" 30-horsepower Touring Car. In base form, this vehicle delivered for approximately $3,800, although price figures do conflict from source to source. The top assembly, which many ordered, cost an additional $150.

# 1909

Designated as Model 2008-A is this Electric Express Wagon with top. It's load capacity was 2,500 pounds. The vehicle "cruised" at speeds of 2 to 9 mph. It could travel 35 miles per charge. The wheelbase measured 111 inches and it weighed 5,150 pounds empty. Its wheels measured 36 inches, and the tires were hard rubber.

"One pachyderm to another," could be the caption as this creature stands on the deck of the 2 ton electric truck. Even in the early days, Studebaker liked to keep its name in front of the public with publicity photos and stunts such as this. Obviously, the company name is nicely implanted on the side of the truck. The driver looks as if he doesn't quite trust the load.

The Studebaker factory brought out this Electric 2-ton vehicle for an early 4th of July parade. The unit carries a selection of toy wagons, also manufactured by the firm, and supposedly shows the Studebaker transition from wagons to automobiles. It is very likely that the children on board are those of employees.

This 1909 Studebaker Electric was displayed during the New York World's Fair in 1940. The owner referred to his vehicle as "Tommy". Note the large Exide battery box under the driver's compartment. The car wears Firestone tires that appear to be almost new. That they carry an inner tube is obvious from the stem in the wheel. Apparently the solid rubber gave up after years of use. This jitney-type vehicle was not a cataloged model. Its unusual design of placing passengers fore and aft of the driver hints that it is probably a one-off or a very limited production design from some unknown body shop.

The 1909 Studebaker-Garford Model "C" Limousine held seven passengers. The 4-cylinder engine developed 30 horsepower. The car came on a 104-inch wheelbase. Roll-up side curtains would protect the front seat occupants in bad weather.

# 1909

Here is the 1909 Studebaker-Garford Model "D" Landaulet. The rear portion of the tonneau compartment collapsed neatly, leaving a center section in a stationary position. The Model D came with a 4-cylinder Garford engine that developed 40 horsepower.

This 1909 Studebaker-Garford Model "C" Touring Car came both as 5 and 7 passenger vehicles. This example is a 5-passenger model that developed 30 horsepower. Its wheelbase was two inches shorter than the Limousine, coming on a 102-inch chassis. A top and windshield were not part of the package, but could be ordered separately.

The 1909 Model "D" Touring Car was only available as a 7-passenger model. It was built on a 104-inch wheelbase, the same as Limousine models. The "D" vehicles used a 285 cubic-inch engine developing 40 horsepower. Note its jump seats between front and rear compartments. It does not appear that these were of the fold-up type as found in the 7-passenger Model C, but look to be permanently fixed seats with an aisle between for the rear seat passengers.

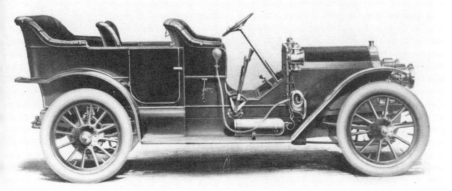

This 1909 Studebaker-Garford Model C Suburban also was a 30 horsepower vehicle. The rear seat of this model was easily removed, creating an area for more storage and in effect, turning the vehicle into a light pickup truck. The top could easily be placed in the up position, but would have to be removed when the rear seat was taken out. The top cost an additional $160, the same as on the other Garfords of this era. In a sense, this was a very early form of the depot hack, a transitional vehicle that eventually led to the development of today's station wagon design.

The 1909 Studebaker-Garford chassis gives a detailed view of its 4-cylinder engine compartment and transmission. The Model "D" chassis came equipped with a pressed steel frame offering more strength to the body of the vehicle. In 1908, Garford marketed this chassis along with fully-bodied cars under the name "Garford." However, Studebaker, which was marketing the same vehicles under the "Studebaker-Garford" name, objected, and Garford withdrew its title, allowing all cars top use the Studebaker-Garford nomenclature exclusively.

MODEL "D" 40 HORSE-POWER CHASSIS

A 1909 Model "C" Roadster was generally classed as a 2-passenger vehicle, but did offer a small "dickey" directly behind the front compartment, which gave seating for a third passenger. That third seat often was called the "Mother-in-Law" seat. This example offered a 30-horsepower engine.

The 1909 Studebaker-Garford Model "C" was available as a Close-Coupled Car. In this model, the arrangement of the seats was closer together. The vehicle used a 104-inch wheelbase and developed 30 horsepower from the 285 cubic-inch 4-cylinder engine.

The Model "B" 7-passenger Touring Car came on a longer wheelbase of 107 inches, making it the largest car for the two-year span. It also used the larger engine of 285 cubic-inches that developed 40 horsepower. The car did not have a windshield as such, but a roll-up curtain with a celluloid window could be dropped in the event of bad weather. But since this celluloid was so difficult to see through, the curtain was usually left rolled up unless definitely needed.

This shot shows the intake side of a 1909 Model "A" 30 horsepower engine. The Garford factory stated the lower half of the aluminum crankcase could be easily removed without disturbing the rest of the engine. The engine was of "T head" design, with the intake valves on one side of the cylinder and the exhaust valves on the other. The valves, which were interchangeable, were operated by dual camshafts. Timing gears ran in brass bearings, while the gears themselves were of fiber with brass shrouds.

The 1909-1910 E.M.F. was classed as the Model C Roadster. It saw production from November, 1908, to June of 1913. A total of 49,399 E.M.F. vehicle were produced during this time frame. With the help of E.M.F., Studebaker ranked in 4th place for 1910.

Available for 1909-10 and likely until the final days with only minimal changes was this Model "20" Flanders, called the 3-speed Suburban. Selling for $800, the vehicle featured a detachable rear seat in order to provide for more luggage or cargo space. The tire size for Flanders cars was 30x3 inches.

It appears that J. L. Carpenter was the agent not only for the E.M.F., but Stearns, according to the dealership sign in the background. This E.M.F. might be leaving the dealership for its first day's outing, as it looks brand new. The event took place in the 1909-1910 era. Interestingly, Studebaker could claim it was the first company to offer a factory recall on their cars. This was done in 1910. The factory replaced the 2-speed transmission with a 3-speed unit, due to the problem of the 2-speed ratio snapping the driveshaft in half.

The 1909-1910 scene probably was also a delivery photo of this E.M.F. vehicle. Note the small dog on the top boot. Is he also getting ready for the ride? This vehicle appears to have been delivered without a windshield. Besides this model, Flanders offered other body styles all in the price range from $750 to $800 price bracket.

The Model 22-G Coupe for 1910 was little changed from the 1906 version. The vehicle operated from a single Westinghouse motor, and carried 970-pounds of Exide batteries in both front and rear compartments. It sold for $1,850, including both a solid removable Coupe top and a folding "Summer Top" of natural leather.

An Electric Model "17-B" Coupe for 1910 was a vehicle that adapted well to all types of weather. Because of this, it was termed an "all year vehicle." The Coupe came with what Studebaker termed "drop windows," which allowed the door and side window glass to lower to sill level through the use of straps and notches. On some models, the front glass (windshield) also could be lowered in a similar manner. It was meant for 2-passenger travel, although many units carried a folding front seat for a third passenger.

For 1910, the Electric Runabout looked basically the same as its predecessors. This example carried the designation of Model "22-A." It was a 2-passenger vehicle chiefly for short excursions, limited of course by its need for frequent battery charges.

A 1910 Flanders "20" is departing from the Flanders' dealership with "Rin Tin Tin" in the passenger seat. The excursion was to Death Valley, California. The vehicle is equipped with United States Tires which, I assume, are the same as U.S. Tires. If so, they really wore well as, through the years, we had U.S. Royal Tires on several cars, and never was there a tire that didn't give excellent mileage.

A clear view of the E.M.F. "30" chassis shows the details of the running gear. A two-speed transmission on the rear axle was used on E.M.F. and Flanders cars. Front fenders were flat across the top, while the rear units had a slight upward flare at their tips.

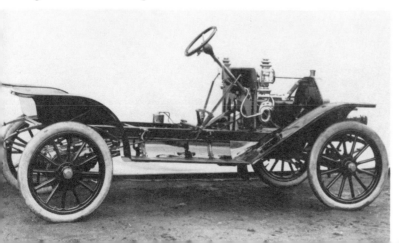

Similar to car manufacturers today, having models over-lapping one another was true even in 1910. Shown here is a Flanders "20" 3-Speed Roadster, looking quite similar to the E.M.F. Fore-Door Roadster. This example carries a tool chest on its running board while the Fore-Door example concealed it within the machine. This Speed Roadster also came without doors, as opposed to the side panels on the Fore-Door. It sold for $750 with two oil sidelamps, oil taillight, and bulb horn. The windshield and top were extra cost items, as were the headlights. The Flanders was built as a make separate from the E.M.F. Priced lower than the E.M.F., it was produced only from 1910 to 1912 when it too became part of Studebaker's buy-out of the overall Everitt-Metzger-Flanders Corp. of Detroit.

Parked in front of the Studebaker, E.M.F. and Flanders dealership in 1910, is this Flanders Model "20" Runabout. This example was equipped with the removable rear seat, which has been removed on this example in order to provide added storage space. This version delivered for $750.

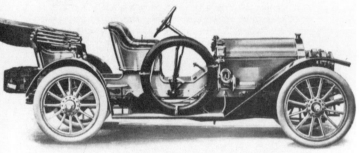

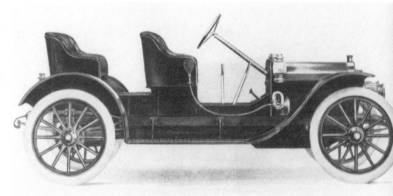

The Studebaker-Garford 40-horsepower Tourabout for 1910-1911 was also known as a G-8. This example was also priced in the $4,000 market, even though it wasn't as impressive looking as the 7-passenger Touring. At this point, all Studebaker-Garford cars used right-hand steering. Tourabouts were the sports cars of the day.

A 1910 Studebaker Flanders Model "20" was available either as a 2-passenger Speedster for $750, or as this 4-passenger example for $790. Flanders' sales amounted to better than 30,000 units during its years of production beginning January 1, 1910, and ending in June of 1913.

It is enjoyable to look at this photo for all the things the dealership offers besides cars for sale. The agency is referred to as the South Bend Automobile and Garage Company. The dealership, besides selling Studebakers, Flanders "20", and Studebaker Electric cars, also sold road guides and an array of parts and accessories like spark plugs, horns, lamps, and various other bits of potpourri, as displayed in the window.

This 1910-1911 Studebaker-Garford 40 horsepower Speed Car was a sporty-looking vehicle offering seating for 3-passengers. The small jump-seat at the rear could be removed if luggage needed to be placed in that area. Known as "mother-in-law" seats, these removable one-passenger affairs were in a sense the forerunners of the rumble seat.

Seen here is the 1910-11 Studebaker-Garford Touring for seven passengers. This example was called the G-40. The G represented Garford, and 40 was the horsepower it developed. This view shows the roomy tonneau with the auxiliary seats that were referred to as "collapsible disappearing seats." The expensive vehicle sold in the $4,000 category.

The 1910-1911 Studebaker-Garford Touring, referred to technically as a G-7, was among the most expensive models of the year, selling for $4,000. If the Cape Top was ordered, it delivered for $4,175. The Series "G" cars were built on a 117.5-inch wheelbase. Also available this year were the Model H and Model M 5-passenger tourers on a 104-inch wheelbase.

Available in 1910 and 1911 was this Studebaker-Garford Tourabout. This example was known as Model G-7. It was technically built only in 1910, but sales continued into 1911. It looked very similar to a G-8, but had enough body differences to warrant being considered a separate model. The spare tire mount is on the running board next to the driver as on the G-8 version, but the tire itself is missing from this example. The 1911 model year saw the end of the Garford models, as far as Studebaker was concerned, as a takeover of the E.M.F. cars gave Studebaker a new source of chassis. Garford, meanwhile, went its own way as an independent make, but only lasted until 1913.

The largest vehicle put out by Studebaker-Garford in 1910-1911 was this 7-passenger Limousine. The vehicle developed 40-horsepower from its T-head 372 cubic-inch engine. The bore and stroke of this vehicle were 4.75 x 5.25. The Limousine rode on the 117.5-inch wheelbase supplied by Garford, and used a rather elaborate Studebaker body. It was priced at $4,750. This year, the cars were also marketed under the Garford name.

A front three-quarter view of the 1910 Studebaker-Garford Limousine shows what a pretentious car looked like in this era. Check the horn mechanism and emergency brake and shifter system. I'll bet someone would enjoy having those carriage lights today, to place in front of their home.

This 1911 Studebaker-Garford Limousine was referred to as the Model "G-840." The final year for Studebaker-Garfords was 1911. After the separation, Garford continued to build vehicles under its own name, but was then purchased by Willys-Overland in 1912. The Garford name continued on cars through 1913, but disappeared after that, although Garford trucks remained on the market for several years thereafter.

This 1910-11 E.M.F. "30" was put through the paces on a rugged excursion from Seguin, Texas to Detroit. The vehicle states "40,000 miles and still running." Since Seguin is less than 1,500 miles from Detroit, this car must have seen plenty of hard Texas driving before starting its epic journey. Considering the road conditions in the U.S. of that era, this was a notable trip. Note the set of long horns on the radiator...and this was supposed to be a recent fad?

Waiting for delivery from the factory, are a group of 1910-11 E.M.F. vehicles. All have been fitted with factory-supplied tops and windshields, which were considered extra-cost options. Such items could be supplied by direct factory order, be a dealer-stocked item, or ordered from a local aftermarket supply house.

This small truck was the 1910-1912 Flanders "20" Delivery Vehicle. It was the only commercial gasoline powered vehicle offered by the Studebaker Corporation up to that date.

The year is uncertain, but no doubt it is in the 1910-12 period. At first it looks like an early-day version of the Joads coming across country. However, it is actually a mail delivery van, possibly handling a Christmas rush. But it looks like the van probably got some pretty hard use everyday. A true statement, "The mail must go through," certainly applies to this photo.

An electric emergency vehicle was specially designed for use by electric traction (street car) companies for repair work. The vehicle was capable of a speed up to 9 mph. Its wheelbase measured 111 inches and it weighed 5,100 pounds. The unit would travel 35 miles per charge. The tires were of solid rubber. The specialty body was cataloged as the Model 2008-B.

Studebaker offered this piano or furniture wagon during its early days of electric vehicles. It apparently had a market, and thus continued to be listed during the 1906 to 1912 era. The Smith & Nixon Piano Company was a large purchaser of this "House on Wheels," being agents for both Steinway and Kurtzmann pianos.

A larger delivery van offered a 111-inch wheelbase. It had a load capacity of 2,500 pounds. The unit itself weighed 5,200 pounds. Called the Model 2006-D, it featured a rather substantial tailgate, which could be used for both loading, or carrying additional cargo when the body was full.

# 1911-1912

Ideal for lumber companies was this truck with a load capacity of 2,500 pounds. It weighed 5,000 pounds. It was in production from 1906 to 1912, when Studebaker got out of the electric vehicle business. Reports show that some of these trucks were still working in major city dock and warehouse areas as late as W.W. II.

A small delivery van was also built from 1906-1912. It had a loading capacity of 1,000 pounds. Its wheelbase was 92 inches and it rode on solid rubber tires. In a sense, this was simply a commercial adaptation of the ambulance body. Apparently fenders were deemed unnecessary on these electric trucks.

Studebaker referred to this unit as a simple delivery wagon. With a load capacity of 2,500 pounds, it could cruise at 9 mph for up to 35 miles. The body was quite fancy, and obviously designed for use by upscale stores of the day.

A different style of furniture wagon also came on a 111-inch wheelbase. It cruised at the astonishing speed of 9 miles per hour, which was about the same top speed of many gasoline-powered heavy trucks of the day. The load capacity was 2,500 pounds and the vehicle itself weighed 5,150 pounds. Roll-up side curtains were designed to protect the cargo, not the driver.

A 1911 Flanders "20" Touring is parked in front of the AAA National Headquarters at Fifty-Fourth Street in New York City. This was the start of the Pathfinder Glidden Tour from New York City to Atlanta and on to Jacksonville, Florida. The company's slogan for the event was "Down the Dixie Trail with a Flanders "20.""

The 1911 Studebaker E.M.F. "30" was available as Series B which was a more top-line vehicle. In open form, it sold for $1,250, or listed at $1,325 with the factory-supplied cape top. A windshield would have been an aftermarket accessory.

With Cape To
$1325

This is a 1911 E.M.F. "30." The front compartment differed from the 1912 models in that it was completely open on the early versions, but had front (or fore) doors on the 1912 issue. Oddly, 1911/12 was the year that many auto manufacturers, including Ford, Buick and Oldsmobile, began to fit their touring cars with front doors.

The South Bend Tribune purchased several of these Flanders Delivery Vans for distributing their newspaper throughout the city and outlying areas. The vehicles sold for under $1,000. Reports are, they were very dependable except for the 2-speed transmission problem mentioned before. The lower rear is equipped with a swing-down tailgate, but a roll-up curtain was used for the upper part of the body. A nice interior touch involved the cargo rub-rails that can be seen here. They protected the inner body sides from cargo rubbing against or banging into the regular body sides.

This model was called the E.M.F. "30" Fore-Door Roadster. It delivered for $1,100. Designed primarily for open driving, it would provide a relatively snug interior when the upper windshield frame and the top was raised...from within the car...and the side curtains were put in place...from without.

E.M.F. Model "30" Fore-Door Touring was the technical name given to this attractive vehicle. It was offered with negligible changes for approximately four and one half years. This unit is from the 1911-1912 era. It sold for $1,100.

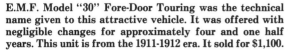

Given a different name for its body style was this Flanders Model "20" for 1912. Formerly called the 3-speed Roadster, the company now referred to it simply as the Speedster. This car, with weight reduced to the last possible ounce, made for a fairly fast vehicle in those days. When the car was introduced, it marked an epoch in the auto industry. It received acclaims from both buyers and spectators alike.

This is the 1912 Flanders Model "20" Fore-Door Roadster. What a lot of things there were to do if the top was to be put in the down position. The cigarette commercial "You've come a long way baby," could well apply here. It delivered for $750.

A late edition 1912 Flanders Roadster Model "20" came equipped with doors not seen on earlier examples. The car is shown well buttoned up for rain, or maybe just cold weather. Although a top with side curtains and a windshield were considered accessories, as were the headlights, most buyers of middle-priced cars were beginning to take these options. Not wanting to mess with a carbide generator for his headlight fuel, the owner of this vehicle has selected a Prest-O-Lite system, which used compressed gas from a tank mounted on the running board rather than a gas producer such as in a carbide system.

Looks like it's a day of remembering when: The 1912 Flanders "20" is seen with Studebaker factory employees looking on as the antique comes off the assembly line. Note the later-day manufacturer's license plate mounted on the cowl which someone forgot to remove. The Flanders came with a two-main bearing engine developing 20 H.P, but it came from a factory in Detroit, not the South Bend assembly line shown here.

This 1912 Studebaker Flanders Model "20" was called the Demi-Tonneau Touring. It sold for $800. The comparable price with the regular Touring for 1912 gave the public a wider selection to choose from.

# 1912

Minus head lamps is this 1912 Flanders Roadster. But it does have the accessory top, windshield, and oil side lamps. Seeing the Starlight Coupe parked next to it, this was obviously taken at a car show in the past few years. Many owners in this era still considered the optional and expensive headlights totally unnecessary, as few people drove after dark anyway.

From the look of utter disgust on her face, I bet its the last old-time car event that she attends. At any rate, it's another view of the 1912 Flanders "20" Roadster.

This 1912 Flanders Model "20" Touring has its top in the down position for a family outing. This was the best of the line, with an $800 price tag, the same as the Demi-Tonneau. The model offered seating for five passengers. Note the bulb horn has now been moved inside the car next to the door in case the driver needs to give a quick squeeze for pedestrians to get out of his way.

The 1912 E.M.F. "30" Fore-Door Demi Tonneau delivered for the same price as the regular Fore-Door Touring... $1,160. This example carries its tool-carrying kit on the running board between the front and rear doors. Also located there is the carbide gas generator which was necessary to operate the headlights. The cowl lamps were fueled by kerosene.

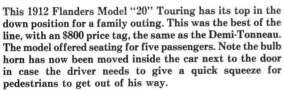

A 1912 E.M.F. is parked on a street in South Bend, Indiana. Apparently it is a local car, according to the license plate on the radiator. Note the hard rubbered Studebaker 5-ton electric truck behind the E.M.F. It states "Studebaker S.B. IND."

The 1912 Flanders Model "20" Coupe was basically the same car from its beginning to its final days. A speedometer and carbide headlamps were classed as extra cost items. People were beginning to venture out more at night, so the headlamps were almost a necessity. This sample sold for $775.

Robertson's Dry Goods and Carpet Company found the 1912 Flanders Delivery Van a very acceptable unit for their type of work. Note the small circular window these vans came equipped with, and the tool box on the side running board. Tire chains must surely have been needed to get through the snow and slush on the day this photo was taken.

This 1912 Flanders was put to work as a home delivery vehicle for the firm of G. Bergstedt of 1402 Kemble Avenue. The city is unknown but if customers needed groceries quickly, they could call their home, as it is also listed on the side of the van: Home Phone 8533 Bell Phone 2445. Things have changed, haven't they! With the Prest-O-Lite headlight set-up, one wonders if they made night deliveries.

The 1912 Flanders "20" engine displays its manifold side. The clutch was of the internal direct cone type, and was leather faced. The transmission gears were mounted in an aluminum housing on the rear axle. A large magneto is evident, which certainly should have provided a good spark. Of L-head design, both intake and exhaust valves were on the left side.

Two 1912 Flanders Delivery cars carrying Indiana license plates appear to be out for another day of hard work. Work was what they were built for, and did they receive it! Note that the windshield folded in half, but when extended to its full height, it did not attach to the roof header. This was to prevent upper body movement from cracking the plate glass.

This 1912 Flanders "20" Delivery Car was used by Parker & Company Caterers. Apparently they at least had two vehicles in their business as this is No. 2. These vehicles employed hickory wood for their artillery wheels. The models used 30x3 inch tires on the front while, for a proper tread pattern, 30x3 inch did best on the rear. It delivered for under $1,000.

The electric ambulance which the factory offered at the turn of the century was continued in production until 1912 as the Model 2004-A. What a slow way to get to the hospital! However, for short-haul city usage, it was probably more dependable than contemporary gasoline-powered outfits. However, those hard rubber tires must have given an interesting ride, especially in a maternity situation.

One of the last Studebaker Electric Commercial vehicles to be delivered was this electric carry-all wagon. It could average between 20-30 miles before recharging. Its speed was generally 5 mph with a full load. Note the models offered on the window of the dealership. The E-M-F sign would indicate that this photo could not have been made before 1908.

Although the largest builder of horse-drawn vehicles in the world. Studebaker was initially very cautious about entering the field of self-propelled vehicles. It's first tentative efforts involved the making of passenger and commercial electric vehicles starting in 1902, but the production was never large and only 1,841 electric vehicles of all types had been built when production was abandoned in 1912.

In the meantime, Studebaker explored the production of gasoline vehicles by entering into an agreement with the Garford Company of Elyria, Ohio. Garford supplied the running gear while Studebaker built the bodies and sold the completed vehicles through its worldwide dealer network. The Studebaker-Garford cars were very large and expensive, generally selling in the $3,000 to $5000 range. A large market simply did not exist for a luxury car of this type and when the arrangement with Garford was terminated in 1911, only 2,481 Studebaker-Garfords had been built.

Nevertheless, Studebaker was convinced that the gasoline automobile was to be a major factor in its future, and the management continued to explore avenues that would lead to the production of substantial numbers of low-priced vehicles. It found an arrangement with the EMF Company of Detroit that was organized in 1908 to build large numbers of a light weight four-cylinder automobile, the EMF-30. Studebaker signed an agreement whereby it was to have exclusive rights for the sale of EMFs. A short time later, EMF purchased other plants to produce still another car, the Flanders-20. By purchasing the outstanding stock of the EMF Company, Studebaker became sole owner in 1910. In January, 1911, the EMF assets were merged with the Studebaker Brothers Manufacturing Company to form the Studebaker Corporation of New Jersey. Cars built in the Detroit EMF plants continued to be sold under the Studebaker-EMF and Studebaker Flanders names until 1912.

Studebaker now had the plants, production capacity, and sales organization to enable it to become a major automobile manufacturer. Fortunately, a very able engineering team came along with the EMF merger. The decision was made to drop all production of electric vehicles and Studebaker-Garfords, and to phase out the EMF-30 and Flanders-20. Thereafter, all vehicles would be designed by Studebaker and manufactured in its own plants. By late 1912, a completely new line consisting of two Fours and a Six were ready for production. These 1913 models were, therefore, the first true Studebaker gasoline cars — ones to bear the Studebaker name exclusively. Although the 1913 cars retained a few of the EMF features, they were basically all-new machines...larger, more powerful, and built with better materials.

Sales of all Studebaker vehicles in 1913 reached 35,410 units, enough to place Studebaker in fourth place in U.S. production behind Ford, Overland, and Buick. Another 35,000 vehicles were turned out in 1914, which probably would have been a better year but for the outbreak of war in Europe which caused a recession in the U.S. Sales of Studebaker cars soared to 46,845 in 1915 and 45,885 in 1916. However, sales dropped slightly in 1917 to 42,000 units due to Studebaker's involvement in W.W. I military production.

The success of Studebaker in the automobile manufacturing field in these teen years was now well established, and the judgement of management to pin its future hopes on the motor car was fully indicated.

*NOTE: Sales figures quoted above are taken from Studebaker corporation reports. They seem to be slightly inflated as they exceed figures taken from other sources. However, the numbers are probably calendar year rather than model year production. They also include commercial vehicle production not included in the production figures for passenger cars.*

This example of the 1913 Studebaker 4-cylinder Roadster was classed as a SA "25" in the group of 1913 cars called Four-Forty. This, in a way, was when Studebaker truly began production of cars...when they finally felt that the gas buggies were here to stay. These vehicles were built under Studebaker's own name. The E.M.F. cars were now history.

A top-down version of Model SA "25" 1913 Studebaker Roadster shows it as nice looking medium-price car. It sold for $875. These vehicles employed a steel housing for the differential and an iron casting for the trans-axle housing. Full side curtains with celluloid panes were supplied with model for use in inclement weather.

The new Studebaker cars for 1913 were outstanding examples of well-engineered quality and simplicity. The principle of unit construction of the rear axle and transmission, which was a prominent feature of the EMF and Flanders, was retained for the 1913 cars. The Model SA-25 Four was produced in two body styles — a 5-passenger Touring car and a 2-passenger Roadster selling for $885 and $875, respectively, at the factory. The larger Four, the Model AA-35, was offered in three body styles: a 6-passenger Touring car at $1,290, a Coupe at $1,850, and a 4-passenger Sedan at $2,050. The Model E-Six was made in two body styles only: a 6-passenger Touring car and a Limousine at prices of $1,550 and $2,500, respectively.

Full-elliptical rear springs were used on the "25" and three-quarter ellipticals were on the rear of the "35" and E-Six. All models used semi-elliptical front springs. Radius rods were used on all cars to remove driving stresses from the springs.

All engines embodied the latest in design with all cylinder blocks cast in one piece of close-grained gray iron. The E-Six is generally credited with being the first large production Six cast en bloc. The exhaust manifold

was cast integral with the block on the Fours, but was bolt-on on the Six. A horizontal draft Holley carburetor was used on all models, with the intake passages water-jacketed within the cylinder casting to insure good volatilization of the gasoline charge.

The water pump and magneto were mounted on opposite ends of a horizontal cross shaft at the front of the engine. This shaft was driven directly by helical gears from the camshaft. This design made the water pump and magneto instantly available for servicing. All cars were equipped with a combination of splash lubrication and oil pump circulation. Oil was pumped to the front end gears and to troughs below the connecting rods where the connecting rod ends splashed the oil to all other engine parts requiring lubrication. A sign feed on the dash indicated to the driver when oil was being distributed by the pump.

Ignition was by a Splitdorf or National low-tension magneto. The "35" and E-Six cars were equipped with a Wagner EM-101 starter-generator of the latest design. A twelve volt battery was used with this installation. In the "start" position a contracting brake caused the engagement of a planetary reduction gear and the starter drove the crankshaft through a chain drive. In the "run" position the planetary gear was released by a spring. The "25" was not equipped for electrical starting or lighting.

A leather faced cone clutch was used on all models. The drive from the clutch to the rear transmission was via a heat treated drive shaft of chromium nickel steel provided with dirt-proof universals at each end.

All models used a selective three-speed transmission with the gears enclosed in an aluminum housing bolted to the front of the rear axle housing. A worm and sector steering gear was employed. Two separate braking systems were used, the service brakes being of the contracting type on the rear wheels, while the emergency brake was hand operated and expanded internally on the rear drums.

Studebaker "25"

The 1913 SA Touring was said to be the last Studebaker produced without a full electrical system. The car was a Model "25" 5-passenger Touring. It came with a 4-cylinder engine, which had a long stroke of 5 inches while the bore was 3__ inches. The car sold for $885. It used a gas starter and carbide lights with kerosene cowl and taillights. The tires were 30x3.5 inch Goodrich, mounted on demountable rims. An extra rim was supplied, but the spare tire was extra.

This 1913 Studebaker Model "35" was classed as a 4-cylinder 6-passenger Touring. New for the company was the use of electric components for the model. It had an electric starter and electric head, cowl, and tail lights. The vehicle had a silk mohair top and included jiffy curtains as standard equipment. Its wheelbase was 116 inches and it sold for $1,290. The tires, by Goodrich, were 34x4 inches.

The 1913 E-6 Touring was a 6-passenger vehicle with a 6-cylinder engine. It employed a 3-inch bore and 5-inch stroke. The car rode on a 121-inch wheelbase. Fully equipped with electrics and top, this car delivered for $1,550.

Studebaker "35"

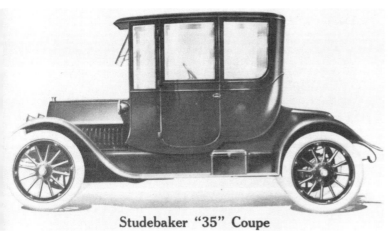

**Studebaker "35" Coupe**

For 1913, this Model "AA" Coupe was electrically fitted in every detail including starter and lights. The coupe body was of all-aluminum. The interior was done in hand-buffed leather, with handmade cushion work, one auxiliary folding seat, and French plate glass windows. The Coupe sold for $1,850.

**Studebaker "35" Sedan**

The 1913 Model "AA 35" Sedan came with an all-aluminum body, plate window glass, English blue broadcloth upholstery, an auxiliary folding seat, and handmade rear seat pillow work. The carriage lights on the side were standard equipment. The vehicle delivered for $2,050. The car was designed in the "center door" style which was so popular for sedans of this era. That meant that the driver and front passenger had to get into the rear section, and then move up to forward seats.

This 1913 EC-6 Touring Car is parked in front of an unidentified Studebaker dealership. Studebaker still employed right hand-hand drive, as exhibited by this future salesman behind the wheel. The tool box is mounted on the running board, ready for a quick repair. The 6-lug demountable rims were standard equipment.

Studebaker came back into the light truck or car/truck field in 1914 with this Model AA-35 Commercial Car. Although technically classed as a truck, the vehicle used all passenger car components for the chassis and running gear, and likewise, all passenger car sheetmetal was used back as far as the B-pillar. Only the delivery car body with its overhanging roof was not of passenger car origin. This example, exported to Europe, wears an early form of turn signal on its windshield post. Now, 80 years later, many drivers still don't know what these signals are for!

The most expensive vehicle for the year was this 7-foot high Studebaker "Six" Limousine referred to technically as the Model "EC". The Limo came equipped with electric dome and corner lights, silk curtains, and a speaking tube from rear-seat passengers to the chauffeur. All other appointments, including all-aluminum body construction, were the same as on the Sedan and Coupe. It sold for $2,500.

**Studebaker "SIX" Limousine**

# 1914

The new 1914 models were introduced about October 1913. Studebaker reduced its product line to two models in 1914 — the SC-Four and the EB-Six. The Four was available in two body types — a 5-passenger Touring car with a factory-delivered price of $1,050 and a Landau Roadster at $1,200. The Six was available in three body styles — a 7-passenger Touring car that delivered at the Detroit factory for $1,575, a Landau Roadster at $1,800, and a 5-passenger Sedan at $2,250.

The 1914 models retained many of the chassis design features of the 1913 cars, including the unit transmission and rear axle, the three-quarter elliptical rear spring design on the Six, and the full-elliptical rear spring on the Four. The basic engine dimensions and designs also remained the same. However, the ignition and starting systems were vastly improved by the adoption, on both Fours and Sixes, of the latest version of the Wagner two-unit electrical system with separate starter and generator. The generator of the 1914 models was fitted on the left side of the engine where it was driven by gears through a flexible coupling. The Wagner starter was located at the right front of the engine where it was driven from the crankshaft through a reduction gear and chain driven clutch.

The Wagner ignition system was a breaker point and coil arrangement with the distributor driven off the right end of the horizontal cross shaft at the front of the engine. The water pump arrangement remained essentially of the same design as used in 1913, driven from the left end of this cross shaft.

The gasoline tank for all cars was moved from the former location under the seat to the cowl section. Since there was no fuel pump, the higher position provided a more positive fuel feed to the carburetor. A new Schebler carburetor was used on both the Four and the Six. With the higher position of the gas tank, the carburetor was provided with a much shorter vertical leg on the intake manifold, permitting a much better fuel mixture distribution to the cylinders.

Of major importance overall, the right-hand steering location found on the 1913 cars was abandoned in favor of left-hand drive for all domestic cars. The wheelbase of the Four was 108 inches; while the Six was 121 inches. Standard tire size was 32x3-1/2 for the Four and 34x4 for the Six. Bodies were finished in dark Studebaker Blue with white striping. Fenders, hood, and running gear were black. An electric horn, extra rim, robe rail, and a complete set of tools were standard equipment on all cars. Bumpers were not standard factory equipment on these cars, but were available in a variety of styles from aftermarket suppliers. Total production of the 1914 cars is given as 17,976 Fours and 7,625 Sixes for a total of 15,601 vehicles of all body types.

This is a Model "SA 25" Roadster out for a drive on a typical dusty, rutted Indiana road of the era. Note the vehicle wears a 1914 Indiana license plate, and is being followed by what appears to be a new Model T Ford Roadster. These models used nickel trim. All Model "25" cars used 30x3-inch B.F. Goodrich tires. It looks as if Dobbin is standing by just in case one of these new-fangled gas buggies decides to die on the spot.

Virtually the same as the 1913 issue in all respects are the 1914 models. This is a Model "SC-4" going through the famous carved out redwood tree at Wawona-Yosemite, California. Note the folks believe in advertising their "pride and joy" 1914 model with the Studebaker pennant displayed on the windshield. The owner must have been rather important to get the 1914 California license "A1."

After its strong showing in 1913, when it took fourth place in sales among domestic automobile manufacturers, Studebaker's projected growth for 1914 slipped a bit because of the recession in the South caused by loss of cotton markets in Europe. Even so, Studebaker retained its fourth place only behind Ford, Overland, and Buick in 1914. By 1915, Dodge was in a virtual tie with Studebaker as the two shared fourth place in sales. Never again was Studebaker to match this high position in the auto industry as the ensuing years were to see it surpassed by Chevrolet, Dodge, Hudson, and others.

It is appropriate that the 1914 and 1915 models are covered together, as the cars of the two model years are quite similar. Studebaker automobile production in these years continued to be centered in the former EMF and Flanders plants in Detroit. The South Bend plant continued in the production of horse-drawn equipment and wagons, still a substantial part of Studebaker's output. However, the South Bend plants also produced springs, castings, bodies, and body parts for the Detroit factories.

By 1914, Studebaker had purchased the remaining outstanding stock of Studebaker of Canada and had taken over full control and operation of the Walkerville, Ontario, automobile plant. Following the outbreak of war in Europe in 1914, Studebaker was one of the first U.S. companies to answer the call for war production. The British War Office placed an order late in 1914 with Studebaker for 3,000 transport wagons for the British Army. Following the prompt delivery of this order, the British War Office later placed an order with Studebaker for the delivery of a substantial number of harnesses, saddles, water carts, and artillery wheels. By 1915, Studebaker was also filling orders for wagons, ambulance carts, and artillery wheels for the French and Russian governments.

Studebaker had a total of 7,934 employees in the U.S. in 1914, which increased to 8,918 in 1915. The average hourly wage in 1914 was $14.67 per week. For the standard 48-hour work week that figures out to about 30 cents per hour.

This 1914 4-cylinder Model SC Touring is virtually the same offering as the 1913 "SA 25". This, obviously, is from a car show with later Studes parked next to it.

In real life, the Studebaker Six Landau Roadster had looks that were the equal of anything in its price class, and much better than many other makes currently on the market. This restored example, missing one headlight, was photographed at a show of the Vintage Car Club in England. Since Studebakers still hung onto right-hand steering, there was no problem in exporting them to countries such as England, Ireland, and even Sweden at that time, where drivers kept to the left.

The 1914 Studebaker EB 6 is shown here in the foreground with top in the up position, and with the top down version displayed in the rear. The model was called a Landau Roadster, and was available for $1,950. Of interesting design are the "X-shaped" landau irons.

# 1914-1915

A 1914 Studebaker EB 6-A Sedan is the same car right down to its seven-foot high roof line as the 1913 model. The only real change came in its price which increased $200. The unit now delivered for $2,250. A thoughtful touch was found in the assist handles on the B-pillar, just below the very ornate coach lamps.

Studebaker found their roadster models to be an instant success, allowing plenty of room for three passengers. It was promoted as a good car for business or pleasure. The leather buttoned seats wore exceptionally well. The top could be raised on a moment's notice. The rather small drivers' seat was located forward of the main seat, leaving plenty of room for two additional passengers. A small padded parcel shelf was located behind the driver's seat.

A 1915 Roadster in the SD line was referred to as the Landau Roadster. It was available in two-passenger form only. The car could be instantly convertible from an open Roadster to a closed vehicle, as the photo shows. It was available for $1,200 in 4-cylinder style or, if the 6-cylinder model was ordered as an ED, the cost was $1,800. Plate glass windows that could be lowered to sill level were used in the doors, but the quarter sections were curtains with celluloid windows.

Brand spankin' new is this 1915 SD-4 Touring. The interior was done in a high-quality buffed leather. The top was at additional cost, but most everyone ordered it. The model, even though basically the same since its introduction two years prior, had increased in price to $1,050.

The 1915 SD Roadster came with an aluminum body, demountable rims, 32x3_-inch Goodrich tires, full elliptic rear springs, and had a large compartment in the rear for tools or minor pieces of luggage. Unlike the Landau Roadster, this model did not have plate glass in the doors.

The 1915 models were introduced in July, 1914. No closed cars were produced. The SD-Four series consisted only of a 5-passenger Touring car and a Roadster. The EC-Six was offered in only two styles — a 5-passenger and a 7-passenger Touring car. The EC-Six was priced at $1,385 for the 5-passenger Touring and $1,450 for the 7-passenger version. The SD-Four delivered at Detroit for $985 for either the Touring model or the Roadster. The 1915 cars were somewhat lighter than their 1914 counterparts. Through the use of improved and stronger materials, there was an average savings in weight of about 100 pounds per vehicle.

The external appearance of the 1915 models was much like the 1914 cars, and mechanical changes were minor. The gasoline tank retained its same location in the cowl, but the filler cap was moved from the external cowl position to the right-hand side of the instrument panel. To-day this seems like a strange bit of design, but during the mid-teens, a relatively high percentage of cars were still filled from gas cans, rather than from gas pumps. Thus, when fueling a car from a can, it was easier to hold the can from a front seat position than it was to balance the can while reaching across fender and cowl. And of course, a pump hose could just as easily fit either location. The cowl lights, which were a prominent feature of the 1914 cars, were eliminated on the 1915 models. The tire size for the Six remained at 34x4, but was increased in size to 33x4 on the Four.

Total production of the 1915 models is given as 33,600 units, broken down as 24,849 SD-Fours and 8,751 ED-Sixes.

This 1915 Studebaker 4-cylinder Model SD Touring is wearing the optional equipment cowl lights, spot lamp, motometer, and special horn, mounted under left head lamp. This example must have been an export car, it being right-hand drive and wearing European license plates. Or, it may just have been an early 1915 issue, still having its steering on the right, as it seems that the switch to left-hand control occurred as an early running change in 1915.

One noticeable difference between the earlier Roadsters of 1913-14 and the 1915 issue is the placement of the headlights. Beginning with the 1915 cars, they are mounted on a higher level, as this model shows. The SD 4-cylinder cars used a 108-inch wheelbase while the EC 6-cylinder vehicle came on a 114-inch wheelbase.

The Berthel Steen dealership certainly was not in the United States. The 1915 SD 4 has right-hand drive and the background shows a foreign car coming out of the dealership, with definite non-English writing on the wall. The cowl lights on this model were an accessory in the U.S., but may have been mandated in some foreign lands.

For the 1915 model run, the Model EC 6-cylinder Touring Car was available as both 5 and 7-passenger vehicles. However, there were no closed vehicles for the year. This car delivered for $1,385 as a 5-passenger, and $1,450 if the 7-passenger touring style were chosen. For 1915 these were the only models available in the EC line. The horsepower rating was 40.

# 1915-1916

Studebaker introduced its new line of 1916 models in June, 1915. Although the new cars were larger, more powerful, and included many mechanical improvements, substantial price reductions were announced. The new Model SF-Four Touring car listed for $885 FOB the Detroit factories, a reduction of $100 compared to the 1915 4-cylinder Touring. Price reductions for the ED-Six models were even more striking. The ED-Six 7-passenger Touring car listed for only $1,050 compared to $1,450 for the 1915 6-cylinder 7-passenger Touring car.

Increased power was achieved by enlarging the cylinder bores of the engines from 3-1/2 inches to 3-7/8 inches. Brake tests showed that the Four developed approximately 44 horsepower and the Six 54 horsepower. Body lines were smoothed to flow in unbroken curves for the full lengths of the bodies. Interiors were much more roomy, due to the wheelbase of the Four being increased a full four inches to 112 inches, while the Six was increased one inch to 122 inches. Contoured front seats were provided in the Touring cars for the driver and front seat passenger. The auxiliary seats were newly designed and fit into recesses in the floor when folded so that more room was provided in the tonneau.

A number of alterations were made in the engine. Most noteworthy of these was relocation of the carburetor to the left side of the engine where a separate intake manifold afforded a shorter and more direct passage for the fuel charge. The former front cross shaft with the water pump on one end and the distributor on the other was eliminated. The water pump was now driven directly from the distributor gear, while the distributor itself was driven from a bevel gear on the front end of the camshaft. The generator location was changed to the right front of the engine where it was driven directly from the crankshaft gear. The basic starting system remained the same as on the 1915 cars. The Four and the Six engines were virtually identical except for the number of cylinders.

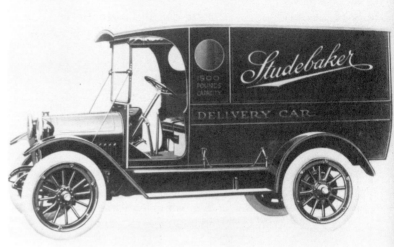

In 1915, the SD Delivery Wagon came with an electric starter, oversize tires of 3 x 4 inches and carried a 1,500-pound weight load. This example was available from 1913-1917. In 1915, this delivery delivered for $1,150.

An interesting unit was this Combination Station Wagon and Baggage Car, as it was technically referred to. For hotel transport or jitney-type usage, padded seats lined both sides, facing the center of the vehicle. When passengers were not on board, the seats could be folded and the back made into a delivery vehicle. It sold in the same $1,086 to $1,150 price range as the delivery cars.

Basically the same vehicle as the Delivery Wagon was this version called the Express Delivery Car for 1915. It sold for $1,085 and proved popular as a vehicle used for picking up stray animals, from which use came its nickname of "dog catcher's wagon." But actually, in these days, the mesh-sided panels were used a lot on delivery vehicles of this type. They offered the advantage of light weight, coupled with screens for cargo protection. Roll-up curtains would be lowered in bad weather.

The Model SF Roadster was available without any changes in both 1916 and 1917. It was classed as a 3-passenger Roadster and sold for $850, making it the lowest priced passenger car available from Studebaker for the year. It also went under the title of Four-Forty One. All Studebaker bodies were finished in 25 separate coats of color and varnish, each baked in and hand applied.

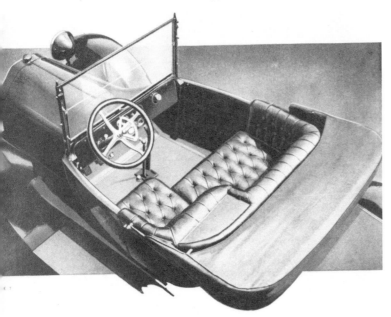

A 1916 Model SF 4-cylinder Roadster shows the seating arrangement for up to three passengers. The top quality tufted leather upholstery has form-fitting cushions and seat backs. All controls were within easy vision of the driver and the steering wheel was of an 18-inch circumference, placed in a natural-tilt position.

This 1916 Studebaker Model SF-4 cylinder Touring came both as a 5 and 7-passenger vehicle. If the 5-passenger seating arrangement were ordered, it sold for $835 while the 7-passenger delivered for $875. The color of this vehicle was dark blue with white striping on the body panels. The hood, fenders, and chassis were done in black enamel. The wheels were done in dark blue, with black hubs and rims, and nickel-plated hubcaps.

There appears to be no record that the SF and ED models that were introduced in June, 1915, were ever called Series 16 models at that time. They were invariably referred to in sales and technical literature as either SF-Four or ED-Six cars, or as Four-Forty and Six-Fifty models. Neither were these vehicles ever referred to as 1915 models, as some have claimed. Both Studebaker, and the trade journals of the day, correctly refer to them as 1916 cars.

In a Studebaker Service Letter dated December 28, 1915, it was announced that several changes would be made in the SF and ED models. Specification for the new cars were announced in the letter, and it was stated that they would henceforth be referred to as Series 17 models to distinguish them from the earlier production cars. At the same time, the earlier production cars were to be referred to as Series 16 models.

The earlier production cars — now known as Series 16 — are readily distinguished from the Series 17 and later models. On the Series 16 the gas tank was located in the cowl where the fuel fed by gravity to the carburetor. Series 17 cars have the gas tank located at the rear of the vehicle, requiring the use of a Stewart vacuum tank to pump fuel to the carburetor. Series 16 cars lack a front splash apron under the radiator, while it is present on later models. The front seat design on Touring cars was changed from a contoured bench seat on Series 16 to individual seats on Series 17 cars. There are a number of other minor changes on Series 17 cars, but the characteristics described above are the most readily apparent.

Production of Studebaker passenger cars was centered in the Detroit factories during this period. No complete cars were built in South Bend. Cars were also assembled in the Walkerville, Ontario, plant from parts shipped from U.S. factories. Only open cars were assembled in Walkerville, however.

The seating capacity of both the 4 and 6-cylinder Touring Cars for 1916 were identical. The wheelbase for the 4-cylinder cars was 112-inches, while 6-cylinder vehicles used the 122-inch wheelbase. When not needed, the auxiliary seats folded into a compartment behind the front seat. Upholstery was in tufted black leather.

The Studebaker Six Open Roadster for 1916 was called an ED Six-Fifty. These roadsters were equipped with a large rear storage compartment, permitting room for extra tires, parcels, and baggage. The compartment offered a corrugated rolled aluminum deck, fitted with trunk straps and fasteners. This was strong enough to place a large trunk on the deck, without marring the finish, in the event an owner wanted to engage in long-distance touring. This example delivered for $1,000.

Studebaker's 1916 Landau Roadster was referred to as Model Six-Fifty in the ED series. The Landau Roadster was also available in the Four-Forty series. Each offered the luxury of a closed car and came with plate glass door windows that would lower to sill level, and a genuine leather top that folded compactly. The top now incorporated the quarter panel section, and only small side curtains were now needed for this area. In all sense of the definition, this was a true convertible. It sold for $1,350 as a Six-Fifty and $1,200 as the Four-Forty.

The 1916 Model ED Six-Fifty 4-passenger Coupe came with an auxiliary seat forward, at the right, which folded under the cowl when not needed. The supporting fixture of this seat disappeared into the floor when not in use. The 1916 models came with an increase of horsepower. The 6-cylinder models now developed 50 horsepower. The tires were again supplied by Goodrich and were 34x4 inches. This model left the dealership for $1,550.

A rear view of the 1916 Model ED Six-Fifty Touring Car shows the vehicle with right-hand steering. It is possible the photo was intended for a foreign catalog, or possibly right-hand cars were still being produced for those customers who didn't want to switch. These models all came equipped with a magnet speedometer, gasoline gauge, battery and oil indicator gauges, and a carburetor adjustment lever on the steering post. The neatly stowed top could be in the up position in a matter of seconds...so said the catalog!

The straight side view of this 1916 7-passenger ED-6 Touring Car best shows off its 122-inch wheelbase. The vehicle decreased in price from the 1915 version by $355. It now sold for $1,085.

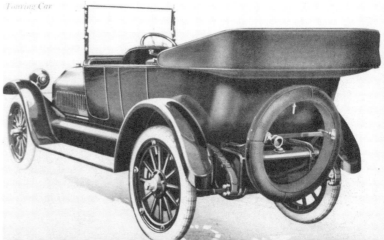

# 1916

The 7-passenger Touring Car model displays its jump seats, which could be concealed in a rear compartment when not needed. The 1916 vehicle came with remodeled and lengthened crown fenders. An increase of 10 horsepower over the previous year was also an addition. The price adjustment put the car on the road for $1,085.

One of the last photos taken of John Mohler Studebaker shows the old gent sitting in a 1916 "ED-6" with James Heaslet, then vice-president of Studebaker. John Mohler lived from 1833 to 1917.

This is another possibly one off version that came on the ED-6 chassis. Some special sedan bodies were done by the Springfield Metal Body Co. This arrangement lasted through 1917. Note the Vee'd windshield. It is truly a "house on wheels". The front door is of the suicide style rather than hinged at the front. Designed to be chauffeur driven, this car contained a division panel between compartments, and was equipped with a speaking tube for giving instructions to the driver.

Even as rare as the 1916 ED 7-passenger Limousine was, this example is even more rare. It appears to have had some special appointments made to it. It isn't an enclosed limousine as there isn't any partition between front and rear. Also, there is no entrance to the rear from the left side. Rear seat passengers had to enter from the right side only, as did the occupant of the right front seat. Possibly it was a one-off creation by some outside body firm, as Studebaker did not build special units at this time.

On the Series 17 models, which were introduced in January 1916, gasoline tanks were moved from the cowl section to the rear, requiring several changes for vacuum tank operation. Other changes were rather minor. On the Touring cars, front seats were changed from a contoured bench type to separate passenger and driver seats. Prices remained about the same. New models included a Sedan on the ED-Six chassis and an Everyweather car in both the Six and Four. An SF-Four Sedan, employing the same body as on the Six, was announced but later withdrawn from production. No closed cars were ever built on the SF-Four chassis.

The Everyweather Car was a clever compromise to provide closed car comfort at low cost. It consisted of a standard open Touring to which a closed body with removable glass windows could be fitted. With the windows in place, the vehicle was essentially a closed Sedan, but with the windows removed it was the equivalent of a Touring car with the top up. For summer use the Everyweather top could be removed easily and replaced with the standard Touring top. The Everyweather top could be ordered separately for fitting to any Touring car at a factory delivered price of $210, or it could

be ordered with any new Touring car at an extra cost of $210.

Few, if any, of the 1916-17 closed car bodies were built by Studebaker. It has been established that Willoughby built some of the Coupe bodies, the Sedan bodies were built by the Springfield Metal Body Company, and the Limousines were built by "one of the oldest and best known body manufacturers in the East" — not further identified.

According to Studebaker Sales Letter No. 765, dated July 26, 1916, the "new" Series 18 cars were to be introduced in September, 1916. Studebaker had projected a large expansion in production for the 1917 SF and ED cars, but with its heavy involvement in war production following the U.S. entry into W.W. I, actual production estimates were almost cut in half.

Production figures given in the compilation below are based on serial number runs. Although close, they do not agree precisely with production data from other sources.

|  | SERIES 16 | SERIES 17 | SERIES 18 |
|---|---|---|---|
| SF-Four | 14,179 | 35,684 | 23,550 |
| ED-Six | 7,259 | 25,509 | 25,994 |

|  | U.S. | CANADA | TOTALS |
|---|---|---|---|
| SF-Four | 73,414 | 8,829 | 82,242 |
| ED-Six | 58,762 | 3,355 | 62,117 |
|  | 132,175 | 12,184 | 144,359 |

A rare car in 1916 was this 6-cylinder 7-passenger Limousine. The body style was continued into 1918. The chauffeur compartment was finished in leather while the passenger area was complimented in a dark Bedford Blue Cord. The deluxe appointments included a vanity with mirrors, foot hassock, lighted rear compartment, and a speaker for the chauffeur. The vehicle delivered for $2,250. Unfortunately none exist today, as far as can be ascertained.

Fifty-Horsepower Six-Cylinder Sedan
Price $1700.00

A new style called the "All Year Sedan" was on the market in 1916. The factory claimed it was an instant success with a backlog of orders. Buyers could special order a choice of color, upholstery, and special equipment. The vehicle came only with two doors, in the center-door concept. Its price was $1,700 F.O.B. Detroit, as the final and complete South Bend assembly plant was still a bit away.

This 1916 4-passenger Touring was classed, due to its smaller interior compartment, as a Chummy Touring by many, even though it wasn't referred to as such by the factory. This example was an ED Six-Fifty and was available for $1,000.

A rugged looking truck is this 1916 vehicle used by the Southern Telephone Co. of Indiana. It must have been a bleak day when they chose to photograph "Old Faithful". Check the chains on the rear wheels and the side curtain to help keep its driver from getting completely frozen and snowed upon. Its a good thing traffic was still light in this era, as those celluloid "windows" in the curtains must have been a delight to see through.

Even though this book is about Studebaker passenger cars, now and then a neat looking commercial vehicle will appear. Here is a 1916 16-passenger bus used for the French Lick Springs Hotel, a prestigious and expensive resort in southern Indiana. The company that furnished the transportation was Rhodes Bros. Livery Service. Note the screened panel on the side for passenger luggage. However, in the background, is the Ellennox Piano Co., located in the Meridian Life Building in Indianapolis. Since the capital city was still too far from the hotel for this type of bus service, it is possible that this was a delivery photo made by some unidentified Indianapolis dealer or body builder which had outfitted this jitney-type hotel bus. In normal operation, the vehicle's route would have been between the French Lick train station and the resort.

The Crowley, Milner Company chose wisely in their purchase of 1916 Model SF commercial vehicles. Little change was seen over those produced from 1913. The most noticeable difference was seen in the headlamp placement, which now apparently gave better visibility due to the higher mounting.

This is a nice looking vehicle even by today's standards. It's the 1916 ED-6 Roadster for 3-passengers. The unit was available for $1,000. A like model also came in the 4-cylinder line and was termed the Four-Forty or Model SF for $850. It remained the same in both 1916-1917 as did the Series ED.

A rear view shows off the nice trunk styling of the 1916-17 ED-6 Roadster. The spare tire was an optional piece of equipment, but with tires and road conditions as they were in those days, practically no one ordered a car without a spare. In addition, the spare also served as a rear bumper, effectively protecting the large rectangular gas tank suspended under the trunk deck. The license was mounted in the center of the bracket, with one tail lamp to its left side. The wooden wheels were painted dark blue, the same as the body, and the small hubcaps were nickel plated.

This rear view shows off another non-factory Studebaker top, which added a little more class to the vehicle. The "ED-6" Touring also sports Houk wire wheels, which makes the vehicle appear lower and gives the appearance of speed even while standing still. In its day, this would have been one sporty vehicle, and it certainly would attract attention at a car show today.

It looks as though the lady is out voicing the great pleasure the new 1916-17 ED-6 Touring has given her. Or maybe she's praying that it will start this time! The car has a non-original Studebaker top, but looks good.

The ED-6 chassis of the 1916-17 models was rather simple and straightforward unit. The frame offered extra strength, which the owners must have appreciated. Note that the transmission was still attached to the differential, rather than being located behind the clutch. The battery was situated under the front seat, on the passenger side. This view does not show the gas tank, which would have been located between the rear frame horns, but suspended from the body.

Production of the Series 18 cars is thought to have commenced in September, 1916, and they are generally considered to be the beginning of the 1917 model year. Mechanical changes in the Series 18 cars were minimal. Studebaker, instead of introducing any significant changes in its line of successful passenger cars, now set out to refine its product line. New color options were to appear in the Series 18 products, as well as new body styles and accessory options.

Prices of the Series 18 cars were slightly higher, and with the entry of the U.S. into the war in Europe in April of 1917, prices continued to climb due to material shortages. By mid-year 1917 about half of the Studebaker facilities were devoted to war production.

To glamorize its passenger car production Studebaker established a custom body department. Initially the output of custom cars seemed to be confined to the Heaslet Special, a new Touring model announced in Sales Letter 768, dated August 30, 1916. It was named for James G. Heaslet, Vice-President of Engineering. The Heaslet Special appeared to be a stock ED-Six Touring car, dolled up a bit and equipped with a cape top of striking appearance. It sold for about $200 more than the stock Touring car, and could be equipped with wire wheels at a slightly higher price.

A sales letter of January 26, 1917, commented further on Studebaker "Specials" as it announced the availability of fifteen Valentine colors for specials built by the custom body department. The same newsletter stated that all specials could be ordered with natural wood wheels at no extra cost or wire wheels at $75 extra per car. It is thought that this marked the first time that Studebaker cars were built with natural wood spoke wheels.

A cryptic note in this sales letter went on to say that "we will not be able to make deliveries of the Bourgionette Touring car until late February, and orders for the Chummy Roadster will not be accepted until March 15." No further mention of the Bourgionette

Touring or Chummy Roadster has been found and, if these models were in fact produced, they remain a mystery to this writer.

New Special Heaslet cars with "extended tops" were scheduled for delivery in late March. The new design 2-passenger Roadster began delivery in early April.

In a sales letter of July 11, 1917, it was announced that the then current production of Touring cars and Roadsters (both Fours and Sixes) were being painted in four colors distributed as follows:

| Purple Lake | 60% |
| Chrome Green | 20% |
| Auto Blue | 10% |
| Battleship Gray | 10% |

The same letter advised that approximately 20 percent of Sixes were being equipped with natural wood wheels, while wire wheels were being made available at $75 additional per car.

A sales letter of October 12, 1917, announced that Houk or Hayes wire wheel equipment could now be furnished for any 1916-17 cars at a cost of $165 for black or $175 for color or white.

Other body styles mentioned in sales department letters for this period include: 1) Brougham with detachable curtain roof over driver at $2,700; 2) Brougham with solid detachable roof over driver at $2,750; and 3) Landaulet at $2,750. Although no descriptions or photos of these cars are available, it is safe to assume that they represent modifications of the standard Limousines.

According to one widely quoted source, production of the ED-Six continued until January, 1918, and the SF-Four until April 1918. However, Service Department Letter No. 281, dated January 8, 1918, states that production of Series 18 cars had already terminated by the time the letter was issued. Sales of Series 18 cars, however, continued for a considerable period of time, and new prices were announced effective January 1, 1918.

This 1916 one-ton delivery van was owned by Robertson Bros. which apparently was a large clothing or department store from the background show window. Apparently the vehicle was ordered without a spare tire. Only the rim came as standard equipment for these units. The 4-cylinder engine developed 40 horsepower for the 1916-17 cars.

Virtually unchanged from its 1915 counterpart is the 1916-17 Model SF Combination Passenger Express Car. For the two-year model run, it sold for $1,025. Note the rear step plate for entrance into the rear compartment. This view shows the seats in a folded position, and the vehicle ready for use as a cargo carrier.

This 1917 Series 18 Model "SF" 4-cylinder Roadster was considered a three-passenger vehicle due to the unusual seating arrangement of the driving compartment. The vehicle delivered $930, but if the 6-cylinder engine were ordered, the price increased to $1,170. The side curtains were standard equipment.

Here is a 1917 Model SF 4-cylinder three-passenger Landau Roadster. This example proved more popular than the plain roadster especially in winter driving as it offered a more snug enclosure. For summer use, the open roadster offered a carefree approach to driving with the top in the down position. The best way to distinguish this model from the plain roadster is by the Landau and the rectangular plate glass windows in the doors. As a Four, it sold for $1,150; the Six delivered for $1,350.

This 1917 Studebaker Model "SF" 4-cylinder was known as the "Everyweather Car." Popular in 1916, it was now back for its second year. This unit looks like it's seen a bit of use in its first year of travel. It is equipped with a front bumper, spotlight, and rear luggage rack, all of which were not part of the $1,700 price tag. In good weather, all of the side panels could be removed, to offer a fully open car, but with a solid top. However, with the panels in place, the windows could not be opened in a conventional manner. Instead, the 2-piece glass had an upper pane that would swing outward for ventilation.

Even the fire department chose the 1917 "ED-6" Roadster. A similar car was available in 1918-19, but was referred to as Model EG. Note the chains are securely placed on the rear tires for that extra bit of traction.

A Model "ED-6" 4-passenger Coupe for 1917-19 looks basically the same as its 1916 predecessor except that the bustle back has a more curvaceous line to it and the price increased from $1,550 to $1,750. The model rode on a 122-inch wheelbase. This model continued to use a folding auxiliary folding seat in the front for the fourth passenger.

The 1917 Studebaker Model "ED-6" Touring Sedan for seven-passengers was available for $1,700. A similar car with the 4-cylinder engine delivered for $940. Each model came equipped with a genuine leather interior and had 25 coats of hand-applied paint and vanish.

This Series 18 "ED-6" 5-passenger Sedan also has been fitted with Houk wheels. These expensive wire wheels appear to be the upscale thing for Studebaker at this time, even though the standard wooden wheels were generally ordered on most vehicles. This example came with a lighter body color and black above the belt-line and black fenders. Note the windshield is in the half opened position only part way up and the steering wheel is on the right side. The car must have been built for export service. This was not a Studebaker body, but appears to have been one built under contract with the Willoughby Co. which was a well-known builder of semi-custom closed car bodies. At this point, Willoughby was supplying a limited run of closed car bodies to Studebaker.

This vehicle is a 1917 Series "18" 6-cylinder 7-passenger Limousine. It is equipped with extra cost Houk wire wheels. The unit measures seven feet tall. The Series 18 models followed a great reputation from the Series 16 and 17 cars which saw a production of over 100,000 vehicles from inception in July of 1915. This example was the most expensive Studebaker offered for the year. It delivered for $2,600.

This 1917 ED-6 chauffeur-driven Town Car is a bit different from the usual 7-passenger models. It is equipped with a cloth top over the chauffeur's compartment, in true Town Car fashion, rather than having the fixed top extend over the front as was the case of most limousine cars. This model appears to be extinct today, or at least no collectors have come up with one. Even in this era, pretentious vehicles of this type were quite rare, being purchased only by the extremely rich. Probably the body was custom made only when a special order was placed by a dealer.

This rare 1917 ED-6 is called a Limousine Brougham. The Landau bars were very uncommon to Studebaker models at this time. This example, like the other Studebaker Limousines of this era, is just history. By the lines in the top, it would appear that the landau irons are functional, and that the rear section could be lowered to provide a semi-open back for pleasant weather excursions. Although the chauffeur's compartment has a solid top, side curtains would have had to been used in bad weather.

Sporting a body by Willoughby & Co. of Utica, N.Y., is this attractive coupe on a Series 18 ED-6 chassis. It appears that during this period, Studebaker no longer produced its own closed car bodies, preferring instead to farm that task out to the numerous body suppliers who were quite happy to build various units to a car manufacturer's specifications. This unit features a split windshield not unlike that found on the center-door sedan in the previous chapter. Probably of semi-custom status, the car has also been fitted with Houk wire wheels, which certainly did not appear out of place on a relatively expensive car such as this.

Although Willoughby is credited with supplying Studebaker's closed coupe bodies in this era, this particular 3-passenger coupe does not appear to be a Willoughby model. Rather it looks like a product from All-Metal Body Co. of Indiana, which was building most of Studebaker's sedan units. Far less costly than the Willoughby bodies, the All-Metal units were still substantial and well styled, and a definite credit to the Studebaker chassis.

This is the famous "Gold Chassis" about which much has been written. The chassis was a stock 1916-17 ED-6. At first it was displayed only as a chassis with nearly all parts plated in gold, except the engine. The chassis was later fitted with a 1917 Heaslet special body and displayed for many years in the Studebaker museum. The ultimate disposition of the "Gold Car" is unknown.

The All-Metal Body Co. was the main supplier of Studebaker's sedan bodies this year, as Studebaker found itself just barely able to keep up with the production of open cars. Considered semi-custom models, these closed cars were built on the ED-6 chassis, and were sometimes fitted with the costly Houk wire wheels shown here. Of unusual styling was the All-Metal sedan, which has a left-hand door for the driver only, while the right-hand door was placed in the center of the body, in center-door fashion. The right-hand front passenger seat was considered an auxiliary, and could be folded against the dash when not needed.

U.S. Mail service also chose Studebaker for their commercial vehicles. This is a one-ton truck with a body now built by Studebaker. Its weight capacity allowed for the vehicle to carry items up to 2,000 pounds with no difficulty. The mesh screen side panels were typical for mail vehicles into the late twenties. Side curtains could be lowered in bad weather. Note that the windshield rises to the roof, but does not attach to it. A small piece of canvas filled the space between the upper windshield frame and the actual roof overhang. The advantage of this design was that severe body flexing on rough roads would not put heavy strain on the plate glass windshield, and thus crack the glass.

This 1918 ambulance came on the ED-6 chassis. The unit road on a 153-inch wheelbase. The body builder is unknown. Note the kerosene lanterns by the driver's compartment and the three-part windshield, two of which are open for ventilating purposes. The center pane was part of the windshield proper, while the upper one was a separate pane, attached to the overhanging roof. A speaking tube leads to the rear portion, allowing the driver to talk to the attendant, or vice-versa. Although still crude by today's standards, this ambulance represents a big improvement over vehicles of only 10 years earlier.

# 1918-1919

As early as 1916, Studebaker management formulated plans for the construction of a completely new, modern plant in South Bend with a projected yearly capacity for the production of 150,000 automobiles. At this time, the South Bend plant was still devoted exclusively to the production of horse-drawn equipment of all kinds, while automobile production was centered only in Detroit. But the Motor City factories, working at full capacity, could only turn out about 60 to 70,000 cars annually. President Erskine was thinking in terms of 200,000 cars per year, at least. Ground was broken December 12, 1916, for what was described as the "great expansion" with plans calling for the construction of numerous buildings over a period of several years. As soon as the first units were completed, the United States entered the war in Europe and the newly-constructed buildings, equipped for forging and machining, were converted to work on war orders for the Ordinance Department of the United States Army. Further construction of the new plant would have to await the cessation of hostilities.

By October of 1918, it was apparent that the war in Europe was nearly over, and construction of the new plant — Plant Two, as it was called — was resumed. In 1919, Studebaker terminated production of its complete line of buggies, carriages, harnesses, and all other horse-drawn equipment with the exception of farm wagons. But a year later, farm wagon production was also halted. After 68 years, the world's most renowned manufacturer of horse-drawn equipment had at last found this part of the business to be unprofitable. Much of the woodworking equipment used for the construction of wagons was ideally suited for automobile body building and was retained for use in the business. Likewise, the factory buildings were also suited for automobile body building so Studebaker was able to make the transition to the Age of the Automobile with a minimum of plant disruption. Thus, old Plant One — the vehicle plant — was converted to the production of parts and automobile bodies which were supplied to the Detroit facilities of the new Plant Two in South Bend.

The New Light Six

While the construction of the new Plant Two was moving ahead, the Studebaker engineering staff was busily engaged in the design of the new car. In the immediate post war period, Studebaker's lowest price model was the SH Light Four which sold for slightly more than $1,000 at the factory. The problems of vibration inherent in the four-cylinder motor, particularly annoying in a closed car, had never been satisfactorily solved up to that time. Hence, Studebaker decided to drop the Four, once and for all, and to produce a new lightweight six-cylinder car to sell in the same price-range as the Four. The new Six embodied a combination of traditionally solid Studebaker design with enough new and daring features to make it interesting. Light Six seemed to be a name that suited the new product ideally, but Studebaker already had a car called the Light Six — the Model EH — which had been in production since early in 1918. Accordingly, the Model EH was renamed the Special Six after the 1919 production year and the all-new Six was called the model EJ Light Six.

The new Light Six, which was to be the sole product of Plant Two, was a break from the Studebaker tradition in that few parts were interchangeable with other products of the Studebaker lines — the special Six and Big Six. The EJ was a completely new design in its own right. Noteworthy features of the new car included: Three-point engine suspension, inclined valves with roller cam followers, aluminum cylinder head of unique patented design with integral intake manifold, thermostatic temperature control, silent chain camshaft drive, and fully machined connecting rods and crankshaft. The basic engine design of the Light Six was the last engineering effort of the great team of Fred M. Zeder, Owen R. Skelton, and Carl Breer, before their departure from Studebaker. The design was to survive for over ten years through the Standard Six cars, the Dictator Six, the GJ Commander Six, and finally the model 53 Erskine and Studebaker Six of 1930. By this

For the 1918-19 model run the designations were changed. Thus, this example is a Light Four, which was technically referred to as the "SH" series. The 112-inch wheelbase was still retained, as well as the 40 horsepower engine. New for the year was a scientifically-designed "hot spot" intake manifold and a very accessible engine, supposedly the easiest for adjustments and least likely to need repairs. The engine now offered a three main bearing crankshaft. This model sold for $995. It was in production from February, 1918, to October, 1919, with a production run of 12,500 vehicles. At that point, 4-cylinder cars were discontinued.

time, numerous changes and improvements had been made, but a careful inspection reveals the block's heritage. The Zeder-Skelton-Breer team, incidentally, left Studebaker to design a totally new car for the then well-known but financially weak Willys-Overland Company. However, before the car could go into production, Willys-Overland was forced to sell off some of its assets to forstall foreclosure on the entire company. Among the assets sold were its plant at Elizabeth, N.J., and the rights to the new Zeder-Skelton-Breer vehicle. Both the factory and the car designs were bought at auction by William C. Durant, who for the second and final time, had recently been stripped of his leadership at General Motors. The car subsequently was put into production the following year under the name Flint (in honor of the Michigan city where Durant was raised) and the vehicle was used as a cornerstone for Durant's third automotive empire. Meanwhile, though Durant had the designs, he did not have the engineers. Zeder, Breer, and Skelton subsequently were hired by the newly reorganized Maxwell firm headed by Walter P. Chrysler. For many years they would provide outstanding engineering for the Chrysler Corp., including the design of the very first car to bear the Chrysler name. As engineers and designers, they had the respect of the entire automotive industry, while at Chrysler they were affectionately known as "The Three Musketeers."

Production Hampered

Production of the new car was slated to begin January 1, 1920, but delays in construction resulted. These were primarily due to the shortages of materials and rail transport in the postwar period. Thus, the first Light Six was not turned out until April 30, 1920, an occasion for much rejoicing on the part of Studebaker management and workers. Production in its first year was limited to about 7,000 units. Due to inflation and

high taxes, prices of the Light Six were well above the $1,000 tag that had been aimed for.

The South Bend Plant Two was a marvel of efficiency for its day. It was one of the few plants in the industry fully integrated for the production of a single model of automobile. The nine separate buildings of Plant Two were built on 85 acres of ground and had a combined floor space of 3,700,000 square feet. There were three huge four-story buildings for storage, body-building, and final assembly. Other large buildings included a stamping plant, forge shop, machine shop, a foundry with a daily capacity of 600 tons of castings, and a car shipping building. A totally new power plant furnished steam and electricity to both Plants One and Two.

The construction of Plant Two required an ultimate outlay of about $15-million, an amount which exceeded available reserves, especially in view of the nearly $8-million in uncollected war production accounts. Therefore, Studebaker financed the construction by the sale of $15-million in ten-year 7% Gold Notes. The debt was retired in only a little over a year by the floating of $15-million in new capital stock.

Studebaker now stood on the threshold of the era of greatest expansion in its history. Within three years the number of vehicles sold was to climb to over 145,000, compared with a total of a little over 51,000 in 1920. And, over half of these were Light Sixes. In 1923 alone, the total value of Studebaker cars produced exceeded the total value of all horse-drawn equipment produced in the first 68 years of operation. Truly the age of the automobile had arrived!

The Light Six was changed relatively little from 1920 through 1924. The Model EM Light Six for 1923 featured an *all steel* Touring Car body, the first all steel body ever built by Studebaker. During 1923 production, after serial number 1,106,001, the aluminum cylinder head was abandoned in favor of a cast iron head of more conventional design. The change required the introduction of a new cylinder block, intake manifold, carburetor, and carburetor controls.

The Light Six was always rather spartan in appointments although, in 1924, bumpers, balloon tires, and nickel-plated radiator shells were offered to attract style-conscious buyers. Slightly over 200,000 Light Sixes were built from April, 1920, to July, 1924, when production was halted to make way for the new version — to be called the Standard Six.

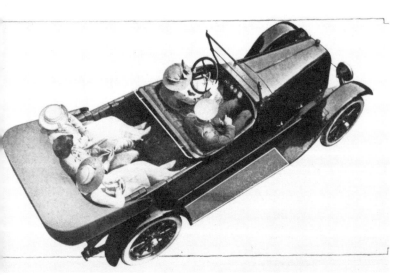

This view of the 1918-19 EH Light Six shows it with a full compliment of passengers. It's skillful body design gave the right amount of length and width for five people to sit comfortably without crowding. But notice the passengers. It looks like the lady of the house is taking three girl friends for an afternoon excursion...and the liveried chauffeur on the right is probably there to fix any flats or other trouble that might occur.

A downward view of the 1918-19 EH Light Six 5-passenger Touring Car gives an all over look at how much interior space the touring offered and how accessible the dash controls were. Note the neat fit of the top boot.

The 1918-19 Light Six would shortly be referred to as the Special Six, but would continue with the same letter designation of "EH." For this time, it was a Series 19 model. The interior seating was genuine leather. The EH Series 19 began production February, 1918, and ended November, 1919, with a production of 25,801 vehicles.

The headlamp lens was a distinguishable note between this Light Six and the Big Six vehicles. These cars came with a more rounded glass, while the Big Six models appeared with a more squared headlight bezel. The Light Six sold for $1,395.

A view taken at the Chicago Speedway in December, 1917, shows the new Series 19, 1918, models from left to right Big Six, Light Six, and Light Four. The cars are participating in a long-distance endurance test. In its day, this high-banked board track provided plenty of excitement for race fans, while between races it was often used as a test bed for many different makes of cars.

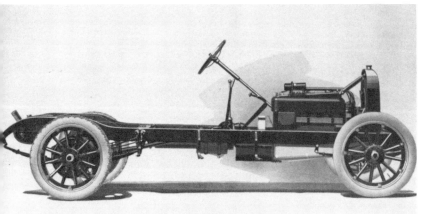

A view of the durable 1918-19 EH Light Six chassis. Company advertising summed it up simply by saying "Strength and Simplicity." Studebakers now used smooth tread on the front tires, while the rear ones were of the new "Safety Tread" design.

The 1918-19 Studebaker EH Light Six Series 19 was introduced in February, 1918, but was discontinued as a Light Six in November of 1919, with a total production under that heading of 25,801 units. After this date, the cars were renamed Special Sixes Series 20, and remained as such until May of 1921, having a run of 45,096 units produced.

An overhead view of the new Big Six Touring Car for 1918-19 shows the extraordinary roominess the 7-passenger vehicle offered. The only color available on Big Six cars for the model run was dark green. Upholstery was in French-plaited genuine black leather. When not in use, the auxiliary seats could be folded into their own compartment behind the front seat.

Now riding on a 126-inch wheelbase is the 1918-19 EG Big Six Touring. The EG "Six" cars Series 19 began production February, 1918, and ended in October, 1919. The total production amounted to 11,757 for the year.

# 1918-1919

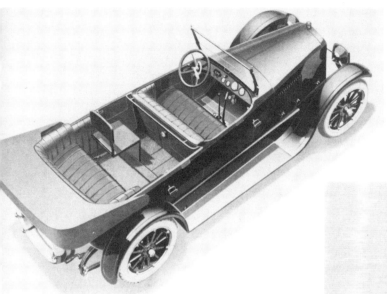

This birds' eye view of the 1918-19 7-passenger Big Six Touring gives a better look at its flat French-plaited, genuine leather upholstery. With one jump seat in the up position, it shows how easy it was for passengers to enter or exit the car. New for the year were a Waltham clock mounted on the dash, a tonneau light with extension cord, and a gypsy top with oval beveled plate glass windows in the rear.

An artist conception of the 1918-19 Series 19 Model EG Touring Sedan was used in contemporary Studebaker magazine ads. The new 4-door model saw an increase to 60 horsepower. It now was on a 126-inch wheelbase and its fuel supply came from a 17-gallon tank.

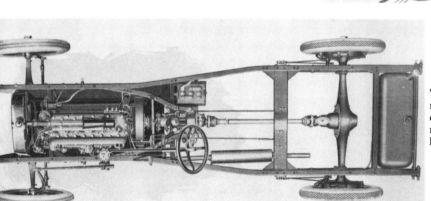

This view of the Big Six chassis shows the transmission now mounted on a sub-frame and Hotchkiss drive being employed. The unit displayed was simple and easy to maintain, whether done by a professional or by the owner himself. Timkin bearings were used throughout.

This is a 1918-19 Model EH Special Six 2-passenger Coupe. Studebaker files show this vehicle was in the planning stage to be manufactured, but whether it ever got to the final approval no one today is certain. This photo is either a heavily retouched prototype or an artist's concept.

# 1920-1922

The 1920-21 3-passenger Light Six Roadster was the lowest priced car that Studebaker produced for this time. Its selling price was $1,435 in 1920-21 and, for 1922, it sold for $1,045. The top material was of an imitation leather material. Its circular window was a rather novel device for those days. The spare tire mounted on the rear was an extra-cost option.

In the 1920 model run, the offerings from Studebaker were classed in three different series: The Light Six was priced from $1,435 for a 3-passenger Roadster; the Special Six EU had prices beginning at $1,685 for a 5-passenger Touring, and the Studebaker EG started with a price of $2,133 for a 7-passenger Touring. The Light Six came with a 207 cubic-inch engine that developed 40 horsepower at 2000 RPM. The bore and stroke were 3-1/8x4-1/2. The tire size was 32x4 inches; the models rode on a 112-inch wheelbase. Four body types were available in the Light Six series. The weight of the Touring Sedan was 2,400 pounds.

The Special Six EU series came with a 288 cubic-inch engine that developed 50 horsepower at 2000 RPM. The bore and stroke were 3-1/2x5, tire size was 32x4 inches, the same as the Light Six and the larger series of EG cars. All Special Six cars used a 119-inch wheelbase. A weight of 2,995 pounds was listed for a 5-passenger Touring.

The top of the line for the year was the EG Series. It came with a 353 cubic-inch six-cylinder engine that developed 65 horsepower at 2000 RPM; its bore and stroke were 3-3/8x5. The EG line rode on a 126-inch wheelbase. Its 7-passenger Touring tipped the scales at 3,175 pounds, making it the heaviest model of the year. A total of 12 models were available for the year. Sadly, production figures and its sales position for the year are not available.

This 1920-22 EJ Light Six Roadster shows how well it was suited to carrying boxed packages. But the front items makes one wonder how long the EJ Roadster will travel before heating up. The side curtains indicate that the day is not overly warm, so maybe radiator air blockage would not be a problem on this trip.

The EJ series of cars remained virtually unchanged for the number of years they were in production, which was 1918 to 1924. This particular model is from the 1920-22 era. The Light Six had a 207.1 cubic-inch engine with a bore and stroke 3-1/8x4-1/2. This Light Six Touring delivered for $1,485 in 1920-21, but in 1922 decreased to $1,045. It weighed 2,400 pounds.

This 1920-22 EJ Light Six Coupe rode on a 112-inch wheelbase and employed 32x4.00-tires, the same as on the two larger series of cars. The wheels consisted of wood spokes and were painted black. Note the top half of the windshield swings out for ventilation.

This unusual item is a 1920-22 Model EJ Light Six. But it does resemble an early hot rod of sorts. The vehicle had been used by the San Francisco Chronicle as a Press Car. Just its appearance probably drew people's attention. Whether it is still in a museum, is unknown.

This U.S. Mail vehicle of the 1920-22 era is an EJ Light Six operating in the Arizona desert. The placard in the back states: "Yes, Arizona is Dry-Dry. The Jack Rabbits Carry Canteens and Frogs Seven Years Old Haven't Learned to Swim Yet - But Salome Water is the Best made. Try some." Evidently, the boys and the Studebaker have tried some and are keeping cool crossing the desert! From the amount of mud splattered on the car, it is evident that the group found some water someplace...and then wondered about the wisdom of removing the fenders and running boards.

The 112-inch Light Six 4-door Sedan for 1920-22 developed 40 horsepower at 2000 rpm. Its production schedule began in April, 1920, and continued to November, 1922. During this time, 83,879 cars were produced in the Light Six line.

# 1920-1922

This sharp looking little rig is a 1920-22 EJ Light Six chassis, with a professional-looking roadster pickup body. Studebaker supposedly did not build a pick-up body at this time, yet this unit was part of a fleet owned by the large Consolidated Edison Co. The possibilities are that either Studebaker built these vehicles as part of a large special order, or an unidentified independent company mounted their own roadster pickups on chassis-cowl units supplied by Studebaker.

This example happens to be a 1920-22 Light Six, done up in a boat-tail version, possibly to be classed as a speedster. Studebaker turned out no such animal at that time. Hailing from Juneau, Alaska, the fenderless wonder might have been an early hot rod, or possibly was designed for the local race circuit, if there was one in Alaska at that time.

The 1920-21 Model EH Special Six 3-passenger Roadster delivered for $1,625. This unit differs somewhat from the Light Six Roadster as it is without the circular windows in its leather top. Window curtains were standard for this model. Those who drove their roadster in wintertime found the window protection a must.

A popular model in the early 1920s was the EH Special Six Touring. It began production in October, 1919, and continued to May, 1921, with a total of 45,096 cars manufactured in various body styles. This 6-cylinder developed 50 horsepower from its 288 cubic-inch engine.

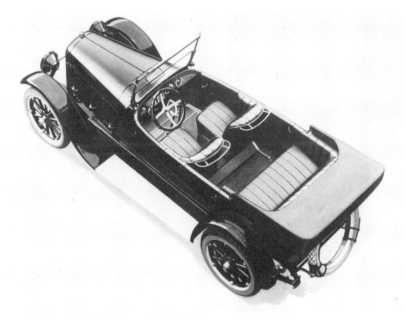

Built during the 1920-22 era is this EH Special Six 4-door, 4-passenger Touring Car. This body style differed from regular touring car by having a divided front seat and a shorter tonneau. It delivered for the same price as the regular touring at $1,455.

In 1920-21 this 4-passenger Coupe style was popular both as car for a businessman who needed more room for his selling supplies, or as a small family car. It delivered for $1,700. Notice that the right front seat was considered an auxiliary, and folded against the dash when not in use. When in use, as shown here, its occupant had to ride facing the rear.

A 1920-21 Special Six Coupe delivered for $1,685. This example came only as a 2-passenger vehicle. Its main difference over the Light Six was that it came on a 7-inch longer chassis, consisting of a 119-inch wheelbase. The unit weighed 2,900 pounds.

Virtually the same offering as the Special Six 4-passenger Coupe was this model, destined for export. Note it is a right-hand drive model. The chief exterior difference between this and the standard model is that the door handle on this version is placed at the rear of the door, rather than in the suicide manner (opening from the front). Probably this body was supplied by Willoughby or some other outside body builder other than All-Metal. Its semi-custom status also makes it a more expensive car selling for $1,920.

The EH 1920-21 4-door Sedan was also one that was shipped overseas after World War I. Studebaker did alright for themselves in the export field. This model sold for $2,010 as an export unit.

The family car was proving to be the most popular. Here is the 1920-21 Model EH Special Six. This example sold for $1,795 and it weighed in at 2,995 pounds. A choice of either leather or mohair upholstery could be ordered for the sedan.

This 1920-21 Model EH Special Six has been fitted with a nicely styled pickup body of non-factory origin. The vehicle probably started life as a Touring Car or Roadster, and was converted to this pick-up or squad car. The conversion is believed to have been done in the shops of the Quebec Fire Dept. At this time, Studebaker did not produce pickup trucks. Note the special spotlight and air horn with which the vehicle is equipped. The tire chains were probably quite necessary, considering the snowy ground upon which the truck sits.

This 1920-21 EH Special Six Sedan may be either a pre-production model or limited production vehicle from one of the independent body builders. The placement of the doors and design of the cowl lights does not match photos of known production models.

The Big Six for 1920-21 was offered both as a 7-passenger Touring Car and as a closed sedan. Production increased on these. The Big Six was known as the Model EG. It began its 1920 run in November, 1919, and continued through to December, 1921. Production figures for this period are not available. The Touring Car sold for $2,135.

Another 1920-21 export vehicle was this EG Big Six 7-passenger Touring. The car came on a 126-inch wheelbase and used the 353 cubic-inch engine that developed 65 horsepower, the same as the state-side vehicles used. This example cost over $2,400, shipped to its port of entry.

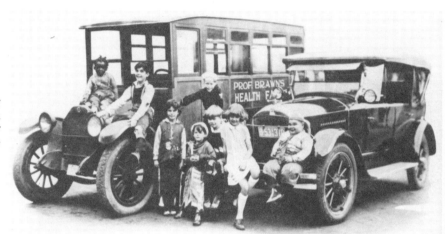

The "Our Gang" comedy movie group is posed in front of a 1920 EG 7-passenger Touring and a Studebaker bus of an earlier era. The Series-90 sports a 1923 license plate. The car is equipped with a rare set of windwings and dual spotlights, all attached to the windshield posts.

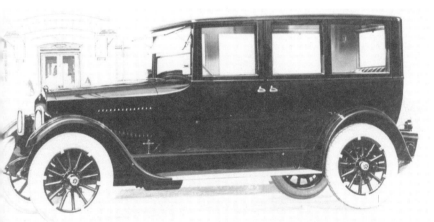

The first closed model in the EG line came with the 1920-21 models. The 7-passenger Sedan proved popular with large families of upper-middle income. The car was available for roughly $2,200. All mechanical devices were virtually what they had been since the EG was introduced in February, 1918.

The frame to this Big Six appears to be an early 1920-21 that was used for sports car and racing events abroad. . . probably in Italy. The chromed headlights, hood, and radiator shell were someone's creation, but certainly not Studebaker's. The identification on the picture reads "Modelo S.R.C. Gran Sport," but it is unknown if this was a one-off or a limited production 4-passenger sports touring car.

STUDEBAKER tipo "Big-Six"
: Modelo S. R. C. gran Sport :

# 1920-1922

Basically being the same offering as in the two previous years was this 1922 EJ Light Six Touring. The 1922 models came with small bullet-shaped cowl lights which the previous cars did not offer. These Light Sixes used an aluminum head which was not totally free of problems. It was the final year for this head to be used. It sold for $1,045, the same as the 3-passenger Roadster.

A 1922 EJ Light Six Roadster had a large space under the rear deck, providing ample room for packages and luggage. Some of the refinements in the Roadster were parking lights set next to the windshield base, a large rectangular window curtain, and convenient inside and outside door handles. A thief-proof transmission lock reduced the rate of theft insurance by 20 percent. Standard non-skid cord tires all around were also included in the regular equipment. The model delivered for $1,045, the same as the Light Six Touring. The only color offered was black with a red stripe around the wheels.

This 1922 EJ Light Six Touring sports a non-factory accessory winter hardtop. Storm curtains opened with the doors. These door curtains were bound on three sides by steel rods to insure a good fit and afford proper protection from the weather. The model came on a 112-inch wheelbase, the same as earlier Light Six vehicles.

Studebaker's 1920-22 Light Six 2-passenger Coupe came equipped with a lock and handle for the rear compartment deck lid. The Coupe was the ideal car for salesmen to carry their samples. The model delivered for $1,375 in 1922.

A 1922 Model EL Special-Six 2-passenger Roadster rode on a 119-inch wheelbase. The engine used a 3 -inch bore and 5-inch stroke, displaced 288 cubic-inches and developed 50 horsepower. The colors available for the 1922 Special Sixes were Studebaker blue, with a black hood, blue wheels, and gold striping on wheels and louvers. Or maroon could be substituted for blue, with the other components in black.

Oddly enough, Studebaker chose different body designations for their models which, by today's standards, don't quite apply. This example they called a Special Six 4-Passenger Roadster, popularly called the Chummy Roadster. The 1922 model seated four passengers comfortably. The front seats are separated making it possible to enter the rear compartment between the seats without much difficulty. For 1922, this was classed as an EL. The 1920-21 cars were EHs. The Chummy Roadster was only available in the Special Six line.

This example appears very much the same as the regular EL Chummy Roadster for 1922, except that the steering wheel is mounted on the right. This was another one of those famous exports Studebaker was famous for shipping to distant lands. Note it carries two small oval windows in the rear compartment rather than the one large plate glass window in the rear curtain. This was probably a running change, caused by a switch in top suppliers, or simply a style variation.

Little change was seen on this 1922 Model EL Special Six 5-passenger Touring over the next couple of years of production. The car offered a newly designed body on a chassis of 119-inch wheelbase. The car's mechanical changes included a detachable head, as in the Light Six and Big Six models, and an improved carburetor with the "hot-spot" intake manifold.

The EL Special-Six 5-passenger Sedan for 1922 saw production from November, 1921, until July, 1924. During that time a total of 111,443 units were built in the various Special Six body styles. This example sold for $1,275 in 1922-23.

The Special-Six Coupe was an elegantly appointed 4-passenger enclosed car. It came with a soft velvet Mohair interior, with top lining, trimming, and floor carpets harmonizing in color and design. Silk roller curtains were provided at the windows and the electric dome light and pillar coach lamps gave the final touch. The folding seat for the fourth passenger was, in reality, a comfortable chair with cushioned seat, back and arms. The model sold for $1,250 in 1922.

The EK Big Six Four-Passenger Speedster for the 1922-24 didn't debut until the 1922 model run. The side-mounted tire equipment, small trunk, and disc wheels with the six lugs were special features of this car. It was upholstered with a high-grade hand-buffed leather that made it a very sporty car in its day. It sold for $1,835 making it one of the most expensive models available for 1922.

One of the rare 1922-24 Model EK Big Six Tourings is displayed at a car show. A quality restoration makes it appear as if the event was in 1922. Everything is as it should be. Note the special cowl lamps and factory style spotlight. The artistically styled headlamps were a Studebaker feature of that era on all models.

The Big-Six Seven Passenger Touring for 1922-24 again was pretty much unchanged. The catalog specifications for 1922 claimed this 126-inch wheelbased car now had 60 horsepower, offered a detachable head with a two-range carburetor, shock absorbers, new clear vision one-piece windshield and windshield wiper, cowl ventilator, cowl lights, courtesy lights, and an eight-day clock. The car went out the door in the $1,850 range.

This 1922-24 EK Big Six wears a non-factory removable winter hardtop. The driver obviously has travelled a bit in inclement weather. The canopy covering the hood and radiator was to keep the heat in the engine compartment, where it would supply the exhaust heater if the car had one. Otherwise, just the plain engine heat going through the firewall and floorboards would still be better than nothing. It also sports accessory step plates on the running board and the rather ugly disc wheels that were beginning to become very popular aftermarket items. Once spring came about, this hardtop could be removed and be replaced with the regular touring car top.

Another series of Big Six models were offered from 1922 to 1924. Shown here is a Big Six Four-Passenger Coupe, Model EK. Its chassis specifications were the same as for touring cars and sedans. Contributing to the smoothness, quiet running and tremendous power which made this engine famous were: the demountable head with its advantages of perfect combustion and high economy; its rugged 4-bearing perfectly balanced crankshaft; the large capacity water jackets, and highly perfected oiling system. This example made its introduction for 1922 and lasted through 1924. The coupe sold in the $1,750 bracket for the next three years.

Now available in its second season was the 1922 EK Big-Six Sedan for 7-passengers. The model was upholstered in rich mohair velvet plush, with headliner and floor carpeting of equal quality. The price continued to remain in the $2,200 range.

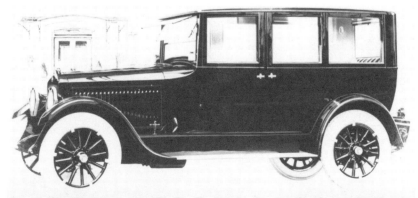

# 1923-1924

In 1923, Studebaker entered the year with the Light Six, Special Six, and Big Six. A total of 13 models were available ranging in price from a 3-passenger Roadster for $975 to a 7-passenger Big Six Sedan for $2,750.

The Light Six cars had a six-cylinder engine of 207.1 cubic inches that developed 40 horsepower at 2000 RPM. The bore and stroke were 3-1/8x4-1/2. The tire size was 31x4. The fuel supply measured 15 gallons, and the car averaged 18 miles per gallon. The vehicles would travel approximately 200 miles per quart of oil. The oil capacity was six quarts. The Light Six rode on a 112-inch wheelbase.

The Special Six came in four models: Roadster, Touring, 4-passenger Coupe, and Sedan. Prices ranged from $1,250 for the Roadster to $2,050 for a 5-passenger Sedan. The Special Six had a 288.6 cubic-inch engine that developed 50 horsepower at 2000 RPM. The bore and stroke were 3-1/2x5. The tire size was 32x4. The fuel supply came from a 17 gallon tank, while the crankcase held a capacity of six quarts. All Special Six models used a 119-inch wheelbase.

The prestige line for 1923 came in five styles. They were priced from $1,750 for a Big Six Touring, to $2,750 in the 7-passenger Sedan version. The Big Six cars used a 353.8 cubic-inch engine that developed 60 horsepower at 2000 RPM. The bore and stroke were 3-7/8x5. The tire size was 33x4-1/2. The Big Six vehicles carried a 17 gallon fuel supply like the Special Six but averaged 13 MPG. The wheelbase was 126 inches.

Production for 1923 was about 150,00 units and it put Studebaker in the seventh place for the year.

Probably photographed on a movie set was this 1923-24 Model E M Light Six Roadster. It sports a California license from 1923, the Automobile Club of Southern California emblem, and a city nameplate often used in the 1920-30 era in California, letting people know where the car was based. The tag on this Studebaker states Hollywood.

This is a true factory photo showing the 1923-24 EM Light Six Roadster for 3-passengers. The model came with a one-piece windshield, giving both driver and passengers clear vision. It was also rainproof, as opposed to the 2-piece units which could leak in a heavy rainstorm. The cowl ventilator was of the new quick action type, which operated by means of a convenient lever.

The big news for 1923 from Studebaker was the return to the cast iron cylinder head. The aluminum affair did not work out too well. Collectors today, rather than try to repair an aluminum head for a 1921-22 car, generally will seek out a cast iron head from a 1923-24 model, finding it to be more beneficial in the long run. This roadster came minus a spare tire which was extra cost. This example delivered as a 2,550-pound car for $975.

Seen wearing the now-fashionable full disc wheels is the 1923-24 Model EM Touring car for 5-passengers. This wheel equipment was optional at extra cost for EM model cars and probably only ten percent came equipped with the accessory. In base form, the Touring sold for the same price as the Roadster, $975.

This is the basic way most 1923-24 EM Tourings looked, fitted with the black wooden spoke wheels. The Light Six cars for the two-year model came painted the same as earlier EJ cars...done in black. However, late 1924 did offer a few maroon models with black fenders.

The Light Six Model EM 5-Passenger Coupe came with distinctive headlights, attractive rectangular coach lamps, and rear corner reading lights which were operated from the instrument board. The 1923 models' rear fenders had more of a flare to them and the new windshield gave a clearer unobstructed view of the road ahead. This model had a small luggage rack at the rear, with nickel-plated rail and aluminum panel guards which added to the utility of the vehicle. This example sold for $1,055.

The 1923-24 Light Six Coupe looked very similar to the previous model. But, like all other 1923 Studebakers, it offered the new all-steel body for the first time. The model came with a genuine leather interior and nickel-finished hardware. A total of 5 models were available in the Light Six line for 1923-24. The two-passenger model delivered for $1,775.

"The Mail Must Go Through." Anyway, many times these 1923-24 Light Sixes were seen being used in rough terrain as this photo shows. The stripped Light Six, due to its light weight, was easy to maneuver in difficult areas such as this.

Studebaker entered the 1924 model year with basically the same offering from the year before.

The Light Six and Special Six models used Kelsey wheels while Budd wheels were employed on the Big Six vehicles. In 1924, the company took pride in its listing of 25 branch offices, 5,000 dealers, and over 3,500 service stations throughout the world. The factory claimed, with the total number of cars in operation, their sales of replacement parts amounted to $13 per car for repairs covering both renewals and accidents.

The price structure changed slightly on the 1924 cars. The lowest priced vehicle was the Light Six 3-passenger Roadster which increased $20 over the 1923 version. It now sold for $995 while the 7-passenger Big Six Sedan decreased from the 1923 price of $2,750 to $2,685. This was the last year for the Light Six series. Beginning in 1925, the low-priced models were called the Standard Six.

Studebaker continued to remain in the seventh position for sales this year.

The most practical and best seller in the Light-Six line was this 5-passenger Sedan for 1923-24. In December, 1922, it went into production with the entire Light Six line, and continued through July of 1924 with 118,002 vehicles produced during this time-frame.

The 1923-24 Special Six Roadster Model EM resembles the lines of the Big Six. However, the Big Six did not offer a Roadster in its line-up. Note the nickel-plated aluminum panel guards mounted on the rear deck. These could serve as a luggage rack, but primarily were intended to protect the deck from scuffing when the top was lowered. This model sold for $1,325, but the disc wheels were an extra cost option. The motor-meter was standard equipment.

This Special Six Model EL Touring sports a nickel radiator which was a distinguishing feature not seen in the Light Six line, or on 1923 Special Six models. The aluminum step plates also were a new feature for the year. Except for the distinctive rear section, this model resembles the Chummy Roadster in appearance. However, the Chummy model did not enter the 1923-24 line of Special Six cars. It was discontinued at the end of 1922.

A 1922-24 Special Six Roadster was available from November, 1921, through July, 1924. These vehicles were designated EL Models and sold for $1,325.

Even in 1923-24, Studebaker showed an interest in racing. Here is an example of a Light Six with its 35 horsepower engine doing its stuff. I'm sure a little altering took place to get the 207 cubic-inch engine ready for the racing event.

A 1924 version of the 1923-24 model run is this Model EL Special Six Touring. The Series 1923-24 began production in December, 1922, and continued to July, 1924, with a 111,443 vehicles manufactured. This Touring model sold for $1,350.

The EH chassis design continued into the Model EL lines with relatively minor changes. The small circular cowl lamps in the corners of the frame, as on this touring model, were a noted and remembered feature of the Special Six.

Two 1923-24 Special Six EL Tourings are on the floor of a dealership. It is possible that this is a foreign dealership, as the car on the right has right-hand drive, and a notation on the bottom of the picture says "Juli 1923" . . . or maybe the dealer simply couldn't spell July. According to signs on the wall, this dealer also handled Philips electric components and Triumph motorcycles.

This 1923 EL Special Six Touring is equipped with disc wheels, optional at extra cost. The side-mounted spares and trunk were not standard equipment for this model.

The well-engineered features of the Light Six were retained on the Standard Six line introduced on September 14, 1924. The engine bore was increased one-quarter inch and the greater displacement with a higher compression ratio — 4.5 compared to 4.38 for the Light Six — gave a rated horsepower of 50 at 2200 RPM for the newer engine. It was also vastly improved by conversion to full pressure lubrication to main, rod, and cam shaft bearings. Instead of the transmission being mounted on a separate sub-frame as on the Light Sixes, it was bolted directly to the flywheel housing which, in turn, bolted to the engine. Numerous other minor changes were required by the adoption of the unit power plant construction.

The new Standard Sixes were equipped with balloon tires as standard equipment and a four-wheel hydraulically-actuated brake system was available as an extra cost option. A fully automatic spark advance system replaced the manual system used earlier, and Alemite pressure lubrication fittings replaced the oil and grease cups of the Light Six. The internal expanding rear emergency brake of the Light Six was abandoned in favor of a contracting brake band operating on a drum at the rear of the transmission.

The 1924 version of the 1923-24 model run shows the nickel-plated radiator which makes it truly a 1924 car. This example is called the EL 5-passenger Coupe with trunk. Overall, it was a very important and distinctive design, as it marked the first of what would become America's best selling body style...the 2-door sedan or 2-door coach, as it was often called. Note the distinctive rectangular coach lamps on the cowl that were popular equipment for the Special Six closed cars.

This is an early 1923 Model EL Special Six 4-door sedan equipped with the painted radiator shell. The model came equipped with the optional disc wheels, rather than the wooden variety. This car rode on 32x4.00-inch tires and had a 119-inch wheelbase.

The Center Car in this group of Studebaker models is a 1923 EL 4-passenger Special Six Coupe. The painted radiator tells us it's an early 1923 version. The vehicle next to it is a 1929 Model FD Commander Sedan.

# 1923-1924

This neat-looking 1923 Special Six was designed as a pickup for use as a service car for Studebaker dealers. For those wishing to have a vehicle of this type at their disposal, Studebaker suggested prospects contact the service department for a set of blueprints. It would be interesting to know how many were actually produced by dealers or in specialty body shops.

What a difference the nickel-plated radiator can make. The car also came equipped with the extra cost bumpers. With these small changes, the 1923-24 Model EL resembled the Big Six cars. This sedan sold for $2,050. Many people felt the lines of these Special Six cars resembled Buicks and small Packards. I agree!

A well-maintained 1924 Special Six poses with its owner, D. A. Pierce, an oil executive from Long Beach, California. Mr. Pierce registered more than 114,000 miles on the speedometer from 1924 to 1929. He purchased it from the Glenn E. Thomas Company in Long Beach. Incidentally, the Thomas dealership is still in business today. They have been a Dodge dealer for well over 40 years.

This special-bodied 1924 open-front limousine or town car was used in Czechoslovakia for government purposes. The body builder of this car is unknown. Also unknown is the very ancient high-wheeler posing with the limousine.

Many manufacturers took liberties with one another in the 1920s and early 1930s, as far as design goes. This 1923-24 EK Big Six Roadster, shares quite a resemblance with a Wills Sainte Claire both in radiator design and the disc wheel set-up. Strangely enough, this appears to have been a very rare car for the model run as it never was catalogued in sales brochures, nor did it make it into the 1923-24 parts books. How many were produced and sold, is unknown.

Studebaker's 1923-24 Model EK Big Six Touring offered the following as standard equipment: extra disc wheel with cord tire and tire cover, nickel-plated bumpers, motometer with an ornamental radiator cap, clock, rear-view mirror, and snubbers (shock absorbers). The car delivered for $1,750.

The Big Six EK 5-passenger Speedster came equipped with a quick-action cowl ventilator, rear view mirror, courtesy lamps, cowl lights, tonneau lamp with long extension cord, combination stop and tail light, a walnut steering wheel with an improved spark and gas control, aluminum-bound running boards with corrugated rubber mats and step pads, aluminum kick plates, grip handles and a clock. The easy way to distinguish the Speedster from other models are the two disc wheels with tires and covers mounted on the fenders out of the way of the doors. This version, along with other Big Sixes, began production in November, 1921, and continued with new models added until July, 1924. During that period of time, 48,892 cars left the factory. The Speedsters were painted in maroon. The car sold for $1,835.

This is an early Model EK Big Six in the 1923-24 model run. The example appears to be a little worse from heavy duty police work. Someone could have at least washed the vehicle for its portrait.

# 1923-1924

Harold Bell Wright, a popular novelist of the first quarter of the 20th Century, stands by his 1924 EK Speedster. The vehicle was purchased from the Elsbery Reynolds Studebaker dealership in Pomona, California, which was one of the largest Studebaker dealerships on the West Coast, at that time.

The Sheriff of Yuma County, Arizona, James Chappell, put many hard miles on this 1923 Big Six Speedster. Note the windshield spotlight at the roof of the car. In this era, touring cars were still the preferred style of most police officers.

One sturdy looking vehicle is this 1923-24 7-passenger Touring. A new feature of the 1923-24 cars was the small courtesy lights at the base of the cowl. The improvements seen for this two-year run included the one-piece rain proof windshield, automatic windshield cleaner and glare-proof visor. A complete tool box, provided with lock, was installed in the left front door. Note that the hood is painted in the same black as the fenders. The body was done in Studebaker blue with gold striping on the hood louvers.

A rear view of the 1923-24 Big Six 5-passenger Coupe shows the car with its spare tire yet to be installed. The door flap was for a handy pocked that was common on cars of this era. It was used for all sorts of items such as maps, gloves, and other small items. Note the window crank and door pull handle. The Coupe delivered for $2,493, which included the handy trunk, shown here with a waterproof covering. The rub rails on the back of the body protected the finish from the trunk rubbing against it on rough roads.

A 1923-24 Big Six 5-passenger Coupe offered luxurious travel at the lowest price with the highest quality. This vehicle offered a handy parcel compartment behind the rear seat and additional luggage space in the rear mounted trunk. Again, this was one of the most important new designs to ever appear on a Studebaker chassis, as it set the ground rules for what would eventually become the best selling car design in America, not only for Studebaker but for the entire automotive industry.

The 7-passenger Big Six Sedan came with the fender-mounted spare tires as standard equipment, and wore a small trunk at the rear. It also came with dome and corner lights, vanity case and smoking set, as well as a flower vase finished in dull silver in keeping with the other interior fittings. It was the most expensive model available for the two-year run, selling for $2,685.

Want to bet he is just leaving the dealership after having his first 1,000-mile check-up on the new 1923-24 EK Big Six 7-passenger Sedan. On the sign of the dealership, the original photo states "Cars washed and greased - drive in." Looking at the mud-caked wheels and doors, one wonders why this owner didn't read the sign.

This 1923 EK Big Six was a non-production vehicle. It does not offer the nickel-plated radiator, nor does it appear to be running on a standard wheelbase. Probably the work of some good but unknown custom body shop, the shortened car must have been a very attractive speedster for the young rich boy behind the wheel.

Those impressive headlights are looking at us again in this view of the 1923-24 Big Six 7-passenger Sedan. The car is equipped with motometer and ornamental radiator cap as standard equipment. All closed models came with a high quality heater in the rear compartment to give the exact temperature desired.

A stately vehicles, for sure, the 7-passenger Big Six Sedans and Speedsters came with the spares mounted in the fenders, giving that extra touch of class Studebaker was always noted for. Of quite high proportions, the rear compartment offered enough headroom for an average man to wear a top hat while riding...to the opera, of course.

# 1925

In 1925, Studebaker entered the year by telling the public "Studebaker models include a car of the right size, style and price to meet the demand of every quality buyer." There were three distinct new models in 15 body types which included an entirely new car called the Duplex. This vehicle offered the advantages of an open car with the protection of an enclosed car. It was available in all three series: the new Standard Six, Special Six, and Big Six. Possibly this model might have been classed as the "Original Studebaker Hardtop".

The Standard Six came with its 242 cubic-inch engine developing 50 horsepower at 2200 RPM. The bore and stroke were 3-3/8x4-1/2. Tire size for the series was 21x5. The fuel came from a 14-gallon tank while the oil capacity was six quarts. The wheelbase measured 113 inches. Prices ranged from $1,125 for a Standard Duplex Roadster to a Standard Six Sedan for $1,595.

The line-up of Special Six models amounted to four. Prices were from $1,450 for a Duplex Roadster, to

$2,150 for a 5-passenger Sedan. The Special Six came with a 289 cubic-inch engine that developed 65 horsepower at 2400 RPM. Its bore and stroke were 3-1/2x5 inches. The fuel supply was from a 19-gallon tank, while it required six quarts of oil for the engine room. Special Sixes rode on a 120-inch wheelbase. The tire size was 20x6.

The Big Six series used the 354 cubic-inch engine that developed 75 horsepower at 2400 RPM. The bore and stroke measured 3-7/8x5. It, like the Special Six, also required a 19-gallon fuel reserve and used six quarts of oil for the crankcase. The wheelbase was 127 inches, while tire size for the Big Six was 20x7. Prices ranged from $1,875 for a Duplex Phaeton, to $2,860 for a Big Six 7-passenger Berline. Four-wheeled brakes were considered an option on the 1925 cars. On the Standard Six, the additional cost was $65 and for the Special Six and Big Six models, the added brakes cost the buyer $75 more. Color choices available for the 1925 were black, gray and blue.

This 1925 Standard Six Duplex Roadster Model ER was delivered to this salesman with bumper equipment and a spare tire. An early model, it used the separate leather-covered flat visor. The firm he represents is the Roth Tobacco Company, which sold "B's Wax Chew and Smoke." The company claimed the tobacco was "Sweet as Honey." But the look on the salesman's face appears he is not convinced of what he sells . . . or maybe he just had too much of it the night before. Also, notice the height of the steering wheel in relation to the cowl height.

Showing Studebaker dependability is this 1925 EQ Special Six Roadster. The unit travelled without a falter for 110 hours from Brisbane to Burketown, Australia, and back, a distance of 3,000 miles. I wonder how it managed in the nighttime without headlights . . . unless the 110 hours were not consecutive. At any rate, the vehicle saw a little dust and mud travelling in the hinterland. Of course, being Australian, this was a right-hand drive car.

Miss Atlantic City of 1925 is nicely posed with this 1925 Special Six Model EQ Duplex Roadster. This example came as a bare-bones model, with the wooden artillery wheels. For sure it is 1925, as the New Jersey license plate shows.

By the time the new Standard Six cars were introduced in September 1924, over 200,000 predecessor Light Sixes were already in the hands of owners. With the change in name came increased power and performance, more luxurious bodies, balloon tires as standard equipment, and the choice of a four-wheel brake system.

Probably the outstanding feature of the Standard Six line was the exclusive Duplex Phaeton body. With a permanent all-steel top, the Duplex afforded the comfort and safety of a closed car combined with the low cost and economy of a Touring car. Roller curtains, permanently fixed to the top structure, could be closed or opened in thirty seconds without the driver leaving his seat.

The optional four-wheel brake system of the 1925 Studebaker cars was actuated by hydraulic pressure developed by a gear pump attached to the rear of the transmission case. Due to the width of the brake drum, it was necessary to use convex disc wheels on cars carrying the four-wheel brake option.

The Model ER Standard Six of 1925 and 1926 proved to be Studebaker's production champion to that time, as over 147,000 were built in two years.

This 1925 EQ Special Six Touring came on the market in July, 1924, and continued to July, 1926, with only minor changes. A total of 53,780 vehicles were produced. The models rode on a 120-inch wheelbase and developed 65 horsepower at 2400 rpm. The tire size was 20x6.20 inches for all Special Sixes.

This 1925 Special Six Duplex Roadster Model EQ resided in Chehalis, Washington, from the license plate and city identification frame on the vehicle. The car definitely does not wear authentic bumpers and also has a small non-Studebaker driving light. Its separate visor makes this an early example of the two-year run.

This Model EQ Special Six 4-passenger Victoria offered the same appointments as the Country Club, but came with a larger rear quarter section. It seemed to appeal more to families with small children, offering more visibility and space in the rear compartment. The vehicle weighed 3,675 pounds and sold for $2,050.

The owner of this 1925 Big Six Phaeton was Luiz Pirolo. He was very proud of his accomplishment where he broke all Brazilian hill-climbing events on May 9, 1925. The car weighed 3,700 pounds and sold for $1,875.

Another time-endurance run that the company took part in was this event which took place on July 12, 1925. The car was put through the paces for an 8 hour, 47 minute run from Barcelona to Madrid, Spain. Note the bulb horn, with its flexible tube running from the base of the hood to the driver's door on this Duplex Phaeton.

Studebaker entered the professional funeral car business in force in 1925, negotiating a contract with the Superior Body Co. of Lima, Ohio. Superior built the bodies and Studebaker furnished the mechanical components, with the final products sold through their respective franchised dealers. This combination ambulance and hearse came on a 158-inch wheelbase. The completed unit delivered for $3,550 less specific interior equipment.

When this photo was taken, this 1925 Studebaker bus had only been in use a few months, but long enough to convince its owner to specialize in Studebaker equipment. This unit served a long distance run, traveling in North Carolina.

# 1925-1926

The two-year run was again seen in certain series for this period. Studebaker offered the Standard, Special, and Big Six series for an over-lapping period of time. The Standard Six Model ER, being the lowest priced car for the two-year run, was available in six models from the 3-passenger Duplex Roadster for $1,125, to the Berline 6-passenger Sedan for $1,650. These models employed the 242 cubic-inch 6-cylinder engine which developed 50 horsepower at 2200 rpm. The bore and stroke were 3-3/8x4-1/2 inches. These models used a 14-gallon fuel tank. They came with 21x5.25-inch tires, and rode on the 113-inch wheelbase. This series was built from August, 1924, through August, 1926, with 147,099 units produced.

The Special Six EQ was available in four models ranging from the Duplex Phaeton for 5-passengers at $1,450 to the 5-passenger Berline selling for $2,225. The engine had a 289 cubic-inch displacement with a 3.5x5-inch bore and stroke which developed 65 horsepower at 2400 rpm. All Special and Big Six models used a 19-gallon fuel

tank. The tire size was 20x6.20 inches and the wheelbase was 120 inches. This series was built from August, 1924, to July, 1926. Production amounted to 53.780 vehicles.

The Big Six EP vehicles were introduced to the public September 14, 1924, and offered the first major change in the Big Six chassis since its announcement in 1918. The basic engine design and dimensions were retained, but conversion was made to full pressure lubrication to mains, connecting rod bearings, and camshaft bearings. The horsepower was now 75 at 2400 rpm. The engine was of 354 cubic-inch displacement which used a bore and stroke of 3-7/8x5 inches. These models were fitted with 20x7.30-inch tires. Most all EP models came on the 127-inch wheelbase. However, some models were offered on the 120-inch wheelbase chassis. Prices ranged from $1,875 for the 7-passenger Duplex Phaeton to $2,800 for the 7-passenger Berline. The Big Six models were in production as 1925-1926 cars from August, 1924, to August, 1926, with a total of 26,267 units manufactured as both Models EP and Models ES.

In 1925-26, this Studebaker Model ER Standard Six Duplex Roadster sold for $1,125 making it the lowest-priced vehicle for the year. The unit employed 5.25x 21-inch tires and rode on a 113-inch wheelbase. Judging by the way Miss Toronto and Miss Winnipeg are bundled up, these Canadian beauty contest winners sure picked a cold day to be riding around in an open roadster.

A nice view of the 1925-26 Standard Six Country Club Coupe shows the early separate sun visor. Some catalogs also referred to this example as a Coupe-Roadster and yet there is nothing about it that could make this a Roadster model. This car came with the extra cost equipment of a spare tire! Many changes took place on these Standard Six models while they were in production. As an example, instrument panels were changed five times during the two-year run. The radiator-hood assembly was altered four times, and each was referred to as a first to fourth design vehicle, making it very difficult for a person restoring one of these models today.

Shown in the snow is a later version of the 1925-26 Standard Six Country Club Coupe. This example of the Q body came with an integral visor. Body color for the closed 1925 vehicles were Light Navaho Gray below the beltline and darker Seminole Gray above, with a parallel light red hairline stripe on the belt molding and a light red stripe on edge of hood louvers. This car was often purchased by doctors and sales people who found it a very dependable and convenient car for their use. It sold for $1,395.

# 1925-1926

Available in both 1925 and 1926 was the Standard Six 2-passenger Country Club Coupe. Shown here are Lanny and Doris Semon with their new "pride and joy" in front of their Hollywood home. This was referred to as a Q body. It had a separate glass visor and was built some time before body No. Q-2,952.

The 1925-26 Standard Six Coach is shown with the F-body, which used the early separate glass visor. These units were built before body No. F-2,900. The car sold for $1,495. It offered passenger space for five people.

The later example of the 1925-26 Standard Six 5-passenger Duplex Phaeton, Model ER used the integral flat leather visor. It delivered for the same price as the earlier Duplex Phaeton, $1,145. With the side curtains removed, the vehicle was as open-aired as a touring car, but still offered passengers a solid top and rear quarters with plate glass windows. This top was similar to the detachable winter hardtops that were offered on the aftermarket, but these could not be removed to convert the car into a fully open style.

The Model ER Standard Six Duplex Phaeton for 1925-26 sold for only $20 more than its Roadster brother, making it an $1,145 car. The 6-cylinder vehicle had a displacement of 242 cubic-inches. All Standard Sixes came with a 14-gallon fuel tank. This example is buttoned up with its wire-supported side curtains. These curtains would open with the doors, but the windows could not be opened for ventilation, which probably explains why the cowl vent is in the full-open position. This is an early version, with the T-body, which used a separate rather large glass visor.

Appearing on the Standard Six Chassis was this example of a special-bodied Brougham. It almost appears to be a "high class" taxi, with disc wheels, Landau irons, carriage lights, and a special light mounted on the top of the visor. The custom body builder is unknown.

This Special Six Duplex Roadster is of the later design, having been built from the summer of 1925 to July of 1926, as indicated by the integral visor. Authentic extra cost bumpers came with the car. The Landau irons were extra cost on early 1925 cars, and then were considered standard equipment on later models. The car sold for $1,450, minus the deluxe options. Duplex Roadsters had a hard top that could not be folded like that of a regular roadster.

The 1925-26 Model EQ Special Six Country Club Coupe was considered a 4-passenger vehicle. It looked much like the Standard Six except for the oval window and additional seating. This Special Six came equipped fancy Landau irons. It rode on a 120-inch wheelbase and sold for $1,935.

A very authentic appearing 1925-26 Duplex Phaeton Model Q is equipped with the optional disc wheels and factory-approved bumpers. The cars came with the 288 cubic-inch engine with a 3__-inch bore by 5-inch stroke. The example, in base form, delivered for $1,495.

This 1925-26 Special Six Model EQ Touring Car has had a few liberties taken. Its top is a non-factory aftermarket item, as is the front bumper. At this time, the disc wheels were extra cost. Note the hood is painted black as are the fenders, while body is done in either Belgian Blue or Chico Drab (dark gray).

An EQ Special Six Duplex Phaeton, built in the 1925-26 model run, went to work for the "Bureau of Fire" of Endicott, New York. Check out the fire extinguisher on the running board, and special siren horn cradled between the front fenders. The chief looks pretty proud of his newly assigned vehicle. The aftermarket winter front attached to this unit probably was a wise option for a car operating in Endicott's cold weather.

The model EQ 1925-26 Special Six 4-door Brougham was easily detectable from a regular Special Six Sedan by its oval rear quarter window with Landau iron. This unit also displays the separate sun visor. The car delivered for $2,225, which was $75 more than the regular 5-passenger Sedan.

A 1925-26 Special Six 5-passenger Sedan weighed 3,855 pounds and came on the 120-inch wheelbase. This example was in the class of EQ models that sold for $2,150.

The 1925-26 EP Big Six Sport Roadster with rumble seat was the proud possession of actor Glenn Hunter, who was staring in "Young Mr. Woodley" at the Belmont Theater, in New York. How about that raccoon coat he sports? Notice the interesting folding armrests on the rumble seat.

Available both in 1925-26 in the EP Series was the Big Six Sport Roadster for $1,795. Note the special rumble seat compartment with the accessory arms on the sides. Disc wheels were beginning to be shown on these units, as was the very novel concept of a rumble seat.

During the 1925-26 model run, the South Bend Fire Department received a new Big Six EP Duplex Roadster. The new model was designed and built especially for fire chiefs. After many years of experience, which Studebaker had in furnishing cars for the fire departments throughout the world, the 1925-26 models were the most successful. The list price F.O.B. factory included a vermillion lacquer finish for $1,750. These cars were sometimes referred to as "Fire Chief" models, but this does not appear to be an official factory designation.

This 1925-26 Big Six 5-passenger Coupe is equipped with the optional disc wheels. This example also came with the special small rear mounted trunk. It used a 127-inch wheelbase, weighed in at 4,030 pounds and delivered for $2,650.

The Big Six line increased the number of models to ten during the 1925-26 run. Seen here is the EP five-passenger Coupe that weighed 4,030 pounds. The 127-inch car delivered for $2,650.

Having travelled a few miles during its time since first leaving the factory is this 1925-26 EP Big Six 2-door Sedan. The year is 1933, according to the license. The owner probably wants to get into the act of having a testimonial to the vehicle's faithful service.

The majestic looking EP Duplex Phaeton of 1925-26 was one of the most popular models available for the two-year span. The most outstanding feature of these Duplex Phaetons in each series was the permanent all-steel top. The Duplex afforded the comfort and safety of a closed car combined with the low-cost and economy of the touring vehicles. This example weighed 3,785 pounds and came on a 127-inch wheelbase. The 7-passenger vehicle delivered for $1,875.

The Big Six Duplex Phaeton was seen again for 1925-26. This particular vehicle is apparently on a trip with its trailer and special cover. This unit is prepared for the roads of the day with two rear-mounted spares. The gentleman in "Plus Fours" is no doubt thanking the banker for a loan to take the trip. Check the American National Bank in the background.

This 1925-26 Model EP Big Six Brougham was delivered minus the small trunk on the rear which was usually found on Brougham models. This example also came on the shorter wheelbase of 120 inches, like the Special Six. The "D" shaped window was a Brougham characteristic, as were the fake Landau irons.

The Glendale, California Chamber of Commerce used this 1925-26 EP Big Six Sedan to encourage people to move to Glendale, citing the proximity to various points of interest in Southern California. The time schedule for getting to various nearby places is listed on the door. For example, Hollywood is only 15 minutes away, while Pasadena is a mere 20 minutes drive. The vehicle is equipped with Eastern Auto Tires as can be seen by the well-lettered "Western Giant Balloon" on the sidewalls.

# 1925-1926

This 1925-26 Model EP Big Six 7-passenger Inside-Drive Limousine is an export vehicle with an oriental license plate. Possibly the vehicle, with its right-hand drive, was destined for Japan. The sun visor also appears different from most Big Six vehicles. The body may very well have not been by Studebaker, but may have been supplied by a custom shop on special order.

This custom built 1925-26 Studebaker Town Car used the 1926 Model EP chassis. Note the wire wheels, speaker from rear to driver, side-mounted mirrors, landau irons, and courtesy lights at the base of the rear door. This would certainly qualify as a classic with the Classic Car Club of America.

This 1925-26 Studebaker Special dirt-track racer was built on a Studebaker Six Chassis. It had been owned by a Studebaker Club member for many years. Its present location and owner are unknown.

This 1925-26 EP Big Six Speedster has its own special built body. Note the curved door line is entirely different from any Studebakers of that era. It also wears a special beltline going from the hood to the rear deck. The custom body builder is unknown. The wheelbase remained 120 inches.

# 1925-1926

Long before the concept of motor homes gained acceptance, many camping-oriented people did many strange things with their automobiles. This 1925-26 Duplex Phaeton is shown with a full-spring bed secured by neat and unnoticeable braces to the top. It was truly a "house on wheels" when the tent was pitched, but watch out for that first step. Obviously, the tent had to be disassembled for traveling.

An interesting photo with no information whatsoever shows this EP Big Six in some foreign land, with what appears to be a wooden touring car body not unlike a contemporary depot hack. Obviously sold as a chassis/cowl unit, the body probably was constructed by some local truck body builder, or possibly even a local cabinet shop. It is difficult to tell where the photo was made, but due to the left hand drive status of the car, Great Britian and Scandinavia (at that time) are ruled out. The license plate likewise gives no hint, but the architecture of the buildings would suggest northern Europe.

This unusual model for 1925-26 served as an ambulance for emergency service when a true ambulance was unavailable. The Big Six gave ample room for two attendants, driver, and a folding cot to carry the patient. The right center door post was removable to allow for loading and unloading of the patient. Since the interiors could be changed relatively easily and quickly, Studebaker referred to this model as "Two cars in one: an Ambulance or a Pallbearers' Car."

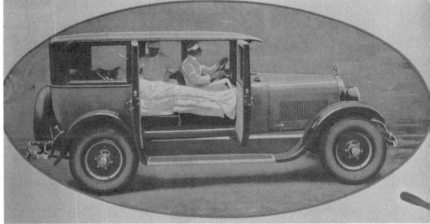

This 1925-26 EP Big Six Combination Sedan was technically referred to as an ambulance or a modified funeral car. It carried all of the appointments necessary, if needed, to be used as an ambulance, but also had enough interior room for a casket. The right hand doors latched into a removable B-pillar. Thus, when open, a very wide aperture allowed for easy movement of either stretcher or casket.

Studebaker now was making a definite entry into the professional car field. It referred to this dignified vehicle as the "Pallbearers Car." It was offered for 1925-26 in the Model EP line, coming on a 127-inch wheelbase. The 8-place seating allowed for the six bearers, plus a minister and the driver. The center seats folded forward to allow access to the rear seat.

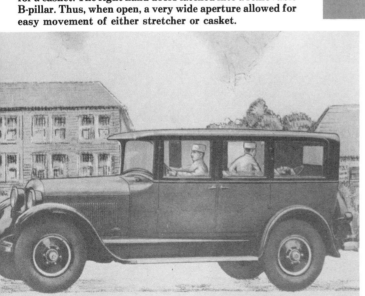

The City of Detroit, Michigan, purchased this 1925-26 Model N bus for the use of the Detroit City Council. Originally, the city had planned to purchase a fleet of touring cars, but it was found that it could save money by purchasing one 12-passenger bus. This example saw use for several years before retirement, probably carrying the councilmen on inspection trips around the city.

The bus line operating this 1925-26 Big Six was the Ashville-Charlotte Blue Ridge Trail Line of North Carolina. The Big Six served its owner for several years of hard service in all kinds of weather in the mountains of the Tar Heel State.

One of the few commercial chassis models in the book is this 1925-26 Big Six Studebaker bus. This unit did admirable work travelling over 200 miles a day on a route that included Indianapolis, Bloomington, and Bedford, Indiana.

This 1925-26 Big Six Duplex Phaeton saw use as a rail car in Mexico. It was converted in Mexico City by J. N. Galbraith Jr. of Mexico Light and Power Company. The unit performed on a run of 36 kilometers between Mexcaca and Beristein, State of Pueblo, for several years.

# 1926

This ER Standard Six Sport Roadster was referred to as a J-body. It also came with a lower belt line for the 1926 models only. In 1926, the price increased to $1,405. This vehicle accommodated three passengers.

Taken at a car show is this 1926 Standard Six ER Touring. This example received factory accessory equipment not usually seen on this model such as bumpers, side mirror, and the special radiator motometer that was associated more with Big Six examples.

The Duplex Roadster in the Standard Six line for 1926 delivered for $1,125. The 113-inch wheelbased car weighed 2,760 pounds. This example came with the integral visor.

The 1926 Tourer Model ER Standard Six was also referred to as a Phaeton. It had a folding top, as this example shows. This is the second design, that offered celluloid curtains in the rear window. Later examples had a glass window in the rear. Note the Atlanta radiator emblem on the vehicle. It also came with the mid-season bullet shaped headlamps.

The Deputy Chief of Passaic, New Jersey received the honor to drive around town in the furnished 1926 ER Standard Six Duplex Roadster. The bumpers supplied are not 1926 Standard Six. If Studebaker, they might be for the following year cars in the Standard Six line.

A 1926 series of ER Standard Six Club Sedans that are available for rental purposes. I used to live in Pasadena, California and, on a recent trip through the town, I checked out this lot in an old City directory at the Pasadena Library. Today a motel sits on this lot. Not a Studebaker was in sight!

In 1926, the designation of the Standard Six Duplex Phaeton was changed in some pieces of sales literature. Basically the same car as in 1925, but for its title. Now this example was called a 5-passenger Sport Phaeton. The models came with the nickel plated radiator as standard equipment.

This 1926 Standard Six Model ER Duplex Phaeton was a record breaker in Honolulu that year. It completed an around-the-island trip of Oahu in 1 hour and 55 minutes which was considered a feat, at that time. In fact, its not too bad a feat even today. The gentlemen on the running board are David Kamaola, Captain of the Oahu Police Department, and D. H. Lake, Sales Manager of the Pond Studebaker dealership in Honolulu.

This late edition 1926 ER Standard Six Duplex Phaeton came with many optional extra cost items like the disc wheels, bumpers, trumpet horn, and rear mounted trunk. The model weighed in at 2,870 pounds.

The 1926 ER Standard Six 4-door Sedan 5-passenger with the integral visor. This version was said for technical reasons to have the "W" Body and came with a mohair interior. The cars with wool fabric upholstery were classed as "S" bodied sedans. Each model was priced at $1595 and weighed 3260 pounds.

This was a low-production Standard Six Brougham Sedan, complete with the oval rear quarter windows. From the sun visor arrangement, it appears to be a 1926 example. It sold for $55 more than a regular sedan at $1,650.

A very rare model is this 1926 Standard Six ER chassis with a special depot hack body. The vehicle was tastefully done. The body builder and number produced are unknown. It appears to be an 8-passenger vehicle, with a row of three folding auxiliary seats adjacent to the rear doors. Probably all rear and center seats were removable for cargo hauling.

This nicely equipped 1926 Duplex Roadster is in the Special Six line. This EQ example wears the optional disc wheels which gives the car a more modern look and an appearance of a lower profile. The fake Landau irons also gives it a more rakish style. The $1,450 price did not include deluxe options.

# 1926

This 1926 Special Six 2-door was known as a 5-passenger Coach or Club Sedan. It was on the market from August, 1924, to July, 1926. The number produced in all styles of Special Sixes for the 2-year run amounted to 53,780.

The license on this vehicle says that its a 1926 unit coming from Indiana. The suburban-type vehicle is on the Special Six chassis and delivered for $1,795. The canopy side covers were a needed piece of equipment in snowy weather such as this. The disc wheels were an added cost item which were not seen very often on a commercial vehicle.

The 1926 Big Six Sheriff Phaeton was a 5-passenger model that delivered for $1,825 and weighing 3,720 pounds. If the 7-passenger version were ordered, it sold for $1,875 and gave a weight of 3,785 pounds. Note the unusual black band this unit wears across its cowl. It appears that this may have been some sort of steel bullet deflector, tightly riveted to the cowling. Genuine leather was used exclusively in these vehicles.

This 1926 Big Six Duplex Roadster came equipped with the integral sun visor. The vehicle weighed 4,030 pounds and rode on a 127-inch wheelbase. It sold in 1926 for $1,850. It uses a true California setting with a tile-roofed house and palm trees for its background.

The 1926 EP Big Six Sport Roadster for four passengers is displayed with the regular wooden artillery wheels rather than the disc set up which made the vehicle look more modern. This unit came without the special canvas tire cover which was seen on most Big Sixes, but instead has what appears to be a spare tire cover of shiny black oilcloth.

The 1926 EP Big Six Duplex Phaeton was one rugged looking vehicle. The appearance of this car makes it look like it would never wear out. It weighed 3,785 pounds and left the dealership for $1,875. Its wheelbase was 127 inches.

Even in Argentina, Studebakers were famous in the 1920s. This is a 1926 Model EP Big Six Brougham belonging to Carmen Berutti, a noted Argentinean theatrical beauty and star of the Portena Operetta. She offered nothing but praise for her new Brougham.

It almost looks like the little lady needs a step ladder to climb into her 1926 Big Six Brougham. The car weighed 4,150 pounds. The vehicle came equipped with fake Landau irons, a practically non-functional fender side-mirror, and bumper equipment. Imagine a small person trying to maneuver a monster like this around town, with mechanical brakes and no power steering.

This 1926 EP Big Six Brougham sported a special oval window in its rear quarter. It also has the rear-mounted spare equipped with the short-lived canvas tire cover and small trunk. This car is shown displayed in a Studebaker dealership. The vehicle only came with an aluminum step plate on the front portion of the running board. Apparently the buyer felt rear passenger foot traffic didn't warrant the additional extra cost item.

Studebaker's most expensive regular production run vehicle for 1926 was this Big Six 7-passenger Berline with enclosed drive features. The car weighed 4,200 pounds, rode on 20x7.30 inch tires and used the 127-inch wheelbase chassis. This example delivered for $2,860. A partition with sliding glass separated the front and rear compartments.

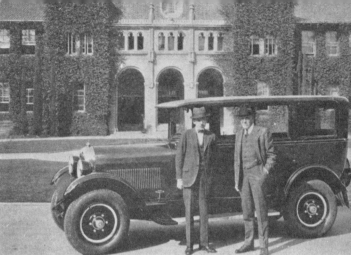

A familiar site to me is this background of the University of Southern California, as I went there to school. Unfortunately, the area where the Stude is parked would be difficult to park, as it is closed off to all vehicles. The gentlemen are Dr. Miller McClintock, head of the A. R. Erskine Traffic Research Bureau, and Dr. E. C. Moore, a director of U.S.C. The vehicle is, naturally, a 1926 Big Six 7-passenger Sedan.

This EP Big Six came on the 127-inch wheelbase and was available only as a 7-passenger sedan. It weighed 4,150 pounds and sold for $2,785. The 5-passenger models were available on a 120-inch wheelbase.

# 1926

This 1926 EP Big Six is rather unusual looking, as it came with non-factory bumpers, wears a winter front cover over the radiator, and is equipped with rare wire wheels. Also, barely discernable, is a front license plate which seems to be composed of Arabic writing . . . is that Salome peering out of the rear door?

Probably the most trim classic-appearing Studebaker for this time period was this 1926 EP custom-built Town Car. The model was displayed in the Rose Room at the Plaza Hotel in New York City by its custom body builders for the year's debut of the new creations. This example wore an aluminum body. No more than eight were produced.

This 1926 Model EP Big Six started life in Quebec, Canada, as a closed car. Sometime later in life a local volunteer fire company converted into a utility pickup or hose car with a homemade bed. It definitely is not a Studebaker creation even though it was done well.

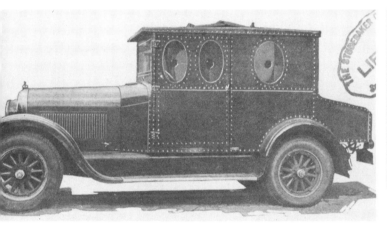

This 1926 Big Six armored Studebaker was the nemesis of bandits in the vicinity of Sioux City, Iowa. Look at all those window gun ports. I never thought Sioux City was that wild a town to require a vehicle of this magnitude to take care of its criminals. The car was built for the Sioux City Police Department. In these days, the "probable cause" ruling wasn't even an idea.

Another view of the 1926 Model EP bullet-proof Big Six shows a 1926 license which says "Official" across the top. I don't imagine the chief felt compelled to drive it home at night when off duty. It is probably still remembered by local "old-timers" in Sioux City today. It may have gone to the scrap drive during W.W. II. Note the opening for a machine gun to do its thing just above the cowl vent. Oddly, neither the tires nor the radiator were given any protection, and these would have been the weak spots in any sort of a chase scene.

This is a 1926 Studebaker Model N commercial chassis with a locally built rear-entrance bus body. The unit came on a 184-inch wheelbase, and used dual rear wheels to help support its heavy load capacity. The bus was sold by the B. J. Penney Ltd. a dealer at Johannesburg, South Africa, to the Standard Omnibus Company to be used in local passenger service between Johannesburg and Norwood. Check the destination placard in the roof of the bus. It is headed for Norwood, South Africa...not Ohio.

# 1926

This luxurious 1926 Studebaker bus was built exclusively for Professor A. W. Seward, an astrologer, to serve him as a traveling studio and home. He referred to himself as the "World's Foremost Astrologer." Note the exterior window awnings the bus employs.

A musical group used this 1926 Studebaker bus. The band, which was planning to tour the country in this vehicle, was H. Ross Franklin of Lake Wawasee, Indiana. The tire cover, rather than advertise Studebaker, tells us they prefer Buescher True-Tone Instruments for the band. Why the group referred to itself as a "Waco Band" is not known.

The 1926-1927 Model N Studebaker hearse came on a 158-inch wheelbase. The vehicle had a Brewster-type windshield that was most distinctive. It carried a body built by Meteor Motor Car Co. of Piqua, Ohio, and was powered by the Big Six engine.

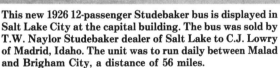

This new 1926 12-passenger Studebaker bus is displayed in Salt Lake City at the capital building. The bus was sold by T.W. Naylor Studebaker dealer of Salt Lake to C.J. Lowry of Madrid, Idaho. The unit was to run daily between Malad and Brigham City, a distance of 56 miles.

The 1926 Studebaker Mourners Sedan provided space for 12 passengers. The vehicle proved to be more economical than requiring a funeral home to purchase additional 7-passenger sedans. Its dignified appearance matched the Studebaker Funeral Car. This version shows cross seats of the sedan-type, but semi-chair-type seats could also be ordered to provide limousine comfort for passengers and drivers. Restful seat cushions and backs were upholstered in genuine leather. Comfort was further enhanced by details of easily adjusted windows, roller window shades, an exhaust heating system, six fresh air ventilators, and space for carrying flowers and wreaths behind the third row of seats when the removable fourth row of seats was taken out. The body was of hardwood framing with metal sheeting. It was 167 inches long and 64 inches wide. A choice of two two-tone color combinations was offered.

The 1927 Studebakers were offered again as Standard Six, Special Six, and Big Six. But this was to be the final year of these three series. Easy identifying marks of the 1927 cars were the disc wheels. These disc wheels were standard equipment because the four-wheel brakes precluded the use of spoke or wire wheels on the front, and apparently only the disc wheels would work. In 1928, by redesigning the front axle, wire or wooden wheels were once more in use. The names President, Commander and Dictator were beginning to appear. In the middle to late 1927 early Commander and Dictator cars for 1928 were introduced. The President title was used on a model of the Big Six cars for 1927. The President Deluxe 7-passenger Sedan was mounted on a Big Six chassis. It was becoming typical in that era to offer more closed body styles.

The Standard Six offered a 242 cubic-inch engine developing 50 horsepower at 2200 rpm. The bore and stroke were 3-3/8x4.5 inches. The Standard Six models used a 14-gallon fuel tank and had a 6-quart oil capacity in its crankcase. The tire size was 31x5.25 inches. The wheelbase was 113 inches. A total of seven models were available ranging in price from $1,160 for a 3-passenger Roadster to $1,385 for a 5-passenger Custom Sedan.

The Special Six used the 289 cubic-inch engine developing 65 horsepower at 2400 rpm. These models had a bore and stroke of 3.5x5 inches. The fuel supply, as on the Big Six series, came from a 19-gallon tank. The cars also had a 6-quart oil capacity. The tire size on both Special and Big Six models was 32x6.75 inches. The wheelbase for Special Six cars was 120 inches. The body types amounted to four models priced from $1,480 for a Duplex Phaeton, to $1,830 for a 5-passenger Brougham.

The Big Six line used the 354 cubic-inch engine developing 75 horsepower at 2400 rpm. The bore and stroke consisted of 3-7/8x5 inches. A total of eight models made up this series, being priced from $1,610 for a Sport Phaeton to the top of the line 7-passenger President Sedan for $2,245. The wheelbases were 120 inches while the President rode on an exclusive 127-inch wheelbase. The company placed in 10th position for the year, from the sale of 76,965 units.

1927 Standard Six

For 1927, Studebaker's lowest price offering was the EU Standard Six. These cars employed a 6-cylinder engine with a bore and stroke of 3-3/8x4.5 from the 242 cubic inch displacement that developed 50 horsepower at 2200 rpm. The tire size was 32x6.00. The fuel came from a 14-gallon tank. At mid-year the Standard Six name was changed to Dictator. Seven models were available in the Standard Six ranging from the Duplex Roadster for three passengers for $1,160, to a Custom Sedan for five passengers for $1,385. All models came on the 113-inch wheelbase. When the name change was made to Dictator, an additional two models became available: a Tourer for 5 passengers at $1,165, and a 7-passenger Tourer for $1,245. As Dictators, the tire size changed to 31x5.25 inches. Chromium parts began to be used on the 1927 models throughout the entire line by the mid-season Dictator debut. The EU Standard Six saw a run of 65,333 units sold from June, 1926, to September, 1927. From early summer of 1927 to August, 1928, a total of 48,339 cars were produced as Dictator models.

Right on target was the early 1927 Standard Six Sport Roadster on the 113-inch wheelbase. The vehicle weighed 3,030 pounds and sold for $1,250. It accommodated three passengers. A Duplex Roadster also was available for $1,160. It weighed 2,965 pounds. This model came in Chapa Blue and Bold Blue.

An easy detection of the Standard Six cars over the larger series was the wheel set up. The Standard Six came with demountable rims using six lugs, while the more expensive models used five-lug disc wheels. This 1927 model sold for $1,225 and weighed 3,200 pounds. It was called the Standard Six Coupe.

The 1927 Model EU two-passenger Coupe, at late season, had its series name changed from Standard Six to Dictator. The Standard models had a production run from June, 1926, to September, 1927, producing 65,333 units.

Providing the lady with a good view of the golf course is this 1927 Model EU Rumble Seat Coupe. The vehicle offered seating for four passengers and technically was known as the "E" body. The tire size for early cars was 32x6.00 inches. When the model became a Dictator, the tire size also changed to 31x5.25 inches. The 1927 cars came with bullet or acorn-shaped headlamps, as this example shows.

The Model EU 1927 Custom Victoria weighed 3,180 pounds and delivered for $1,335. It offered interior seating for four passengers. This model was available in two color choices: a lower body, Tuchi Gray; a beltline in Kinick Green, and the balance of the body in black. The second choice had the lower body and beltline in Hopi Drab, and the balance of the body in Croation Green. The model was received well by the public.

The 1927 Standard Six Rumble Seat Coupe was referred to as the Model EU. Later in the season, like all Standard Sixes, it was referred to as the Dictator. Note the door to the golf bag compartment on this vehicle.

Notre Dame's famous football coach Knute Rockne and some of his Fighting Irish are pushing a 1927 Custom Victoria off the field . . . possibly to make way for football practice?

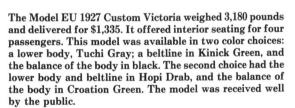

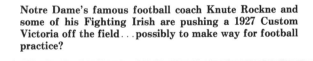

This gent seems to be quite proud of his 1927 Standard Six Custom Victoria. The disc wheels were seen on these models because the new four-wheel brake mechanism precluded the use of spoke or wire wheels on the front. Only the disc wheel would work. However, on these models, a true full-disc wheel was not used. Rather, the disc was designed similar to the old wood spoke wheels, and could not be removed from the hub. Instead, a now-archaic type of removable rim was used, fastened by the six lugs around the perimeter. In 1928, by a redesigning of the front axle, either the wire or wooden wheels were once again available.

For 1927, this early version EU was known as the Standard Six Custom Sedan. The mid-season title became Dictator. The body letter designation was called "W". The color choice on this model was Pewamo Blue below the beltline, and a Limousine Blue beltline between the moldings. The balance of the body was done in black. This model weighed 3,225 pounds and delivered for $1,385. It seated five passengers.

The 1927 ES Custom Sedan for five passengers appears to be very close to the EU Dictator Sedan, with both using the 120-inch wheelbase chassis. The differences were seen under the hood. The color combination for the Custom Sedan was upper and lower moldings and the body above done in black; between moldings done in Kinick Green; and the main body below the molding in Tuchi Gray. The unit sold for $30 less than the Custom Brougham at $1,755.

This special bodied 1927 Standard Six was used by the Darling Shop of 234 West Sixth St., Los Angeles, as a gimick-type of delivery vehicle for their florist business. This was the era of novelty delivery truck bodies for specific types of businesses, and such things as shoes, milk bottles, candy boxes, and even cameras could be found in truck form, making deliveries in cities all across America. This vehicle did not get the disc wheel treatment, but sports front brake drums, and thus indicates that it is a very late 1927 chassis, with the new 1928 front axle and brake design.

This 1927 special bodied pickup carries all the niceties of a Model EU Standard Six. However, it is a non-production vehicle because Studebaker built "No such animal" at that time. The spare tire would fit on the left front fender. The bracket equipment is there to carry the spare. This was probably a Studebaker design exercise, possibly with the intent of producing such a vehicle in 1928 or 1929. Note that a special door has been used, which does not match the molding of the hood and cowl.

In 1927, the Specialty Body Co. created this example of a rather luxurious 6-passenger depot hack. It came on a Standard Six Chassis Model EU, but was not part of Studebaker's selling program and was not catalogued for the year. A touch of custom-car class is found in the wide wicker-filled belt molding. Roll-up side curtains were used for weather protection.

This is a 1927 Studebaker commercial chassis referred to as Model EY. This example used all the mechanical components found in the Model EA cars. Very few were ever produced. The 9-passenger body also appears to be from Specialty Body Co., and is quite similar to the other example shown here. The swing-down tailgate, with its wicker belt molding, would provide space for carrying extra luggage, or for easy removal of the third row of seats when 6-passenger capacity was sufficient.

This unit is sort of a maverick. It is classed as a 1927 commercial panel with Standard Six cowl lights. The bumpers are from 1927, but the radiator core is the flat style as on 1928s, and body style is more 1925-26. So take your pick. It appears that the vehicle is in the engineering or testing department, and is running on some sort of dynamometer. Possibly it was a factory cobble-job used for testing certain components.

This 1927 Studebaker hearse came on a 146-inch wheelbase and was referred to as the Arlington. This model was to become one of Studebaker's most popular vehicles in the professional car line. It delivered for $2,986. The Dictator Six engine was used for these vehicles. Approximately 300 were produced over a period of time.

1927 Commander

Studebaker used the Commander nameplate on its second line of cars beginning with the 1927 models. These vehicles were placed just below the President in price and size. The first Commander was the Model EW Big Six introduced in January, 1927, as a replacement for the 120-inch wheelbase Model ES Big Six of 1926. The longer wheelbase (127-inch) Big Six President continued for most of 1927. The EW cars had a 3-7/8x5 bore and stroke, providing 353.8 cubic-inch displacement. The engine developed 75 horsepower at 2400 rpm. The Commanders rode on 31x 5.25-inch tires. The EW was so much like its predecessor ES model that they are almost indistinguishable except for one notable feature. The ES cars were equipped with disc wheels having six stud

nuts, while the EW models had five studs and used 32x6.75-inch tires.

Because of the reduced weight and economics of manufacture, the EW models were priced substantially lower than corresponding ES cars. The ES Brougham was priced at $1,985, but the EW version was initially $1,785 F.O.B. South Bend. And, a price reduction to $1,495 at the factory was announced in September, 1927.

Body types available in the Commander line were: Sedan Brougham, Custom Coupe for 2 passengers, Custom Coupe for 4 passengers (with rumble seat), Victoria, Chancellor Victoria, and Sport Roadster. A total of 63,516 units were built as EW-ES Commanders for 1927-1928.

An early type 1927 Roadster is shown here. This was the conflicting model-change time at Studebaker. This model began in December, 1926, and continued to October, 1927, with a production of 40,668 vehicles. Some refer to these cars as early 1927 and late model 1927s and some are said to be 1928s. Take your pick. At any rate, this is an early 1927 EW Roadster that weighed 3,480 pounds, came on a 120-inch wheelbase and sold for $1,630.

The "Lovelies" are from the Ziegfield Follies, circa 1927. The model EU Roadster is of the later design, as the larger parking lights were used when the cars began to be referred to as Commanders. Probably this was considered quite a risque picture when made in 1927.

A late 1927 EW Commander 4-passenger Roadster is shown with the rumble seat in the open position, windshield in the down position, top in the down position and, in other words, you don't mind being blown about! Chrome was beginning to be used with the arrival of these 1927 cars in each series.

A 1927 Commander Roadster, with Eddie Hearn at the wheel, finished in second position at this event at the Atlantic City Speedway, a well-known board track. When the vehicle was stripped, as this car is, it could do about 80 mph with stock Studebaker running gear. In this era, stock car racing meant exactly that...stock cars, totally unmodified except for fender removal.

The early 1927 Rumble Seat Sport Coupe was still known as the Special Six. The small acorn parking lights are the best telltale feature. This 4-passenger vehicle sold for $1,325 and weighed 3,125 pounds. The rumble seat passengers look well bundled up, and with good reason...it could get mighty cold back there.

This is the 1927 EW Commander or, if you wish, you may call it a Special Six, as it still retains the early acorn parking lights. The model is a 4-passenger Coupe with rumble seat, as indicated by the step-plates on the rear fender and the golf bag door on the right side. It delivered for $1,305 and weighed 3,145 pounds.

A 1927 Model EW Special Six Coupe for two passengers had a substantial trunk compartment, but only for storage, not passengers. This example delivered for $1,275. Access to the trunk was made a bit difficult by the rear-mounted spare.

Even Ab Jenkins, the famous record-breaking driver, did the honors of standing by a 1927 late Special Six or, if you prefer, early Commander Custom Victoria. The Atalanta radiator mascot was still very much in use for the 1927 models.

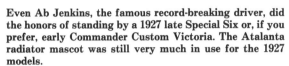

This was the ES Victoria Big Six first design, which appeared in December, 1926. The vehicle sold for $1,735 and accommodated seating for four passengers. It weighed 3,705 pounds which apparently was too heavy a car for its engine. So, shortly after the first part of January, 1927, the Commander 8 was used for power.

I do hope he's keeping warm. The car is a 1927 Commander Custom Victoria weighing 3,570 pounds and selling for $1,495 which was $160 additional above the Standard, or Dictator Six price.

The late season 1927 EW Commander 5-passenger Sedan came with the free-standing larger acorn parking lights. Somehow this car got packed into the ruts of a still-unpaved suburban street, probably to demonstrate its traction. Note the small tassel on the rear window shade to raise or lower the curtain.

This 1927 EW Commander model travelled the famous board track speedway at Atlantic City. The vehicle was driven by Eddie Hearn in what was described as a sensational high-speed endurance event lasting from July 21 to August 9, 1927. At one point, the car was wrecked. However, it was back in commission in about 20 minutes with the help of skilled craftsmen.

A 1927 EW Commander Sedan of the early style delivered for $1,820. This vehicle came on the 120-inch wheelbase like other 1927 EWs and weighed 3,600 pounds.

This 1927 EW Commander has been put through the paces for a new car. The 1927 license shows it to be from Utah. How could anyone abuse a car to that extent? From the fender bracket it displays, it appears to have had a side-mount at one time. Even the headlight is out of adjustment, and the right spotlight appears to have lost its lens.

# 1927

## 1927 President

The name "President" was first used by Studebaker denote its top-of-the-line Model ES Big Six Custom dan which was displayed July 23, 1926. The President remained the company's most expensive car rough 1942. The change from the preceding EP Big x was chiefly seen in the body design, which resulted lower profile bodies with rounded roofs and panels, d two-tone lacquer paint. Double bar bumpers; im- oved dual-beam headlights; no-draft ventilation, and pistol grip parking brake handle were the most ticeable changes. Mechanical four-wheel brakes and sc wheels were standard equipment on all the "Presi- nt" models. The engine compartment was basically e same as the previous Big Six cars.

The ES President was offered as a 7-passenger sedan two color combinations: black with a light green ltline striped in yellow, while the other was Croation een with an ebony beltline, and striped in ivory. Later

in the season, a two-tone gray and brown combination was offered when three limousine models and a 7-passenger touring car made their appearance.

In addition to these 127-inch wheelbase cars, there were 120-inch wheelbase models. The ES 5-passenger Sedan (referred to as the Custom Brougham), Custom Victoria, President Tourer, Sports Roadster, Sheriff, Duplex Roadster, and a later model Duplex Phaeton were cataloged, but whether the Duplex Phaeton ever got into production on the 127-inch wheelbase is uncertain.

Some historians refer to these cars as 1926-27 models, while others rank them as separate year vehicles. Studebaker did not assign separate year models to its production as did many other manufacturers, so the 127-inch cars were in production from June, 1926, to October, 1927, with production at 9,405 units. The 120-inch wheelbase ES cars were only available from June, 1926, to November, 1926, with a production run of only 7,949 cars.

The 1927 ES Sport Roadster for four passengers sold for $1,700, which was $90 more than the Touring which seems odd. This was a rare model even when new. According to promotional material, Studebaker supposedly wished it that way to keep it as a special model made for special people...sure! The fact is that roadster styles simply were not selling as they had in the past. More and more buyers now preferred the comfort of closed cars over the wind-blown experience of roadsters and touring cars. This is a late ES with chromed headlamps and the new bumper design which not too many displayed.

This 1926-27 early ES Sport Roadster is equipped with a rumble seat and has the rare wire wheel accessory package available on 1926 models. Apparently this car isn't equipped with the 1927 front brake set up which required the disc wheels. The 4-passenger vehicle sold for $1,680 and weighed 3,485 pounds. It was built on a 120-inch wheelbase.

Here sits an export vehicle with right-hand drive. The 1927 ES Sport Roadster is another one of those inbetween, neither "fish nor fowl" models as it carries the later bumper, but still has the painted bullet headlights. Note the bracket on the right rear fender for the tail light and license assembly. This is where they were mounted on the export cars. It also employs a small courtesy lamp in the aluminum step plate on the running board.

This 1927 ES President Touring came on a 120-inch wheelbase, weighed 3,580 pounds, and left the dealership for $1,610. This is the mid-season 1927 version, wearing the small acorn-style cowl lamps. The roof material was of a high quality canvas like the Hartz cloth used today on quality restorations.

This view is of the 1927 ES President Touring with its top in the folded position and the windshield lowered. The mid-season cars began coming with chromed headlamps as the example displays. Bumper equipment would really add to the cars' appearance, but was still considered an added-cost accessory. Note that these models used true disc wheels, which were removable from the hub, as opposed to the removable rims found on the lighter models.

This 1927 ES President Tourer was designated in many foreign publications as the rare President 8 Tourer of 1927. The 8-cylinder cars were still a few months away. This vehicle was still in the Big Six category, using the 354 cubic-inch engine. Photographed somewhere in Europe, this car apparently went into the service of some official governing body, judging from the flag on the radiator cap and the red flasher light on the right windshield post. A conventional spotlight occupies the left post.

For 1927, the ES Sheriff Touring was a both powerful and dependable "work-horse." This example used the double bumpers and drum headlamps. The windshield is in a slightly open position, while the large visor gives a rather unusual look to the otherwise nice lines of this big open car.

This 1927 ES President 7-passenger Touring is equipped with the extra cost bumpers which certainly give the look of a finished product. It came with mid-year double bar bumpers and chromed headlamps. The center seats could be folded out of the way when only five or less passengers were being carried.

The ES Big Six shows a slightly different fender line from those employed on Commanders. Each came on the 120-inch wheelbase. The fender line and difference of 5 or 6 wheel lugs per wheel, as discussed earlier, were the only noticeable changes.

Although this example looks very much like the ES Big Six for the year, coming on the same 120-inch wheelbase, it actually is the Commander Custom Victoria. Looking at the exterior, the Commander used five wheel lugs and the ES Big Six used six lugs, so that pretty well sums it up.

This example of the 1927 Big Six is the shorter wheel-based Model ES 5-passenger Sedan. It came on a 120-inch wheelbase and was produced from June, 1926, to November, 1926, for a total of only 7,949 vehicles. This example came equipped with the rare Pines winterfront radiator louvers, factory spotlight, and disc wheels.

This short wheelbased Model ES President for 1927 is a rare car as it is equipped with wire wheels rarely seen on 1927 cars due to the front axle, four-wheel brake set-up. Apparently this car was a very late build, coming out after the new front axle design was approved, but before the true 1928 models were on tap. This sedan used the 120-inch wheelbase.

Studebaker's big advertising campaign in 1927 stressed telling the public that lubrication of their vehicles was important, but that owners needed to visit the lube rack only once every 2,000 to 2,500 miles of driving. This was opposed to the 500-mile lubrication schedule that many other auto manufacturers recommended. Seen here is a 27 ES Custom Sedan being lubricated on one the outside lifts that were still commonplace at many small stations right up until the 1950s. Today, one would be hard pressed to find such an outside lift.

This 1927 ES Custom Sedan was purchased for police high-speed pursuits. That running board mounted spotlight appears to be from another era, but probably was as powerful a light as one could get in 1927. This is another one of those "gray area models" — equipped with older style bumpers, but it also has later chromed headlights. The engine in these cars was capable of traveling at speeds of 80 m.p.h., all day without tiring. What the additional hood mascot — the skunk —is needed for, I haven't a clue.

A 1927 early Big Six 5-passenger Custom Brougham used the early style bumpers with painted bullet shape head lamps. This example delivered for $1,985, F.O.B. the factory.

This example is another Studebaker puzzle. The model is a 1927 President Big Six Custom Brougham, considered a late model by certain features, and an early one by others. It carries late model bumpers, early style headlamps and free-standing larger cowl lamps as seen on late 1927 vehicles. The vehicle like other Big Six Broughams shown here delivered for $1,985.

A 1927 ES 7-passenger Big Six Sedan entered the market in June, 1926, and remained until October, 1927, before being phased out to be renamed the President Series. A total of 9,405 vehicles were manufactured. The 7-passenger weighed 4,050 pounds and sold for $2,245.

The 1927 ES Big Six 7-passenger Sedan, was now titled "President" and was a model within the Big Six line. This example is extremely close in appearance to the regular Big Six models at the end of the Big Six series. Standing by the rare car is Albert Erskine on the right, and an unidentified Studebaker executive. This version came with chromed headlamps, whereas many other Big Six examples still had painted lamps. Probably the company was using up supplies before the chrome units were put into production, as introduction of these lights seems to have been a running change.

This was the first 1927 President 7-passenger Sedan delivered in Cleveland, Ohio. The owner was State Senator George H. Bender who took delivery from the local Cleveland Studebaker-Erskine dealership.

This is a late model Big Six or, if you wish, early President Model FA 7-passenger Sedan. It sports the newer bumper design, chromed headlamps, but still retains the Atalanta goddess radiator mascot. It came on the 131-inch wheelbase used on 1928 cars. This example made its introduction in December, 1927, and lasted until October, 1928. The number produced was 13,186 units.

Studebaker offered so many styles that overlapped one another during this era that it makes it difficult to show each one. This example of a 1927 ES 7-passenger Limousine came as a driver-owned vehicle; with a window partition; without a window partition, or as a chauffeur enclosed-drive limousine. Shown here is the latter, selling for $2,245. It is riding on either the 127 or 131-inch wheelbase as the chassis length increased on later models.

Seen behind the wheel of the 1927 President he drove during his career as a movie director in Hollywood is Count Ilya Tolstoy. Again, it's a mid-season model, having older bumpers with the Studebaker medallion in the center, and chromed bullet-shaped headlamps. Tolstoy was the son of the famous Russian novelist.

This 1927 Studebaker hearse employed the Big Six engine, rode on a 158-inch wheelbase and used a body from the Meteor Motor Car Co. This firm later became the Miller-Meteor Division of Wayne Corp. of Piqua, Ohio, in 1956.

A combination Funeral Car and Ambulance was purchased by the Saxton-Daniels-Mastick Co. of Cleveland, Ohio in 1927. This vehicle was the first one sold in Cleveland in 1927. The owners praised its service both as an Ambulance and a Funeral Car. The unit was not only used in Cleveland, but in surrounding cities, as well. Easily removable interior fittings made conversion from hearse to ambulance and back again a relatively simple job. This type of ambulance was not really set-up for emergency work, but was more of a patient transporter.

This 1927 Studebaker Funeral Car was decided upon by the Racine, Wisconsin funeral directors, Bayerman and King, because of its dignity and appearance, silent operation and low cost. The directors stated they were more than pleased with the purchase after having it in operation for several months. The unit was delivered through Century Motor Company of Racine, Wisconsin, the local Studebaker dealer at that time.

This 184-inch wheelbase Studebaker bus had a 19-passenger (including driver) seating capacity. The seating arrangement consisted of a semi chair-type with entrance only on the right from four doors. The body builder for these buses was the Kingston Body Co. of Kingston, New York. All rows of seats had their own door except those directly over the rear axle. Passengers in these seats had to fold down the right seat in the row ahead. Notice the step plate over the rear fender to help the driver in loading the roof-top luggage/cargo area.

This is a 1927 Big Six Model N 15-passenger (including driver) bus. Studebaker referred to it as the cross-seat sedan type. It used the 152-inch wheelbase. Deluxe fitted buses of this type were used in inter-city work, usually between smaller towns and cities, rather than in inner-city operations. The roof-top corral was for carrying luggage, parcels, mail, and whatever else would generate some additional profit.

1927 Erskine Model 50

The Erskine first made its debut in 1927 as a Model 50, receiving the title of "The Little Aristocrat". Without a doubt the most striking feature of the Erskine Six was its supposed European styling. Studebaker felt there was a market in America for a car that was built in America but which had a European flavor to its design. The radiator molding, sweep of the fenders, hood, and the general body lines gave them car what the factory felt the country needed.

The Erskine had its own factory, being built in Detroit. It received its name from the president of Studebaker at the time, Albert R. Erskine. The vehicle practically was an assembled car with its engine being a Continental. Many other parts were purchased out of Studebaker's stock. The 6-cylinder engine had a 140 cubic-inch displacement that developed 40 horsepower at 3200 RPM. The bore and stroke were 2-5/8x4.5 inches. The tire size was 28x4.40 inches. The wheelbase was 107 inches. The factory cataloged four body types; a Custom 4-door Sedan for $975, a Tourer at $945, a Custom Coupe with rumble seat for four at $930 and a 2-passenger Coupe for $910. The cars came from the design studio of R.H. Dietrich. All plans for heavy European orders never materialized, mainly due to the high price that was put on the car just for stateside delivery, let alone European shipping. Erskine finished with 24,893 vehicles delivered.

The sharp looking 1927 Cabriolet is equipped, at extra cost, with the optional wire wheels. The Continental engine could deliver up to 60 mph with gas mileage in the 30 miles per gallon range. Note the small built-in box on the front right fender, this is where the battery was contained. For its time, Erskine was far ahead of most manufacturers, many of which placed the battery in a most inconvenient location, such as under the front seat or beneath the floor boards. The tire cover on this vehicle is of canvas and has a much more tailored look than the oil cloth example on the coupe. Note the two colors on the rumble seat deck. Apparently this car, seen in the factory lot, was undergoing some special paint experimentation, and was not yet ready for shipment.

On this side of the 1927 Erskine is another built-in front fender unit. Here the compartment is for tools and jack. Such were the neat little things that were offered on these cars. This Roadster example came late in the season, and was not listed in the catalog for 1927.

Really sporty for its day was the 4-passenger Rumble Seat Roadster with the extra cost wire wheels. The main tire supplier for Erskine was Firestone which this example wears.

Albert Erskine commissioned Raymond Dietrich to design this new car for 1927. He wanted Dietrich to produce a car with a European flavor, that would sell both in the states and abroad. This is what came from his talented hands. The only thing against the design was the fact that it was too costly! Despite having many things in its favor, the Erskine was just too expensive to try and compete with Ford and Chevy. This Tourer delivered for $945, compared with a Chevrolet for $525 or a Model T Ford for $380. Of course, it was far more of a car than was a Model T.

This Tourer version for 1927 possibly is a special custom as it displays a different paint combination from other Tourers. The paint is different on the hood and on the beltline to the rear of the vehicle. The car certainly does have a look of something from Europe. The wire wheels were still extra cost for Tourers, as well as other models. Note the strange wire wheels. Unlike the standard types shown on the roadster, these are fixed to the axle via the hub nuts, and are fitted with demountable rims, such as found on wood-spoke wheels.

What a change there is in the appearance of this Tourer against those with wire wheels. This vehicle looks much older and doesn't have a spritely get up and go that the wire-wheeled Tourer offers. Also note that the paint job on this version is in a solid color, except for the black fenders and aprons, and not in the more sporty two-tone combinations of the other varieties.

The first year for the Erskine saw some cute looking little cars come on the market. Seen here is the lowest-priced model for the year, the Model 50 2-passenger Coupe, selling for $910.

The 1927 Erskine Coupe, like all Erskines, used a 107-inch wheelbase. The cover for the spare tire had "Erskine" nicely imprinted in the oil cloth. It was an extra-cost accessory, selling for $1.75. The spare tire was also an extra-cost item, but the extra rim and mounting bracket was included in the car's price. The tire cover's wearing qualities were short-lived. Note the large family Studebaker parked on the driveway behind.

This is a 1927 Erskine Rumble Seat Coupe for four passengers. The 146 cubic-inch engine developed 40 horsepower. The bumpers displayed on this example were extra cost items not included in its F.O.B. price of $930.

The 1927 Erskine Six Custom Club Sedan had seating for five passengers. It was not cataloged for the 1927 market, but the sketch did appear in later advertising. It was to sell for the same $975 price as the 5-passenger Custom Sedan.

Being a smaller car than a Studebaker, the rumble seats of the Erskin appeared a bit cramped. These models rode on 28x4.40-inch tires. Seat material in the rumble seat was imitation leather while interior material was done in Mohair. The 1927 cars were referred to as the Little Aristocrat. Maybe that's what the beau with the fancy hat thinks of himself.

The 1927 Erskine was delivered from December, 1926, to December, 1927, recording a run of 24,893 vehicles manufactured. But the cars didn't have a real long life expectancy due to a low torque engine combined with a high axle ratio of 5.125. After a few thousand miles of hard driving, the small 146 cubic-inch engine gave up and so did the sales, which began to plummet.

It looks like this Model 50 Erskine is taking the young folks on a trip with their camping gear strapped to the left door with the help of the running board carrier. Also, a fair supply of equipment is carried between the front fenders, low enough not to overheat the radiator and engine compartment. In this era of few motels, long auto trips were usually synonymous with long camping trips.

This 1927 Model 50 Sedan was classed as the regular Erskine Six. It is minus the extra frills such as a contrasting color on the beltline and has a less impressive interior. The vehicle was classed as a sub-model to the higher priced Custom Sedan selling for $945.

The dolled up Erskine Six Custom 4-door Sedan was the best seller among the Erskine line for 1927. The model is shown in base form, with wooden artillery wheels, and contrasting beltline color extending to the roof. It is also fitted with the extra cost bumpers.

# 1927

The 1927 4-door Sedan is shown with the optional at extra cost wire wheels. It sold for $975 in base form. The cars came as assembled units using a Continental engine that had a bore and stroke of 2-5/8x4-1/2 inches.

This customized 1927 Erskine has a fabric-covered body by Weymann. The unit was delivered to the Auto Commerce Co. of Prague, Czechoslovakia, as a 7-passenger Limousine. It could be called an early "Stretch Limo," as it was built on a 116-inch wheelbase. Features included a leather front compartment and division panel with sliding glass. For some reason the car was right-hand drive, even though Czechoslovakia drove on the right. The original cost is unknown.

Trying to show its rugged dependability, Erskine demonstrated a mile a minute run on the proving ground. The fifth wheel illustrated was used with an electrical timing device to give accurate performance figures on speed, acceleration, and deceleration. These facts didn't hold true for a long period of time as the small engine couldn't cope with continued high speed.

This 1927 "Erskine House on Wheels" supposedly exhibited modern "Scientific Streamlining". Erskine claimed this vehicle was capable of maintaining a speed of 45 mph all day long without a falter. The car used an extended Erskine chassis and stock engine beneath its strange, top-heavy looking body. No information could be found regarding the builder.

With the Dictator name first introduced in mid-1927, its first full year was as a 1928 model. The Dictator nameplate continued through the 1937 model run.

For 1928, Studebaker offered the Dictator in nine models ranging from a 5-passenger Tourer for $1,165 to a Royal Sedan selling for $1,295. The model designation for 1928 Dictators was GE. The cars continued to use the 242 cubic-inch engine which developed 50 horsepower. Virtually, these were the same cars as the mid-season 1927 model. A total of 48,339 Dictators were produced during 1927-28.

The 1928 Commanders were referred to as Model GB. They used a 353.8 cubic-inch engine, with a bore and stroke the same as in 1927 cars, but having an increase in horsepower from 75 to 85. The wheelbase also increased from 120 to 121 inches later in the year with the introduction of Model GH Big Six. This was the final year for this power plant to be used. A total of 31,276 units of both GB and GH series were produced during the 1928 model run.

The 1928 Presidents were classified as Models FA and FB. It makes things a bit difficult for historians and restorers of Studebaker cars of this period because there was the FA model and a later model, the FB. The FA came with a 313 cubic-inch 8-cylinder engine. The bore and stroke were 3-3/8x4-3/8 inches, which developed 100 horsepower at 2600 rpm. The compression ratio was 4.9:1. The engine contained a 2-5/8-inch diameter crankshaft that was carried on five large bronze-backed main bearings.

The bodies of the Model FA cars resembled the earlier ES Presidents. The five and 7-passenger sedans showed little of the square bulky lines of many sedans of that era. Newly designed headlamps, cowl lamps, and bumpers were employed. All exterior bright work was done in chrome plating. A circular wreath was fitted to the fender crossbar with a distinctive "8" to let the public know this was a Studebaker with 8-cylinders! The interior was done in two-tone Bedford cord or broadcloth, or mohair. Window frames were finished in walnut with silver medallions at the center of the lower edges. The instrument panel came in a two-tone walnut. The standard instruments consisted of an 8-day clock, speedometer, electric gas gauge, ammeter, oil pressure gauge, and temperature gauge.

The FA body styles were regular 5-passenger and 7-passenger Sedans, a State Sedan for five and, shortly after production began, a State 7-passenger Sedan was offered. The regular and 7-passenger sedans sold for $1,985, while State 5 and 7-passenger model cars went home for $2,250. A 7-passenger State Limousine also became available, delivering for $2,450. This was Studebaker's most expensive car for the year. Toward the end of the model run, the FA President line expanded to include a State Tourer and State Cabriolet listed at $2,485 and $2,195, respectively. Coming so late in the season, the State Tourer may have been put out only in catalog form, as it appears doubtful that the car ever got into production. The price of the regular Tourer was $200 less than the State Tourer. All regular models were equipped with wooden wheels and rear mounted spare, while State vehicles came with six wire wheels and side-mounted spares. All five-passenger sedans were delivered with a trunk, and seven-passenger State models were fitted with a folding trunk rack. These models rode on a 135-inch wheelbase.

The Model FB President arrived as a mid-season model for 1928. It, along with the Commander, Dictator, and the newly-introduced Erskine, all were completely restyled. At the same time, the President Eight engine was redesigned with a larger bore. It now had a 336 cubic-inch displacement and was rated at 109 horsepower. The Model FB came on a 121-inch wheelbase. These models ranged in price from $1,685 to $1,850. The restyled bodies came with a new "polo cap" visor rather than a visor which was an extension of the roof line. A new radiator was fitted, and redesigned headlamps were used with a winged motif at the top. This winged style feature carried over to the radiator and also to the cowl lamps. The former Atalanta radiator cap used on 1927 and early 1928 models was phased out. The main chassis changes, other than the larger engine, was the introduction of Fafnir ball bearing shackles on all Studebaker cars with the exception of the Erskine.

The FB body styles consisted of State and regular 5-passenger Sedans, State Victoria, State Cabriolet, and a State Roadster. The FB closed cars were virtually the same offerings as the GH Commanders except for the 8-cylinder engine. The FA Presidents continued in production, but were equipped with the FB engine for the most part. A few FA cars with the new body style were continued in production with the older FA engines — probably to use up the remaining engines of the earlier production.

This mid-year offering has never been fully resolved. Ordinarily when a mid-year car is introduced, it takes on the registration of the following year if that model will continue for a full year's run. However, in Studebaker's case, the FA, FB and Commander GH were terminated before the end of 1928. So, if these models were classed as 1929s, it would continue to confuse everyone as to the model year, since true 1929 cars were radically different from these styles. It's really not the best situation to offer two identical model years to entirely different models.

As was the case during this era, Studebaker preferred to make a change when the factory felt it wise, and by offering such a change as a model designation rather than a model year assignment. A total of 26,372 President FA and FB cars were produced during this period of December, 1927, and October, 1928.

Looking a great deal like the Dictator Coupe is this Cabriolet with seating for four passengers. The Landau irons are fake, meaning the top could not be lowered. The windshield was similar to those of other closed cars, and was not the fold-down type found on roadsters and touring models. The interior of this model was in imitation leather. The unit delivered for $1,245.

# 1928

The 1928 Model GE Dictator 6 Business Coupe for two passengers sold for $1,195. For $100 more, a buyer could have a Sport Coupe accommodating four passengers with the aid of the rumble seat. The 242 cubic-inch engine developed 50 horsepower at 2200 rpm.

A second design 1928 GE Dictator Royal 4-door Sedan offered a more deluxe interior than the first series vehicles and yet the price remained the same. These models offered the same mohair interior, while the less expensive Bedford Cord was available in Commander sedans and coupes. This unit came with 31x5.25-inch tires. The sidemounts add to its looks, but they also added to the price if a customer wished this option. The wire wheels also were an extra-cost option. This model was the first Dictator to offer the larger free-standing cowl lights.

The first design 1928 Dictator 4-door Sedan weighed 3,235 pounds and sold for $1,195. The first Dictators for 1928 appeared in September, 1927, and the model was continued with two additional series through October, 1928. A total of 48,339 Dictators in all models were produced in 1928. The first series cars still retained the bullet-shaped cowl lamps. This was a distinguishing mark between it and the two later series. The upholstery was of a long-wearing mohair.

Representing the third design among the 1928 Dictator line, was this 5-passenger Sedan. It was the first series not to have the Atalanta mascot hood ornament. The model came on the 113-inch wheelbase. The fuel capacity was the same as on Commanders, a 14-gallon tank. Wood-spoke wheels with 5-lug demountable rims were standard. The "Atalanta" mascot is often wrongly spelled "Atlanta," in reference to the Georgia city. Actually, the name Atalanta is derived from Greek mythology, and refers to a swift-footed maiden known for tempting suitors into races, which of course she won.

A pretty car in 1928 was this Model GB Commander Sport Roadster. The vehicle weighed 2,900 pounds, rode on a 31x5.25-inch tires and was delivered for $1,595, including the rumble seat, which rated it as a 4-passenger car.

Not as popular as the 4-passenger model was this 2-passenger version of the roadster. It sold for $1,550, but the wire wheels were an extra cost option which certainly added to the car's appearance. The GB Commanders had a short model run, arriving on the market in October, 1927, and lasting only until June, 1928. The production run amounted to 22,848 vehicles.

A rare model even when new was the 1928 Commander GB Roadster. It offered seating for four passengers and sold for $1,595. This well-restored vehicle has even won its Senior Award Badge from the AACA, as the oval plaque on the radiator shows.

It looks like this export version of a 1928 GB Commander Sport Roadster with right-hand drive got sidetracked on its way heading for the shipping docks. Note its special fender-mounted side mirror and the small golf bag compartment door on the rear quarter panel.

Sometimes Studebaker would refer to this 1928 GB as a Big Six Tourer. Evidently, the company wished to keep this name in the public's eye for as long as they could before totally phasing it out for the new 1929 models due shortly. The Tourer example delivered for $1,625 in base form. Note that both roadsters and touring cars continued to use a hinged windshield that would fold flat across the cowl.

This 1928 GB Commander Tourer, with its right-hand drive, obviously was destined for overseas or Caribbean duty. Note the heavy contrasting beltline color and the rear-mounted tail lamp license assembly on the opposite side from state-side vehicles.

This is the GB Commander Cabriolet for 1928. The early cars came on the 120-inch wheelbase and, when the later GH series was introduced, the wheelbase increased by one inch. The 353 cubic-inch engine increased its horsepower over the 1927 models to 85. Note the two-tone paint arrangement from cowl backward, entirely different from fenders and hood. Also, this is an early version with painted headlamp rims. The strange paint scheme makes one wonder if this was actually a production car. It may have been an early prototype, staged for a publicity photo, possibly for an artist to use for a catalog or advertising rendering.

This is a 2nd Series 1928 GB Sport Coupe. Only small changes are noted, such as the cowl lights being moved down to the beltline on the cowl. Also, the grip or door handles don't have the curved flair that the earlier cars offered. This model delivered for $1,495 as a 4-passenger vehicle, with rumble seat.

Shown here is a 2-passenger model GB Coupe. This was a popular car with sales people, as the relatively large storage compartment could be used to keep samples and small sales articles. The Commander model was the lowest priced vehicle in the series, selling for $1,450. Note that the two coupes were photographed in exactly the same location, but the 4-passenger was shot in winter, with snow on the ground, while this 2-passenger appears to have had its picture taken in the spring.

Shown with its rumble seat in the up position is this 1928 Commander 4-passenger Rumble Seat Coupe. It is one of the in-between cars again, as this example came with the chromed headlamps which gave a more finished look to the front-end assembly. The rumble seat deck was a fairly large unit, providing a higher back for the passengers than was found on the rumble seats of many other makes.

A very early 1928 Commander Victoria for four passengers shows some early features not seen on later models. It carries the 1927 bullet-style parking lamps and lacks the chromed welting between the hood and cowl. The leather covered rear top quarters and decorative landau irons were only used on 1st and 2nd series cars due to a change in the side panel and roofline design of the later vehicles.

This is a 1st Series GB 1928 Commander Victoria for four passengers. The Victoria came with mohair upholstery and carpeted flooring, giving its interior a more deluxe appearance. The model weighed 3,594 pounds and sold for $1,495. The distinguishing mark telling it's a 1st series is that the middle beltline isn't painted in a contrasting color, as was the case with later models. The Victoria also came in the Dictator line as well. It used the regular Dictator wheelbase of 113 inches with the same mechanical appointments as other Dictators, and sold for $1,175.

# 1928

A 2nd Series 1928 Commander Victoria shows the middle beltline toned in a contrasting color from the rest of the car. It also has parking lamps mounted lower on the cowl at the beltline. As did the Cabriolet, the Victoria also used a set of attractive but non-functional decorative landau irons.

The late season Commander Victoria was known as a GH model. Gone is the Atalanta radiator mascot, headlamps are now chromed in all models, and the cowl lights are free standing and mounted on the lower edge of the cowl. But the big change is seen on the roof quarter panel, which is no longer curved at the top end, but is now a more squared window. Also, this panel was now made of steel and finished in body color, rather than being leather covered. This change also meant the end of the fashionable Landau irons as they just wouldn't fit the new style top. An upscale Victoria with special trim was also available. Called a Regal, it sold for $1,625.

Considered a good family car was the 1928 Studebaker Commander Model GB Club Sedan. This three-quarter rear view gives a sideview of the oilcloth tire cover was a dealer-supplied accessory to help keep the sun from deteriorating the rubber of the spare tire. The model delivered for $1,450. Painted headlights mean that its an early car for 1928.

A three-quarter front view of the 1928 GB Club Sedan shows small bullet shaped cowl lights and only one bar crossing from headlights, rather than double bars as used on later examples. The 6-cylinder engine had a compression ratio of 4.25:1. It developed 85 horsepower at 2400 rpm. The same model came in the Dictator line for $1,175.

The most popular model in the 1928 Commander line was this GB Sedan for five passengers. The vehicle weighed 3600 pounds and delivered for $1,495. This model came with the later styling, including chromed headlamps. It used the new 121-inch wheelbase chassis.

This Commander version of the GB series 4-door Sedan is one that still used the small bullet shaped cowl lights and painted headlamps. It does employ the wider contrasting painted beltline. This model used the older 120-inch wheel base.

The 1st design 1928 Model GB Commander Regal 4-door Sedan offered more deluxe interior appointments than regular models. The train engineer looks like he would just as soon be behind the wheel of the Commander as take on the locomotive.

What a difference sidemounts can make in a car's appearance. This Regal 4-door model also sports a factory spotlight and a very rare set of front vent panes. These items were seldom seen on Studebakers of that era. The standard wheels were of wood-spoke design, fitted with demountable rims.

This is the Model GH Commander 4-door Sedan for 1928. Quickly looking at the car reminds me a great deal of a 1928-29 Chrysler 65 which my parents owned at that time. From the photos I've seen, this model Studebaker resembles it quite a bit. Note the small window tassels on the rear curtains. People were now able to select a wider range of colors for their cars, rather than having all sedans finished in blue, coupes in tan, etc. Studebaker was right in there, too, with a great variety of colors to choose from.

# 1928

One of the most up-to-date looking cars of that time was this version of the Commander GH Regal Sedan. The model came equipped with wire wheels and side-mounted spares which were part of an accessory package. This was the most expensive closed model in the Commander line. It sold for $1,625, the same as the Regal Victoria. The wire wheels made the vehicle look lower and sleeker than the wooden wheeled cars. There were only 8,000 Regals built in the 1928 Commander line.

Here is the 1928 President FA Cabriolet, 1st design. This 4-passenger model used the 131-inch wheelbase and delivered for $2,195. The FA Cabriolet top did not fold as did those of later FB models, and the landau irons were strictly decorative. The FB Cabriolet came on the 121-inch wheelbase. It made its appearance shortly after the introduction of the FB State and regular 5-passenger Sedan.

A different view of the classic 1928 President 8 FA State Cabriolet. This model was never produced in the 2nd design. The early State Cabriolet did not list the color choices that were available. Color combinations of mid-year FA and FB models amounted to eight choices, but whether all variations were available in all body styles, is not known.

"Miss Studebaker," was known in real life as Jewel McCarley. She won the title of Miss San Antonio and represented the city in the international contest held in Galveston, Texas. She was sponsored by the San Antonio Studebaker dealer . . . Winerich Motor Sales Company. The model is the 131-inch 1928 President Model FA Cabriolet.

# 1928

Model FA 1928 Studebaker President Sedans were built on a wheelbase of 131 inches. This 5-passenger model carried a trunk on the rear as standard equipment. The trunk was 42-inches wide, 18__-inches high, and 10__-inches long at the top, and 16.5-inches long at its base. A larger trunk was also available at extra cost. Both were fitted to conform with the folding trunk rack.

Here is the 1928 FA President 8, 7-passenger State Tourer wearing the famous Atalanta radiator cap mascot. The side mounts and wire wheels were standard equipment on the Tourer. Not many were produced, and the exact number is not certain. Those lucky enough to own one paid $2,485, making it Studebaker's most expensive car for the year. It ranks as a true classic today, according to the Classic Car Club of America.

A 1928 President 8 State Sedan for five passengers is shown here as an enclosed owner-driven model. This model could be ordered either with a leather or Bedford Cord front interior while the rear stayed in the cloth pattern. This model sold for the same $2,250 price tag as the State Sedan, but was minus the glass division window.

The familiar Irving S. Cobb, with one of his famous stogies, is standing beside his early 1928 FA President Sedan. Again, it is one of the first to lack a headlight bar for the oval "8" wreath. Instead, this unit is mounted on the new chromed fender brace or tie-bar. The model also has the three bumper braces across the double bumper bars. According to the road sign, this photo was staged somewhere along Route 60 in Kentucky.

This is a 1928 President 8 Model FA. This was the last body design before Serial No.6002765. The FA cars rode on a 131-inch wheelbase. The large oval "8" emblem on the fender cross bar was later relocated to the headlamp cross-bar. This change necessitated a revision in headlamp design. Only the first 2,000 Presidents came with this type of cross-bar.

# 1928

This 1928 FA President Sedan may have been the means of transporting the pilots and passengers from the airfield to the hangar or terminal. The car claims to be part of Pacific Air Transport, Inc., a division of Boeing Air Lines. It came equipped with wooden artillery wheels, side mounted spare rim, and extra large trunk.

This is a classic looking 1928 President 8, 7-passenger Sedan. This is the owner-driver version, listed at $1,985. The President 8 had a 313 cubic-inch engine that developed 100 horsepower. The "owner-driver" designation usually meant that the same upholstery was used throughout the car. Vehicles meant for chauffeur operation usually had leather front compartments or seats, and cloth rear compartments.

The mid-season President 8 on the 121-inch wheelbase had been face-lifted to a degree. Gone was the old style visor which had been an extension of the roofline. The new style was called a "polo" or "military" visor, and was of a much shorter depth. A new radiator was also fitted, and new headlamps were used which had a winged motif at the top.

Just one more model to help confuse the issue...this is a 1928 Model FA President 7-passenger Limousine of the late type. This example came with an FB engine that developed 109 horsepower at 2600 rpm. The event the car is participating in had something to do with Stanford University, as the school's pennants are draped over the hood and its flags are mounted on the spare tires. It can be assumed that this car had a leather front compartment and was fitted with a divider window behind the driver.

This is the 1928 Model FA President State Sedan on the longer wheelbase of 131 inches. It was a 7-passenger Sedan, minus the glass partition found in the limousine version. This provided lots of leg room for rear-seat passengers. The vehicle weighed in at 4,200 pounds and sold for $2,250.

The second most expensive President built in 1928 was this State 7-passenger Limousine. The vehicle weighed approximately 4,400 pounds and sold for $2,450. The interior was done in leather for front compartment, and highest quality Bedford Cord for rear compartment.

A Studebaker President 8 with a custom landau-limousine body was placed at the disposal of the Sultan of Morocco by Marcel Addor, the Studebaker distributor in Lausanne during the Sultan's visit to Lake Geneva, Switzerland. Note how the rear landau roof folds down. It is not known if the body was from a European or an American custom shop, though the lines indicate a definite American influence.

This 1928 FB President State Roadster was a 4-passenger vehicle of excellent styling. But sales were fewer than anticipated and not too many left the dealerships. The sporty car came equipped with a rear-mounted spare and five wire wheels as standard equipment. This model rode on a 121-inch wheelbase. It sold for approximately $1,800.

# 1928

The 1928 President State Cabriolet FB utilized the 121-inch wheelbase chassis. It was available with a folding top and rumble seat. The landau irons were functional, and the side mounts and wire wheels were standard equipment for this model. For some reason, this car was delivered with only one bumper face bar while most all came with three. Possibly it was another one of those mid-season changes.

After his football days at Notre Dame, the famous Knute Rockne joined Studebaker in an executive capacity until his untimely death in a plane crash. Here he stands besides a late 1928 FB Victoria 4-passenger President. This example is minus the Atalanta goddess, which was replaced by a small radiator cap. It also displays the later all-metal rear quarter window panel, and the small "military type" visor rather than the extended visor which was integral with the roofline.

This 1928 President FB 5-passenger Sedan is equipped with the headlight bar upon which the "8" oval wreath is displayed. This says it is a late model. The rear of the car also has the accessory trunk attached to the folding rack.

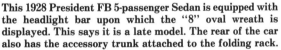

This example was one of the short-lived Model FB President 5-passenger Sedans that was in production from June, 1928, until October, 1928. It was dropped after the 8-cylinder Commander made its appearance as a 1929-30 Model in December, 1928.

The one horsepower model is checking out a 1928 President FB 5-passenger Sedan that rode on the shorter wheelbase of 121 inches. Actually, this was a late season model that some considered to be on the earlier Commander Chassis which increased its wheelbase from 120 to 121 inches. The FB cars came into production in June, 1928, and only lasted until October, 1928. But, for the five short months, the company still produced more FB cars than FA models that were manufactured through the full 1928 model run. FA car production was 13,186 units. The FBs saw a run of 13,386 built.

The 1928 Model FB 5-passenger President State sold for $1,985. Like the FA models, it used Bendix three-shoe mechanical brakes expanding on all four wheels. Its tire size was 31x6.20.

The President 7-passenger FA bore the look of a luxury limousine when equipped with side mounts, wire wheels, and the factory spotlight, all of which were rare items at that time.

This 1928 GB commander Roadster looks much like a 1927 Commander EW. The door advertising claims the vehicle ran 25,000 miles in 23,000 minutes. Actually there were three cars (two Sport Roadsters and a Commander Sedan) that did this endurance run. The Roadsters traveled better than 65 m.p.h. and the Sedan better than 61 m.p.h. The event took place at the Atlantic City track. This clocked event included time for refueling, replenishing oil, and changing tires. This was another one of Studebaker's bits of documentation. The company really loved to present these records to the public, to let potential buyers know what great vehicles Studebaker built. This sort of promotion went on until the very end of the company. Note the three trumpet horns mounted under the right headlamp.

One of Studebaker's greatest feats came from these four 1928 Presidents that took on Atlantic City, N.J., in July, 1928. These four cars pounded the Atlantic City board track for 19 days and 18 nights at constant speeds of better than 68 m.p.h. The totally stock cars drove 30,000 miles in 27,000 consecutive minutes. The leader of the pack was none other than Ab Jenkins.

# 1928

Paul G. Hoffman is here doing the congratulating for another Studebaker racing event. This time it was a 30,000-mile event that took place in 26,326 minutes. Again it took place in Atlantic City, N.J., shortly after the "Big One" earlier that month. The Atlantic City Speedway held the event from July 25 to August 8, 1928.

Studebaker, being noted for racing events in the late 1920s and early 1930s, showed off this FB Roadster and the two Sedans in the winners circle after the Atlantic City event of 19 days and 18 nights in July, 1928.

Car number 3 was one of the four vehicles that took part in the 19 day, 18 night July, 1928, Atlantic City board track event. The cars averaged better than 68 m.p.h. It looks like this FB Sedan is in for some fuel and water, both of which can be seen spilled in puddles beneath the car.

This Model GD early 1928 Commander Funeral Car rode on a 146-inch wheelbase. The model is an Arlington style hearse built by the Superior Coach Corp. of Lima, Ohio. This Studebaker was referred to as the "DeLuxe" as far as professional vehicles were concerned. These models carried the slogan: "Powered for the back road" as Studebaker advertising claimed. It carried a Big Six engine under the hood. The funeral car delivered for $2,985. Similar styles were also available in ambulance form, or as combination (hearse/ambulance) cars.

The commercial 1928 Studebaker GD one-ton vehicle came with a 6-cylinder Dictator engine, and rode on a 140-inch chassis. The 68 horsepower engine probably was doing its fair share of work for the day. Depending on equipment ordered, the unit delivered for approximately $1,100. The spare tire was carried under the rear compartment. Owned by an unnamed tobacco company, the unit was used to deliver Prawn Cigarettes, packed 10 to a box, according to the truck lettering.

It's a 1928 Model GD Commercial, but it carries the passenger car front end. The lines look very much like a 1927 model, with disc wheels, demountable rims, and all, but it is registered as an early 1928. This vehicle carries its spare tire with canvas covering in the front left fender well as standard equipment. The model rode on the 140-inch wheelbase, also.

The 1928 GD Commercial Car with Dictator running gear came on the regular 140-inch wheelbase. The chromed radiator gave a little splash to this vehicle. The bumpers, motometer and Pines winterfront radiator equipment were all extra cost items.

The unit originally was a 1928 President Regular Sedan for seven passengers. The 131-inch wheelbase vehicle was converted to rail service, but information is lacking as to who did the conversion, or what railroad played home to this distinctive vehicle. It was probably intended only for the exclusive use of railroad executives.

# 1928

## PIERCE ARROW

Pierce Arrow has always been one of my all time favorite cars. Possibly it was the novel structure of the headlights in the fenders that made me always have a special attraction to them. At any rate, I'm glad they had a short merger with Studebaker which makes me enjoy working on this book even more. The company wasn't in the greatest position financially in the late 1920s and the merger with Studebaker seemed to be the answer to everything. Even though the companies joined forces, Pierce Arrow continued to build cars only in its Buffalo, New York facility. Studebaker owned Pierce Arrow from 1928 until 1933 and continued its line of cars somewhat as an autonomous separate entity. Pierce introduced its 366 cubic-inch, 8-cylinder engine in 1929, followed by two V-12s in 1932. This high-priced engine introduction could not have been done at a worse time, with the Depression putting its clutches not only on the automobile industry, but on rich and poor alike. And, in 1933, with Studebaker in receivership, Pierce Arrow was in no better shape than they were before. So, it was back to the drawing board, as it were, in 1934. Pierce Arrow was on its own once again, until its final days in 1938. Shown here are a few photos of Pierce Arrows during the Studebaker days. This book makes no approach to giving a definitive Pierce Arrow story, but only touches briefly on a few cars that were issued while the company was under the wing of Studebaker.

This 1928 Model "81" Runabout Roadster was one of the first to come out under Studebaker ownership. Note the rumble seat in the open position and the sharp looking canvas covered trunk attached to the fold-down luggage rack above the rear bumper. Pierce Arrow produced approximately 5,500 cars in 1928, all being 6-cylinder models. This series developed 75 horsepower, while the Series 36 cars gave 100 H.P.

The Model "81" Runabout Roadster is shown with its top in the up position. This model rode on a 130-inch wheelbase. It weighed about 3,500 pounds and delivered in the price range of $3,300. This was the last year for the 6-cylinder engine.

1928 Erskine Model 51

For 1928 Erskine, felt a shot in the arm was needed to help increase sales. So the cubic-inch displacement was increased to 160.4, with the six cylinders now developing 43 horsepower at 3200 RPM. The bore and stroke changed to 2.75x4.5 inches. Tire size this year was 29x 4.73 inches. The vehicles continued to ride on the 107-inch wheelbase. The fuel supply came from a 10-gallon tank.

For the year, "The Little Aristocrat" name was downplayed and the 1928 models were referred to as the Erskine American 6. Probably this was done to let people know this was truly an American-built car. Technically, it was Model 51.

Small changes were made such as having the instrument panel contain a hydrostatic gasoline gauge and an ammeter. The front seats were now adjustable fore and aft to three positions. The bodies received increased head room and increased length. The front end received some small changes with a narrower, deep radiator of greater beauty. Fender styling consisted of a more crowned appearance, and an embossed panel on the hood extended from the radiator ornament to the cowl, widening to meet the body belt which was finished in a contrasting color.

The first of five models to be available for 1928 was the 2-door Sedan, referred to as a Club Sedan, and selling for $795. The model was finished in fawn and sable, with gold and red striping with maroon wheels. The other styles available were the Coupe, Sport Roadster, 5-passenger Sedan selling at $885, and the Royal Sedan, the latter being the top of the line, going out the door for $995. Sales continued to slip and for the year. Erskine sold 22,275 cars, putting it in 19th position for the year.

Here is the 1928 Erskine Cabriolet, referred to as the Model 51. It was now in its second year of production. This year's cars even offered a Bedford cord interior if the owner didn't plan on putting the top down. If he did, the imitation leather was the better way to go. This example sold for $825 as a 4-passenger model.

Looking quickly at it you might think it was a Model A Ford Tudor Sedan. Actually, the wire wheels give this impression. Actually, its the Custom line Club Sedan for 1928 that delivered for $30 more than the regular Club Sedan which priced this car at $825.

The 1928 Club Sedan was available again this year both in regular version and Custom. This happens to be the regular model, selling for $795. The new engine now came with an increased displacement of 160.4 cubic inches with a bore and stroke of 2.75x4.5 inches.

I bet she had a difficult time boarding the driver's seat. This 1928 Model 51 Sedan has just been serviced by the local Mobil Oil dealer. Note all the Mobil memorabilia in the background of the Erskine Sedan. The purpose of the large running board box in not known.

One of the noticeable changes on the 1928 Erskine was the fact that there was no built-in battery box on the right front fender. For some reason, the designers chose to conceal the battery, making it more difficult to service. This example was the Custom American "6" selling for $885 F.O.B. Detroit.

This 1928 Erskine Model 51 Panel Delivery must have been an early 1928 product, as it still wears Indiana license plates for 1927. The panel listed for $825 F.O.B. Detroit. The 1928 models were on the market from November, 1927, to December, 1928. The actual total production was less than in 1927 with only 22,273 being assembled, putting Erskine in 19th position for sales.

It was not a big seller, but it gave good economical service around town. This Erskine Screen Side 1928 Delivery could be ordered as a full panel truck, or for vegetable home delivery service, it could be purchased without the screen sides. I remember one in Pasadena, California, when I was a little kid. The owner turned it in on a 1936 Chevrolet Vegetable Delivery and got $5 trade in. How things have changed!

This 1928 Erskine Panel Delivery was also produced in 1929. It rode on a 109-inch wheelbase. This example was delivered to Neil Neilsen, a leading florist in Mankato, Minnesota. It was sold by the Clements Automobile Company of Mankato, which was a leading Studebaker-Erskine dealer in Minnesota. Sidemounted spare rims were standard on all Erskine commercial vehicles.

# 1929

Studebaker entered the 1929 market with 26 models among its three series of cars. Prices ranged from a -passenger Dictator Coupe for $1,045 to the State Limousine at $2,495.

The 1929 cars made their appearance in the fall of 928, all at different dates so that each would receive ts fair share of the debut.

The Dictator cars once again came with the 242 cubic-nch 6-cylinder engine of 3-3/8x4.5-inch bore and stroke. The engine developed 67 horsepower at 2800 rpm. The uel came from a 16-gallon tank. Dictators rode on the ame 113-inch wheelbase as on the previous year's car. The tire size was 20x5.50 inches. The Dictator model designation was GE for the 1927 through very early 929 models. These cars were produced from September, 927, to January, 1929, with a total of 48,339 units sold. Later model Dictators made their appearance starting n June, 1929, and ran through May, 1930. These were he new-style 6-cylinder Dictators called GLs. Beginning in May of 1929 was the arrival of Dictators in -cylinder fashion. Known as Model FC, these cars were produced through August, 1930. The total run of these two series amounted to 40,276 cars sold.

Again, because of late model introduction, it is hard o pinpoint models of one year or the other. At any rate, 6 models were available between 6 and 8-cylinder Dictators, ranging in price from $1,000 for a Coupe to 1,395 for the 8-cylinder Dictator Brougham. The wheelbase increased to 115 inches and tire size changed to 19x5.50 inches. Both the Sixes and Eights used a 14-gallon fuel tank. Engine-wise these two versions were not that much apart. Both offered the same 221-cubic inch displacement. The bore and stroke for he 6-cylinder block was 3-3/8x4-1/8 while 8-cylinder models were 3-1/16x3.75. The Six developed 68 horsepower at 3200 rpm, while the Eight came with 70 horsepower at the same rpm.

The 6-cylinder Commander models began production in December of 1928 and continued through April of 1930. The 8-cylinder series also made its debut in December, 1928, but lasted through June, 1930. The 6-cylinder Commanders developed 74 horsepower at 3000 rpm from their 248 cubic-inch engine while the 8-cylinder version offered 80 horsepower at 3600 rpm from a displacement of 250 cubic-inches. Commanders used the same tire size as the Dictators. The wheel base remained the same as on earlier Commanders — 121 inches. The Commanders used the same 14-gallon fuel reserve as the Dictator models. Total production of 1929 Commander cars amounted to 40,658 units.

The 1929 Presidents began their 18-month model run with Models FE and FH in December, 1928. A heavy advertising campaign, showing the endurance and speed records of which these cars were capable, took place in July and August of 1928 when they ran a total of 30,000 miles in 16 days at an average speed of 68 mph without a falter. This was a great plus in Studebaker's sales program for the year.

The new President models were longer and lower than their predecessors due to a new double-drop frame. Both FE and FH cars were powered by an improved Eight that now turned out 115 horsepower at 3200 rpm from its displacement of 336 cubic inches. The bore and stroke were 3.5x4-3/8 inches. The President FH models rode on 20x6.00-inch tires and had a 125-inch wheelbase, while the FE cars came equipped with 19x6.50-inch tires. The FE wheelbase was 135 inches. The fuel supply for President models came from a 16-gallon tank.

A total of 12 styles were available, ranging in price from $1,765 for a FH Sport Roadster to $2,495 for the FE 7-passenger State Limousine. Oddly enough, there were no President Coupes produced in the 1929-1930 model run. The Convertible Coupe was as close as the factory came to a coupe style. A total of 26,267 FH and FE cars were produced during this 18-month model run.

This 1929 Dictator Tourer, Model GE, apparently has been out for a little "spin". With its number 7 on the hood, trophy displayed on the fold-down windshield, and non-U.S. license plate, it has apparently taken some honor at an unnamed foreign racing event. It still wears the 1927-28 Atalanta radiator ornament not used for 1929 cars.

# 1929

This 1929 Dictator 5-passenger Tourer, also known as a Phaeton, weighed 2,955 pounds and sold for $1,145. This example rode on a 113-inch wheelbase. Late model GL cars increased the wheelbase to 115 inches. The tire size was 19x5.50 inches. The Dictator models used a 16-gallon fuel tank.

This early 1929 Dictator GE Cabriolet for four passengers is equipped with accessory side mounts and wire wheels. The tire size was 20x5.50 inches. It weighed 2,940 pounds and sold for $1,145. The top could not be lowered, and the Landau irons were just a piece of attractive ornamentation.

A Cabriolet for two passengers was available early in 1929. Minus the rumble compartment, it wasn't as big a seller as the 4-passenger variety. It sold for $1,125 and was equipped the same as the 4-passenger style, but minus the rumble seat.

Studebakers lowest priced car for 1929 was this Model GE 2-passenger Coupe selling for $1,000. A 4-passenger Rumble Seat Coupe also was available for $1,075. The Dictator Six made its debut as the Model GL in June, 1929, and continued until May, 1930, with a run of 16,359 cars produced. The GE cars were a continuation from 1928 and into early 1929.

This was the lowest priced Dictator 4-door Sedan built. It is a very early model called a Touring Sedan for five passengers. It even carries the battery placed on the right front fender similar to the Erskine. It was available for $1,040, but the bumper equipment was additional.

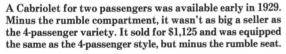

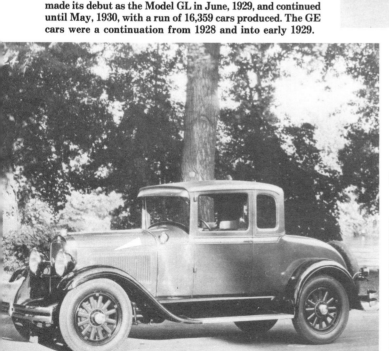

An early 1929 GE Dictator Sedan is shown equipped with the early style wire wheels and small hub caps. With this equipment, the car almost resembles an overgrown Model A Ford. In base form this model sold for $1,165. The bore and stroke of these 242 cubic-inch engined cars was 3.75x4.5 inches. Later GL models used the 221 cubic-inch displacement engine which had a bore and stroke of 3.75x4.25 inches.

Another view of an early GE Dictator Six shows the "S" mounted in the headlight bar, while later editions came with a "6" mounted in the circular emblem ring. Very late Dictator 8 Model FCs carried an "8" in the oval ring.

Call it an early station wagon if you wish. Studebaker referred to it as a commercial vehicle, the Standard Dictator 6, Model GN20. It carried a slightly modified body on a 115-inch wheelbase. Very few were produced in the 1929-1930 model run. The 4-door body had a swing-down tailgate and had two sets of easily removable seats behind the driver's seat. Roll-up windows gave the driver and front passenger weather protection, but roll-up side curtains were used for the rear passengers (or cargo when the seats were removed). The vehicle is shown here with the center seat in place for its furry passenger, while the rear seat has been removed to provide cargo space.

Sitting in the rail yard is one of those late 1929, or possibly early 1930, Dictators. Its a 5-passenger Regal Tourer. This model had minor changes along the way. It came equipped with door handles having a slight curve to them, which earlier models did not have, and the hub caps have a white center around the "S", while earlier models were painted in red. The 242 cubic-inch engine now developed 67 horsepower at 3200 rpm. As a Regal, it sold for $1,265 and weighed 3,075 pounds.

The 1929 GE Dictator Regal Victoria came on the 113-inch wheelbase. This car also was available as a regular Victoria for $1,165. The Regal name added $100 to the price, going out the door for $1,265 as a 4-passenger vehicle. Most all were equipped with natural wood-spoke wheels and a rear mount spare. However, a few did arrive with side mounts and even fewer offered the more costly wire wheel set up. The wider contrasting color distinction on the beltline shows this is equipped as a Regal model.

The Regal Dictator 5-passenger Sedan delivered at $1,265 during the 1929 model run, the same as a Regal Victoria. The sidemounts and wire wheels were part of the Regal package along with an upgraded broadcloth interior. This was also available in Brougham models which sold for $1,295, thus being the most expensive Dictator Six styles available. The 8-cylinder Dictator line delivered the same car for $100 additional.

Studebaker's late season 1929-1930 Model FC 8-cylinder cars came on 115-inch wheelbases. This model made its appearance in May, 1929, and continued until August, 1930, with a production run of 16,359 cars. It sold for $1,285. There seemed to be a great resemblance of this model with Buicks of the same era.

The 1929-30 Dictator PL 6-cylinder line came out in June, 1929, and was part of the overlapping year sales until May, 1930. A total of 17,564 units were manufactured during this time period. It sold for $1,165, the same as early model GEs. In addition to the attractive wire wheels and sidemounts, this version also sports the rare wind wings on the front doors, while the running boards have been fitted with cast aluminum step plates.

# 1929

The headlamp bar tells it all. Most people had to look to tell the difference if it was a "6" or an "8". The caption on the back of the original photo stated "1929 GJ," therefore, this car has 6-cylinders with a horsepower rating of 75 at 3000 rpm.

The 1929-30 Dictator Model FC 8-cylinder Regal Sedan was actually overlapping into the Commander line of vehicles. This model weighed 3,230 pounds and sold for $1,395.

Looking the same as the 8-cylinder version is this Commander Six Model GJ Convertible Cabriolet for 1929-30. This unit, also a 4-passenger vehicle, weighed 3,215 pounds and delivered for $1,545. This view was taken at a dealership where two other 1929-30 models are displayed. Cabriolets came with the wire wheels and sidemount tires as standard equipment.

The 1929 Commander 5-passenger Phaeton came as both a 6 and 8-cylinder vehicle. The Six weighed 3,200 pounds and sold for $1,495. If the Eight were ordered, it weighed 3,250 pounds and left the dealership for $100 additional, or $1,595. The upholstery was imitation leather, unless the owner specified differently.

Here is the 1929 Commander 6-cylinder Model GJ Victoria. The 4-passenger vehicle weighed 3,130 pounds and went out the door for $1,425. This model carried the spare tire mounted on the rear compartment. Natural wood wheels were standard equipment.

Here is the 1929-30 Commander FD 8 Roadster that entered the market for an 18-month span. This series began production December, 1928, and lasted until June, 1930. A total of 24,639 Commander 8 vehicles were manufactured in this period. The car continued to use the 2-way windshield, which could either be swung open from the top, or folded flat across the cowl.

What a sleek looking vehicle is this 1929-30 Commander 8 Roadster, Model FD. The 120-inch car weighed 3,040 pounds and sold for $1,595. It appears this vehicle may have been painted a dark green with black fenders and wheels. The fold down windshield still was popular with those not minding the wind in their face. Note the 1930-style wheels on this very late model. The wheel lugs now reside behind the large hub caps, rather than being exposed as they were when the small hub design was used.

None other than the famous Al Jolson is shown behind the wheel of his late 1929 Commander 8 FD Convertible Cabriolet. The 8-cylinder car weighed 3,240 pounds and sold for $1,695. It had seating for four passengers. Unlike the roadster, which had a fairly neat folding top, the Cabriolet top bulked into a substantial pile of material when folded.

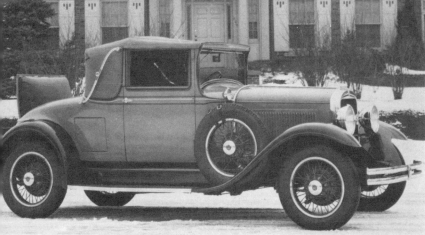

This view of the 1929 Commander 8 Convertible Cabriolet shows the top in the up position and Landau irons in place. It now gives the appearance of a well tailored, compact looking unit. The golf compartment door led to a handy storage space for things other than clubs, if the owner wasn't a golfer.

This is the 1929 GJ Commander Six. It also sold as an Eight. The prices were $1,345 for a 6-cylinder weighing 3,105 pounds. The 8-cylinder weighed 3,130 pounds and delivered for $1,495. These figures were for 2-passenger cars. A 4-passenger rumble seat version also was available for $80 additional in each series. This Windsor Fire Department Chief's Car came with non-authentic disc wheels.

This 1929 Victoria is the 8-cylinder version. It is equipped with extra cost wire wheels and side mounted spares. The FD model came with mohair or Bedford Cord upholstery, which the purchaser had his choice of when ordering. The vehicle weighed 3,170 pounds and delivered for $1,513.

The 1929-30 Commander 8 Club Sedan weighed 3,440 pounds and sold for $1,695. A like model in the Dictator 8 line sold for $1,395. Appearing exactly the same except for the oval ring showing a "6" was a Commander Club Sedan that weighed 3,390 pounds and carried a $1,575 price tag. As a 6-cylinder Dictator it weighed in at 3,250 pounds and delivered for $1,295. A 115-inch wheelbase was employed on all the Dictators, while the Commander came on a 120-inch chassis.

A 1929 Commander Brougham was available in both 6 and 8-cylinder versions. Most buyers ordered the 8-cylinder variety of the 5-passenger intimate sedan. Brougham models came with side mounts, wire wheels and a rear-mounted trunk as standard equipment. The Sixes weighed 3,390 pounds and sold for $1,575. The Eight, equipped the same, weighed 3,240 pounds and delivered for $1,695. This example came with a special leather clothed top at extra cost, and sports very unusual visors over each door window.

A very late season FD Commander 8 Brougham was available with Regal styling that wasn't available on the 6-cylinder car. This special model, besides having an extra plush interior, also came with nickel plated windshield frames, as this model shows. The few small deluxe appointments added a little more to its cost, selling for $1,725. A total of 24,639 Model FD Commanders were produced during this 18-month stay.

The great Scotsman Harry Lauder stands beside a 1929-30 Commander Sedan, Model FD, which was given to him for his use while making one of his many tours of the United States during 1929-30. Being that Scots are supposedly very thrifty people, I bet that's why Studebaker chose the tie-in of its thriftiness with the reputation of the famed Scottish singer and comedian.

Here in front of the Studebaker administration building, once again, are two gentlemen who don't believe in taking their hands out of their pockets. The vehicle is the late Model FD Regal Commander Sedan. This model saw production from December, 1928, until June, 1930. The options, at extra cost, are side mounts and the wire wheels. The 120-inch car weighed 3,385 pounds and sold for $1,695.

This is a 1929-30 Model FD Commander on the same 120-inch wheelbase as the 5-passenger Sedan. However, this example is the Regal 7-passenger Sedan. It was the most expensive model in the Commander line, selling for $1,845. Wire wheels and sidemounts were considered standard equipment for this vehicle.

This 1929 President 8 Roadster stopped by for a little Texaco soup before going on for the rest of some unidentified race. Being stripped down added a few more miles per hour for the President and its driver. The headlights have been replaced by two small spotlights mounted on the cowl, in the remains of the windshield stantion.

Stripped for sure is this 1929 President Roadster with all unnecessary hardware removed. These were great cars during the 1929-30 race season. The cars broke scores of records, never had an engine seal broken, and averaged speeds of 70 m.p.h. Ab Jenkins and his team set 12 records in this time period.

Number 7 was the famous roadster that set the endurance run at Atlantic City for the July event of 1929. It averaged better than a mile a minute for 19 nights and 18 days.

This was the President Model FB that came on the 121-inch wheelbase. The car used 20 x 6.00-inch tires and weighed in at approximately 3700 pounds. The model delivered for $1,885. Notice the unique 2-tone paint scheme that was used on many roadster models this year. Fenders, hood, cowl, and rear panel were in one color (usually dark) while the wheels, doors, and body were in a secondary color.

The Model FB President State Roadster was one of the new model designations for 1928-1929. This example, along with the President FA and the Commander GH cars classed as 1929s, were discontinued before the end of 1928. Only 13,186 of the FB 121-inch wheelbase cars were produced for the 1928-1929 model run.

The 1929 Model FB Roadster received a few changes in its transitional late 1928 period. These included new fenders with more crown, a flat radiator cap, redesigned head and cowl lights, and new spring shackels. The unusual two-tone paint combinations proved to be quite popular, considering the limited appeal of this attractive car, and were used exclusively on this model.

The sporty President Model FH Sport Roadster for 1929, or it might be considered by some to be a 1930, came with five wire wheels. These FH cars came with a radiator having thermostatically controlled shutters, narrow bead fenders, and larger hub caps. The FH cars had a 115 horsepower engine, rated at 3200 rpm. The wheelbase was 125 inches. No lightweight, the vehicle weighed 4,050 pounds.

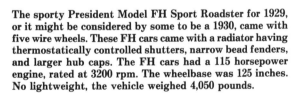

Look at that plush leather upholstery this 1929 President Roadster came equipped with. Note how the front portion of the rumble compartment opens forward making it easier for rear seat passengers to be comfortably "trapped." Once the passengers were seated, the forward panel would be pulled down, and thus provide lap protection for the rear occupants.

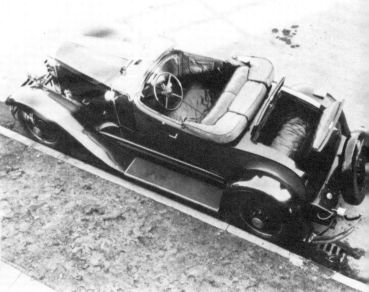

Another celebrity is shown in the passenger seat of this 1929 President Roadster. The gentleman is none other than, at that time, General Eisenhower. This unit was one of those coming with hood painted the same color as fenders while the body is finished in a contrasting color.

Another timed record event occurred for Studebaker. This 1929 President Roadster has Peter Auseklis, the Studebaker-Erskine dealer from Latvia, at the wheel with a Dr. Intlemann. The pair set a new record between Riga and Koenigsberg with a Studebaker Roadster. The time for the event was officially recognized by the International Association of Paris at 4 hours and 50 minutes.

This restored handsome looking President Roadster, Model FH, probably looks better now than when new. It originally came only with a rear mounted spare and wire wheels, but check out all the right accessories for that era; radiator stone guard, spotlights, fender mounted side mirror, Trippe driving lights, and those whitewalls that add the final touch.

A 1929 President FH Cabriolet came with a raised panel by the splash pan. It's beltline was straight, making it a different vehicle from previous convertible models. This Cabriolet was also one inch shorter than the Cabriolet of a year earlier.

# 1929

This 1929 President 8, shown at the famed Brookland's Race Track in Brookland, England, wears an attractive British custom touring body by an unidentified builder. The team was ready to go...and did they go with another win under their belt for Studebaker. This time it was in an endurance run consisting of several consecutive races at the famous track west of London.

These are the two President Eights which did honors for themselves in the 1929 Double Twelve Endurance Run at Brookland's track. The chassis were strictly stock, while the touring bodies were English built. The Double Twelve event consisted of two consecutive twelve-hour daytime races. In other words, the cars went for 24 hours of participation during the two-day endurance trial.

This 1929-30 Studebaker FH President Cabriolet, equipped with an Aerocar passenger trailer, was one of 11 used by Transcontinental Air Transport in cooperation with the Pennsylvania Railroad. How it worked was like this: If one were to travel, say from Pennsylvania to Los Angeles, it could take four days if going by train. To make the trip much easier, a passenger could leave Pennsylvania by air in the day time; travel until dark (planes didn't fly at night); arrive at an airport and be picked up in the President with the trailer that accommodated eleven passengers, and then go to that city's train depot and travel by train through the night. The next morning a new Studebaker/Aerocar would meet the passengers, take them to the local air terminal, and once more they'd fly during daylight hours, hopefully reaching Los Angeles in two days of travel time rather than four. Sounds a bit complicated, but that was how it was done for a "fast" trip in 1929.

This was the FH Short wheelbased President 8 State Victoria for 1929-30. It rode on the 125-inch wheelbase and was powered by the improved straight eight engine that turned out 115 horsepower. This vehicle weighed 4,015 pounds and sold for $1,975. As the State Victoria in the FE series it tipped the scale at 4,360 pounds and delivered for $2,295. Its wheelbase was 135 inches. Both were impressive looking cars, but the price a little high and thus not many were sold.

The Flagship of the B. F. Goodrich Rubber Company's Silver Fleet was this 1929 President Straight Eight Sedan. It was part of a cavalcade of automobiles that made a tour of the U.S. telling all of the great features B. F. Goodrich Tires offered. Note the rubber company's door logo and the windshield placard telling it's the "Flagship."

Demonstrating the power the new President FH had to offer, this dealer took a sedan on a rather wild hillclimb. On the outside are seven men, while how many more are on the inside nobody knows. This event is similar to one performed on an Erskine a short time before at Stone Mountain, near Atlanta, Georgia, which is said to be the world's largest rock.

Looking very similar to the FE President is this FH model. The basic difference in their appearance was the wheelbase. This example rode on a ten inch shorter chassis of 125 inches. It delivered for $1,765 and weighed 4,045 pounds. The car is shown here with the extra cost spare tire. Note the interesting two tone treatment, with the fenders, apron, and beltline done in a light shade and the body and hood in a dark hue.

This 1929 Model FH Studebaker State 5-passenger Sedan obviously is equipped with products supplied by United Motors services. They would include A.C. Delco batteries, a Harrison car heater, and a North East speedometer. The sedan is also equipped with a factory spotlight, wind wings, step plate, aftermarket trunk, and extended horns which appear to protrude out to the bumper. It looks as if some sort of loud speaker has been installed in place of the rear quarter window.

Basically the same car, appearance-wise, as the wooden spoked, rear mounted spare version, is this FH President short wheelbased sedan. This example was the Regal Sedan. The sidemounts and wire wheels were part of the package for Regal models. This example weighed 4,160 pounds and sold for $1,975.

The 1929 President Regal State Sedan looks the same as the regular Regal Sedan, except for a few higher-priced appointments. Some of these cars even came with leather tops, as this example shows. Very few ever got off the production line and price was never divulged. This right hand drive model was an export car. The chauffeur was not included.

This 1929 President 8, 7-passenger Phaeton was photographed by Honigsberg and Son, the distributors of Studebaker and Erskine in Shanghai. The chief of the Shanghai Fire Department sits proudly in his new President. Not too long after this photo was made, Shanghai became involved in China's vicious civil war, and it is anybody's guess what happened to this beautiful car.

When the symphonic band of the Royal Belgian Guard arrived in New York City, it was escorted to City Hall in Studebakers. After the official welcome, the band started on tour of the country. Captain Prevost, leader of the band, is standing in the rear of the 7-passenger President Phaeton that led the procession.

This is a Model FE President Tourer for 1929-30. This vehicle was the first President sold in Calcutta, India for 1929. The vehicle was sold through The Great Indian Motor Works Ltd. to P.D. Mullick, one of the richest landowners in the city, shown beside the driver. Note the older style Studebaker script nameplate mounted on the radiator and its right hand drive steering wheel.

The 1929-30 Model FE style L1 was a Tourer for seven passengers. This car came with a rear mounted spare and wood-spoke wheels, and demountable rims. It was an elegant open car, but evidently it was produced in limited quantity, as few have survived. The vehicle weighed 4,065 pounds and sold for $1,845. The L2 version of the car was referred to as a State Tourer. It weighed 4,210 pounds and the 135-inch wheelbase beauty delivered for $2,145.

A nice side view shows off the 1929 FE President State Brougham for five passengers. This example only came on the 135-inch wheelbase. It was available with a leather top with either broadcloth or mohair upholstery, or with a Burbank top with a Broadcloth interior. In base form, the 4,360-pound car delivered for $2,295. The landau irons were strictly decorative. The trunk, demountable from a folding rack, was finished in the same material as used on the top.

Imagine having a vehicle like this out on the green . . . it sure doesn't look like a golf cart. It's one sharp looking 1929 President State Tourer. This version weighed 4,210 pounds. The 7-passenger car came on a 135-inch wheelbase, delivering for $1,845. A regular Tourer also was available for $1,245. It also as a 7-passenger car and weighed 4,065 pounds. The regular Tourer was equipped with a rear mounted spare and wood-spoke wheels.

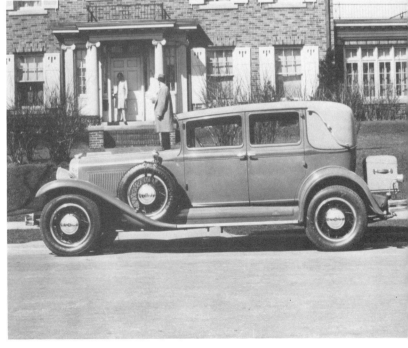

Many manufacturers referred to this body style as a Club Sedan, but not Studebaker. A Club Sedan to them meant a 2-door Sedan. Studebaker thought of this style as a Brougham. This body style with its enclosed rear quarter panel, padded top, and decorative landau irons, came in each series from Dictator Six to President 8. This one is even equipped with a spot light.

The long wheelbased 7-passenger President FE in regular fashion came with demountable rims, a rear mounted spare, and wooden artillery wheels. The sedan weighed 4,210 pounds and delivered for $1,995 F.O.B. The interior was done in either top grade mohair or Bedford cord, at the owner's choice. A spare tire was still at extra cost as this model shows, but the spare rim was supplied with the car. This series offered a larger rear quarter window than those of early examples for the year.

The 1929 FE President State 7-passenger Sedan weighed 4,310 pounds and sold for $2,245. The vehicle rode on the 135-inch wheelbase. The tire size was 6.50x19 inches as on all FE models. These President cars came with a 16-gallon fuel tank.

This car is the long wheelbased 1929 regular President Sedan for 7-passengers. The event shown here was a welcome mat reception for the famous marching band leader John Phillip Sousa. He is shown exiting from the rear compartment.

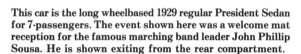

He's right in style with his 1929 President Model FE long wheelbase 7-passenger Sedan. This unit weighed 4,235 pounds and carried a price tag of $1,995 which was probably one great value for its day. This model differed somewhat from other 7-passenger sedans in that the interior appointments were not quite as luxurious as the Limousine models.

This is the FE President State owner-driver Limousine for 1929. The model rode on a 135-inch wheelbase. It was called an X-2 in the FE lineup. The car weighed 4,370 pounds and sold for $2,295. This example wore a top quality Bedford cloth interior throughout since the division window was excluded from this model.

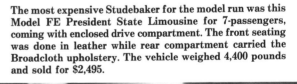

The 1929 FE President seven-passenger Limousine had a leather front compartment. It could be ordered with or without a division window between compartments. However, the speaker tube right behind the chauffeur would indicate that this car did have the divider glass. It carried all the same components as the owner driven Limousine right down to weight and price. Note this unit is headed for overseas, with the chauffeur manipulating the right-hand steering wheel.

The most expensive Studebaker for the model run was this Model FE President State Limousine for 7-passengers, coming with enclosed drive compartment. The front seating was done in leather while rear compartment carried the Broadcloth upholstery. The vehicle weighed 4,400 pounds and sold for $2,495.

The 1929 President Eight Limousine which was on display at the Grand Salon de Automobile of Paris was a real eye-catcher. The exterior of the vehicle was done in San Marco blue and lustrous black, with all bright work and hardware in gold and the roof in gold lacquer. The door beltline was in golden scroll on a black lacquered belt with the "double L" crest on the door panel, characteristic of the Louis XIV period. This was a one off vehicle.

An interior view of 1929 Limousine shows off the exquisite fittings of the era. The rear was fitted with parquet flooring under a heavy bearskin rug. Richly upholstered hassocks were used in place of conventional foot rests. The seating area was doeskin broadcloth with Louis XIV Grand Medallion needlepoint lace on the upholstered arm rest, which could be folded into the seat back. All interior cabinet work was hand carved walnut, and the hardware was finished in gold.

This is the 1929-30 President Funeral Service Car. It came on a 135-inch wheelbase in the FE lineup of vehicles. The Superior Coach Corp. of Lima, Ohio, were the chief producers of Studebaker funeral vehicles and very likely were the craftsmen for this vehicle. Funeral service cars were essentially deluxe panel trucks, outfitted to carry a funeral director's equipment to the funeral site, or to carry a body in a non-hearse transportation role.

How would you like to have this on your property to take care of the premises? Well, that's just how this vehicle was used. A retired capitalist, by the name of Noel Arnold, of Pasadena, California, purchased this unit to be put in service on his estate. He felt there was no need to hide it from guests as it commanded many admiring glances, besides rendering efficient service in a variety of capacities. Studebaker, in their dealer bulletins, often mentioned service vehicles of this type being used on large estates throughout this country.

# 1929

The 1929 Erskine Six, Model 52, came with smart new body styles, a longer wheelbase of 109 inches, and increased roominess and comfort. Mechanically, the cars were basically the same as offered in 1928. The changes did consist of hydraulic shock absorbers, long chrome vanadium rear springs and well-shaped deeply cushioned seats which did make the Erskine an exceptionally smooth riding car for its size. Tire size for the 1929 models was 20x4.75 inches. This year saw the company offering five models with a 2-door Club Sedan being the lowest priced model for the year, selling at $775. It was followed by Cabriolets available both as 2 or 4 passenger units and two 4-door Sedans referred to as a 5-passenger Sedan and the Royal Sedan for 5-passengers coming in an enclosed rear quarter window version. Both sedans tipped the scale at 2,600 pounds. The fuel supply for the 1929 models continued to come from a 10-gallon tank.

Sales continued to slip badly for Erskine. According to MOTOR ANNUAL, the company finished in 30th position for the year with 7,261 units sold.

Erskine's Detroit body production line is where this 1929 Cabriolet (in the foreground) is being assembled. It appears a few more man hours took place on each car's assembly, than is seen today.

Seen here is a 1929 Cabriolet Model 52 in 2-passenger version. Note the tilt to the spare tire. This was the beginning of Studebaker's famous "extended look" which gave the cars a longer appearance from the rear. Since there is no rumble seat, there isn't any need for step pads on the rear fender. The deck lid opened from the bottom. This example also has optional wire wheels for that touch of class.

The Erskine for 1929 offered the Cabriolet as both a regular and a Sport model. This example was the regular, with a stationary top. The Landau irons for this model was fake. This example weighed 2,520 pounds. It is shown here equipped with extra cost bumpers, spare tire, and the oil cloth spare tire cover.

One of the late 1929 Erskine Cabriolets was this model, available as either a 2 or 4-passenger unit. This example happened to be a 4-passenger, as indicated by the rear fender step pad. Some authorities also believed it to be classed as a Royal since it is equipped with the sporty wire wheels and sidemounts. The Cabriolets delivered in the $875 range but, with the depression doing its thing, these 2 and 4-passenger models were not big sellers.

The 1929 Erskine Club Sedan or, as some preferred to call it, the Coach, Model 52, was the lowest priced car Erskine offered for 1929. It delivered for $775.

A left side view of the 1929 Erskine Club Sedan shows how the rear side window could be lowered about half way down. The vehicle was mechanically about the same as the previous year, except for hydraulic shock absorbers being introduced. Also, the wheelbase was increased to 109 inches.

Erskine's best seller for 1929 was this 4-door Sedan that delivered for $845. The Sedan versions weighed 2,600 pounds. They, like each Erskine, came with a 10-gallon fuel tank.

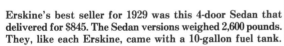

Even though sales were better than in the two previous years, with 25,565 units delivered, the company finished lower on the sales ladder than in its years before. Now, it ranked in the 30th position. That sweep at the bottom of the cowl was a Dietrich touch, for which he was noted.

The wire wheels and sidemounts were basically seen on the Royal models. This, however, is a Custom 4-door Sedan selling for more than the regular 4-door by $15. It went out the door for $860, without the wire wheels.

Seen in an overseas setting is one of those models that Erskine himself had hoped would flood the market in Europe. Unfortunately, it never happened. This right-hand drive vehicle also is equipped with rare lights beneath the headlamps, and has a special extra light mounted on the left in place of the parking light.

The greatest Erskine creation came in 1929 with this example that Studebaker displayed along with a President Eight Limousine at the annual Salon de Automobile in Paris. This Erskine, with richly patterned tapestry upholstery and bronze lacquered hardware, was the ultimate for a low-priced car on display at the Salon. The exterior was done in three shades of French violet, with black upperworks, silver roof and window reveals, and running board shields and belt in a futuristic pattern emphasizing the modern art motif that Erskine was trying to create. Only one example was ever produced.

The 1929 Erskine Panel Delivery was a dependable little livery unit for such things as it's doing — delivering baked goods and groceries. This was classed as a half-ton delivery unit, selling for $850. It used the passenger car mechanical components and from the cowl forward used all the passenger car ingredients.

A nicely restored 1929 Pierce Arrow Roadster represents the company's lowest-priced car for the year. It sold for $2,875. This was classed as Model 133, a number which referred to its 133-inch wheelbase.

One of Pierce-Arrow's best years was 1929. This fact was chiefly due to the new 8-cylinder engine that developed 125 horsepower at 3200 rpm. This example, a 5-passenger Sedan, delivered for $2,975. Pierce Arrow produced 9,840 vehicles for the model year run, to the great delight of those Studebaker executives who had been in favor of the acquisition. Sadly, the days of glory were to end very quickly.

This beautiful 1930 Model "A-144" 7-passenger Touring weighed 4,700 pounds and delivered for $3,750 F.O.B. Buffalo, New York. Being Model 144, it rode on a 144-inch wheelbase. Incidentally, talk about depreciation. This car was purchased used in 1933 following a trade-in on a new Lincoln. It left the used car lot for $500. What a steal!

### 1930 Erskine Model 53

This was the swan song year for Erskine, despite being called "The Dynamic New Erskine". With the Depression putting its clutches into the automobile industry, Erskine did all it could do to try and stay alive, but it still wasn't good enough. The company discontinued its Continental engine in place of the 205 cubic-inch engine from Studebaker which developed 70 horsepower at 3200 RPM. The bore and stroke from this engine was 3.25x4-1/8 inches. The fuel supply was increased to a 14-gallon tank. The last models also came on a 114-inch wheelbase. Erskine came with a 1.25-inch Schebler carburetor with Studebaker's semi-automatic spring-loaded choke. The tire size for these models was 5.25x19 inches. One novel device used for the year was an acoustic muffler, designed to give unusual silence with minor back pressure. In this muffler was a long unobstructed pipe with many perforations, surrounding a jacket containing steel wool.

A total of eight models were available for the year ranging in price from $895 for a 2-passenger Coupe, to $1,095 for a Regal Land Sedan for 5-passengers. The company did not complete the full 1930 sales year and production figures placed Erskine in 23rd position with 8,757 units sold.

Even in its final year, Erskine continued to offer a variety of cars. This Royal Brougham, Model 53, delivering for $1,095. It was the most expensive Erskine. Some changes were made this year, the major one being that the Continental engine was now replaced with Studebaker's 205 cubic-inch 6-cylinder engine that developed 70 horsepower. It also saw a wheelbase increase to 114-inches.

The middle line 1930 Erskine Custom Sedan used the same mechanical features as the regular and Royal models. It's highly advertised feature was the acoustic muffler, which supposedly offered complete silence. This unit, equipped minus the sidemounts and wire wheels, sold for $995. Note that new and more modern wire wheels were now being used. These had the lug nuts hidden behind the large hub caps, rather than having exposed lugs and small caps.

It's still an Erskine! This is not a Studebaker Model 53, which is what the lowest-priced Studebaker Six became known as. The Erskine coat-of-arms is seen on the top of the radiator. Erskine sales ended before the close of the model run, putting them in the 23rd sales slot. The Erskine sales for 1930 also included the Studebaker Six, which took over the remainder of the season with 22,371 vehicles manufactured.

The 1930 Studebakers came in three versions. The 6-cylinder cars were offered in Dictator and Commander models only. The Dictator vehicles developed 68 horsepower with the 6-cylinder block and 70 horsepower in 8-cylinder form. Each engine was rated at a maximum of 3200 rpm. The Commander, in 6-cylinder form, was rated at 75 horses at 3000 rpm, while the 8-cylinder models were rated at 80 horses at 3600 rpm. In the Commander series, the Six had a displacement of 248 cubic inches, which was almost as much as the 250 cubic inches credited to the Eight.

The upscale President line came only with an 8-cylinder engine. Displacing 336 cubic inches, it was rated at 115 horsepower at 3200 rpm.

The Dictator and Commander vehicles were equipped with 14 gallon gas tanks, while the President models had a 16 gallon fuel supply. Both Dictator and Commander cars rode on 5.50x19 inch tires. President models were offered with 6.00x20 inch tires on the regular line while the senior Presidents used 6.50x19 inch tires. Four different chassis were used. The senior Presidents utilized a 135-inch wheelbase while regular Presidents came on a 125-inch wheelbase. The Dictator cars used a 115-inch wheelbase and Commanders were built on a 121-inch base.

Altogether, 50 different models were made available among the three series. This includes similar models varying between 6 and 8-cylinder cars, but still represents a wide range of vehicles when compared to many other manufacturers. The factory prices ranged from $1,045 for the 2-passenger Dictator Coupe to $2,495 for the 7-passenger President Limousine. Studebaker placed in the 11th sales position nationally for the calendar year, with 51,640 cars being sold.

This 1930 Model 53 Roaster is equipped with wooden artillery wheels. It was quite a sporty looking little car for its day, but would have benefitted greatly from a set of extra-cost wire wheels and side mounts. As is, the vehicle sold for $895. The one-man top was easy for up and down operation. It offered seating as a two-passenger vehicle.

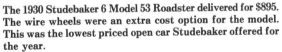

The 1930 Studebaker 6 Model 53 Roadster delivered for $895. The wire wheels were an extra cost option for the model. This was the lowest priced open car Studebaker offered for the year.

Here is a Model 53 Touring car that delivered for $965. It was also available as a Dictator 6 for $1,145, Dictator 8 for $1,285, Commander 6 at $1,395, Commander 8 for $1,495, and President Touring for 7-passengers selling at $1,845. In each series, the quality improved to compensate for the increase in price, while the body also became much larger on the bigger cars.

The 1930 model Studebakers were still in the lapping-over stage...going into another year with very little change. This was a 1930 Model 53 Club Sedan which had been the Erskine model, until that make ceased production. Now Model 53s were given to the Studebaker Six. This example was one of the lowest-priced cars the factory had available for the year. It delivered for $850.

One thing noticeable on the lower-priced 1930 Model 53 Studebakers is the arrangement of the hood louvers. They are done in groups of three with seven sectors on each side panel. Check out that roof rack! Since this car was used on a rural U.S. mail route, the rack was probably put to good use in carrying mail order packages to remote farm families.

The Model 53 Studebaker for 1930 was a descendant of the Erskine. This mid-season title was needed in helping phase out the Erskines. As both the office window and logo on the cab tell us, this unit belonged to the Indiana DeLuxe Cab Company. The model delivered for $965. The spare tire was an extra cost item, and this one came without it.

Not only did the Indiana DeLuxe Cab Company offer Model 53s, but so too did the Yellow Cab Company. Here a fleet of them are waiting for their call to duty. This same background will also appear for 1931 models. Apparently, the Yellow Cab Co. had a contract with Studebaker for yearly change-over.

This side-mounted Model 53, being a carryover of the Erskine from early 1930, was referred to as a Regal Sedan. It was built on the 114-inch wheelbase. This example sold for $1,065 and offered occupancy for 5-passengers. The side mounts and wire wheels were extra-cost options.

This example for 1930 is just a bit more deluxe than its Regal brother so it was called the Model 53 DeLuxe Regal. It offered a little more style to its interior, and had pin-striping which doesn't show too well in this photo. This added an additional $30 to its price. The car sold for $1,095.

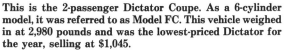

This is the 2-passenger Dictator Coupe. As a 6-cylinder model, it was referred to as Model FC. This vehicle weighed in at 2,980 pounds and was the lowest-priced Dictator for the year, selling at $1,045.

Classed as a Model GL Dictator was this Club Sedan. For the 1929-1930 model run, production began in June, 1929, and lasted until May, 1930. In the entire GL line, production amounted to 17,561 units.

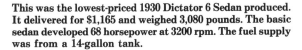

This was the lowest-priced 1930 Dictator 6 Sedan produced. It delivered for $1,165 and weighed 3,080 pounds. The basic sedan developed 68 horsepower at 3200 rpm. The fuel supply was from a 14-gallon tank.

This is the 1930 Dictator 6 Sedan available as a Regal model with 2-tone paint, natural wood wheels, and a more deluxe interior. The model sold for $1,265. As a Six, it weighed 3,209 pounds; the Eight was only 30 pounds heavier.

The 1930 Dictator Coupes each rode on a 115-inch wheelbase. The 6-cylinder 2-passenger Coupe delivered for $1,045, and the 4-passenger went home for $1,095. As an 8-cylinder, the 2-passenger sold for $1,235, while a 4-passenger Coupe brought $1,285. This example is the Dictator 8 4-passenger model that weighed 3,010 pounds. Its Model designation was FD. Studebaker also offered two and 4-passenger Coupes in the Commander line, both as 6 and 8-cylinder cars. The prices ranged from $1,345 for a 2-passenger 6-cylinder, to $1,545 for the 4-passenger Commander 8. No coupes were available in the President series this year.

Looking identical to the Dictator 6 Model GL, is this 8-cylinder Dictator FC which carried an 8-cylinder engine under its "bonnet". The eight delivered for $1,195 and weighed 2,990 pounds. Model FCs were in production from June of 1929 through August of 1930, seeing a production run of 16,359 cars assembled.

This is the 1930 Model FC Dictator 8 Brougham that was a well-received unit for those seeking a 4-door Sedan. This car delivered for $1,395, the same as a Regal Sedan. It weighed 3,275 pounds. The vehicle employed 5.50x19-inch tires. Basically, the Broughams were delivered with side mounts, wire wheels, and the trunk accessory. One item that the late season 8-cylinder models carried that was not seen on 6-cylinder models was the headlight bar seen on this vehicle.

This is a model FC 1930 Dictator 8 Sedan, delivering for $1,285. The conservative model weighed 3,095 pounds. The painted black wooden artillery wheels gave a somber tone to the vehicle. Note the embossed canvas oilcloth spare tire cover. Often times, dealers put these on the cars they delivered with their name inscribed for a "free ad."

Looking more stylish with its wire wheels and side-mounted spares is this 1930 Regal Dictator 8 which sold for $1,395. There was only a $130 price-difference between it and the 6-cylinder models, including the accessory package that this vehicle wears.

This 1930 Regal Commander 8 Model FD sold for $1,695. If a Regal Commander 6 Model GJ were ordered, the tab was $1,545. The Eight weighed 3,385 pounds and the Six was 3,335 pounds. Note the contrasting color scheme that this Commander employs, especially around the beltline. The wire wheels give a lower profile to the car.

The 1929-30 Commander 6 Model GJ Roadster was exactly the same as the 8, as far as body goes, except for the 6-cylinder emblem on the headlight bar. One wonders if Miss Michigan was given the car after her tour of duty was completed, or if she was simply allowed to pose in it for publicity shots. The Commander 6 Roadster delivered for $1,495.

This 1930 Commander 8 Regal Brougham offered many of the deluxe appointments seen on the President line, such as center fold-down seat armrests, clock, and fully adjustable steering wheel, to name a few. The Sedan weighed 3,440 pounds and delivered for $1,695. A comparable 6-cylinder Commander Brougham was also available for $1,575.

This view of the 1929-30 Model FD Commander Brougham resembles the President Brougham a great deal except this vehicle does not have a raised panel by the running board, which was standard on President cars. This was probably an export model to India, according to the lady posing by the vehicle. Note its foreign license and right-hand drive. That open windshield must have provided real "flow-through" ventilation.

This 1929-1930 Model FD Commander 8 Brougham is equipped with the side-mount spares. Note the short-lived oilcloth canvas tire cover with the Studebaker logo imprinted on it, and the driver's window shade.

This is the 1930 Commander 8 FD Sedan that weighed 3,255 pounds in basic form. It carried a selling price of $1,515. The same car was available as a 6-cylinder for $1,445 and weighed 3235 pounds. The tire size for all Commander units was 5.50x19.

The late model 1930 Commander Sedan was available both in 6 or 8-cylinder fashion. This new example doesn't have the usual sun visor that was seen on 1930 cars, and its hub caps are slightly larger. The kid is pulling a neat toy Bulldog Mack fire engine, that today would make a fine collector piece in itself.

The 1930 President Cabriolet Model FH was built on a 125-inch wheelbase. The 8-cylinder model developed 115 horsepower from the 322 cubic-inch engine. The car weighed 3,970 pounds and delivered in a 4-passenger style for $1,975.

The Deputy Imperial Potentate of the Masonic Temple of Rochester, New York, appears to be enjoying his chance to drive the 1930 President Phaeton. This model came either as a 5 or 7-passenger vehicle delivering for $1,795 for the 5-passenger, and $1,895 in 7-passenger version, or $2,145 if the 7-passenger State Touring were ordered. Note the white canvas tire cover with the imprinted Studebaker logo and the V-shaped rear windshield with folding wind wings. This was not a dual-cowl phaeton, but simply a touring car with rear windshield.

The deluxe example of a 1930 President Brougham Model FE came on a 135-inch wheelbase, weighed 4,360 pounds, and carried a price of $2,295. This model came with a leather top, which was an extra cost item.

Check out this classic. It's an export vehicle with right-steering wheel and the license bracket attached to the right tail lamp. The Landau irons came with the model, when the extra-cost leather roof was ordered. The President Brougham only came on the 135-inch wheelbase.

A 1930 President Brougham is parked next to a 1930 Martin Dart, a mini-type car slated for production of 250,000 units to be sold at $200 each. However, only about a half-dozen prototype cars were produced by the M.P. Moller Co. of Hagerstown, Md., before the whole Dart idea died. The designer, J.V Martin, seemed fascinated with little cars, and continued to introduce them up until the late 1940s. The complete story of Martin and his cars is covered in the ENCYCLOPEDIA OF AMERICAN CARS, 1930 TO 1942 by James H. Moloney, and published by Crestline/Motorbooks International.

This 1929-30 President Sedan Model FH was built on the shorter wheelbase of 125-inches. The model sold for $1,765. The car is parked in front of the U.S. Immigration Service, but the large decal on the car's door, indicates that some of the officials are from the National Automobile Club. The car wears accessory driving lights and California license plates. The gentleman on the far right probably is part of the California/Mexico border patrol.

This is a 1929-1930 President FH 5-passenger Sedan in basic style, without any of the nice amenities usually associated with the President models. It was the lowest-priced President available for 1929-30, selling for $1,765 as a 5-passenger sedan. It weighed 4045 pounds.

A 1930 President 7-passenger Limousine could be ordered either as an owner-driven vehicle or Chauffeured enclosed-drive model. It sold for $2,295 as a regular 7-passenger, or $2,495 as the Enclosed Drive Limousine. The more expensive model offered a partition between compartments, and a leather front seat, while the owner-driven style was fitted in regular sedan form. Note that this example came minus cowl lamps, and employs a single bar bumpers in place of the typical double bars seen on most 1930 models.

What a classic design this 1930 President FE offered. The car came with stock Studebaker hood, fenders, bumpers, head lamps, and radiator. The body is aluminum, and its setting is definitely Europe. The blurred body name on the back of the original photo claims Graber of Switzerland to have completed the full-custom job. The car is right-hand drive. Of interest are the attractive European-style wire wheels and sidemounts, and the visors over each side window and the windshield.

A straight-on front view of the 1930 7-passenger Touring gives the car an almost intimidating appearance. This year Pierce-Arrow had 17 different cataloged body styles on the market...three on the 132-inch wheelbase; four on the 134-inch base; five on the 139-inch unit, and five on this 144-incher. And these did not include the custom bodies available from the multitude of coach building firms still in business in that era.

The 1930 Pierce-Arrow Town Car in the Model A series was available for $7,500 which was next to the top of the line, the French Brougham for $8,200. All Model A cars used the 144-inch wheelbase chassis and the 132 horsepower version of the straight-eight engine.

Some people still preferred the drum headlamps. So Pierce Arrow was willing to accommodate. When drum headlamps were supplied, fender mounted parking lights were used. Both versions sold for the same price. This 1930 example was a Model "C" coming on a 132-inch wheelbase and referred to as a Roadster with Rumble Seat. Selling for $2,875, it was the lowest priced Pierce-Arrow of the year. The Model C cars came with seven groups of narrow hood louvers while, the Model A and B cars were supplied with five hinged hood doors.

This Sport Phaeton is in the Model B class for 1930, as it has the seven groups of three louvers on the side of the hood. Rather than the single bar bumpers which the larger series employed, this unit is equipped with the two-bar set up. It was built on a 134-inch wheelbase chassis, using 19x6.50 inch tires.

The Group "B" 1930 Pierce-Arrow 5-passenger Club Sedan rode on the 139-inch wheelbase. This was considered one of the Salon models, meaning that it was cataloged by Pierce-Arrow, but would be built on special order only, usually with distinctive upholstery and fittings designed to the customer's specifications. New for Pierce, as most all the automobile manufacturers, was the device of Free Wheeling which allowed the car to coast as if in neutral when the foot was taken from the gas. Eventually free wheeling was outlawed in all states because it negated any braking effect that the engine had, especially on downhill grades.

The Group "B" 1930 Pierce Arrow 7-passenger Salon Model Enclosed Drive Limousine rode on the 139-inch wheelbase. Note the special colored diamond seen on the whitewalls. This was a B. F. Goodrich and Vogue Tyre trademark for several years. All Group B cars used the 8-cylinder engine of 125 horsepower. The 139-inch wheelbase chassis would not reappear in 1931, being replaced instead by a 142-inch unit.

This year there were few changes to differentiate the new issue from the 1930 models. Generally, the cars were more rounded in the styling department, which was a definite plus. Generally, the Dictator became a bit smaller, while all other models grew in length.

The popular Dictator line once more came in 6 or 8-cylinder form, and was now the only 6-cylinder Studebaker. The Dictator Six had a 205 cubic inch engine that developed 70 horsepower at 3200 rpm. The Dictator Eight developed 81 horsepower from its 221 cubic inch engine, again at 3200 rpm. This was a slight power increase for the Six, and a nice boost for the Eight. All Dictators were built on a slightly shortened wheelbase of 114 inches, and their tire size was decreased to 5.25x19 inches. Once more, a 14 gallon fuel tank was used.

The Commander line now appeared only in 8-cylinder form, with the Six being discontinued. Its block of 25[?] cubic inches developed 101 horsepower. All Commanders now rode on a new 124-inch wheelbase, use[?] 6.00x19 inch tires, and were equipped with 17-gallon fue[?] tanks.

The top of the line again was the President serie[?] which was offered in both 130 and 136-inch wheelbas[?] lengths. The President series used an 8-cylinder engin[?] of 337 cubic inches which developed 122 horsepower a[?] 3200 rpm. All Presidents used 6.50x18 inch tires an[?] were equipped with 20.5-gallon fuel tanks.

In the engineering department, a 3-speed syn[?] chromesh transmission made its debut on the entire lin[?] while the new free-wheeling concept was also used fo[?] the first time. Studebaker managed to sell 48,921 car[?] during this depression year, which was enough to pu[?] the company into the 10th sales slot nationally.

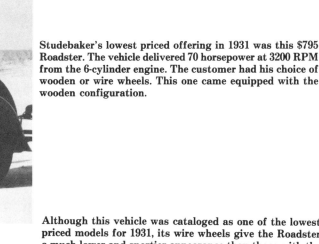

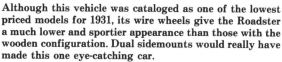

Studebaker's lowest priced offering in 1931 was this $795 Roadster. The vehicle delivered 70 horsepower at 3200 RPM from the 6-cylinder engine. The customer had his choice of wooden or wire wheels. This one came equipped with the wooden configuration.

With top up is the Studebaker 6 Model 54 Roadster. The wheelbase for Studebaker Sixes was 114 inches. This example weighed 2,850 pounds.

Although this vehicle was cataloged as one of the lowest priced models for 1931, its wire wheels give the Roadster a much lower and sportier appearance than those with the wooden configuration. Dual sidemounts would really have made this one eye-catching car.

The lowest priced Coupe available from Studebaker in 1931 was this 6-cylinder Business Coupe. It sold for $845 and weighed 2,835 pounds. Helping to distinguish a Model 54 from a Dictator 8 are the bumper designs. The 6-cylinder cars came with double-bar bumpers with a deep central "V", while 8-cylinder models wore the one-piece bumper. The Business Coupe used a trunk deck rather than a rumble seat.

A 1931 6-cylinder Studebaker Sedan for 5-passengers was factory priced at $895. The 4-door weighed 2,950 pounds. If the wooden wheels were used, the customer had his choice of either varnished natural wood or painted. This owner apparently felt the conservative car looked better with painted black wheels.

For still another year, Studebaker was in the taxi business. These 6-cylinder Model 54s are anxiously awaiting for a phone call to leave the Yellow Cab headquarters to get out and prove their stuff. The 6-cylinder engine was a very dependable unit. The "No. 67" on the rear door would indicate that these units were part of a rather substantial fleet.

Looking basically the same as a Studebaker 6 is the Dictator 8, Model 61 side-mounted Coupe. It was listed at $1,095 as a 2-passenger vehicle or $1,150 if the 4-passenger version were ordered. The side-mounted spares and trunk were optional extra cost pieces of equipment. Use of the optional free-standing trunk would indicate that this model probably was equipped with the rumble seat.

This example of the Studebaker 6 was delivered with the side-mounted spares and wire wheels for an additional $103 to its base price. Bendix mechanical brakes were used on the Sixes as well as on Commander and President cars.

# 1931

This Model 61 Dictator 8 Coupe has the "old man" wooden wheels. This actually was the 2-passenger Business Coupe available for $1,095. It weighed 2,950 pounds. The 8-cylinder engine developed 81 horse-power at 3200 rpm.

Only noticeable difference between the Business Coupe and the Sport Coupe in this photo is the golf compartment door which is displayed on the right rear quarter. This 4-passenger model delivered for $1,150. It weighed 3,010 pounds.

A 1931 Model 61 Dictator Sedan for 5-passengers. This vehicle was available for $1,150. Of the Dictator 8's, this model was the most popular. A total of 10,823 Dictator 8's were manufactured for the model run which began June, 1930, and lasted through September 1931. Some people refer to these as 1930-1931 cars.

This Dictator 8 was considered the Regal Sedan style for the Dictator line. It weighed 3,290 pounds and delivered for $1,250. It was also available in the Studebaker 6 line for $995, where it weighed 3,110 pounds.

Classified as a Model 70 Commander Victoria was this attractive 2-door. Coming on a wheelbase ten-inches longer than the Dictator cars, this model had inside seating capacity for 4-passengers. It weighed 3,390 pounds and sold for $1,585. Side-mounted tire equipment was available at extra cost, as were wire wheels.

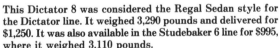

With its California license plates already mounted, this owner is ready to tread west from the South Bend factory in his new 5-passenger Commander Sedan. The vehicle weighed 3,520 pounds and, in base form, sold for $1,585. Factory pick-up was not all that unusual in this era, but seldom did one come from California for a new car.

Put to work in South Bend as the Fire Chief's car is this six-wheeled 1931 Commander 5-passenger Sedan. The vehicle came with the wire wheels, which no doubt kept a rookie fireman busy keeping them clean.

One way to get the public's attention was by using a loud speaker system to tell about all the fine qualities the Studebaker had to offer. Here is a 1931 Model 70 Commander 8 Sedan announcing the Free-Wheeling for which it was famous. Note the speaker in the driver's hand as he parades through town. Studebaker had more sales devices than many other auto manufacturers, to get the public into their corner.

The new 1931 Commander Regal Brougham certainly was a regal looking car. This body style also was referred to as a Close-Coupled Sedan. The model weighed 3,660 pounds and sold for the same price as the regular Regal Sedan . . . $1,785. Side mounts were an extra cost item for this car, but certainly did add that little extra touch.

Parked in front of a Studebaker dealership is this 1931 Model 70 Commander Regal Sedan for 5-passengers. The car weighed 3,660 pounds and delivered for $1,785. There is a small piece of today's memorabilia posted on a light post similar to one in the author's Studebaker literature collection. It states: Eastside, Westside, everyplace you see Studebakers.

This 1931 Commander Regal Sedan came on a 124-inch wheelbase. This vehicle even has the very attractive metal tire covers over its extra cost side-mounted equipment. The lady has a Wisconsin license plate mounted on the front bracket. She apparently has just taken delivery from the factory and is heading home.

The classic lines of the 1931 Studebaker President Roadsters is enhanced by the contrasting color arrangement on this vehicle. A safe assumption is that it was done in Absinthe Green for body color, with a beltline and fenders of Coach Green, with Cream wire wheels. What a knockout!

This short wheelbase Model 80 President Roadster is being transported on a Studebaker truck capable of a carrying capacity of two tons. Even though it is brand new, one must wonder where all the dirt came from on its wheels? Note the art deco Studebaker dealership in the background.

This 1931 Studebaker President Roadster was one of three used to promote the Elks Magazine, the Elks 68th National Convention at Seattle, and also advertise Studebaker's new free-wheeling. Driven from New York to Seattle, the cars undoubtedly stopped at many an Elks Lodge enroute, where the Studebakers probably were greatly admired. The national convention for the Elks took place July 6-9, 1931. Note the fold-down windshield, twin spotlights, and special-built factory accessory trunk that this President employs. In 1982, the Studebaker Drivers Club and Antique Studebaker Club held their convention in Seattle. Too bad they couldn't have once again run three of these beauties from New York to the West Coast.

I've enjoyed looking at this photo for the detail in it. How about the vines growing over the gas pumps? I think — as kids would say, today — NOT! The car is a 1931 Model 80 President Roadster which was used for a Warner Bros. movie called "The Millionaire." It starred David Manners, Evelyn Knapp and George Arliss. For the movie, the car was called an "Alden" and a radiator cap and hub caps were to wear an "A" inscription. In this era, no movie company would think of calling any car by its rightful name.

This 1931 President 8 Four Seasons Convertible Roadster was photographed in front of Studebaker's South Bend administration building. The barrel on the front of the Model 80, and the canister on the side state "From New York to Rome, Italy." This would indicate the crew was set for a relatively long drive and sea journey. But why the skull and cross bones on the canister? The pilots' helmets would indicate that much top-down driving was planned. Incidentally, the car carries New Jersey license plates. One wonders if it ever reached Italy.

This was the lowest priced 1931 President available for the year. The 130-inch wheel based car sold for $1,850. It was a lot of car for only two occupants. The model weighed 3,995 pounds.

Studebaker's lowest priced President Sedan came as this Model 80 on a 130-inch wheelbase. It delivered for $1,850 and weighed 4,230 pounds. These models were part of Studebaker's production run that often overlapped for more than the regular yearly run. As an example, this particular model saw production for 15 months beginning in June 1930 and ending in September 1931. Often called a 1930-1931 car.

A Model 80 1931 President Sedan is parked in front of this small unidentified dealership. The little boy in his replica horseshoe-radiator Bugatti is probably the dealer's son. Note the window advertising banner telling you to "Free Wheel with Studebaker." Makes one wonder how many Presidents the dealership sold in 1931?

This 1931 7-passenger Sedan was put into daily use operating between El Paso, Texas, and Silver City, New Mexico, a distance of about 150 miles each way. The Free-Wheeling unit was given the best testimonial it could receive over its years of use. The sedan came from the Glenn Foster Studebaker dealership in El Paso. The wooden wheels were rather rare on the President line and gave a very heavy look to an already huge car. Possibly for such rough mileage as this vehicle was subjected too, the owners preferred the stronger wood spoke wheels over the prettier but less substantial wire models. Or, the wood spoke units might simply have been more cost effective.

Studebaker offered six versions of the President Sedan for 1931. This example was a 7-passenger State Limousine for 7-passengers. It was the most expensive model Studebaker offered for 1931. The car weighed 4,580 pounds and sold for $2,600.

The 1931 President Sedan poses with a couple of rather unsavory looking characters. From the angle at which the car was photographed, it is difficult to tell whether it is a Model 80 or 90. Look at all that beautiful chrome to keep polished. The background is obviously Washington, D.C., and the car has District of Columbia 1931 license plates, so maybe those characters are some of the politicians of the day.

Parked in front of the Studebaker dealership is this Model 80 President State Roadster. The vehicle sold for $1,950. The 130-inch car weighed 4,130 pounds, and used a rumble seat as standard equipment.

This 1931 President State Tourer Model 90 was in production from June 1930 until September 1931. During its 15-month manufacturing period only 2,762 units were built. Can you imagine the ladies in their finery being driven down the road with the windshield in its down position? Only if the chauffeur kept the speed under 20 mph. The double white-walls really add to the already classic appearance.

The State Tourer was a 7-passenger model delivering for $2,150. The vehicle weighed 4,265 pounds and came on a 136-inch wheelbase. The 8-cylinder engine developed 122 horsepower at 3200 rpm from the 337 cubic-inch engine. Folding auxiliary seats in the rear provided seating for two extra passengers, while two fit comfortably in the front and three could occupy the spacious rear seat. Upholstery was in genuine leather.

A slightly different background view was decided upon to show off the Studebaker Corporation's administration building. These men may all have been factory officials, or South Bend's leading citizens. They've chosen the 7-passenger State Tourer, chauffeur-driven, to go out for lunch.

The President State Coupe also was built on the 130-inch wheelbase, but it was only available as a 4-passenger car. Note the golf bag door on the side panel. This unit tipped in at 4,200 pounds and went home for $2,050. But, with depression clouds hanging heavy, not many went home. A total of 6,340 Model 80s were produced for the year 1930-31.

This pretty young thing is showing how easy it is to place golf equipment in the special compartment of the 1931 Model 80 President State Coupe. This example looked far nicer with the wire wheels and side mounts, than when equipped with wooden wheels. This particular vehicle also sports the fold-down luggage rack. Note the small "F" inscription on the tire sidewall. This car like, most Studebakers, came equipped with Firestone tires. Note that even the most expensive Studebakers still had only a single left-hand taillight.

Available only as a Model 90 in the President line was this State Victoria. The "behemoth" rode on a 136-inch wheelbase and weighed 4,275 pounds. The vehicle sold for $2,350 and had a seating capacity for five. The fuel supply came from a 20.5 gallon tank. See the wreath on the front door of the house. This car may have been a nice Christmas present. The lady certainly looks pleased.

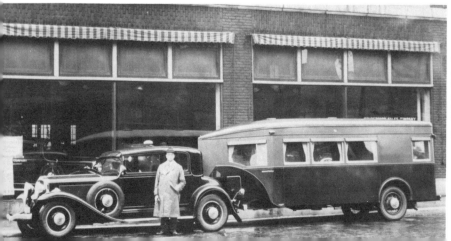

This 1931 State Victoria is well equipped with spotlight, outside rearview mirror, side-mounted tires, and an attached "home away from home." The goose-neck trailer is mounted where the usual trunk would be installed. Note new Studebakers on display in the showroom behind the President. Travel trailers of this type were a very rare sight in the early 1930s.

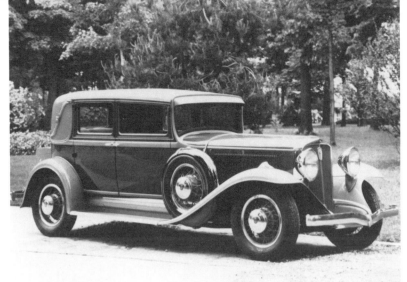

Always the most appealing body style in any sedan model was the Club Sedan, Close-Coupled Sedan or, as Studebaker referred to this example, the President State Brougham. This unit came as a Model 90 on a 136-inch wheelbase and sold for the same price as the State Sedan...$2,350. The vehicle delivered with the landau irons as part of it regular equipment. The model is quite similar to one of Studebaker's affiliates in 1931 — the Pierce Arrow. Put the headlights out on the fenders and you might think you were looking at one of the big Pierce models..

This Model 80 President Sedan is wearing the side-mounted tire equipment with only part of the metal cover in use. Note the white sidewall exposed in the fender well. Such metal covers added a nice touch of class and did protect the tires from the elements, but could be a real nuisance when removing the spare. Those dual horns really add a classic touch.

Jack Dempsey must have had a liking for Studebakers, as he is shown later in this book standing by another acquisition. Here he is by his new Model 80 State Sedan that was delivered for $2,050. This example came with the canvas-covered tire cover carrying the Studebaker logo. It must have been a warm day with the windshield in the extended out position.

The 1931 President Model 90 State Sedan for 7-passengers came on a 136-inch wheelbase, weighed 4,520 pounds, and delivered for $2,350. It was a lot of car for the money! It is strange that a model in this category doesn't have the metal spare tire covers. The vehicle was classed as an owner driven limousine.

This 1931 Model 90 President State Sedan is equipped with the rare radiator stone guard. This chauffeur-driven vehicle weighed 4,520 pounds and delivered in base form for $2,350. Seating allowed for 7-passengers in the 136-inch vehicle. This example came with a division window between passengers and chauffeur. Possibly a late delivery, the car wears 1932 Pennsylvania license plates.

Ab Jenkins is shown doing his thing in a rather mud-spattered 1931 President Roadster. He obviously is participating in some unidentified cross country race, for which he was famous. Note the side-mounted spare tire was removed from the left fender well, while the right one is in place. Was it out due to a blowout, or was it just to save extra weight? Ab later became known for his record speed runs on the Utah Salt Flats in both Auburns and Duesenbergs.

Cliff Bergere, a famous race driver of the time is shown driving the 1931 President Roadster to promote Studebaker's new Free-Wheeling device. He and race drivers Tony Gulotta, and Ab Jenkins drove identical cars all over the country to major hill climbs, where they demonstrated the great qualities Studebaker cars had to offer.

This display was voted the most interesting mechanical exhibit at 1931 auto shows throughout the country. The Studebaker President Eight chassis revealed the operation of Free-Wheeling. Two speedometers — one coupled to the motor, the other to the drive shaft — illustrated how this new device operated. It turned four miles of engine effort into five miles of actual travel.

Cliff Bergere is shown at the wheel of his red Studebaker Special just before the flag was waved for the start of the 1931 Indianapolis performance. Next to Cliff, sits his mechanic, Vern Lake, also a veteran at this speedway and at dirt tracks around the country. For the 1931 event, Bergere placed third.

Tony Gulotta drove No. 37 in the 1931 Indianapolis event. This car was the Hunt Special, or also known as the Hunt-Jenkins car. The vehicle was not officially built by Studebaker, but did have Studebaker components. The racer qualified at 112 MPH and finished in the 18th position. He spun out on the 167th lap. To that point, Gulotta was in 2nd and 3rd place for most of the race.

The Hunt Special is shown with Tony Gulotta at the wheel, ready for the 1931 Indianapolis race. The car raced as No. 18. It was entered by D.A. "Ab" Jenkins, a famous driver himself, known for his record shattering speed runs, both cross-country and on the Utah salt flats. The car used a Studebaker engine and a Rigling chassis. It qualified 19th at 111.72 mph, but was involved in a wreck on lap 167, and thus was only credited with 18th finishing position.

A pair of 1931 Studebaker Six Panel Delivery vehicles are parked in front of the local Studebaker dealership. These units came on a 115-inch wheelbase and delivered for $845.

# 1931

A 1931 Studebaker Six Panel Delivery was the pride of the Rosary Florist Ltd. of Winnipeg. Throughout its history, Studebaker had maintained a strong dealership network in Canada. Check out the driver's hat, fur coat, and knee-high boots. What was considered a uniform then would be classed as a costume today.

A group of three 1931 Canadian Studebakers have been loaded on a transport. The two front cars are Dictator Model 61s, and in back is a Studebaker Six Model 54. The trucking firm is Rasland Transporting operating between Toronto and Windsor. These apparently left the Walkerville, Ontario, assembly plant a short while before this picture was taken.

I took this photo well over 30 years ago of noted race driver Phil Hill's 1931 LeBaron bodied Convertible Cabriolet. The car has been in his family since new. Today, the vehicle sports a set of whitewalls which adds greatly to its appearance.

The 1931 Pierce-Arrow Model 41 engine had a 3__x5-inch bore and stroke. The 8-cylinder block developed 132 horsepower. The tire size for the Model 41s was 18x7.1 inches. This Roadster example weighed in the 5,000 pound category.

A LeBaron-bodied 1931 Pierce-Arrow Model 41 Club Sedan is shown arriving at a car show. No small vehicle, it was built on the 144-inch wheelbase. This example weighed in at 5,200 pounds. Most everyone was now choosing wire wheels such as this example wears. Pierce-Arrow also cataloged two other Club Sedans this year, one on the Model 43 chassis of 137-inch wheelbase, and the other on the Model 42 chassis of 142-inch base.

# 1931

The trademark always associated with Pierce-Arrow was the headlight in the fender treatment. Seen here is that example from noted race driver Phil Hill's 1931 Model 41 Convertible Town Cabriolet on the new 142-inch wheelbase chassis. The engine shown is the Model 42 version of the 8-cyliner block. It developed 132 hp.

This 4-passenger Convertible Victoria for 1931 has a body by LeBaron. Even a Pierce-Arrow came without a spare tire in those days. This is a Model 41 with clean massive lines to its body. This example rode on a 147-inch wheelbase. A widely copied design, this style of body was also produced by Brunn, Dietrich, and Waterhouse, with the latter version probably being the most lavish of the lot.

This 1931 Pierce Arrow Model 41 was a 4-passenger Convertible Coupe in the Salon grouping of semi-custom bodies. It was the only Convertible Coupe available in the Series 41 cars. It delivered in the $4,200 price-range and with the Depression worsening, it was admired more than purchased. The body appears to be by Derham.

# 1932

## ROCKNE

The Rockne was a product of Studebaker, being built in 1932 and 1933. The car was named after the famous Notre Dame football coach, Knute Rockne. Rockne himself, played a part at Studebaker during the late 1920s and very early 1930s, until his untimely death in a plane crash which occurred shortly before the car was introduced. The Model "65" car was at first produced in the old Detroit facility and remained there until Studebaker switched Rockne production to South Bend in April, 1933, where the "75" had been built. This was done for pure economics. Still, Rockne ended manufacturing in July, 1933.

Actually, there were two Rocknes in 1932 and both were sixes. One developed 66 horsepower at 3200 rpm from a 190 cubic-inch engine, and the other used a 205 cubic-inch displacement with the same rpms to developed 72 horsepower. The former rode on a 110-inch wheelbase while the latter used a 114-inch chassis. The production of these cars amounted to 20,169 units for the two-year life span. The 110-inch Rockne was designed by Ralph Vail and Roy Cole while the larger model was from the talented hands of Studebaker's famous Barney Roos. For 1932, Rockne used the term "65" and "75" to distinguish the two series. But in 1933, the two names were discontinued and only one model was available called the Rockne "10". It used the wheelbase of the Rockne "65" from 1932. For the 1933 cars, the Rockne 10 increased its horsepower to 70 at 3200 rpm.

This sharp Convertible Roadster is in the 1932 Model 65 series. The "Jumbo" balloon tires and special wheels are not factory equipment, but many dealers supplied them if owners requested. They gave a softer ride, though made slow-speed steering difficult. General Tire was a great producer of the "jumbos".

The 1932 Rockne "65" Convertible Roadster, minus the sidemounts, lost much of the appeal of the sportier car. In this form, it sold for $720. This example also came with only one horn bugle mounted under the left headlamp.

A 1932 Model 65 Convertible Roadster is shown with its top in the up position. The sidemounts in the fender wells add a little to its basic $720 price. The open car was second to their most expensive vehicle for 1932, only outdone by the rare Convertible Sedan for $740.

This group looks as if they are ready for some warm weather driving, with everything open and down. The "65" Convertible Roadster sports the rumble seat in the open position, top down, and windshield in the open position for that additional breath of air. Possibly one of those hot humid South Bend days?

This is Rockne's lowest priced car for 1932, a Model "65". It certainly must be one of the first models available for 1932 as it doesn't even have one trumpet horn. The radiator mascot must be of an early design also. It left Detroit for $585 as a two-passenger Couple model.

The 1932 "65" Rockne Coupe poses in front of a Studebaker Rockne dealership. The gentleman leaning against the fender is Harold Vance. The other man may be the dealer himself. Maybe they are discussing all the fine attributes the Rockne has to offer. This model sold for $585 as a two-passenger vehicle.

This cute coupe was a compact little car riding on its 110-inch wheelbase. The Model "65" used 5.25x18 inch tires and had a fuel supply of 12 gallons. It weighed 2,565 pounds.

The front end is easy to distinguish on the 1932 Rockne "65" and 1933 Model 10 models. No other car had the V-grille insert and the sloping hood louvers. This 2-door "65" delivered for $635 equipped with sidemounts in the fender wells. The plain version with a rear-mounted spare sold for $610. Sales were not too brisk for either model.

This is the Rumble Seat Rockne Coupe for 1932 that accommodated four passengers. Note the step pads on the right rear fender leading into the rumble compartment. This model sold for $620. Rockne was proud of its "Switch Key Starting," and the fact that all models used a fully synchronized transmission with free wheeling included at no extra cost.

Probably the best selling Rockne for 1932 was the Model "65" 5-passenger Sedan. It weighed 2,595 pounds and sold for $635 in base form. Note the angle at which the spare is installed. It helps give a look of more length to the rear, and also offers added protection from rear bumps. Studebaker did the same thing on some of their models at this time.

The 1932 Rockne "65" is shown in front three-quarter view. Interestingly enough, these vehicles were designed by Ralph Vail and Roy Cole initially to be built for Willys-Overland. Unfortunately, for Willys-Overland, the design never got to them. That was to Studebaker's good fortune as the car had lots of style to its body. There is quite a family resemblance with this car and 1932-1933 Studebakers.

This 1932 Rockne "75" Convertible Roadster was a car that offered size, power, style and looked like it cost far more than it actually did. The top went up or down in a matter of seconds. This unit delivered for $775. If a person preferred an open companion car to this model, there was a "75" Convertible Sedan that sold for $795 F.O.B. the factory. This latter model was probably the most rare of all Rocknes, and it is doubtful any survive today.

The 1932 Rockne "75" Coupe was a smart-appearing car and reportedly very easy to drive and maneuver in traffic. It was available as a 2-passenger vehicle for $685 with a spacious storage compartment. The 4-passenger rumble seat models delivered for $720.

Not as popular as the Model "65" was this better-appointed Model "75" DeLuxe 1932 Rockne. It came on a 4-inch longer wheelbase of 114 inches and was supplied with 5.50x18-inch tires. The number of models available in the "75" series amounted to 12. Actually, this was six separate styles as each model carried a deluxe version and a standard mate. Here is the Model "75" 4-door 5-passenger Deluxe Sedan which sold for $680. A standard example delivered for $635. The Model "75"'s were never built in Detroit, but came from the South Bend plant right from the beginning. Most noticeable differences on this model over the smaller cars are its longer wheelbase, more vertical hood louvers, and the chromed parking lamps on the fenders, the latter being available only on deluxe cars. The "75" models were very similar to the small Studebakers of 1932-33.

This 1932 Model "75" 4-door Sedan rode on the larger 114-inch wheelbase. It was considered to be the standard version in the line-up. Note how the artist's rendering didn't place the spare tire quite in its proper angle. It should be far more tilted, giving the rear end a look of more length. This standard example sold F.O.B. South Bend for $635.

This very trim looking 1932 Rockne "65" Panel Delivery is equipped with an accessory roof rack, though it is almost certain that the florist had little use for the extra-cost rack. I can just picture a bouquet of roses holding in place on the roof rack.

The 1932 Model "65" Panel Delivery has just been delivered in South Bend. This owner, too, came to Indiana to pick up the vehicle and have his picture taken in front of Studebaker's administration building. The panel was then enroute to its home base in Raleigh, North Carolina.

It was a good looking light delivery panel when new, but when did you see your last one? Popularity and sales were the main things that eluded Rockne throughout its life. A neat little unit to own, this vehicle no doubt saw hard use with the weight of paper in its rear section, delivering the Morning Herald and the Leader Republican to newsstands and route boys in Gloversville and Johnstown, New York. Including the sidemount, it listed for $695 F.O.B. Detroit.

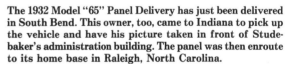

This 1932 Coupe came as a Dictator 6 for 2-passengers, or for 4-passengers when wearing a rumble seat. It also appeared as a Regal model, with the same seating capacities. An 8-cylinder version was also available. Prices ranged from $840 for a 2-passenger Dictator Coupe in the Six line, to $1,135 for the 8-cylinder Dictator 4-passenger Coupe. Each came on a 117-inch wheelbase. Besides these Dictators, the factory offered a similarly styled version as Commander Eights in the regular Commander line for $1,350 and, as a Regal model, with the price increased to $1,690. The Commander cars only came with a rumble seat as 4-passenger vehicles. They rode on a 125-inch wheelbase.

In 1932 Studebaker found itself in a much better position than many other auto manufacturers. Despite the worsening of the world-wide depression, the newly introduced economy-type Rockne was helping greatly with the cash flow. Only trimming slightly, the company still offered a total of 48 available styles, though it is doubtful if any dealer at any one time would have all 48 models in stock.

Again, as in the previous years, the Dictator Six was the low-price offering, with a Business Coupe now being available at $840. The Six was now rated at 80 horsepower, a jump of 10, while the Dictator Eight was rated at 85 horses, also a slight increase. Aside from the engines, all Dictators were essentially the same cars. All now had a new chassis of 117-inch wheelbase, an increase of three inches, rode on 5.50x18 tires, and used 15-gallon fuel tanks.

The new Commanders also grew slightly, now being built on 125-inch wheelbase chassis. Available only in 8-cylinder form, the Commander engines were still rated at 101 horsepower at 3200 rpm. Tires were reduced from 6.0x19 to 6.0x18, but the fuel supply remained at 15 gallons.

The 8-cylinder President engine also was unchanged and continued to develop 122 horsepower at 3200 rpm. However, the short models were dropped, and all Presidents now appeared on the 135-inch wheelbase. The car used 6.5x18 tires and retained the 20.5-gallon fuel tank. Incidentally, these President models are recognized as true classics by the Classic Car Club of America.

Sales records for the year were 44,325, which also included the new Rockne. Despite a loss of 4,596 cars, other companies were doing even far worse in this depression economy, and as a result, Studebaker moved up to the sixth sales slot in the national rankings.

Looking the same as the Model 61 Dictator 8 is this Studebaker 6 Rumble Seat Coupe Model 55. The beach scene was photographed at Santa Monica, California. The car carries California license plates with DIR on the plate telling the car is no doubt a demonstrator from a Studebaker dealership. Probably it came from one of the Paul G. Hoffman enterprises.

Nicely styled is this 1932 Dictator Convertible Sedan that was available as a Six for $955, or as an Eight sold for $1,095. The wire wheel equipment was optional at no extra cost. Both Six and Eight rode on 5.50x18-inch tires. The Six offered an engine of 80 horsepower, while the Eight developed only five more horses. Both calculations were made at 3200 RPM. Free-Wheeling was available at extra cost on all Dictator cars.

A bare bones 1932 St. Regis Brougham was classed as a Model 55 when built as a Studebaker Six. What a difference when whitewalls and the chrome steel spoked wheels were supplied. The unit sold for $890 in base form.

A 1932 Studebaker 6 or, if you prefer, Model 55, delivered for $890 as the regular sedan but, if a Regal model was ordered, the price increased to $995. It came on the same 117-inch wheelbase as the Dictator 8. This car was one of the most popular models produced by Studebaker in 1932.

# 1932

The 1932 Studebaker Six Regal St. Regis is shown here with accessory equipment generally devoted to the higher priced models. This Regal example sold for $995. If the lower priced St. Regis were ordered, it could be delivered for $890. Note how wide the door is for easy access into the rear compartment.

Rin-Tin-Tin apparently also liked the 1932 Regal St. Regis Brougham. This car, as a Dictator 6, was referred to as Model 55, and Dictator 8 classified as a Model 62. The Regal versions sold for $995 in 6-cylinder style while the 8-cylinder example delivered for $1,135. The body style proved to be a good seller in spite of the depression. This vehicle came equipped with accessories that set it off nicely, such as trumpet horns, whitewalls, and chromium spoked wheels. A regular St. Regis also was on the market for $890 and $1,030 respectively.

This is a 1932 Regal Dictator Rumble Seat Coupe for 4-passengers. This model was available either as a Six or an Eight. Prices were $995 for a Six and $1,135 if the Regal Eight was ordered. Note the fender step pads to aid in climbing into the rumble seat. The whitewalls and trumpet horns were classed as extra cost items.

The 1932 Dictator 8 Convertible Roadster, classed as a Model "52", came either as a regular model for $1,030 or as a Regal version for $1,135. Both styles were available only as 4-passenger cars with rumble seat. This example is the more expensive Regal equipped with a rear-mounted spare tire.

This 1932 Model 62 Dictator 8 Convertible Roadster is equipped with the rear-mounted spare. Most were painted with a contrasting fender color and, if wire wheels were ordered as on this vehicle, they too were done in a different shade. The 8-cylinder version had a compression ratio of 5:1 and the Six had a compression ratio of 5.1:1. Interiors of the open Dictators were done in a leatherette material.

# 1932

A Model 62 Dictator Convertible Roadster delivered for $1,030 in 8-cylinder fashion. The Model 55 went out the door as a Dictator 6 for $890. Both used the 117-inch wheelbase. Each series began production in November 1931 and ended in November 1932. The 6-cylinder cars had a production run of 13,647 units while 8-cylinders had a run of only 6,021 cars built. Convertible Roadsters used roll-up windows in the doors.

This three-quarter front right view of the 1932 Dictator Convertible Sedan shows off its accessory equipment such as the chromium spoked wheels and trumpet horns which were easily damaged by either a car backing into them, or by some envious person who took pleasure in snapping them off at the base. The lowering of the top was best done with the help of a second person.

The true businessman's coupe was this Model 61 Dictator 8 Coupe. The rear-mounted spare was generally ordered when a company owned vehicle was delivered for its salesmen to drive.

The 1932 Model 62 Dictator 8 Rumble Seat Coupe was a nice looking car and sold well especially with young people. The Dictator Eight sold 6,021 units during its production from November 1931 to November 32. Its light body made for a fast car with its 81 horsepower engine.

The 1932 Model 62 Dictator 8 Sedan for $1,030 also came as a Regal model for $1,135, offering more deluxe appointments. If equipped with a rear-mounted spare like this vehicle, many people preferred the split rear bumpers which aided the owner if a tire needed to be changed. Cars with sidemounts usually wore a one-piece rear bumper.

The 1932 Studebaker Commander Eight Convertible Sedan sold as a regular Commander for $1,465 and as a Regal model for $1,570. This happens to be the Regal variety. Notice the large chrome plated door hinges on the B-pillar. No hidden hinges for this style. Chromed spoke wheels and dual horns help to present a classic profile, but a set of metal tire covers with mounted rearview mirrors would really have completed the picture.

Studebaker's Convertible Sedan in the Commander series was available both as a regular model for $1,467 and $1,570 if the Regal version was ordered. This happens to be the Regal wearing the chromed steel spoked wheels. Free-Wheeling was a feature classed as standard equipment on Commander cars, as well as on the President. The detachable trunk on the folding trunk rack provides ice lines for the rear of this car.

This 1932 Commander Model 71 4-door Sedan is being used as an everyday work horse by the Atlanta Baggage and Cab Co. The Atlanta, Georgia, based taxi company had employed Studebakers for several years due to their economical qualities and rugged performance.

Looking almost the same as a Regal Commander Sedan is this regular Commander Sedan sporting the side-mounted tire configuration minus the metal tire covers. This unit delivered with the optional at no extra cost wire wheels for $1,350. The main difference between this and Regal cars was in the interior appointments.

# 1932

Often times the Commander and President models looked very much alike depending on the angle that the car might be parked. The means of a quick identification is to count the hood louvers. The Presidents employed 36. This example is a Commander Sedan with the fold-down trunk rack.

This 4-door Regal Commander Sedan is equipped with side-mounted tires and the accessory metal tire covers. In base form, the Regal Sedan delivered for $1,455. It resembled the Dictator line a good deal in all but its wheelbase which was 125-inches. The Commander cars all came on 6.00 x 18-inch tires. The line used broadcloth upholstery with a folding center arm rest as was also done on Regal Broughams. Some of the Regal models refinements included silken curtains, cowl and door pockets, foot rest, robe rail, cowl ventilator, dual ash receivers, adjustable steering wheel and wiring for radio installation.

A regular Commander Eight Sedan is shown wearing the deluxe chrome steel spoked wheels and whitewall tires as part of its accessory package. The basic sedan sold for $1,350 minus the deluxe equipment. The vehicle was classed as a Model 71.

Not many people driving Commanders in 1932 were as fortunate as this pair to have their chauffeur waiting to take them home from the polo course. This Regal Commander Sedan was not equipped with a built-in trunk, but instead used a fold-down luggage rack, upon which the trunk could be attached. The cost of the car was $1,455. The optional trunk was quite practical as it proved to be more popular for storage than simply tying luggage to an open rack.

The factory offered this 1932 President Convertible Roaster as its lowest priced model for the year. It sold in base form for $1,690. This 4-passenger vehicle came as a new style for 1932. A clock, electric gas gauge, and pass-around cigar lighter were considered new selling features offered as standard equipment on the President. The chrome spare tire cover and twin spot lamps really add a note of character. Although called a roadster, the car was a true convertible, with wind-up windows in the doors.

The 1932 President Convertible Sedan, was referred to as a Model 91. A winter day in front of the South Bend administrative building is the setting for this 5-passenger vehicle. The car delivered for $1,820 with the chrome steel spoked wheels classed as standard equipment for open cars in the President line. President models, as well as Commander cars, came equipped with two-way hydraulic shock absorbers. There was a thermostatic valve which regulated the action, regardless of oil temperature, so that the control in warm and cold weather remained the same.

With top down, these five gentlemen seem to be enjoying a spin in the President Convertible Sedan. The true name Studebaker gave to the trumpet horns, which this vehicle wears, was the "Salon Chime Horns." These were standard equipment on President models. Note that all doors on this model hinged at the B-pillar.

This example of the President Convertible Sedan was the less expensive of the two Presidents classed as open 4-door models. This was the $1,820 model. This version displays how the rear door opens easily for entering and exiting. It came minus many of the dolled up accessories seen on most Presidents, but still wore the chrome spoke wheels and beautiful dual sidemounts.

A 1932 President Coupe, Model 91 was the lowest priced President available for the year. It could be delivered for $1,690. President Coupes were only available as 4-passenger models, with trunk-back versions not being listed. A total of 14 models were available in the President line for the year. Many were overlapping models within the series.

Here is a 1932 St. Regis Brougham in the President series. This is classed as the lower-priced version selling for $1,690. Even in the President line, metal spare tire covers were classed as an accessory at extra cost. Fundamentally, the engine had not been changed from the previous year, but all crankshafts were counter-weighted and engines in each series were mounted in rubber.

Looks like "Our Gang" went for Studebakers, too! Hopefully they didn't put the vehicle into Free-Wheeling, or merrily down the road they would go. This example is the lowest priced President Sedan for 1932. It sold for $1,690 and was a 6-passenger model. The President cars had an 8-cylinder engine that developed 122 horsepower at 3200 rpm. Note those chime horns nicely placed under those famous Studebaker headlamps.

For 1932, the Presidents were in production from November 1931 through December 1932. A total of only 2,399 saw production. Among them was this 7-passenger that sold for $1,790 in the U.S., but probably was quite a bit more expensive when delivered to its new owners somewhere in Japan. A total of six versions in the President line were manufactured. They were: Regular 6-passenger Sedan, 7-passenger Sedan, State Sedan for six, Limousine for seven, State Sedan for seven and the State Limousine for seven selling for $1,995, being the most expensive offering for 1932.

Here is a very impressive way to keep from having the radiator and tires being riddled with bullets. This example is a President Sedan being used by the South Bend Police Department. The car also came with a bullet-proof windshield. Note the spotlight equipment and two red lights mounted in the rear window. Does this car make a political statement for the era?

A Model 91 President Regal St. Regis Brougham came on the market as a new model in 1932. It was classed as a smart-looking, wide door, five-passenger vehicle. This model never came off as the "Old Maids" 2-door Coach. It delivered for $1,795. This like other President, models rode on 6.50x18-inch tires.

This 1932 President State Convertible Roadster for 4-passengers came on the 135-inch wheelbase. I'd say this gentleman is rather proud of what he just purchased for $1,795. Note that the rear license plate is mounted under the tail lamp. On President models, twin rear-mounted tail lamps were considered standard equipment.

# 1932

A nice full side view show the excellent styling of this Classic 1932 State Convertible Roadster. With the rumble seat in the open position, shows how easy it is to enter the compartment with the help of the fender step plate. Also notice the golf bag door on the quarter panel. This example came equipped with the full metal tire cover. Fewer than 100 of this model were produced in 1932.

This Model 19 President State Convertible Sedan was the most expensive open model Studebaker built for 1932. It sold for $1,925 and offered seating for 5-passengers. When the top was lowered, which took some work, it folded into a nicely tailored package, as on this car. The President came with a 20.5-gallon fuel capacity. It took eight quarts of oil to fill the crankcase of this 337 cubic-inch engine.

These folks are out for one of their first winter rides in their new President State St. Regis Brougham. This was the most expensive Brougham offered for the year. It cost an even $100 more than the President St. Regis Brougham for $1,895. Not many saw this style in their garage. If people were buying the Presidents, they usually chose the Sedans.

This is a State Coupe in the President line. It weighed 4,200 pounds and sold for $1,795. As a coupe, the sales were not as great as the factory would have liked. Coupe purchasers preferred the Commander if they were buying an 8-cylinder vehicle. It, like other Studebaker models for the year, came with Startix, an automatic starting switch which went into action when the ignition was turned on.

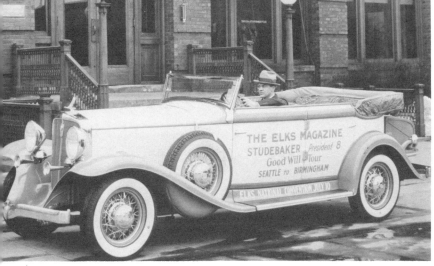

For 1932, the Elks chose this 1932 President Eight State Convertible Sedan for their yearly goodwill tour. The classic convertible sold for $1,925. The event lasted 30 days going from Seattle, Wash. to Birmingham, Ala, by a rather wandering route. The 8,000-mile excursion ended on July 10th, at the National Convention in Birmingham.

Is this supposed to be "hats off" to the 1932 President State Convertible Sedan? A more intimate appeal is generated with the top in the up position. Getting the top in either the up or down position was truly not a one-man operation. This is a model recognized by the Classic Car Club of America as a bona fide classic.

One of the 2,399 Presidents delivered included this 6-passenger State Sedan that was classed as an owner driven vehicle. The car delivered for $1,795. The weight of this vehicle came to 4,500 pounds.

The most expensive car produced by Studebaker in 1932 was this 7-passenger President State Limousine. It delivered for $1,995. The vehicle weighed 4,695 pounds. Strangely enough, the car came without the metal tire covers, which were still considered an extra-cost option even on the highest-buck car.

The 1932 President State Sedan for 7-passengers delivered for $1,895. It was the second most expensive model Studebaker offered for the model run. The President cars coming with side-mounted spares had a folding trunk rack mounted on the rear end as standard equipment.

The event is Indianapolis, 1932, the gentleman behind the wheel of the Studebaker Special is Pete Kreis with his mechanic Aaron Vance. They did not finish the race as they were eliminated at the 445th mile (lap 178) in a single-car wreck. Only the body was able to be saved. A replica of this vehicle is supposedly still around. Despite the wreck, Kreis was credited with 15th place. He had a qualifying speed of 110.27 mph, which saw sufficient to start in 17th place.

Cliff Bergere, in his Studebaker Special, made the best showing of the entire Studebaker team at this year's Indianapolis 500. In the 1932 event on Memorial Day, he placed third with an average speed of 102.662 mph and a qualifying speed of 111.5 mph, which put him in the 10th starting position. In later years, this car was totally restored and kept at the Studebaker museum as a show piece. Also on the Studebaker team this year were Tony Gulotta, who finished 13th, and Luther Johnson, who lost a wheel on lap 164, but was credited with 16th place. Unlike today's races which are limited to 33 cars, the 1932 event had 40 entrants on the track.

The car is the famous No. 37 belonging to Zeke Meyer who finished in 6th position for the 1932 Indianapolis classic. His average speed was 98.476 mph, while his qualifying run was at 110.74 mph. All of these Studebaker Specials were team cars entered by the Studebaker Co. itself, and all were built on special Rigling racing chassis.

This 1932 Studebaker Special was one of the five team cars that were entered in the Indy 500-mile race. Number 22, with Cliff Bergere at the wheel, finished in 3rd position at a record speed of 102.662 mph. It was the highest speed ever to that date for a stock block engine. His mechanic once again is Vern Lake.

Another 1932 Studebaker Special team car shows Tony Gulotta as the driver, and Carl Riscigno as the mechanic. The car finished in the 13th position for the 1932 Indy 500. It qualified at 108.896 mph. The race cars were powered by a 336 cubic-inch engine. The vehicles were about 85 percent stock Studebaker parts and chassis. The racing bodies and frames were by Herman Rigling.

This was the 1932 Pierce-Arrow Sport Phaeton. Its lines were similar to those of the previous three years, but not quite so squared off in design. The big news from Pierce was its newly introduced V-12 engines. The engines were of 398 and 429 cubic-inch displacements developing 140 and 150 horsepower, respectively. This example as a Model 54 8-cylinder Sport Phaeton delivered for $3,050. If the V-12 version were ordered as Model 53, it delivered for $3,850, being the most expensive model in the "53" lineup.

For 1932, this 7-passenger Sedan came in each of the three series: Model 54 sold for $2,750; Model 53 delivered for $3,550; and the top of the line, Model "52" which this example happens to be, went home for $4,085.

A new series of upscale cars this year gave Studebaker four distinct series. The new line was the Speedway President, which became the top level of the President Eight series. Also remaining on the floor were the Dictator Six and the Commander Eight, along with the Rockne, which will be discussed as a separate make. All models featured totally new styling with sweeping skirted fenders, a slanting grille, and beavertail rear end design.

The Dictator was now available only as a Six, with prices ranging from the $840 2-passenger Business Coupe to the $1,015 Convertible. The chassis retained its 117-inch wheelbase, but the engine was now rated at 85 horsepower at 3200 rpm. Tire size was down to 5.50x17, and the fuel tank on both the Dictators and the Commanders was now reduced to 14 gallons capacity.

The Commander also shared the same 117-inch chassis of the Dictator, but it wore 6.00x17 tires and its 8-cylinder engine was rated at 100 horsepower at 3800 rpm.

The President Eight used a new chassis of 125-inch wheelbase, and carried a revised engine now rated at 110 horsepower at 3000 rpm. Tire size was 6.50x17, and the fuel tank held 17.5 gallons.

The new Speedway President, which appeared this year only, utilized the old President chassis of 135-inch wheelbase. The 8-cylinder engine was rated at 132 horsepower at 3400 rpm. Tires were 7.0x17, and the fuel tank held 20.5 gallons. Speedway President cars were the most expensive Studebakers, ranging from $1,625 to $2,040. Definitely not among the best sellers, production amounted to only 635 before the line was discontinued.

All of the new styled models used mechanical brakes with the Bendix vacuum power-operated assist system. Also offered on all models were automatic shock absorbers, automatic choke control, and ball bearing spring shackles.

Again, 48 different models were made available among the four series, not counting the soon-to-disappear Rockne. Despite its deepening financial troubles, Studebaker maintained its same 6th sales position for the second year in a row, with the sales of 43,024 cars, a reduction of only 1,301 from 1932.

The 1933 Rockne "10" Roadster was available both as a regular model for $725 and in deluxe fashion for $775. Each offered seating for four passengers with the help of the rumble seat. This Deluxe model weighed 2,735 pounds and sold for a $775 price tab. Not many went out the door marked sold, as the Depression was gaining on the auto industry more each month.

A mock-up of the 1933 Rockne "10" is shown in Studebaker's South Bend styling studio. Not an operational vehicle, the car needs block supports under its front axle. The bumpers and front fender lines differ from those on regular production models.

# 1933

The 1933 Rockne "10" 2-door, 5-passenger Sedan, possibly referred to as a Club Sedan in the Studebaker terminology, was also known as Model 31. This example sold for $595 as a regular 2-door and, if the deluxe version were ordered, it left the dealership for $640.

This rendering came from a 1933 sales brochure. It is difficult to tell the differences between the 1932 Rockne "65" and the Rockne "10" of 1933 from this photo alone, as the styling and bodies are virtually the same. Actually the bodies were about one inch lower this year because of the switch to 17-inch wheels. After Studebaker went into receivership on March 10, 1933, the Rockne "10" production was moved from Detroit to South Bend to reduce expenses. Production continued at a reduced level until July when the Rockne was discontinued. The Rockne "10" engine then remained in use on the 1934 Dictator, while its basic design continued until 1951 to power various Studebaker vehicles, and then was used as a truck engine for nearly 10 more years.

I can picture this 1933 Rockne "10" coming in a two-tone combination of brown fenders and roof, and tan body. This was a popular Studebaker color scheme that many chose at that time for both it and the Rockne. This was the deluxe version that sold for $710 with sidemounts and two-tone paint, both considered standard equipment.

The 1933 Rockne "10" Panel Delivery used a totally different body style than the Panels of 1932. However, information is confusing, and this may not have been a true factory production vehicle, but might have been a chassis-cowl unit fitted with a special body.

In 1933, this Model 56 Studebaker Six Coupe for two passengers was the lowest priced car the factory offered. It sold for $840, weighed 3,140 pounds and rode on 6.00x17-inch tires. The wire wheels were optional equipment at no extra cost.

This car looks exactly the same as the 2-passenger Coupe except that this version had seating in the rumble seat compartment for two additional passengers. It sold for $50 more than the trunk-deck model, or $890, and weighed 3,210 pounds. Regal Coupes also were available in both 2 and 4-passenger versions selling for $945 and $995 respectively. Note the golf bag door on the side of this unit.

The 1933 Studebaker Six St. Regis Brougham came on a 117-inch wheelbase and could be delivered for $915. A Regal version also was available for $1,020. The same models came in the Commander line. They looked the same, except for the 8-cylinder engine. A Commander St. Regis went home for $1,075 and its dolled-up sister, the Regal St. Regis cost $1,180. It weighed 3,475 pounds.

This is a Model 56 Studebaker Six Sedan which was the lowest priced 4-door Studebaker offered for 1933. It sold for $915. The 117-inch wheelbase car weighed 3,310 pounds. Note the rakish angle at which the spare tire is mounted. Most sedans that came with the rear-mounted spare also were seen with split rear bumpers for easier tire changes. However, the full bumper could be ordered. The spot light this unit is equipped with was a factory-approved accessory.

This is a three-quarter front view of the 1933 Studebaker Six Regal Sedan. Those awesome headlamps were a Studebaker tell-tale trademark during the early 1930s. The fender-mounted parking lamps were in keeping with the headlamp configuration. The 6-cylinder engine developed 85 horsepower at 3200 rpm.

A three-quarter rear view shows a nice treatment of the luggage rack equipment. When the models were ordered with side-mounted spare tires, the luggage rack was automatically part of the accessory package. This is a Model 56 Regal Sedan weighing 3,435 pounds and selling for $1,020. Note a few snow flurries on the roof of the car that got there ahead of the photographer. These give graphic proof of the cross-rib design under the fabric top.

The 1933 Studebaker Six Suburban Model 56 was not a South Bend creation. The body builder for the model was Cantrell of Long Island, N.Y. Studebaker contracted for only a limited number of the bodies to be built as, at that time, there wasn't a great demand for vehicles of this type. This particular unit was purchased by the U.S. Department of Agriculture.

What a sharp looking car! This 1933 Commander 8 Convertible Sedan was the most expensive model in the Commander line for 1933, selling for $1,300. The interior was done in Spanish grain leather with imitation leather for door paneling. With the depression taking its hold on more people, the sales were few. The naval commander must feel right at home in the Commander model. Note the foreign license plate. Most Studebakers had the license plate mounted on the left, rather than on the right like the model displays.

# 1933

The Studebaker Commander 8, Model 73, was available in four versions of 2 and 4-passenger coupes in the regular model, and 2 and 4-passenger in the Regal style. Regular models sold for $1,000 and $1,050, respectively. This model is the regular 2-passenger coupe on the 117-inch wheelbase.

It was another one of those snowy days when the factory photographer chose to photograph one of the new models. This is a 1933 Commander St. Regis Brougham selling for $1,180. A less expensive model with fewer garnishings delivered for $1,075.

The least expensive Commander Sedan for the season was this regular 4-door model. It could be delivered for $1,075. Oddly enough, considering the depression economy, at its best the Regal Sedan was more saleable than this lower-priced model. Kelsey-Hayes wire wheels were standard equipment on this car.

This three-quarter left front view of a Model 73 Commander Sedan displays the new sloping grille which attracted many customers. This was the most popular model in the Commander line, which had a production run from November, 1932, through July, 1933. Commander sales amounted to 3,841 vehicles.

The 1933 Regal Commander Coupe for four passengers was the most expensive coupe in the Commander line. It sold for $1,155. It employed a 14-gallon fuel tank, which was the same as used on the Six models. In the President line, it was only available in 4-passenger form, but it came as a regular coupe and also as a Regal 4-passenger. These sold for $1,325 and $1,425, respectively.

A nicely-dressed Commander 6-wheeled Regal Sedan weighed 3,385 pounds and sold for $1,180. The 8-cylinder car came with a 236 cubic-inch engine that developed 100 horsepower at 3800 rpm. The striking two-tone paint job and chrome steel-spoke wheels made this one fine looking sedan.

Classed in the Model 82 category along with all 1933 Presidents is this regular Sedan which rode on a 125-inch wheelbase. The vehicle sold for $1,385. Comfortably, the car seated five but was termed a 6-passenger model. Presidents were available in two different series. This model rode on a 125-inch wheelbase.

A total of ten models were available in the President line for 1933, ranging in price from $1,325 for a 4-passenger Coupe to $1,650 for a Regal Convertible Sedan. This example fit in the middle of the road selling for $1,490. The model was the Berline Limousine cataloged for the same price as the straight Regal Sedan.

The 1933 President Regal Roadster came on the 125-inch wheelbase and sold for $1,490. It found few buyers only because times were rough! The body style also was available for $1,385 as a plain roadster. Both offered seating for 4-passengers, and used roll-up windows in the doors.

The 1933 Regal St. Regis Brougham in the President series weighed 3,655 pounds and sold for $1,490. The same car in the President line, with fewer deluxe appointments and called just the St. Regis Brougham, could be purchased for $1,385. Note the model is equipped with side mounts, but lacks the deluxe tire covers which cost additional if the owner chose them.

This President Sedan appears to have been one of those models done in a color combination I always liked...which was a tan with a contrasting darker brown window trim. It also appears to have chrome spoked wheels. It is a Regal Sedan which was the biggest seller in the President line and could be delivered for $1,490. The Regal Sedan weighed 3,720 pounds.

The Model 92 President Speedway State Convertible Sedan weighed 4,600 pounds, thus being the heaviest car the company produced for 1933. It sold for $1,960. Besides this State example, a regular Speedway Convertible Sedan was offered delivering for $1,855. It too rode on the 135-inch wheelbase.

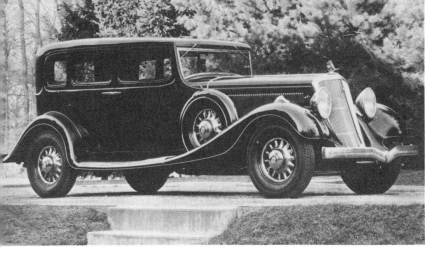

# 1933

The 1933 President Speedway line showed this side-mounted example as its lowest priced car in the series, going for $1,685. All Speedway models came with the side-mounted spares with tire covers as standard equipment.

President Speedways were called Model 92s for 1933. This example is the most expensive car Studebaker produced for the year. It was the State Limousine for 7-passengers selling for $2,040. All Speedway models rode on 7.00x17-inch tires. In the Speedway line there were six sedans ranging in price for $1,685, to the top of the line limousine.

This sedan, classed in the President Speedway Series, sold for $1,790. The vehicle weighed 4,465 pounds and looked quite similar to the regular Presidents except for a wheelbase 10 inches longer. Then, under the hood a big difference took place. All Speedway models employed a 337 cubic-inch engine developing 132 horsepower at 3400 rpm.

The Superior Body Co. of Lima, Ohio, continued to do professional car body building for Studebaker. This beautiful open-front 1933 example was referred to as the "Arlington Coach." It was equipped with an 8-cylinder Commander engine developing 100 horsepower at 3800 rpm. The wheelbase was 152 inches. The hearse sold for $2,995. It also came as a 6-cylinder model, but few were ever produced. The service car, which Superior offered in 1933, was referred to as the "Elmwood."

This photo shows L. L. Corum and Jimmie Louden in the Studebaker race car preparing for the 1933 Indianapolis event. This shot of the car was taken before it was re-bodied. In point of racing years at Indianapolis, "Slim" Corum lead the group. His first race at Indianapolis was in 1922. He also drove in 1923, 1924, 1926, and 1930. In 1927, he entered but did not start. He won first place teamed with Joe Boyer in 1924. "Slim" was born in Indianapolis and lived there his entire life except for excursions to different race tracks. But 1933 was not his best year. He finished 12th after starting in 18th place.

In the 1933 Memorial Day event, Tony Gulotta and Carl Riscignio were the first of the Studebaker team to finish. They came in 7th after starting in 12th place. Tony was a veteran of the Studebaker team in terms of races driven. Although he was only 29, the race of 1933 was the eighth at Indianapolis for this Louisiana native.

As a money winner for the 1933 Studebaker team, the honors went to Cliff Bergere. He had six Indianapolis races to his credit and finished out of the money only two times. Cliff took third place in 1932, but in 1933 was able to only claim the 11th spot after starting in 9th position. Residing in Hollywood, when not racing, he was employed as a stunt driver for the movies. His chief mechanic was Vern Lake. The 1933 race was the last which saw participation by Studebaker. Despite the 5-car team placing an amazing 7th, 9th, 10th, 11th, and 12th, finances within the company brought the costly team sponsorship to an end at the close of this season.

Zeke Meyer and Walter Mitchell were both veterans at Indianapolis. Zeke had competed in two previous Indy races and a large number of contests at other tracks during the previous 18 years. This 1933 event, driving #9 for Studebaker, saw him come in 9th after starting in 16th place. Meyer hailed from Germantown, Pa.

Model 1247 belonged to the special cataloged Pierce-Arrows for 1933. This example was the Custom Salon Enclosed Drive Limousine. The V-12 engine was increased to 462 cubic-inch displacement and now developed 175 horsepower for this series. The compression ratio was now 6 to 1.

This is the beautiful 1933 Pierce Arrow Custom Salon Convertible Coupe for four passengers. It was equipped with a rumble seat. This example rode on 17x7.50 tires. It weighed approximately 5,500 pounds and sold for $5,600, or slightly more than $1 per pound.

One thing about the rear view of this V-12 Model 1247 Pierce Arrow Convertible Coupe is that it has a styling touch similar to the Rockne and Studebaker, with the spare tire mounted at the same sharp angle on the rear. Certainly Pierce didn't need to extend the rear end to its already massive 147-inch wheelbase, but the protruding spare would have kept careless parkers from bumping the tail of this beauty. And besides, it does look good. The split rear bumper arrangement ceased with the 1933 cars. From that point on, a full-width rear bumper would provide the same body protection as the protruding spare tire.

The 1933 Pierce Arrow Club Sedan, Model 1236, was a 12-cylinder car riding on a 136-inch wheelbase. This example delivered for $3,095. At the end of this year, following Studebaker's bankruptcy and the untimely suicide death of Albert Erskine, Pierce-Arrow once again went up for auction. It was purchased by a group of bankers in its home town of Buffalo, N.Y.

# 1933

The Model 1242 Custom Salon Club Brougham drew its nomenclature from the fact that it used the 175 horsepower V-12 engine and was built on a 142-inch wheelbase... hence 1242. Note the small lamp below the door used as a courtesy light. This example weighed 5,200 pounds and delivered for $4,150. The same car could be ordered on the 137-inch wheelbase for $3,650. Both offered seating for five passengers.

A beautiful original 1933 Pierce-Arrow V-12 Club Sedan was photographed by Bernie Weis, a good friend of mine, in 1954. It was in like-new condition at that time. It's another of those "Oh, how I wonder where it is today" stories that we all know about. Behind it is Bernie's 836 Pierce Arrow Sedan. I believe the photo was taken in Rochester, New York, even though the car wears New Jersey license plates.

I took this photo back in 1952 of this gentleman and his 1933 Pierce Arrow. He was the original owner until his death. A few years later, the car was shipped to the East Coast. I have often wondered where it might be today. It was painted in medium blue, black fenders, with cream wire wheels.

A three-quarter rear view shows off the integral trunk of the 1933 V-12 Pierce-Arrow Club Sedan. This was Pierce's last year under the Studebaker merger. Both companies were in bad financial difficulties. In April 1933, Studebaker went into receivership and Pierce-Arrow went its own way until 1938, when the death blow took another one of America's great cars. A total of 2,152 Pierce Arrows were produced in 1933.

This is a familiar view of the 1933 Pierce Silver Arrow, looking straight down on this classic beauty. The style had a production of only five vehicles. The Silver Arrow tipped the scale at 5,729 pounds. It rode on 17x7.00 inch tires and came on a 139-inch wheelbase.

The classic-looking Pierce Silver Arrow offered some unusual design features that were later considered quite in keeping with the modern day car, including such things as fender skirts, recessed door handles, slab-sided body panels, and a "V" shaped windshield. The spare tire was also hidden, being lodged in the front fender panel. This vehicle was the forerunner to the production Silver Arrows which came as 1934 and 1935 models with either 8-cylinder or V-12 engines.

Because of worsening financial situations within the company, Studebaker was forced to tighten its belt and discontinue several of the models that had been available in 1933. As a result, only 28 models were on the sales floor this year, as compared with 48 available styles in 1933. Also gone was the expensive and pretentious Speedway President series and the semi-independent Rockne. This year, Studebaker offered only three series.

Smallest in the line was the Dictator Six, Studebaker's only 6-cylinder car. This year its engine was rated at 88 horsepower at 3600 rpm. Downsized from 1933, the car now rode on a new chassis of 114-inch wheelbase, though it retained its 5.5x17 tires. Its gas tank was increased to 14.5 gallons.

The Commander Eight came with an engine upgraded to 103 horsepower at 4000 rpm. All Commanders grew slightly, and now used a new chassis of 119-inch wheelbase.

Meanwhile, the President Eight shrunk by two inches, being built on a chassis shortened to 123-inch wheelbase. Its engine was still rated at 110 horsepower but the rating was made at 3600 rpm rather than 3000.

Tires on the Commander were 5.0x17, while the President used 6.5x17 rubber. Both series used 17.5-gallon fuel tanks. Mechanical features of the 1934 cars consisted of aluminum heads with a 6.3:1 compression ratio, aluminum pistons, automatic manifold heat control, automatic choke, and a thermostatically controlled cooling system. The Dictator Six series used "Steeldraulic" brakes, while all of the Eights were equipped with Bendix brakes, which Studebaker seemed to prefer in the long run. All brake systems remained mechanical.

Again, prices were down, with the range going from $725 for a Dictator Regal Coupe to $1,145 for a President Regal Sedan. A multi-million dollar ad campaign helped bring calendar year sales up to 46,103, but since other car companies were also doing good this year, Studebaker saw its ranking slip down to 9th position.

The Dictator Roadster in regular fashion for five passengers sold for $695. This model weighed in at 2,950 pounds. The side-mounted tire equipment came only as an extra cost item. The Dictator cars used Steeldraulic mechanical brakes, a 14.5-gallon fuel supply, and Budd steel-spoke wheels.

This was a Dictator St. Regis Brougham that sold for $695. A like version was available in the Commander line for $200 additional. Neither model had a large following. The Dictator used 5.70x17-inch tires while Commanders came with 6.00x17s.

Studebaker's lowest-priced car for 1934 was the 3-passenger Dictator Coupe, selling for $645. All Dictator models were classified as Model A. This unit tipped the scale at 2,796 pounds. The car offered a good size storage compartment in its trunk. Besides the regular Coupe, a Regal version was available in the Dictator line for $675. This car also accommodated three passengers. In the coupe models, regular and Regal Coupes could also be ordered in the Commander line from $845 to $875. The President models also were available from $1,045 to $1,075. In both series, 5-passenger Coupes also made their entry for the year.

The 2-door Dictator St. Regis Brougham was offered for the first time as a small carrier for independent ambulance services. The wide opening door made for easy access in getting a patient on a stretcher in or out of the vehicle. The front right seat was easily removed and the left half of the back seat could be used by an attendant. Note the side pocket in the door panel. This was often a feature of lower priced cars.

A Dictator Sedan was the lowest-priced 4-door Studebaker offered for 1934. The model delivered for $695. Note the spotlight mounted at the windshield cowl. It doesn't appear to focus on anything of much importance, and in fact, looks like somebody has broken it off at its base.

Was this really an "unmarked car" used by South Bend Police Department? At any rate, it is a 6-wheeled Dictator Sedan used for police duty. The sidemounts look good, but were extremely difficult to get around when engine work was required. Most mechanics preferred to remove the spares for easier engine maintenance.

The famous Loewy design was first seen on these 1934 Land Cruiser Sedans. This body style was available in each series for 1934. This example is in the Dictator line selling for the same price as the regular Regal Sedan at $745. The fender skirts were classed as part of the regular package.

Boarding a freight car for its destination to a Studebaker dealer somewhere in the U.S.A. this vehicle wears the rare wire wheels which weren't being ordered by many customers in 1934. The bumpers were installed after the train ride and put on the car at the dealership in most cases. Railroads were still the most popular method of moving new cars from factory to distant dealerships, though those agencies in northern Illinois, Indiana, Ohio, and southern Michigan more often resorted to drive-away fleets or truck transport.

A piggy-back ride or a short haul, probably from the factory, is here being given to this 1934 Dictator Sedan. Surely it's not a breakdown of a brand-new vehicle. The truck is a current model "Big Chief" which will soon be fitted with an aftermarket body.

This six-wheeled Regal Roadster in the Dictator line is equipped for five passengers. It sold for $725. It also came on the market as a less fancy vehicle, also accommodating five passengers, for $695. The side-mount equipment was optional at extra cost.

This 1934 Studebaker was classed as a Regal Sedan selling for $745. The horizontal hood louvers were seen on mid-season cars in each series and referred to as "year ahead models." The change took place in early May of 1934. The Dictators were produced from September, 1933, to October, 1934, with a production run of 45,851 units.

This 1934 Dictator 6-wheeled Regal Sedan is all decked out in its circus attire. Even the windshield is open to give extra ventilation. The side mount accessory added $85 to the basic cost, but the clown's costume was not a factory-approved item.

A typical two-tone creation often seen on Loewy designed models is displayed on this Land Cruiser sedan at a Studebaker introduction. The skirts really add to the vehicle's side and rear appearance.

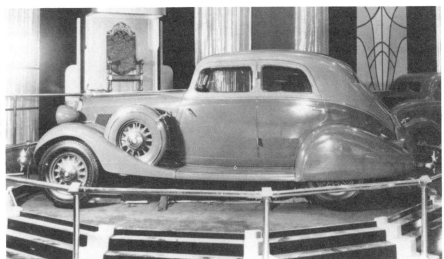

Parked in front of the South Bend administrative offices, like so many other Studebaker publicity shots, sits this 1934 Commander Roaster. It resembles the President model a great deal, except that the President came on a 123-inch wheelbase. Both Commander and President models used Bendix mechanical brakes with a power brake assist at no extra cost. The actual number of Roadsters produced in 1934 is unknown.

This 1934 Commander 3-passenger Coupe delivered for $845. Looking quickly at it, this model looked almost the same as the rumble seat version except for where the trunk handle was located and the lack of fender step plates which were required to enter a rumble seat. This vehicle even came with a factory spotlight, an extra cost accessory of limited appeal.

# 1934

The 1934 Commander Coupe was available with a rumble seat in both regular style or as a Regal model. The lower priced version delivered for $895 and the Regal went home for $925. Both offered seating for five passengers. The same automobiles came as a Dictator for $695 and $725 respectively. The only difference was in the engine compartment and wheelbase of 114 inches for a Dictator and 119 inches on the Commander.

This 2-door model was available in both Dictator and Commander style. As a Dictator, it sold for $710 with built-in trunk. The Commander was the same car as far as appearance goes, but was five inches longer and delivered for $905 with the side-mounted tire equipment. The spare tires give the car a more aristocratic look.

The counterpart of the Dictator, was this six-wheeled side-mounted Commander 2-door on a 119-inch wheelbase. The Commander model used a 17.5 gallon fuel tank, the same as President models. Studebaker provided safety glass in windshield and ventilating wings of all models. It was also available in all windows at a slightly extra cost, affording complete protection from the danger of flying glass to driver and passengers.

Look at all the check stickers on the windshield showing that this 1934 Commander has received its final okay before being shipped from the factory. Note the easy-access hood grip plainly visible on this model. This was the typical hood release used on all Studebakers for the era.

This was Studebaker's lowest-priced Commander Sedan for 1934. Yet it wears the accessory side-mounted wheel package which added additional dollars to its price. In base form, the 8-cylinder sedan delivered for $895.

Studebaker also made available Roadsters in each series. This is a Commander Regal Roadster for five passengers. It delivered for $925. A less deluxe version was available for $895. As a President, the unit came in regular style for $1,095 or in Regal version with side-mounted tires for $1,125.

This early 1934 Commander Regal St. Regis Brougham wears a 1933 New York license plate. This version of the Brougham sold for $895. A Regal St. Regis Brougham could also be ordered for $945. Few buyers chose this 2-door body style.

This 1934 Commander Regal St. Regis Brougham had a built-in trunk as standard equipment. It delivered for $895. This model was accepted better than the plain 2-door "trunkless" models. All 1934 Commanders were classed as Model B cars.

# 1934

Looking basically the same as the Regal Dictator is this Regal Commander for 1934. This 6-passenger sedan came on a 119-inch wheelbase. All Studebaker sedans for the year came with suicide doors on the front and rear doors opening from the back. The Budd steel wheels were standard equipment on all models for the year. The built-in trunk was seen on most all models, though a few cars did carry the rear mounted spare, minus the trunk.

Very proud of his new 6-wheeled Regal Commander sedan is this elderly Californian, posing for an agency delivery photo. The vehicle weighed 3,300 pounds and came with power brakes as standard equipment. This example delivered for $945. This was the first year for Studebaker to offer windshield wipers that pivoted from the bottom of the windshield. Twin wipers were available on all Dictator and Commander cars at a slight additional cost, but were standard on the Presidents.

A 1934 Regal Land Cruiser Sedan in the Commander line delivered for $895 and was an excellent buy for the time. It, like all Commanders, came with a full compartment of instrument gauges: ammeter, fuel, oil, and temperature gauge. In addition to the speedometer, package compartment, and ash tray, space for a clock and radio were provided.

Even Tarzan and Studebaker were friends. Parked by the familiar Studebaker headquarters doors is this Commander Sedan in regular fashion minus the built-in trunk. This was an official car from Metro Goldwyn Mayer movie studios operating under Studebaker's sponsorship. The car was supposedly used by Tarzan's mate for an "All American Tour". Note the siren unit by the front left door. Who the people are is anybody's guess, but they certainly are not Tarzan or his mate.

A 1934 President Coupe was available in four versions. The 2 or 4-passenger regular Coupes delivered for $1,045 and $1095, respectively. The deluxe models, which proved more popular in the Regal line, also came as 2 and 4-passenger vehicles selling for $1,075 and $1,125. This 2-passenger trunk model was classed in the regular President line. It weighed 3,280 pounds.

Being put through the paces is this 1934 President Sedan, classed as the lowest-priced President 4-door of the model run. The vehicle was used in conjunction with Union Oil Co. for a 60-day, 60,000-mile road test. Here it looks as if the car has already been driven a hard 60,000 miles. Note where the trumpet horns were placed. Rather than being in their usual spot, they were mounted directly above the bumper brackets. No explanation is given.

Note the trumpet horns on this sedan. It is the best means of identifying it as a member of the President line. This is the lowest priced President Sedan, delivering for $1,075. It came minus the built-in trunk. Very few of the model were manufactured.

This nicely equipped President Sedan with its side-mounted equipment, factory driving lights, and the special roof rack sits outside the administrative office of the South Bend factory. The car was operated by Universal Newsreels, which probably used the roof platform as a camera base when photographing special assignments.

# 1934

The top of the line for 1934 was this President Land Cruiser Sedan, equipped with its bumper guard accessories. The center driving light also was classed as an approved factory piece of extra cost equipment. This version is done in the two-tone paint combination. It sold for $1,145.

This 1934 President Land Cruiser came with a single-tone paint arrangement. It was available either way at no extra cost. The safety plate glass used on Studebaker cars at that time had a central substance sandwiched between inner and outer panes of glass. This plastic-like material often discolored into a yellow glow, or it would frost a bluish-white, making it difficult to see through. I recall as a kid someone in our neighborhood had one of these sharp cars. But, it always bugged me seeing the rear window glass being frosted white. Basically, the vehicle appeared to be in quite nice shape for a car then approximately ten years old. Today, of course, most 10-year old cars are still quite presentable, unless they have really been mistreated.

Looking basically the same as the 123-inch President Coupe in regular line is this Regal Coupe in the top line vehicles. On the 4-passenger models, extra passengers would sit comfortably in the rumble seat compartment. However, the trunk deck handle immediately behind the spare tire tells that this is a 2-place car. This model went out the door for $1,125.

The owner of this 1934 "7-wheeled" President Regal Sedan must have had a fear of frequent flat tires or blow-outs. Besides the side mounts, this car also carries a spare attached to the built-in trunk. As a President, it came in the group of cars referred to as Model C. As a base President, minus the extra cost tire equipment, it sold for $1,095.

This was one of the 1934 Studebaker models that helped put the company back on its feet. A six million dollar loan was granted through the efforts of Paul G. Hoffman to put the company in a more solvent position. One of Studebaker's advertising slogans this year read "From the Speedway Comes the Stamina," but it should have read "From the Bankers Comes a New Life."

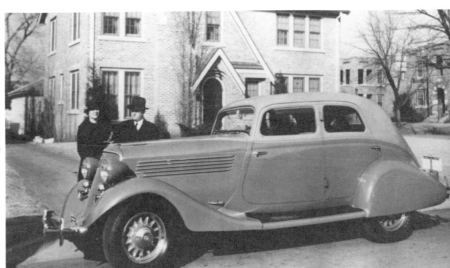

This couple probably was classed as "well to do" when, in the depths of the depression, they could pose with their new President Land Cruiser Sedan. The two-toned beauty apparently was a late season delivery since it is equipped with the horizontal hood louvers making this one of the "year ahead models" for 1934.

Here is a three-quarter rear view of the stylish 1934 President Land Cruiser Sedan. As beautiful a car as it was, the trunk compartment left something to be desired especially when the vehicle did not have tires mounted in the fender wells. However, the 4-piece rear window was quite unique, to say the least.

The 1934 President Regal Sedan delivered for the same price as the Land Cruiser model at $1,145. Both were comparable as far as the number sold. Each rode on the 123-inch wheelbase using 6.50x17-inch tires.

This is the President Regal Berline Limousine for six passengers. The model offered deluxe appointments equal to cars much higher in price. A commodious rear seat for three came with a folding center arm rest as well as side arm rests. The driving compartment was separated from passenger compartment by an easily raised or lowered window which completely disappeared if the owner so desired. This vehicle wears 1934 Iowa license plates. The background appears to be farm land lying fallow for the winter. This really does not seem to be a natural setting for such a pretentious car.

This 1934 President Regal Sedan was an export vehicle. It wears the small parking lamps mounted on top of the fenders, came without the trumpet horns, and carries a license plate from England. It also is, naturally, a right-hand drive car. Note that the rear license plate is mounted on the right fender.

A special built body is seen here. It is a Dictator 4-door open touring. Such a model was not part of the production line from Studebaker. How many were built and who the manufacturer was, is unknown. Quickly looking at the vehicle, it reminds one of a 1934 Ford Phaeton.

This 1934 Open Studebaker was in the Commander series. It was stated on the original photo that the body was by Graber, a well known European custom body builder located in Switzerland. The small painted, rather than chrome, road lamp was an after market piece of equipment. The number built is unknown.

This special bodied 9-passenger scenic touring vehicle was the property of White Cars of Cairns PTY Limited, located in Queensland, Australia. The steering mechanism was right-hand drive. All passengers entered from three left-hand doors. The vehicle used the Warner Free-Wheeling as on regular production models, and came with Commander 221 cubic-inch engine that developed 103 horsepower at 4000 rpm.

This 1934 Studebaker Commander Eight with a Superior body was designated as the "Mission." This hearse had a casket compartment over 100 inches long, 54-inch side doors, and a low loading height of only 27 inches. The spacious interior was quite similar to the "Arlington" interior.

This is another 1934 Studebaker President with a Superior body. This version was called "The Arlington." It offered a very streamlined design that pleased many undertakers. The vehicle employed the 110-horsepower engine with its cylinder head and pistons made of aluminum to make for lighter weight.

Giving a good view of the 1934 President Superior hearse is this photo of a side-loader platform named the "Sidroll." It operated automatically with press of a button once the casket was placed in position. Superior was the first to offer this convenience, while others followed with similar devices shortly after.

Studebaker offered this 1934 Superior service car to mortuaries throughout the country. This unit came on a Dictator chassis. It developed 88 horsepower from the 6-cylinder engine and it rode on 5.50x17-inch tires. Note the carriage lights behind the right door. The nameplate of a funeral home could be mounted on the cowl just above the windshield. However, on this example, the plate simply reads "Funeral Coach."

Basically using the same body as the Superior hearse is this Superior ambulance that came on the President chassis. The wheelbase was 153 inches and the vehicle used the 110 horsepower President engine. As far as ambulance and mortuary vehicles go, the Superior coaches held the limelight in 1934 with their well-designed vehicles. Note the chrome Budd wheels on this ambulance. They make for a very sharp looking machine.

Studebaker's entry into the station wagon business in 1934 was not done in great abundance or with much enthusiasm. The company referred to the wagon as a Suburban. This example came on the Dictator chassis. The side and rear window compartments did not come with roll down windows, but used an isinglass that did not weather too well. It discolored and cracked in a short while. Studebaker used the U.S.B.F. body company as its supplier for the wagon bodies.

A rather novel photo shows three 1934 models being delivered. Folks living in South Bend back in the 1920s and 1930s probably saw this type of delivery quite often. Note the third car had a tow-bar attached to its front end. Full semi-trailer car carriers were still in the future. One must wonder why the towed car has no protective sheeting over its front, to prevent those open dual wheels from kicking stones into the grille, headlights, and even the windshield.

For 1935 Studebaker used the basic design of its already streamlined fleet of 1934 cars, but gave them a slightly more chiseled look. Mechanically, the company's big news was the use of hydraulic brakes to replace the somewhat archaic mechanicals that had been in use up until now. Also appearing later in the year was a "Hill Holder," which locked the brakes when the clutch was pressed. This was very useful in areas where steep hills and traffic lights intermixed, because after a stop, it allowed the driver to remove his foot from the brake pedal to the gas without the car rolling backward. Also on the mechanical side was a new "Planar" independent front suspension system, and on the President models only, overdrive was offered as standard equipment. And, within the bodies, a more plush interior than ever before appeared in all series.

After slashing several models from its line-up in 1934, the company began to introduce new models once more. The same three series were continued, but now a total of 35 models were included in the offerings. Among the series, the Dictator Six line offered 13 body styles ranging from a $695 3-passenger Coupe to a Dictator Land Cruiser for $885. The Commander Eights came in 11 body versions, starting with a 3-passenger Coupe for $930 to a Commander Land Cruiser Sedan for $1,085. And in the President line, 11 models also ranged from a pretentious 3-passenger Coupe for $1,245 to a President Regal Berline Sedan for $1,445.

Basically, the Dictator Six was the same car as in the previous year. It gave the public the same 88 hp 6-cylinder engine, still rated at 3600 rpm. The wheelbase remained 114 inches, the fuel capacity remained 14.5 gallons, but the tire size was now 6.0x16.

Commander Eight cars had a slight increase in horsepower. They now delivered 107 horses at 3800 rpm. The wheelbase continued at 119 inches, but the fuel tank was the 14.5-gallon unit shared with the Dictator series. While the tire size was reduced to 6.50x16. Despite the fact that the Commander fit between the Dictator and President in both sales and price position, the series was destined to be terminated at the end of this year.

The President also continued with its chassis of 123-inch wheelbase, and continued to use its own 8-cylinder engine rated at 110 hp at 3600 rpm. It also retained its 17.5-gallon fuel tank, but its tire size was reduced to 7.0x16.

Despite its sales climbing by 2,959 cars to a calendar year total of 49,062, Studebaker continued to slide downward again in sales position, and once more was rated as 11th in the nation. The slip in position was not due to Studebaker's sales decreasing, but to the fact that by percentage, other makes were doing even better as the nation slowly began to crawl out from under its depression economy.

In 1935, Studebaker made available this Coupe as a 3 or 5-passenger model in the Dictator, Commander, and President lines of cars. This is the lowest-priced model for the year, the Dictator 3-passenger Coupe that sold for $695. As a five-passenger version, it delivered for $20 more at $750. Regal Coupes also were available for roughly $780.

A pair of 1935 Dictators are getting set for an African Safari. Note that the cars have their hoods strapped down and these are not to be opened until a given time during this event. Both cars performed well and not one ever heated up. Note also that the cars are equipped with wire wheels, rather than the regular steel spoked wheels which were standard equipment.

The 1935 Dictator St. Regis Sedan for five sold for $720. It came on a 114-inch wheelbase and sold well, in spite of the depression, to families where economics played an important part.

Besides being used as the regular St. Regis Sedan, this 2-door model also saw use by small town ambulance services. Note how compactly the stretcher fits into the vehicle with wide-door opening. On this model, the rear seat could be left in place for use by an attendant. When not in service as an ambulance, its front seat could be easily re-installed for regular passenger car use. The vehicle weighed 2,912 pounds. All Dictators rode on 6.00x16-inch tires.

The 1935 Dictator Sedan was classed in the 1-A Series. It was the lowest-priced Dictator sedan selling for $750. The 1-A models began production December, 1934, and continued through September, 1935, with a production run of 11,742 units sold. Total Studebaker sales amounted to 49,062 cars sold, placing the company in 11th position for the 1935 calendar year.

The 1935 Studebaker Dictator Custom Sedan for six sold for $785, making it the best-selling car in the Dictator line. In addition to this model, there was a plain Dictator Sedan for $750 with fewer deluxe appointments, while a Custom St. Regis with all the frills went home for $855.

# 1935

Studebaker Regal Roadster

Studebaker Custom St. Regis Sedan

Available as either a Dictator or Commander, this Custom St. Regis sold for $785 as a Dictator and $955 if ordered as a Commander. The only noticeable differences were in wheelbases. The Dictator had a 114-inch wheelbase and the Commander rode on a 119-inch chassis. Raise the hood and you saw an 8-cylinder engine if it was a Commander, and 6-cylinders if a Dictator.

The rare 1935 Dictator Regal Roadster delivered for $780. Being a Regal model, the side-mounted spares were standard equipment. The regular Dictator Roadster sold for $750 and came with a rear-mounted spare as regular equipment. This deluxe series of Dictator was referred to as Series A and was produced from December, 1934, to September, 1935, with a total of 23,550 units sold.

For 1935, this Commander six-wheeled sedan was a refined version of its 1934 selling mate. The optional side-mounts gave an extended look to the front end. The new radiator enclosure, new teardrop headlamps, new hood louver treatment, new bumpers, and new hubcaps, gave the models a nicely improved facelift for the model year.

The Naval Commander fits the picture quite well with his new Commander Coupe. The unit sold for $895 making it the lowest-priced Commander for the year. Commanders were produced from November, 1934, to September, 1935, with a total production of 6,085 units sold.

This restored 1935 Regal Roadster is in the Commander line. The 5-passenger car sold for $980, when new. It is a rare car today and certainly the owner is aware of it. This was the year Studebaker introduced the front-end suspension that stayed with their cars for several years. The device was referred to as the Planar Independent Suspension, and also was known as the "Miracle Ride".

Looking basically the same as the Dictator models is this Commander Regal Coupe coming in both 3 and 5-passenger styles. This is the 3-passenger with trunk deck. If a 5-passenger style was ordered, the rumble seat would make up the added seating. The Commanders came on a 119-inch wheelbase. The price for this unit was $930 while as a 5-passenger, it delivered for $980.

A famed star in 1935 was the popular Mickey Rooney, here standing on the running board of a Land Cruiser Commander. This was the most expensive Commander of the year, selling at $1,085. The fender skirts were standard on all Land Cruisers. This model rode on the 119-inch wheelbase, the same as other Commanders. This body style was also available as a Dictator, as well as in the President line. The sidemounts were an additional cost item.

The most popular model in the 1935 Commander line up was this Custom Sedan delivering for $985. Its 8-cylinder engine developed 107 horsepower at 3800 rpm. The Commander models were referred to as Model 1-Bs. The fuel tank held a 14.5 gallon supply in the Commander line.

A 1935 sliding roof compartment was available on Commander and President vehicles. Very few ever reached the production line. If any exist today, it is doubtful. In its infancy such a roof would have had its problems, especially on a rainy day. Thirty years later, such roofs were hailed as a "great new styling innovation."

An interior view shows the 1935 Commander dashboard being done in walnut grained decal. The luxuriously cushioned, adjustable seat was 50 full inches wide and accommodated three adults comfortably. Unlike many makes which put the parking/emergency brake next to the shift, Studebaker put this lever on the left, where it was out of the way of the middle passenger.

Studebaker President Eight

The President Eight Regal Roadster for five delivered for $1,325. If a person didn't need the extra frills, a basic Roadster also was on the market for $30 less. It sold for $1,295, with an interior of cloth or leather being optional. The side-mounted tires were extra cost equipment. Presidents for 1935 were classed as Model 1-Cs.

The President Coupe for 3 or 5-passengers ranged in price from $1,245 for a regular model, to $1,325 for a 5-passenger Regal Coupe. Actually, there were four versions made available. Namely, 3 and 5-passenger regular coupes and 3 and 5-passenger Regal Coupes. An offering, made available on these coupes as well as all President models, were multi-beam three stage headlamps that threw light beams at any of three levels to the left of the road when passing an oncoming car. Dual tail lamps, aerodynamically "fared" into the fenders, were also standard equipment.

Studebaker President Eight

How about that bullet-proof radiator and tire screens that this 1935 President wears? These President models were often used as unmarked cars in large cities for police and special visiting dignitaries. A bullet-proof windshield generally was part of the extra cost package. The supplier of the special armor-plating package was not identified.

As for the sedans in the President line, there were five for 1935. This happens to be the most popular model, the Regal Sedan selling for $1,345. All President cars offered luxurious interiors with thick carpeting front and rear. A silken rear-window curtain was concealed behind the rear seat, and door pockets, grip cords, robe cords, and hassocks were standard. The front seat adjusted at a slight push of the button.

# 1935

The top of the line Land Cruiser came in the President series. This model used the 123-inch wheelbase. It rode on a 123-inch wheelbase. The tire size was 7.00 x 16 inches. The Land Cruiser delivered for $1,430. This design was the creation of Raymond Loewy. What else can one say, but that it's another one of his great works of art, with a flowing style very unique for the era.

The small trumpet horns are the distinctive notes seen on the 1935 President. This beauty took some of its lines from the Pierce Silver Arrow, from that same era. The President hood ornament adds to the classic front end. The model held the spare tire in a lower compartment beneath the regular trunk space, if side-mounted tires weren't ordered.

The 1935 Studebaker Custom Berline Limousine was basically a 6-passenger vehicle. It was the company's second most expensive car of the year, selling for $1,430. Only the Regal Berline topped it in price, going for $1,445. The Regal Berline offered a leather front interior, if the owner desired a chauffeur-driven type of vehicle.

Studebaker President Eight

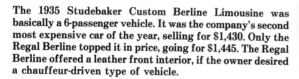

The Arlington funeral coach rode on the Dictator chassis. It sold to funeral homes for $1,850. The Superior Company of Lima, Ohio, held Studebaker as one of their big accounts at this time. The style reveals nice appointments and fittings, and expert coachwork which kept Superior's ranking as one of the best in the funeral car business.

# 1935

Utilizing the 1935 Studebaker Dictator chassis is this Superior Service Car using the 88 horsepower 6-cylinder engine. Even with the additional weight, this vehicle rode on the regular 5.50x17-inch tires. Since most funerals during this era were held in the home of the deceased, such service cars were quite necessary for funeral directors to carry all of the equipment necessary to conduct the ceremony...such as chairs, altar, casket stand, flower trays, etc.

This 1935 Studebaker/Superior funeral car was referred to as the Westminster. It offered a combination of distinguished appearance, luxurious interiors, utility features, and mechanical excellence that made it the "one" complete funeral car. This funeral coach was available on the President 8 chassis at $2,490.

This Superior funeral car on the President Chassis came with a large casket compartment that was over 100 inches long. The side doors of the car were 54-inches wide, with a rear-door loading height of only 27 inches from ground level. Superior side-loading vehicles featured an improved "Sidroll" platform that saved 4 inches of inside height and eliminated the need for a casket bench. The Sidroll was an extra cost option Superior made available on all of its models.

A side view of the Superior coach shows how wide the actual doors are, making for easy access for removing the casket. The rear end of this vehicle has a more streamlined design than most funeral coaches of the time. Although the owner of this car was listed as William A. Harris Funeral Director, there was no notation as to the home city.

# 1935

A fleet of 1935 President ambulances was operated by Sanidad Militar Regimento No. 2 Maximo Gomez. These vehicles were all delivered for use in Mexico City. The body builder was Superior of Lima, Ohio. The roof line these units employ is ahead of its time. All came equipped with regular steel Budd wheels which Studebaker employed on all their vehicles.

This 1935 President 8 Superior Ambulance had the advanced styling seen on all Superior coaches of the time. The beaver-tail rear end was common on equipment delivered by Superior, as well as a few other funeral and ambulance builders during the mid to late 1930s.

The trumpet horns and President hood ornament tells us this Superior-built ambulance is riding on an 8-cylinder President chassis. It was referred to as the Samaritan and sold for $2,665. Note where the rear license plate is mounted. I'll bet it didn't stay there very long without getting bent. The siren equipment is neatly placed on the front right bumper brace. The bumper guards were optional equipment.

This 1935 President 8 funeral service car belongs to the City of Columbus, Ohio, according to the door nameplate. This body style was called the Elmhurst and delivered for $1,905. The side-mounted spare tire equipment did not receive the extra cost metal tire covers. It must have been a hot day when this photo was taken as the side door windows are down and the windshield is in the open position. Since it is doubtful if the City of Columbus engaged in funeral work, this car must have been assigned to some other department, where a prestige-type of delivery car was mandated. The siren on the front bumper hints that it was part of the city's fire or police departments.

# 1936

Studebaker had always seemed to be a few steps ahead of its competition, and this certainly held true with the 1936 and 1937 Coupes with the "Batwing" rear windows. Probably because of the sometimes unique designs, this author has always been partial to Studebaker styling from the mid-1930s onward.

In a total rethinking of marketing strategies, the company this year offered only 13 models, spread over only two series. These were the Dictator Six and the President Eight, with the Commander Eight being left behind with the 1935 models. Both series shared the same new body design, displaying a chrome diecast grille, louvered hood, and split windshield. For the first time, no open cars were offered this year. The lowest price model was the 3-passenger Dictator Coupe selling for $695, while the most expensive offering for the year was the President Touring Sedan, which carried a price tag of $1,065.

All models in both series were nicely appointed. Design features included overdrive with free-wheeling, "Startix" independent sprung front wheels, and an all-steel roof. Standard items for the President, which could also be purchased as accessories for the Dictator, included cigar lighters, dual sun visors, dual horns, full chrome wheel covers, dual taillamps, and a banjo steering wheel.

The Dictator came with a 90 horse engine (3400 rpm) while the President developed 115 horses at a similar rpm. Wheelbases were 116 inches for the Dictator and 125 inches for the President series. The 6-cylinder cars used 6.0x16 inch tires while the Eights employed 6.50x16s. Both series shared the same 18-gallon fuel tanks. Fuel economy was touted, especially after Studebaker placed well in the Gilmore Economy Run and in many other succeeding economy events.

During the year, the company sold 85,026 vehicles, which was an amazing increase of 35,964 over the previous year. Not only did this show that the public certainly accepted the new styling, it also moved Studebaker back into the 9th place in the national sales picture.

A bare bones basic 3-passenger Coupe was in the Dictator series for 1936. The Dictators for the year were referred to as Model 3-As when in basic form. The body designed was of a completely new style for 1936. The chrome plated diecast grille proved to be a real eye-catcher for the company. The factory placed ninth for the year with 85,026 units sold.

This gentleman apparently is signing the contract to take delivery of his new 1936 Dictator 3-passenger Coupe. This was the lowest priced car the company offered for the year. It sold for $695. The Loewy-designed coupe was being delivered from the K. A. Murray Studebaker dealership. The cowboy on the license plate tells us the Murray dealership must have been in the State of Wyoming.

A popular movie star in the 1930s was the proud owner of this 1936 Dictator 5-passenger Coupe. Her name was Norma Shearer, and she is seen here as she enters the movie studio for another day of work. The 5-passenger delivered for ten dollars more than its 3-passenger cousin, at $705.

# 1936

This example of the 1936 Dictator 2-door Sedan was mainly offered as a business vehicle. This St. Regis Brougham could be available for carrying extra large loads by easily removing the rear seat. This gave form to an extra large built-in luggage compartment. When the spare was carried in the fender well, it gave even more carrying capacity as in the trunks of most other cars. This model sold for $705.

The 1936 Dictator St. Regis Cruising Sedan for six passengers also came available as a mini-ambulance by removing the right half of the front seat and employing a stretcher. Some small town private ambulance firms made use of this equipment during the depression when funds weren't there for more expensive ambulances. In regular style, the car delivered for $715.

Demonstrating how easy it is to remove a patient from the Dictator St. Regis Cruising Sedan, these attendants appear to have had much experience. These 1936 Dictators rode on a 116-inch wheelbase and used 6.00x16-inch tires.

Did Mom and Pop just drive into the filling station to show off their new Dictator Sedan which sold for $745. It doesn't appear the vehicle is receiving any "liquid refreshment." My dad always referred to this type of gas station customer as an "I.W.W." — Information, Wind and Water.

Demonstrating how easy this agile one-wheeled trailer could be for transporting luggage, business supplies, etc. is this Series 3-A Dictator Sedan which sold for $720. The trailer appears to be weighing down the new Dictator. Note the special guard on the rear bumper of the trailer. All lines blend well together from the front of the car to the rear of the trailer. These unique units bolted firmly to the rear bumper, with the pivoting single wheel acting in the same role as the ball hitch on a normal trailer. They were great for light loads, and very easy to back up, as long as the driver remembered the trailer was there when squeezing into a tight parking place.

A fleet of Studebaker police units. The information at the top of the photo states "Studebaker Radio Patrol." Whether this was another "P.R." device possibly for South Bend, or maybe the factory employed its own police patrol, is anybody's guess. Anyway, probably the police chief rated the new light-colored Dictator and his "henchmen" followed with the other dark-colored Dictators. The 1935 at the end of the row was either too good of a car to turn in, or the low man on the totem pole rated last year's model.

One of those special two-toned models Studebaker was famous for in 1936 is this Dictator Custom St. Regis Brougham. The 6-passenger 2-door model was not classed in the same category as the business model and yet prices were the same $705.

The Dictator Custom Sedan for Six was the lowest priced sedan the company offered in 1936. It sold for $725. Most buyers preferred the hump trunk models to this slant-back style.

*Studebaker Dictator*

# 1936

This Dictator Sedan for 1936 happens to be a St. Regis version which was the most expensive model in the Dictator line. When in the deluxe line, the car was referred to as the 4-A series. A total of 22,029 Dictator cars in all versions of the 4-A series were produced in 1936.

This fellow obviously likes accessories on his new car. Check out that badge bar across the front bumper. The center-mount driving light is an approved Studebaker accessory. However, in factory literature for 1936 Studebakers, nowhere does it show the trumpet horns, small fender lights, or fender skirts. Possibly the skirts came as leftover 1935 models, or aftermarket items. At any rate, this man seems quite proud of his new acquisition.

How about this for a special bodied 1936 Studebaker? It is a Dictator that turned from a 4-door Sedan into a special bodied convertible sedan. Note the front suicide doors and the rear-opening rear doors. How many were produced and by whom are unknown. Also note the small fender parking lamps.

The Logan Fire Department purchased this classic styled President Coupe for the Fire Chief. It came equipped with the rare side-mounted spare tires, but minus the deluxe spare covers. It also shows various other items needed for its fire patrols: siren, spotlight, and red driving light mounted on the bumper bracket. White sidewall tires and the deluxe wheel-trim rings are nice added touches, but not needed for fire duty.

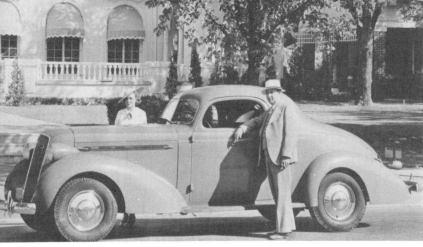

Studebaker's lowest-priced President for 1936 was this 3-passenger Coupe, selling for $945. It was designated as a Model 2-C. Note the full chrome wheel discs that this model wears. The name President is used in the center of the disc. Even though classed as an accessory, most all President cars came equipped with these wheel covers.

From this view, the President Coupe for five appears the same as the 3-passenger version except for a rumble seat and step pads on the right fender to help enter the rear compartment. This example delivered for $970. Production began in October, 1935, and ended in June, 1936, with a total of 7,297 vehicles produced in the President line. Note the long antenna bar under the running board. This beauty apparently is equipped with a radio since this is where the antenna gave the best reception.

This 1936 President St. Regis Cruising Sedan came on the 125-inch wheelbase and used 6.50x16-inch tires. Note this example came equipped without the deluxe wheel discs, but does have the factory chrome trim rings. It also was delivered minus the bumper vertical guards. The 2-door sold for $1,015, but did not entice as many buyers as the 4-door models.

A rare version of the 1936 President was this Custom (flat trunk) Sedan. This model was used as another publicity feature. Both Studebaker and the Cleveland, Ohio Police Department took part in the venture of safety for the state. Oddly enough, the car is not equipped with any police equipment. The sedan, in regular decor, sold for $1,030.

# 1936

Conservation at its best! This gentleman probably ordered a black sedan figuring it went well with his black hat and black top coat. The only noticeable accessories the vehicle utilizes are the wheel-trim rings. Who would ever think of a set of white sidewalls to give it a touch of "pizazz"? The President employed a 250 cubic-inch 8-cylinder engine that developed 115 horsepower at 3600 rpm.

The six-wheeled 1936 President Cruising Sedan was the most expensive model the factory offered for the year. The car delivered for $1,065 in base form. The side-mount tire equipment, metal covers, and full wheel discs were available at extra cost.

The pilot in his full regalia appears to either be getting ready to leave his side-mounted President Sedan for a spin in the air, or has just landed from his flight and hopefully he's going to take the car for a much needed wash job. The vehicle is well equipped with vertical bumper guards, wheel trim rings and side-mounted spares.

This 1936 Dictator Cruising Sedan is somewhat different from the regular models. Looking closely at the vehicle, you'll see its an export car with the right-hand drive. The license plate is mounted on the right side rather than on the left, where Studebaker always chose to attach the plate. The license also appears to be from a foreign country.

This is actually a mock-up of a 1936 Studebaker St. Regis Cruising Sedan, photographed in Studebaker's styling studio. Oddly enough, the photo below it shows the left side as a 4-door Sedan. This is because it's the same clay model just showing a sedan on one side and the 2-door version on the other. Often this was done to study the feasibility of using the same basic body shell for both styles. Virtually every major auto manufacturer did the same type of model building.

This is the left side of the Dictator Cruising Sedan in mock-up. Note that the trunk emblem is different from the oval lazy "S" that came on regular production models.

Showing the durability Studebaker offered with their new all-steel roof, these "pachyderms" may have been told to tread lightly. This 1936 Dictator is finished in one of the special two-tone paint combinations that were made popular for the model run.

In 1936, the Superior Coach Builders continued to build bodies for Studebaker. The frosted glass rear quarter windows contained a sunburst pattern with a cross in the center of the golden rays. The vehicle rode on a 145-inch wheelbase. The Superior combination car was designed for those owners who wanted an ambulance that could double as a hearse, or vice-versa. It was extremely attractive with its streamlined body and oval side windows, but note the strange cut of the rear door, sweeping down below the coach light. The model came with President running gear.

# 1936

This is a view of the 1936 Studebaker Superior combination coach with its side door opened to show the room the streamlined vehicle offered to those having to remove either the stretcher, as shown here, or a full casket when a side-loading was desirable. Note the special brocaded door paneling employed on this coach.

This Superior funeral coach used the Dictator engine and did not have as many deluxe appointments as the combination car. Note the small coach lamps between the front and rear side doors and the cut of the door itself. The rear opening door was wider than many coaches of this class.

A longer wheelbase 1936 Studebaker Superior funeral coach, this unit came on a 153-inch wheelbase. But, it offered the same deluxe appointments as seen on the Superior model of 145-inch wheelbase. The oval side door windows were basically a feature on all Superior units of that time.

This 1936 Superior ambulance still came with its own Studebaker nameplates on the grille and on the hub caps. Rarely did a product leave the Superior facility without wearing all the Superior nameplates. The President came with regular 8-cylinder appointments.

Having retooled the entire line in 1936, this year's Studebakers received only a streamlined facelift. The changes to a more pointed grille, an alligator hood opening from the front, and extended louvers added even more beauty to an already good-looking car.

As in 1936, Studebaker offered only two series of cars, the Dictator Six coming in seven models and the President Eight available in six styles. Prices ranged from $665 for a Dictator 3-passenger Coupe to $1,065 for the 8-cylinder President Cruising Sedan. For the second year in a row, there were no convertible models available.

Mechanically, the cars were the same as the previous year's models. Accessories were plentiful for the 1937 buyers and many people took advantage of dealer or aftermarket items to add even more style to an already sharp looking run of cars.

In an interesting note, this would be the last year for the Dictator Series. The 6-cylinder series would reappear in 1938, but would once more bear the name "Commander." Apparently with a nut named Adolph devastating the face of Europe, many people felt that the name "Dictator" no longer fit into the accepted American scene. Even then, there were certain words that just were not politically correct.

Despite the still-fresh stylings, sales slipped by 4,033 this year, dropping to 80,993 units. Although this in itself wasn't particularly bad, other companies did so well that Studebaker fell to 13th position in the national sales slot.

The lowest-priced Studebaker for 1937 was this 3-passenger Dictator Business coupe. The vehicle sold for $665, minus the double whitewall tires shown here. The plane is a Waterman Arrowmobile, a semi-experimental unit which backers hoped to put into production. In theory, it was supposed to fly to a location, drop its wings, and then be operable as a car.

The 1937 Dictator Custom 2-door Sedan came as a business vehicle for many types of use. Here it was being used as a mini-ambulance. Note: with the lack of the folding front right half seat, a stretcher could be placed in the vehicle by removing the rear seat. By placing the spare tire in the fender well, more carrying capacity became available in the trunk area. In some models, the right half of the front seat was used as a left rear seat for an attendant.

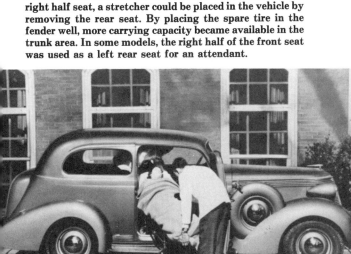

Rarely seen, even when new, was a side-mounted Dictator 2-door Sedan. This is a Custom series. The absence of bumper guards, and the lack of a right-fender tail lamp tells its in the more economical line.

The 1937 Studebaker Dictator Custom Sedan appears to be carrying a healthy load of foot pads and inner soles for the famous Dr. Scholls foot comfort service. Some spring overloaders might have been helpful for the rear end. This 2-door model often was referred to as Custom Coupe for five. It sold for $715.

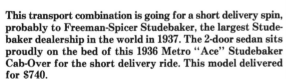

Again, using the P.R. department to its fullest, Studebaker offered cars for Driver Education programs. This fleet was delivered to the Chicago Board of Education for the Lane Technical School. All models are Dictator 2-door Sedans. Surprisingly when cars were sold for large sale purposes rarely did they come with deluxe options. But these units all carry the extra cost bumper guard equipment.

This transport combination is going for a short delivery spin, probably to Freeman-Spicer Studebaker, the largest Studebaker dealership in the world in 1937. The 2-door sedan sits proudly on the bed of this 1936 Metro "Ace" Studebaker Cab-Over for the short delivery ride. This model delivered for $740.

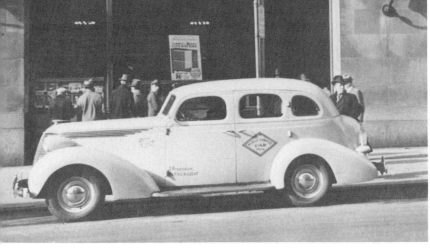

Being put to good use by the Public Service Cab Co. of Phoenix is this 1937 Dictator Sedan in the series of 5-A vehicles. The Dictator model used the 90 horsepower engine rated at 3400 rpm. Studebaker taxi vehicles proved to be popular through the years, mainly due to their economical qualities.

Parked by the ocean is the slant-back 1937 Dictator Custom Sedan for six. The vehicle rode on the 116-inch wheelbase. Production began in August, 1936, continuing to July of 1937. A total of 50,001 of the standard version Dictators were produced for the model run.

A 1937 Dictator St. Regis 4-door Sedan was one of the more popular models for the model run. This unit sold for $765. This car is equipped with twin windshield wipers, bumper guards, license frame to protect its new 1937 California license plate, and also sports a highly collectible Triple-A badge mounted directly below the famous Studebaker oval emblem. The dog was not a factory option.

Another familiar view of the South Bend administrative offices shows directly behind this new 1937 Dictator Cruising Sedan. This vehicle was the most expensive Dictator for the year. It sold for $795. This was Studebaker's first year to offer the alligator hood. This novel device eventually became popular with all manufacturers, and mechanics especially appreciated it.

# 1937

The distinguished looking 1937 President Coupe for five has always been a favorite model of this author. I love those "Bat Wing" rear windows that were a Raymond Loewy specialty. This example was classed in the series of 3-C cars being built from August 1936 to July 1937. A total of 39,001 Presidents were produced for the model run. As a five-passenger coupe, it was delivered for $995. The three-passenger version was available for $965. Both versions offered a huge trunk space.

The famous George Vanderbilt Cup Race was held on July 3, 1937. Seen here, from the Italian Racing Team, is Scuderia Ferrari. He is driving through the courtesy of the H. M. Williams Studebaker Agency, located at Broadway and 56th Street, New York City. The agency obviously was putting the 1937 President out for a day's display. Note the New York dealer license plate that the President shows.

Paul G. Hoffman and Harold Vance stand beside a 1937 President Sedan as the vehicle begins a test run for Texaco Oil Company. Note the front driving lights and accessory bumper guard equipment, especially the loud speaker equipment coming from the trunk compartment. Was the loud speaker for night driving, to gently hint to following drivers that they should dim their lights? Haven't we all wished for such an attachment?

Again, the factory entered the yearly Elks Magazine Safety Tour for which Studebaker had become famous for sponsoring. This year it was the President Sedan making the official July tour, going from Boston to Denver. From the stand in front of the factory office and the General Dual-10 logo on the sidemount, it appears that Quaker State Oil and General Tire also got in the act.

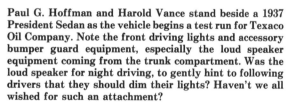

A 1937 President Cruising Sedan was also put to good use for the Vanderbilt Cup Race. The gentleman behind the wheel is Tazio Nuvolari, winner of the previous year's event, and one of the most famous racing drivers of the day. The car also was used with courtesy of Studebaker and the New York City dealer H. M. Williams. Most President models came equipped with the full wheel disc covers which were classed as optional equipment. This Cruising Sedan was the most expensive Studebaker for the year. It delivered for $1,065.

A rare body style in the President line is this St. Regis Custom Sedan. The gentleman about to take delivery of it is none other than Joe Lewis, the famous prize fighter. The unit sold for $1,015, but the actual number built is not known. The car is apparently on display inside the administrative offices. By using a high-powered magnifier, I detected the name on the office window being the same as mine (Moloney).

Jack Dempsey stands proudly beside his new 1937 President Cruising Sedan. This top of the line sedan delivered for $1,065. The fender-mounted siren is not a factory approved accessory, as are the full wheel discs, trim wings, and white sidewalls. This model rode on a 125-inch wheelbase and used 6.50x16-inch tires. No information was given as to Dempsey's need for a siren.

This 1937 President 6-passenger Cruising Sedan with a sun roof is probably the rarest model of Studebakers built in the 1930s. How many were actually built is unknown. This example also sports fender-well spare tires and the rare fender parking lamps. I'm sure it must also be equipped with the optional Hill Holder which became a Studebaker first.

This is the President St. Regis Cruising Sedan which sold for $30 less than the top of the line Cruising Sedan for six. This model delivered for $1,035. It used the 8-cylinder engine developing 115 horsepower at 3600 RPM. It too did duty at the Vanderbilt Cup race, being used as one of the cars for race officials.

Look at those factory-approved accessories on the 1937 President Regal Sedan. The side-mounted fender wells, alone, make this a very much sought after vehicle today. The hood ornament when given a slight twist opened the new style alligator hood which Studebaker advertised heavily as being one of the first in the industry to offer. Behind the car, and of even more interest than the Studebaker, is one of the famous China Clipper transports, which the then world-famous Pan American Airlines used on its lengthy Pacific routes. At the time this was the largest flying boat in commercial service.

Studebaker referred to its station wagon as the Suburban for 1937. The car was available in a variety of colors, while the doors, side and rear panels were finished in natural wood. The vehicle could comfortably seat eight people. The unit was classed as a model in the Coupe-Express line of cars with it being listed as one of the 3,125 models being produced. It was only available with Dictator running gear. The body builder was U.S.B.F.

A new model for 1937 was the Coupe-Express. Studebaker's newest innovation was this dual-purpose car. It offered passenger car comfort and a commercial car that was more convenient and efficient than a coupe. It offered seating for 3-passengers. The automatic Hill-Holder was also available on this model. If the owner wished, 6.50x16-inch tires were available at extra cost. Regular production used 6.00x16-inch tires.

# 1937

This version of the Coupe Express could be ordered as a refrigerated unit or an early "Roach Wagon." It would be a nice unit to take to a car show just for its unusualness. All Coupe-Express models came with the spare tire mounted in the front right fender.

Seen in regular fashion is the 1937 Coupe Express Model J-5. This model was only manufactured from January, 1937, through July, 1937, with a total of 3,125 being produced. This unit came with the rare steel spoked wheels while disc wheels were more popular by 1937. In base form, it sold for $695.

A different style of Coupe Express was this version, called a Canopy Express. The Coupe Express vehicles were known as Model J-5s. This canopy cost an additional $105 installed, but it is not known if that included the screened sides. This style of truck was often referred to as a "Dog Catcher's Wagon," as they were often used by the Humane Societies for picking up stray animals. Not many were produced.

What a neat way for a Newark, N.J., photo studio and supply store to advertise. This unit displayed a large version of their commercial camera to put its point across. One wonders how much business was generated from this sales device?

The body builders for funeral directors seem to have the right touch in choosing titles for the vehicles to give that extra bit of class at a time when needed. This Superior-built vehicle was referred to as the Elmhurst Service Car if mounted on the Dictator Six chassis. If the President Eight chassis were employed, the service vehicle was called the Elmwood. Both styles used the 145-inch wheelbase.

# 1937

The Superior Studebaker ambulance for 1937 more than not employed the President running gear. At a time for speedy travel, the 8-cylinder engine proved to be more efficient than the 6-cylinder. As with the hearse models, it came on the 145-inch wheelbase. Note the siren mounted on the lower left fender, but no roof lights, only a left-mounted spot lamp.

This handsome looking hearse is a 1937 Studebaker with body by Superior. It technically was called the Limousine Funeral Car and came with velour draperies on the side compartments. The side-mounted tires, full wheel discs, and whitewalls were optional equipment and they do help to set it off, even for the "last ride."

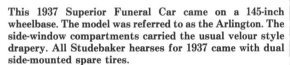

This 1937 Superior Funeral Car came on a 145-inch wheelbase. The model was referred to as the Arlington. The side-window compartments carried the usual velour style drapery. All Studebaker hearses for 1937 came with dual side-mounted spare tires.

A more conservative Studebaker Superior hearse is seen here with its carved side-window paneling. The carvings on this hearse actually were stamped metal. This whole panel was removable to convert it to a limousine-style unit. Either the Dictator or President running gear were available. Most funeral homes preferred the President appointments over the Dictator.

During this era, two years was about the limit that most automobile manufacturers would hold onto a given body style. Competition kept all companies on the edge, as overall sales still were not that great. As a result, each automotive company tried its best to have something new and fresh to offer its followers and entice new customers. Thus, at Studebaker, for 1938 another body change took place.

The company once again offered three series, after limiting itself to two lines since the 1935 models. As mentioned in the previous chapter, the Dictator was one. It was replaced by the Studebaker Six, sometimes called the Commander Six. The top line continued to be the President Series, but a new middle ground, retaking the name Commander, once more occupied the sales charts. When the name Commander Six is applied, the middle ground seems to have taken the name State Commander. Also, a sub-series of the President line was the State President, a slightly better trimmed division whose name appeared interchjangeable with the President. Both the Six and the State Commander models used the same 6-cylinder engines, which now developed 90 horses at 3400 rpm. They came with 6.0x16 tires on their Budd wheels, and as did all Studebakers this year, used an 18-gallon fuel tank. The main difference between the Studebaker Six and the State Commander, as far as appearances go, seemed to be in the design of the headlamps. The Six came with round lights mounted on top of the fender catwalks, while Commanders shared their style of an oblong teardrop effect with the Presidents.

The famous Studebaker Hill Holder was available at extra cost on the Six Series, but was standard equipment on the State Commanders and the Presidents. Optional equipment available at extra cost on all State Commander and President models was the vacuum actuated "Miracle Shift." The control for this unit was mounted in the center of the lower part of the dash, which left the floor clear for easier seating of three front seat passengers. Not an automatic shift, the vacuum unit assisted the driver in making smoother up and down shifts, but did not do away with the need for a floor clutch or for normal manual shifting. With the introduction of column shifts in 1939, this unit had no further use.

The company offered a total of 16 models ranging in price from $834 for the 3-passenger Commander Six Coupe to the top of the line State President Eight Convertible Sedan for $1,385. The convertible sedan was back for essentially a one-year offering, in either State Commander or State President form. The car would reappear in 1939 promotional material, but it is believed few if any beyond prototypes were built in 1939 form. This would be the last convertible sedan built by Studebaker, even though specialty body builders did produce a few at a later date. Who wouldn't want to own one of these convertibles today? In fact, when was the

last time that anyone even saw such a car?

The year 1938 was a poor one for the auto industry in general and was particularly poor for the independents. Studebaker's sales fell an amazing 34,786 units, ending the calendar year at 46,207 cars. Still that was enough to actually move Studebaker up to 10th place in the national sales picture, as other companies did even worse.

In 1938 Studebaker once again introduced the style leader among the coupe designs. This was another Loewy creation. Seen here is the lowest priced model for the year replacing the Dictator. It was called the Studebaker Six, available only as a 3-passenger Coupe that weighed 3,190 pounds and delivered for $843. The bumper guards were an accessory item for all "Six" cars.

The Studebaker Six Club Sedan for 1938 was this two-door model that sold for $933. It was the lowest priced Club Sedan sold by Studebaker for the year. This model offered the sleek flowing lines of a sport coupe, but gave the roominess of a sedan. An interesting feature available on all models for the year was that the front seat not only moved backward and forward, but also up and down to accommodate the height of the driver. This was a really helpful innovation that sadly would all but disappear until power seats began their rise to popularity in the mid-1950s.

The 1938 Studebaker Six Cruiser Sedan was the most popular model in the "Six" line of cars. It sold for $943. The easy detection of this series against the Commander and President cars is found in the round head lamps as opposed to the streamlined "faired" lamps the other two series employed. The Studebaker Six rode on the same wheelbase as Commander cars, which was 116.5 inches. These models were referred to as series 7-A cars. A total of 19,260 units were produced among the different models in the "Six" lineup.

A rare model was the 1938 Studebaker Suburban as this station wagon was called. It was classed as a model in the "Six" series of cars. The body builder for the vehicle was the U. S. B. and F. body company. The wagon carried its single spare mounted in the right front fender well. The wood paneling was done in oak on a steel-framed body. Roll-up windows were used in all four doors.

Studebaker's 1938 Commander Coupe was available as a three-passenger model for $912. The Commander cars for 1938 were designated as the 7-A models, the same as the "Six" series. The Coupe offered a wide and deep upholstered shelf behind the three-passenger seat which was useful for small traveling cases, packages, or coats and hats.

Resembling the "Six" a great deal is this Commander series 6-passenger Club Sedan. The basic exterior difference is the streamlined headlamps that this series offered. The absence of bumper guards tells us that these were an extra cost item for the Commander cars. The Club Sedan delivered for $977.

The most popular model in the Commander line was this 1938 4-door Sedan. This model used the famous 226 cubic-inch engine, developing 90 horsepower at 3400 rpm. Talk about a loaded unit! Look at those factory accessories, including the grille guard, bumper guards, radio antenna, door mounted side mirror, wheel discs, wheel trim rings, fender mounted parking lamps, and the very rare oscillating stop signal lantern which illuminated and swung back and forth until the brake pedal was released. Minus all these accessories, the Commander Cruising Sedan delivered for $987.

Rarely ever seen on 1938 Studebakers are the side-mounted spare tire kits. This unit doesn't display even one other approved accessory. Because of the new fender lines, the height of the spares gives an out-of-proportion appearance to the rest of the car's good looks. Unlike the sidemounts of a few years earlier, these did nothing to enhance the car's appearance.

Studebaker was interested in Driver Education even back in 1938. Shown here is a Commander Sedan fitted with a special dual control device, which allowed the teacher to take over in a situation that the student could not handle. This car is well equipped with the approved accessories such as the side cowl antenna, whitewall tires, bumper guards, and the fabric radiator cover which was adjustable for all temperatures. These covers were popular in cold northern climates, as they helped the engine to run warmer, and thus provide more hot water for the heater

Available for only a one-year stay was the 1938 Convertible Sedan in both Commander and President models. This is a Commander example. Both series came with an interior of narrow tufted custom-type leather seat material, with hard-wearing leatherette door panels. Note the full wheel decor and the rare fender guide which is artistically modeled to harmonize with the hood ornament. A total of 22,053 Commander cars were built in all styles for 1938.

A 1938 Commander Convertible Sedan is shown with the top down. This was the Commander's most expensive vehicle for the year, selling at $1,185. It appears strange that Studebaker advertised this model heavily throughout 1938 in all the major magazines, then discontinued it at the end of the model run. But, this was another low year for all manufacturers, with the depression coming back to take its hold even further. Buyers just weren't there, even for the pragmatic cars, let alone for a sharp looking but very expensive and totally impractical model such as this.

The 1938 President Coupe came with a 110-horsepower engine, rated at 3600 rpm. The tire size was 6.50x16 inches, or at extra cost, 7.00x16s were available. The car came with twin sun visors, dual windshield wipers, and a pair of tail lamps mounted in the fenders. Centered on the trunk was the license plate. For the first time this came with a trunk light mounted beneath the license plate, which also illuminated the name Studebaker. This vehicle was the lowest priced President for the year. It sold for $1,058.

A handsome looking 1938 President Club Sedan is parked next to this Loewy-designed New York Central locomotive. Evidently the idea was to compare its power with that of the well-known steam engine, which was used to pull the famed "Broadway Limited" on its daily runs between New York and Chicago. Who could out run whom? Note how the parking lights are very similar to the newly-designed headlamps. This configuration lasted for only one year.

The 1938 President State Club Sedan was one of the sportiest looking cars of the year. Due to its 2-door safety, this model proved to be very popular with families having small children who might be tempted to open rear doors. The Club Sedan went out of the dealership for $1,123. The rear quarter windows acted the same as the front wing window vents, as far as giving the right amount of ventilation to the passengers.

Another "Official Car" was sponsored by Studebaker. This time it was for Colonel Clarence Chamberlain, world famous Trans-Atlantic Flier, who is standing beside the new 1938 President and his aircraft. Note how the wind wings opened on Studebaker's of this era. Only Studebaker offered this style of slanting vent that supposedly prevented rain from entering the driving compartment.

The most expensive car in Studebaker's lineup for 1938 was the President Convertible Sedan, selling for $1,385. How many were produced is not known, but the number must have been very small. Only certain colors were made available to the Convertible Sedan. The choices were: Tulip Cream exterior with green interior; Clay Rust exterior with brown interior; black exterior with vermillion interior, and Palm Beach Tan exterior with a maroon interior. If these did not suit the customer, other choices were available on special order and at extra cost.

The Planar independent suspension was standard equipment on this 1938 Convertible Sedan, as on all other Studebakers for the year. This suspension system was referred to as the "Miracle Ride." This model is the President Convertible Sedan, also known as Model 4-C. It came on the 122-inch wheelbase.

Always being on the lookout for an P.R. event was a reputation Studebaker enjoyed. The company liked having its cars displayed with "Official Car" on the door, at any gathering, in order to tell the public that all was well. Here the Convertible Sedan is acting as the host car for the South Bend Horse Show. From the positioning of the camera, it almost looks as if the horse is in the driver's seat.

The most popular car in the President line for 1938 was this Cruising Sedan. It sold for $10 more than the Club Sedan, being priced at $1,133. A new feature introduced on the 1938 cars in the President line was the Duplex aero-type carburetor. This new device helped to keep the cars from vapor locking in hot weather. Incidentally, this photo shows the President parked in front of a fashionable store named Bullocks, in Westwood Village, California. As of this writing, the store is still there. Besides Bullocks, Westwood is also the home of UCLA!

Seen here is the 1938 President Cruising Sedan in just a little different version. Note the wider trim belt of stainless steel on the door line and the unusual driving lamps mounted on the front bumper brackets. Different stories have come up about this photo: First, that it's an export model only; Second, it was specially built for some unnamed home office executive and, Third, it is an early pre-production example of what was to be a 1938 model. Take your pick. Too bad the photo can't talk. Anyway, it is a stately looking vehicle.

The Coupe Express for 1938 is shown in this book for two reasons, even though some may refer to it as a small pickup truck, and this book isn't dealing with trucks, per se. First off, as the author, I like the design; and secondly, it carries the passenger car front end. The total of these Model K-5s produced from October, 1937, to July, 1938, amounted to an even 1,000. The spare tire mounted in the right fender well was a standard piece of equipment. The canvas canopy was an extra cost option. It is not known if this beauty was based in Windsor, Ontario, or Windsor, Connecticut.

This is a different version of the 1938 Coupe Express classed within the "Six" series of cars. The open bed was the standard version for this half-ton express. These models rode on 6.00x16 inch tires, the same as the regular passenger cars. Possibly this is another Canadian example, as the name on the door states "London"...possibly Ontario?

A really dolled up 1938 Coupe Express is seen here wearing all deluxe Studebaker approved accessories from fog lamps, grille guard, spot light, and the rare vent cowl, to roof mounted antenna. The half-ton's gross vehicle rating was 4,500 pounds. The chassis, cab, and body road weight was 3,200 pounds. The interior of the Coupe-Express was done in cloth but, if the customer wished, a leather-type fabric upholstery was optional at no extra cost. The owner of this vehicle is Harry Keller, from somewhere in California.

The Bender Body Company of Cleveland, Ohio, was another one of the main suppliers of ambulance and funeral coaches which built on Studebaker chassis for a number of years. This example was constructed on a stretched President chassis, and used the 8-cylinder engine that developed 110 horsepower. The wheelbase was 154 inches. This ambulance was called the "Samaritan" by the Bender Company.

The 1938 Bender Westminster hearse was also built on a stretched President chassis. This vehicle is fitted with all factory approved equipment, including fog lamps, spotlight, and parking lamps. As with the ambulance, which shared the same basic Bender body shell, the wheelbase for this unit measured 154 inches. The regular 8-cylinder engine was used. These units were usually sold by Studebaker dealers, but specialty professional car dealers could also order them direct from the factory.

This 1938 Studebaker hearse is another example from the Bender Body Co. The company was glad to receive the additional units in their contract, which had been divided between Superior and themselves in previous years. This example, using President running gear, gave better performance than the Commander cars could offer from the 6-cylinder engine. Note the lack of regular running boards which made it easier for the removal of a casket from the side doors. This example is equipped with a siren if the occasion required it to be put into use for ambulance duty. Probably the vehicle was what was then known as a "Combination Car"...one that had removable interior fittings, and could be converted from ambulance to hearse, or vice versa, with relative ease. Such vehicles were popular in small cities, where a full-time ambulance or hearse was economically impractical. The spare tire is mounted in the front right fender similar to the Suburban Wagon and Coupe Express.

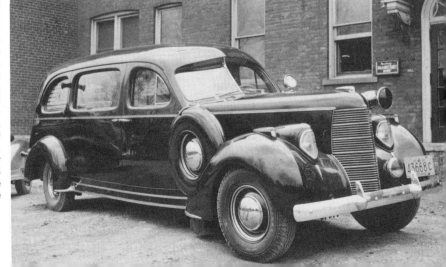

The big news at South Bend didn't come until mid-season this year. But when it did come, it was in the form of a totally new car called the Champion. Essentially the Champion was to the Studebaker of 1939 what the Rockne had been to Studebaker in 1932...only the Champion was successful.

With the discontinuation of the lowest level 6-cylinder line at the end of 1938, the new and much smaller Champion filled the sales slot formerly occupied by the base model. Utilizing a chassis of 110-inch wheelbase, the Champions were available in a total of six models, divided over plain and DeLuxe series, ranging from the plain Business Coupe for $660 to the nicely appointed DeLuxe Cruising Sedan for $800. The tire size was 5.50x16, and the fuel tank held 15 gallons. Again, Budd wheels were used on all Studebakers, including the Champions.

One of the main selling points of the Champion was the economy it offered. Helping in this claim was its performance in this year's Gilmore Economy Run, where it was named the overall winner. Succeeding Gilmore runs in subsequent years would produce similar results. Providing this economy was a new 6-cylinder engine of 164.3 cubic inches which produced 78 horsepower at 4000 rpm. The engine had a bore and stroke of 3x3-7/8 inches.

The regular Commander Six remained as Studebaker's mid-level offering. These cars used the same engines as in 1938, which developed 90 horsepower at 3400 rpm. The wheelbase was 116.5 inches, and standard tires were 6.0x16, though optional 6.25x16 rubber was available. Both Commanders and Presidents gained

greatly in appearance through newly designed front fenders with integral headlights, and new hoods which swept gracefully into very attractive two-piece grilles of thin chromed vertical bars.

The President line, sometimes called the State President, continued to be Studebaker's prestige vehicles. They used their own exclusive chassis of 122 inches, rode on 6.50x16 tires, and were equipped with Studebaker's only 8-cylinder engine, which produced 110 horsepower at 3600 rpm. Most expensive of the lot, President prices ranged from $1,035 for the 3-passenger Custom Coupe to $1,460 for the Convertible Sedan. However, it is not certain if any convertible sedans were actually sold this year, or if the display models were simply prototype cars used for promotional purposes.

This year Studebaker's deluxe appointments included a new fresh air heating and ventilating system, built into the body under the front seat. A new overdrive also became available, which allowed the driver to immediately shift into overdrive. And, the end of the floor shift came about, as each series offered a column gear shift as standard equipment.

With the help of the new Champion, Studebaker sales increased greatly, rising to a remarkable 106,470 units. This represented a gain of 60,263 automobiles, an increase that itself was 1.5-times greater than the total 1938 production. As a result, Studebaker moved into 8th place in the national sales standings for the calendar year.

New for 1939 was the Champion line that came as a mid-year offering. Seen here is the lowest priced model for the season. It is the Custom 3-passenger Coupe that weighed 2,260 pounds and came with a 164.3 cubic-inch 6-cylinder engine that developed 78 horsepower. The model sold for $660. If a 5-passenger model was ordered, the price increased $20. This 1939 Champion Coupe carried a bumper-to-bumper banner telling all that "Champion Leads the Way."

Studebaker furnished a fleet of official staff vehicles for the National Air Races, which were being held September 2 to 4, 1939, at Cleveland, Ohio. This type of P.R. work was something the factory always took part in with great pleasure. Note the neat United Airlines DC-3 in the background. These planes, called "Mainliners" by United, were the flagships of that company's New York to Chicago route. DC-3s seem to have a life expectancy enjoyed by few other mechanical marvels, and thus it is quite possible that this particular plane still survives somewhere in the world...or third world. Can the same be said for the coupe?

# 1939

This 1939 Champion Custom Club Sedan was the lower priced Club Sedan. It weighed 2,330 pounds and cost the owner $700. As a DeLuxe Champion, the vehicle sold for $720. The Champions used 5.50x16-inch tires and rode on a 110-inch wheelbase.

Coast to Coast performance and dependability was what this advertisement claimed for the 1939 Champion Custom 2-door Sedan. It took 14,511 minutes or, would you believe, a little over ten days to go from Coast to Coast. This was a Triple A sanctioned event.

Paul G. Hoffman and Harold S. Vance proudly stand by their new model which put Studebaker back on the road to recovery. This 1939 Champion Custom Cruising Sedan was the lower priced Sedan, delivering for $740.

No, this was not the 1939 "Miss America Pageant." Well, anyway, the car is a 1939 Champion Club Sedan waiting for the holder of a lucky 10-cent ticket to drive it home. Sorry, the girls have to stay.

# 1939

This is a 1939 DeLuxe Champion Cruising Sedan. The unit weighed 2,375 pounds and, being the most expensive Champion for 1939, delivered for $800. The DeLuxe Champions came with broadcloth upholstery, rear seat ash receiver, stainless steel body finishing strip, dual windshield wipers, dual sun visors, dual tail lamps, front door arm rests, carpet on the lower inside of the doors, grained garnish moldings with tenite panel, ventilating rear quarter windows, chrome strips and circle door handle trim.

This is the 1939 Champion DeLuxe Coupe for 3-passengers. It sold for $720, and was popular for fleet use, as attested to by this example owned by the Standard Oil Co. of Indiana. Late in the season, it was available as a 5-passenger model as was the Custom Coupe. Both employed fold-away opera seats behind the split front seat. This example is equipped with unusual circular bumper guards mounted at the ends of the bumpers.

A 1939 Champion DeLuxe 2-door Sedan was the more expensive model as far as 2-door Sedans went. This example weighed 2,345 pounds and cost the owner $760. The Champion models made their introduction in the spring of 1939. The plant began producing in January of 1939 and closed down for 1940 retooling in July of 1939. A total of 33,905 Champions were produced within that time frame.

A model designed as a delivery vehicle for upscale stores was this Champion Club Sedan Delivery, with blanked out rear side windows and an open rear compartment fitted for carrying light cargo. Colburn's Fur Shop, which owned this example, put these window panels to good use to advertise their business. This 1939 Champion is well equipped with all deluxe appointments such as grille guard, whitewall tires, trim rings, and twin side mirrors.

The 1939 Champion Pick-Up Coupe was both practical and economical. The pick-up box fit snugly into the rear deck. This unit was supplied to Studebaker by the Edwards Iron Works of South Bend. A total of 1,200 were produced.

A long-haul drive-away truck stops in front of a dealership with a delivery of new 1939 Champions. The distributor is Chapman Motor Company operating out of Jacksonville, Florida. The models are a Custom Club Sedan and Custom Cruising Sedan on the top, while the tractor is a current Studebaker truck. Note the typical dealership building of that era in the background. It was nice to see the cars enclosed in a building rather than having 500 vehicles sprawled out all over a lot, like dealerships today.

More 1939s are going to a dealership on a Studebaker transport truck. The top vehicles are a 3-passenger Coupe and a Custom Club Sedan. The truck is owned by Maris Automobile Transport of Windsor (Ontario?) so it is possible that these are Canadian Studebakers.

It looks like this was a very early example of what the 1939 Commander Club Sedan was to look like. This pre-production model appears to be void of stainless belt line trim, and the bumper guard equipment is missing. This is a Custom model weighing 3,160 pounds and selling for $955.

The 1939 Commander Coupe was available as a Custom Coupe for 3-passengers, weighing 3,045 pounds and selling for $815. If it was ordered as a DeLuxe, the weight was 3,080 pounds and the selling price was $900. Commanders came with a 226 cubic-inch engine developing 90 horsepower.

# 1939

Truly a one off was this 1939 Commander Convertible Sedan. It almost makes one think that the company had one body left from 1938 Convertible Sedan production and, putting a 1939 front on it, brought it out to see what the reaction might have been. Although it would have been one of the best looking Studebakers of the year, its sales potential probably would have been no better than in 1938...in other words, terrible.

Probably one of the most unusual vehicles to appear in Studebaker guise is this export model, fitted with a gas processor. After World War II began in Europe, gasoline became almost impossible to find in many countries occupied by Nazi Germany. As a result, gas generators of various kinds became available. Usually quite bulky and inefficient, these generators converted wood chips into a butane-like fuel which would at least get the cars from point A to point B. The generators had to be stoked frequently, and reportedly gave a lasting smoke-house aroma to both vehicle and operator. Since the generator occupied the entire trunk area, the spare had to be stored on the roof, while the wood probably went on the back seat. And, once the tires wore out, the vehicle would have been out of business for the duration.

The 1939 President State Coupe came only as a 3-passenger car weighing 3,300 pounds and selling for $1,035, making it the lowest priced President for the year. A plentitude of accessories were available on all 1939 models, including a touch control automatically tuned radio, electric clock, automatic windshield cleaner, controllable spot light, and fog light. Even Studebaker luggage was available singly, or in sets of three.

Studebaker's 1939 State President Club Sedan weighed 3,390 pounds and carried a price tag of $1,100. The 1939 Presidents were produced from September, 1938, until August, 1939, with a production run of 8,205 vehicles. The seating capacity was for six passengers.

The Paul G. Hoffman Studebaker dealership in Los Angeles sponsored this 1939 Commander 4-door State Cruising Sedan for the Gilmore Yosemite Economy Run. The Commander weighed 3,200 pounds and sold for $965. Note the chains on the rear wheels of this vehicle. Since the car is shown in the famed Yosemite National Park at the end of the run, it can be assumed that some snowy mountain driving was encountered enroute. The Standard equipment on the Commander cars for 1939 included Planar independent wheel suspension, Automatic Hill Holder, and Hancock Rotary door latches. Sedans were the most popular model in the Commander line. The Commanders were produced from August, 1938, entering dealerships in September, and continued in production until August, 1939. Commander sales amounted to 43,724 units for the model run.

The 1939 President Cruising Sedan weighed 3,440 pounds. It was the most expensive car Studebaker offered for 1939, listing at $1,110. Its 8-cylinder engine developed 110 horsepower at 3600 rpm, and the fuel tank held 18 gallons.

This 1939 President Cruising Sedan is equipped with side mounted spares and a right-hand spot light. Obviously it is meant for export use. It also wears small driving lamps and special flaps mounted on the front fenders. These flaps look suspiciously like the bullet deflectors shown on some of the police models in the earlier chapters, but there is no information as to the true function of these items.

Here is a rare model, since Studebaker didn't actually build station wagons, per se. This 1939 body was placed on the Commander chassis. The body builder was McVoy and Sons. A spare tire was concealed, with its storage being in the rear floor compartment. How many were produced, is unknown.

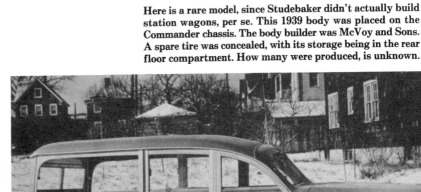

# 1939

True, this isn't a truck book, but neither is the model a true truck since it carries a passenger car front end. This 1939 Commander Coupe Express was rated as a half-ton vehicle. It was equipped the same as regular Commander models, using the 226 cubic-inch engine that developed 90 horsepower. In standard form, the vehicle came only in black. However, it was available at extra cost in Beverly Blue, Dovetone Gray, Cardinal Red, Revere Blue, Forest Green, Chrome Yellow, and Fern Green. These units came with the spare tire mounted in the front right fender. This particular example was owned by the Forest P. Jennings Studebaker Agency, located somewhere in Texas.

This neat looking 1939 Commander Coupe Express came with an original canopy shell fitted with what appears to be solid sides for total protection from inclement weather. This unit also has the deluxe metal spare tire cover and grille guard which were factory-approved extra cost accessories.

A company named Bender Coachworks of Cleveland, Ohio, did funeral and ambulance coachwork on stretched Studebaker chassis during this time. This 1939 funeral coach was one of a few models built by Bender. The contoured roof line was one of the special features. Extra wide rear side doors made it easier for attendants to manipulate the removal of the casket. Most models came equipped with fender skirts with the Studebaker emblem mounted at the bottom. These vehicles were sold by both Studebaker and independent professional car dealers.

Looking quite similar to the Bender hearse is this Bender ambulance, which used the same basic body shell as the hearse. It is equipped with warning siren lights mounted in the roof, and the familiar grille and fender accessory equipment. Spotlights also are additional pieces of necessary equipment. The fender skirts add an additional bit of class to the vehicle. The price of this Bender ambulance on the 1939 Studebaker President chassis is unavailable. The Bender line offered on the Studebaker chassis included the Westminster and Arlington funeral coaches and ambulances, and the Elwood and Elmhurst service cars.

# 1940

As could be expected, the new Champion continued to be the big money maker for Studebaker this year. Economy was still its main selling feature, and plenty of advertising was done along this line in magazines, on the radio, and on billboards. One of the main advertising themes was the fact that the little car averaged 27.25 mpg in a recent Gilmore Economy Run, completing the test at an average speed of 40 mph. The unchanged engine was still the 164.3 cubic inch block that developed 78 hp at 4000 rpm.

The new Commanders and Presidents once more benefitted from redesigned fenders and grilles, again more massive and streamlined. Still built on a 116.25-inch wheelbase, the Commanders continued to utilize their 226 cubic inch 6-cylinder engine that developed 90 hp at 3400 rpm. They shared the 18-gallon fuel tank with the Presidents, but the Budd wheels took 6.25x16 tires while the President's took 6.50x16. The President series, sometimes referred to as State President, was still built on a 122-inch wheelbase chassis, and its 8-cylinder engine of 250.4 cubic inches was still rated at 110 hp at 3600 rpm.

Studebaker claimed a total of 28 models this year. Actually, this figure is misleading as 10 of these so-called models really were simply sub-series upgrades brought about by a new two-tone paint scheme with accompanying interior trim, while 12 others resulted from the four styles in the Champion line being spread over Custom, Custom Deluxe, and Deluxe sub-series. In its price range, Studebakers went from the 3-passenger Champion Custom Coupe at $660 to $1,135 for the President Sedan in the Deluxe Two-Tone sub-series.

Again, primarily due to the Champion, Studebaker saw its calendar year production rise, going up over 10,000 units to a new high of 117,091. This was certainly enough to keep Studebaker in the 8th sales position.

This is the 1940 Champion Custom Coupe. It was available as a 3-passenger or 5-passenger vehicle. The two small opera seats could be neatly folded in the back compartment when not in use. As a 3-passenger, it sold for $660 and, if the opera seat model was ordered, it delivered for $695. The 5-passenger was the more popular version.

This 1940 Champion Custom Cruising Sedan, wearing its 1940 Indiana license plates, is parked while the young couple is getting ready to do a little fishing. He apparently is demonstrating how the antenna could be used for a fishing pole. The car delivered for $740. Who today would go fishing with a necktie on? The Champion 4-door sedan rode on a 110-inch wheelbase. A total of 66,284 1940 Champion models made their appearance for the model run.

A rare unit designed for sales people was the 2-door Champion Delivery Sedan, available either as a Custom or DeLuxe. This particular model is classed by some as the Sedan Delivery. It had the rear window quarters blanked out, while the rear portion of the interior had no seat, but was totally fitted for cargo hauling. Note the special bumper accessory guards on the rear bumper. This unit was owned by a spice and seasonings dealer out of Bellville, Ill.

The 1940 Champion DeLuxe Club Sedan was a very popular model with families having small children. The vehicle weighed 2,340 pounds and sold for $745. The two-tone paint option was available at extra cost and was becoming popular with Studebaker owners.

A young star in 1940, by the name of none other than Judy Garland, stands proudly by her first car, a 1940 Champion DeLuxe Business Coupe. The car weighed 2,360 pounds and sold for $740.

The 1940 Studebaker Champion 4-door Sedans generally were not seen parading around town with all of this hoopla spread over their bodies. This DeLuxe Cruising Sedan was used for advertising "Smashing, Crashing and Rolling Automobiles" event sponsored by Jack Derby's Hell Drivers. One benefit of the event was that it was a fund raiser for the Harryanna Crippled Children's Hospital, sponsored by the Benevolent Order of Elks. The show took place Sunday, December 10, 1939, shortly after the 1940 models made their debut. The car is nicely equipped with fog lamps, grille guard, and cowl mounted antenna. For sure, this model had no intention of participating in the thrill show, except to possibly make a parade or pace lap. Such thrill shows were very popular in the decades just before and after World War II, but died in the early 1960s as television and movies produced stunts that the shows couldn't even dream of duplicating on local fair grounds tracks.

The 1940 Champion DeLuxe Cruising Sedan was the more popular 4-door Sedan in the Champion line. It weighed 2,375 pounds and could be driven home for $785, being the most expensive Champion for the year. This vehicle carries the deluxe grille guard and factory approved fog lamps. According to the U.S. map painted on the side, it was either engaged in or getting ready for some long distance promotional tour. It is wearing Utah license plates.

This is the 1940 Commander DeLuxe Cruising Sedan which weighed 3,200 pounds and sold for $965. Commander models rode on a 116-inch wheelbase. Note that the example is considered a two-tone model, with the window sills done in a contrasting color to the body. Total Commander sales for 1940 amounted to 34,477 units. The Commander Custom Sedan was the lower priced version available for $55 less than DeLuxe Cruising Sedan.

The 1940 President Coupe was available as a 3-passenger car, or could be ordered with small opera seats making it a 5-passenger vehicle. The 3-passenger sold for $1,055 and the 5-passenger was available for $1,205. Both versions rode on the 122-inch wheelbase.

The President State Club Sedan was actually a 2-door Sedan, but did not give the appearance of the "Old Maids Coach." It was actually a good looking vehicle that drew a fair amount of buyers to its corner. It weighed 3,370 pounds and sold for $1,055. A total of 6,444 President Cars were manufactured spread over the three body styles in 1940. The Club Sedan also was available as a Commander, weighing 3,125 pounds and selling for $925.

Another Studebaker received the honor of being photographed in front of the home office. This example was one of the official cars used for the 1940 running of the 28th Annual Memorial Day Indianapolis 500 mile race. It is the President 4-door Sedan.

Probably it is a doctor who is very proud of his new 1940 President 4-door Sedan. The vehicle is parked next to the Saunders Memorial Hospital. The President is equipped with full wheel discs, trim rings, and the accessory grille guard. Note the special stamped running board with the "S" implanted in the center below the B-pillar. This was done on many President models during this era. A note that helps distinguish Presidents from Commanders, besides the President's longer wheelbase, is the heavier meshed grille pattern used on the Presidents. This vehicle was the top of the line, weighing 3,440 pounds and selling for $1,095.

# 1940

This rear view shows off the Shrock 1940 President Speedster. I was privileged to drive this unit at their home in Coalsport, Pa., in the interim of Carlisle and Hershey, 1992. What a car! The vehicle uses the regular 122-inch wheel base. With top down, the 1940 President Speedster cuts quite a figure. It also sports all Studebaker approved accessories for the year, too, but South Bend never saw anything resembling this beautiful boat-tail.

Another one-off 1940 Studebaker is this beautiful example. It started out life as a President Club Sedan, before it was in an accident. Through the skilled craftsmanship of two gentlemen named Dave and Tom Shrock, it was put back together as this "pride and joy" for their Studebaker collection. It used the regular President 8-cylinder engine with overdrive developing 110 horsepower. From this angle, the car could easily be mistaken for a Lincoln-Zephyr.

This view is of the 1940 President Speedster's dashboard. Nothing is altered from the stock dash, and everything is in its keeping for the period. Genuine red leather upholstery was used on seats and door panels. The dash was done in cream, the same as the exterior.

Its really classic looking, but who would want to ride in it, unless as a necessity? This ambulance is from a company named Bender, from Cleveland, Ohio, which had supplied bodies to Studebaker for several years for both ambulance and funeral car service. This ambulance is nicely decked out with deluxe trim rings, whitewalls, fog lamps, spotlight, side-mounted spares, and even fender skirts. The skirts wouldn't be too practical for a snow-laden night or a blowout during an emergency call. The price for the unit is unavailable. The model used the President engine and running gear.

Truly a one-off is this handsome 1940 President Convertible Sedan with body by Derham of Rosemont, Pa. Studebaker did not build any open cars of their own in 1940. In fact, the 1938 Convertible Sedan, shown in that portion of the book, was Studebaker's last open car until 1947.

# 1941

Author's Note: Even authors have favorites, and thus not only have a thing about all 1941 cars, but the 1941 Studebakers really rank at the top of my preference ladder. Their clean lines, special two-toned bodies, and the large array of factory approved accessories really make them special "lookers" as far as I am concerned. The only thing I ever had against them was a Studebaker salesman who came to our house one Saturday afternoon in 1941. He thought that my mother had called him to come to the house and he wanted to take us out for a demonstration ride in the new Champion. All hell broke loose when I was told to go to the door and explain who had called. All I had wanted was for the agency to send me a catalog on the new models, but he failed to see the humor in this request. In fact, when he saw his 10 year old kid in front of him, he became furious. My father never did forgive him or the agency for his reaction, and secretly, I felt that I shouldn't care for Studebakers either. To this day I can still recall the event very clearly. However, all was forgiven on my part, and shortly after, I started liking Studebakers once again, minus one particular salesman, of course.

As to the 1941 models, Studebaker again offered three lines, the Champion, Commander, and President. These were sub-divided into Champion Custom, Custom Deluxe, and Deluxe-Tone; Commander Custom, Deluxe-Tone, and Skyway, and President Custom, Deluxe Tone, and Skyway. The result was 30 separate models, albeit there was not that much difference between the various trim levels.

A complete upgrading took place with the 1941 models. The Champion engine was now a 170 cubic inch Six developing 117 hp at 4000 rpm. The Commander remained a 6-cylinder car, but its 226 cubic inch block was rated at 94 hp at 3600 rpm. The large President retained its 250 cubic inch straight-8 engine, but it was now rated at 117 hp at 4000 rpm.

The Champions retained the 15 gallon fuel supply, while the full-size models still had an 18 gallon tank. Exterior styling saw a revision of the frontal area, plus totally new fenders and greatly revised bodies featuring a lack of exterior running boards. All styling was by Raymond Loewy. The Champions used their old 110-inch wheelbase chassis, but the wheelbase length of the larger models was increased to 119 inches for the Commander and 124.5 inches for the President series. Champions came with the same 5.50x16 tires; Commanders used 6.25x16 size, and the President employed 7.0x16 tires for the model run.

To help sales, a new variety of upholstery combinations and harmonizing color treatments added to customer appeal. A choice of three kinds of upholstery in eight colors was available among the different series, and new single and two-tone paint combinations proved to be very popular.

Prices ranged from $690 for a 3-passenger Champion Coupe to $1,235 for the President Skyway Land Cruiser 4-door Sedan. Sales climbed again, with the calendar year total hitting 119,325. However, this was not enough to hold 8th place, and so Studebaker once more found itself in 9th ranking in the national sales.

A 1941 Studebaker Champion Custom Coupe for 3-passengers went to work as a salesman's car for the United Dressed Beef Co. of New York. It delivered for $660, being the lowest priced 1941 Studebaker for the year. It came on the 110-inch wheelbase, weighing 2,290 pounds. A 15-gallon fuel tank was employed on the Champion line.

This 1941 Custom 5-passenger Coupe delivered for $725, and weighed 2,335 pounds. The door decal on the vehicle says it belongs to American District Telegraph Co., a fire and burglary alarm service that is still in business today. Note that the Custom models don't carry the stainless rocker molding, like the DeLuxe line.

Again, the South Bend Police picked Studebaker for its patrol vehicles. This 1941 Champion Club Sedan looks like it just came in from a blistery cold snowy night. This is the $730 Custom model which was the lower priced Club Sedan that weighed 2,390 pounds. Behind it is a relatively rare 1937 Chrysler Royal Six Sedan, the only Chrysler 4-door to use fastback styling. It is known that 1,200 such Chryslers were built, but it is not certain how many Custom Club Sedans left the plant.

A 1941 Champion Custom 4-door Cruising Sedan looks much like its DeLuxe brother, except for trim and interior appointments. The unit weighed 2,435 pounds and carried a price of $770. The engines were the same...170 cubic inches, developing 80 horsepower at 4000 rpm.

A basic 1941 Champion Custom Club Sedan sold for $730. A total of 84,910 Champions cars were produced for the 1941 model run. This example came equipped with only one windshield wiper.

The middle series of 1941 Champion Custom DeLuxe Coupes were available in 3 or 5-passenger models. The 3-passenger sold for $720 and 5-passenger models delivered for $755. Champion models were produced from August, 1940, to July, 1941.

# 1941

The 1941 Champion DeLuxe was available as a 3 or 5-passenger Coupe. The 3-passenger sold for $755, while the 5-passenger delivered for $790. Both rode on the 110-inch wheelbase. This example displays Studebaker's fashionable two-tone paint combination in the belt line. Looks like the "Fightin' Irish" are getting ready for a Saturday afternoon clobber.

The neat appearance of this 1941 Champion Custom DeLuxe Cruising Sedan offered an array of harmonizing exterior and interior colors. This was a model in the middle class of Champion vehicles selling for $800. It rode on the regular 110-inch wheelbase.

The Commander Cruising Sedan, as shown here, came in three versions: This example, being the lowest priced model for $985; the Delux-tone Cruising Sedan (applies to two-tone models) for $1,050, and the Skyway Cruising Sedan for $1,075.

Studebaker's most popular Champion model for 1941 was this DeLuxe Cruising Sedan. It weighed 2,415 pounds and sold for $835, making it the most expensive Champion for the year. The two-tone belt line was an option many people ordered. Whitewalls also were an option.

This is the 1941 Commander Custom Sedan Coupe. It was the lower priced Sedan Coupe in the Commander line. It weighed 3,160 pounds and sold for $965, making it the lowest priced Commander model for 1941.

This is the lowest priced 1941 Commander Custom Land Cruiser. Note it doesn't come with the fender stainless trim like other Commander models. The 6-passenger sedan weighed 3,160 pounds and delivered for $1,030. A total of 41,996 Commander models were built in 1941.

The 1941 Commander Delux-tone Cruising Sedan weighed 3,125 pounds and delivered for $1,050. Note: This model wears the header mounted antenna not seen on many 1941 Studebakers. It also sports the front fender spears.

Outside the home office sits a fleet of 1941 Commander Sedans waiting for these gentlemen to take the keys and head for their designated areas. The two-tone paint combinations were not factory, but probably were done as a fleet company's order.

The 1941 Commander Skyway Sedan-Coupe was the more popular version of the Sedan Coupes in the Commander line. This model weighed 3,240 pounds and sold for $1,055. It, too, came on the 119-inch wheelbase. The Commanders sported a 226 cubic-inch engine that developed 94 horsepower.

The newly styled body for 1941 is shown here. This is a 1941 Commander DeLux-tone Land Cruiser Sedan. This model sports the fender stainless trim as standard equipment. The car weighed 3,260 pounds and carried a price tag of $1,095. This type of sedan was a very popular style among many manufacturers at the time, including Chrysler and General Motors.

This three-quarter view shows off the nice frontal appearance of this California-based Commander Skyway Land Cruiser Sedan. This was the most expensive model in the 1941 Commander lineup, selling for $1,105.

This President Custom Cruising Sedan was the lowest priced President on the market in 1941. It delivered for $1,115. The vehicle weighed 3,385 pounds and came on the 124-inch wheel base.

Shown beside a pool party is this 1941 President Custom Land Cruiser. The Custom models offered the fender skirts only as an extra cost feature. This model weighed 3,405 pounds and sold for $1,030.

For 1941 the President Deluxe-tone Cruising Sedan was priced at $1,180. This example rode on 7.00x16-inch tires. A total of 6,994 Presidents were delivered for the 1941 model run. Note the side cowl vent that became a feature for Studebaker, beginning with the 1941 cars and continuing in certain body styles right through until the last car got off the line.

# 1941

The 1941 President DeLux-tone Cruising Sedan was developed under the direction of Raymond Loewy. It offered the customer five exterior two-tone combinations and three harmonizing interior color combinations. A choice of leather or cloth bolsters also was optional.

The 1941 President Skyway Sedan-Coupe looked virtually the same as the Commander except for its wheelbase. President models rode on the 124-inch wheelbase and had the 8-cylinder engine developing 117 horsepower. The Skyway Coupes in both series employed the one-piece windshield. This example is equipped with fender skirts, white sidewall tires, full wheel decor, and the directional parking lamp units. It sold for $1,185.

All Commander and President models carried the center piece front bumper guard equipment. But the outer bumper guards and end tips, which were optional equipment, gave the car a wider appearance. The Skyway Sedan Coupes came as two-tone models at no extra cost. Stainless strips in the rear quarter scuff pads were standard.

The top of the line for Cruising Sedan models is this President Skyway Cruiser. It weighed 3,500 pounds and carried a price tag of $1,205. Note the lack of belt line and hood side trim molding on the Skyway models. Fender skirts were part of the package.

# 1941

Studebaker's most expensive model for 1941 was the President Skyway Land Cruiser 4-door Sedan. The model delivered with skirts, full wheel discs and trim rings, and with whitewall tires for $1,235. It weighed in at 3,520 pounds.

This must have been an early version or a prototype for the President line for 1941. It came equipped with the optional stainless trim on the bottom of the fenders and carried special Studebaker emblems mounted on the fender skirts. This two-tone President, done in black and cream, was one of Loewy's special paint combinations. such paint jobs were a big help in selling the cars. He seemed to know what pleased the public.

The depth of the 1941 Champion Coupe's trunk is easily seen here where a person six feet tall could curl up for a long winter's nap. The spare tire and tools were stored beneath the luggage shelf. Actually, this unit was not a basic camper, but was promoted as a way to use such coupes for emergency ambulance service. Not designed to replace standard ambulances, such units would have been used only in major disasters where regular ambulance services were strained beyond capacity. The metal fixture surrounding the person was fixed solidly to the trunk floor. Its sole purpose was to hold the removable stretcher in place while the victim was being transported.

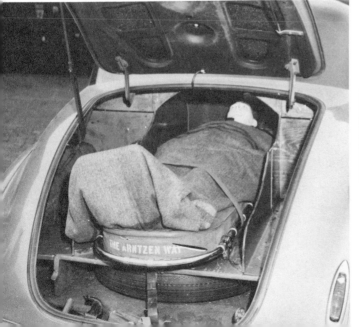

This vehicle was Studebaker's answer for a pick-up coupe... take one coupe, remove trunk deck, and slide in a box! The smart appearance of the 1941 Champion Coupe, when converted to a pick-up, made it a credit to any business. A tarpaulin canvas top was also available at extra cost. The removable pick-up box could be handled by one person. It measured 65 inches long on the floor and was 31 inches wide.

If Studebaker made a mistake in 1942, it was in giving extensive renovations to the Champion and a total new face to both the Commanders and Presidents. Barely had the model year gotten underway, when the infamous day of Dec. 7, came about, and headlines concerning Pearl Harbor and World War II obliterated the nation's further thoughts of any cars, let alone Studebaker.

New on the 1942 Commander and President models was the entire run of front sheet metal; the grille, and the parking lamps. These lamps were now situated within the ends of the grille, directly below the headlights. Meanwhile, the Champion parking lights were incorporated into the headlight unit. New bumpers were designed for each series. The Commander and President models carried the license within guards centered in the bumpers, both front and rear. Champion models used this same form only on the front, while the rear license plate remained mounted on the trunk, where it had been in the previous years. Both the Commander and President lines retained three trim levels, now known as Custom, Deluxe, and Skyway, but the Champion line offered only Custom and Deluxe models.

Mechanically, the big news was a new automatic transmission, available only on the Commander and President models. Called "Turbo-Matic," it consisted of a fluid coupling, vacuum operated clutch, and a conventional 3-speed transmission with a kick-down overdrive. The clutch pedal was eliminated, and the need for manual shifting virtually done away with. The gear selector was of the normal column-mounted type. However, Second gear was referred to as "Traffic Range," while High was called "Cruising Range." After reaching a speed of 15 mph, the transmission would automatically go into overdrive. When the accelerator was pressed all the way down, it then returned to High. Very few of these units were ever delivered due first to customer resistance and secondly to all of the shortages caused by raw materials going into military production.

In other mechanics, the cars were essentially the same as in 1941. However, a rather gimmick-like item was a new radio with the station selector mounted on the steering column for easy reach of the driver.

Because of material shortages and war-time inflation, Studebaker prices increased roughly $100 per model over the 1941 cars. The Champion 3-passenger Coupe now sold for $785, while the top of the line President Skyway Land Cruiser went home for $1,340. Because car production was curtailed in January, 1942, in order to switch to war related items, only 9,285 cars rolled out of South Bend for the calendar year. Still, this was enough to place Studebaker back into 8th place in the national ranks.

For 1942, the Champion received a nice frontal facelift. This is the lowest priced example, a 3-passenger Coupe in the Custom series, selling for $785, and weighing 2,440 pounds. It also came as a 5-passenger Coupe for $820 and weighed an additional 25 pounds. Note the military theme. With war clouds blanketing Europe, military backdrops were becoming popular in ads and publicity photos.

The New York City Police Department was fortunate enough to have a fleet order in before regular 1942 car production ceased. They ordered a healthy number of Custom 3 and 5-passenger Coupes for city patrol. Note these models have shaded headlamps mandated for blackout night driving. The eyelids kept the light pointed toward the ground, and prevented it from shining upward, in the event of a night air attack. The models still received chrome components.

The 1942 Champion Custom Club Sedan for 6-passenger weighed 2,495 pounds and sent out the door for $815. This model didn't receive as much bright trim as the new Deluxstyle. The absence of rocker moldings and rubber scuff pads are the noticeable differences on this car.

The lower priced 1942 Champion Custom Cruising Sedan weighed 2,520 pounds and sold for $845. Champion production amounted to 29,678 units for its short model run. The bright work wasn't as plentiful as on 1941 cars, and disappeared completely before the end of the run as wartime mandates dried up the supply of raw materials.

This is the new top of the line Champion Double Date Coupe for 1942. It weighed 2,475 pounds and sold for $845. The fender skirts were an accessory. It also came as a Custom with less trim, costing $810. The stainless trim beneath the window line was a distinguishing mark between this and custom coupes.

This is the more expensive 1942 Champion Deluxstyle Club Sedan. It delivered for $850 and weighed 2,520 pounds. Very few were produced between August, 1941, and January, 1942. This is an early production model with the extra cost whitewalls. Being the Deluxstyle, the rubber scuff shields and rocker moldings were standard.

Seen in the factory parking area for "Brass Hat" employees, sits this top of the line Champion Delux Cruising Sedan. It definitely is an early production model with all its pre-World War II bright work in place. It delivered for $880, making it the most expensive Champion for 1942. It continued with the 170 cubic-inch engine that developed 80 horsepower.

The 1942 Commander Custom Sedan Coupe was the lowest priced Commander for the year. It weighed 3,200 pounds and sold for $1,075. It doesn't carry as much bright trim as the Skyway Coupes did. A Deluxstyle Sedan Coupe sold for $1,120 and the Skyway Sedan Coupe delivered for $1,155.

This 1942 Commander Custom Cruising Sedan weighed 3,265 pounds and delivered for $1,095. It employed the regular 6-cylinder engine that developed 94 horsepower.

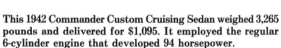

The 1942 Commander Deluxstyle Land Cruiser rode on the 119-inch wheelbase. Weighing 3,305 pounds, it sold for $1,175. Studebaker continued using its self-stabilizing planar suspension that it introduced back in 1935, and also its double-acting hydraulic shock absorbers, assuring a very smooth ride. In addition to this Deluxstyle there was the Sky Land Cruiser Sedan which was the most expensive Commander for the year, selling for $1,210 and weighing 3,540 pounds.

This 1942 Deluxstyle Commander Cruising Sedan is done in one of its optional two-tone paint combinations. This unit weighed 3,280 pounds and delivered for $1,140. Commander sales for 1942 amounted to 17,500. "Deluxstyle" was a newly coined word used this year only.

A 1942 Commander Skyway Sedan-Coupe was the most expensive of this style in Commander form. It delivered for $1,155 and weighed 3,240 pounds. This unit carries the skirts, plastic wheel trim rings, and directional lights, located in the fender marker above the headlamp unit.

Looking very much like its smaller brother, the Commander, is this 1942 President Custom Cruising Sedan. The most noticeable difference was the additional five inches in the wheelbase. This 124-inch car weighed 3,485 pounds and sold for $1,225. Its mate, the DeLuxe Cruising Sedan, weighed fifteen pounds more and delivered for $1,270.

Nicely accessorized with as many extra cost items as could be ordered, is this 1942 President Custom Land Cruiser. The vehicle displays the white plastic wheel trim, skirts, and directional signals. Being the lowest-priced President Sedan, it delivered for $1,130.

# 1942

Totally blocking a good view of an early B-17 bomber is the 1942 President Deluxstyle Sedan Coupe that weighed 3,455 pounds and sold for $1,250. This was the middle-priced model of the President Sedan Coupes. The President Custom delivered for $1,205 and top model Skyway Sedan Coupe went out for $1,285. The interior of the Deluxstyle models came in a choice of Canda cloth or a soft worsted cord with welted in piping in a contrasting color. Upholstery fabrics were available in gray or tan.

The 1942 President Deluxstyle Land Cruiser Sedan weighed 3,515 pounds delivered for $1,305. It was the middle model of President Sedans for 1942. It was fortunate enough to receive a set of whitewall, which marks it as a very early 1942 model.

This 1942 President Skyway Sedan Coupe was the most expensive of the Sedan Coupes. It listed for $1,285 and weighed 3,475 pounds. Most of these models were beginning to be delivered with fewer deluxe items. As an example, this model usually came with fender skirts...but not so on this one. This model also lacks the hood and body belt line stainless trim, which was the distinguishing mark between it and other Sedan-Coupe models. A total of only 3,500 Presidents were manufactured in the short model run.

A very early 1942 President Skyway Land Cruiser Sedan is equipped with whitewall tires, but is minus the deluxe wheel trim that Land Cruisers generally had. It does have the full rocker trim molding extending into the front fenders, which mid-season cars didn't receive. The stainless beltline trim is unusual for this model.

Here sits the top of the line for 1942. It's the Skyway Land Cruiser Sedan riding on its 124-inch wheelbase. This model weighed 3,540 pounds, being the heaviest vehicle for 1942 from Studebaker, and also the most expensive, selling at $1,340. Note: Since whitewalls were almost non-existent on 1942 cars, this unit sports the white plastic beauty rims. It also has the fender-mounted directional signals. The President Skyway Land Cruiser came with fender skirts as standard equipment, but these were optional on other models. It is minus the stainless trim at the bottom fender line which was omitted on mid-season cars.

This was the last Studebaker to roll down the line before the assembly geared for full wartime production. The photo was taken January 31, 1942. Note the "blackout" grille. Also, the headlamp bezels haven't been installed. The model is a President Skyway Sedan.

This example was what a proposed 1942 or possibly a 1943 Studebaker was to look like if World War II hadn't entered the scene. The vehicle came with a lower rub molding and DeSoto (circa 1942) enclosed headlamps. The car was the work of Bob Bourke, a designer under the direction of Raymond Loewy

# 1943 - 1945

Although Studebaker was exclusively engaged in war production from January, 1942, onward, it actually had become involved with defense work by late 1940. The K-Series of trucks that Studebaker initially supplied to the Allied forces were commonplace in Europe, and often were found in the hands of the German Army as that force engaged in its early conquests. These vehicles were virtually indestructible, and it seems that the Germans knew a good vehicle when they saw it, and therefore confiscated as many as they could possibly find. Maybe too, they just liked the Teutonic ring of the name "Studebaker."

By February, 1942, the South Bend plant was totally involved with government contracts. During the years of 1942 to 1945, over $1.2 billion was spent with Stude-

baker. Much of this came from the production of 197,678 trucks; 25,124 copies of the famous amphibious carriers known as the Weasel, and 63,789 Curtiss-Wright engines built under contract for the B-17 bombers.

With these contracts, Studebaker was able to give its stockholders a dividend check in 1943, for the first time since their day of going into receivership. During 1944, the government sales were at a record high of $415 million. From 1943 to July, 1945, when the war clouds finally cleared, the U.S. Army leased the 800-acre proving grounds at South Bend to test various trucks, cargo carriers, transport vehicles, half tracks, etc.

Was Studebaker doing its part to help the country during these war-torn years? It seems that the answer is obvious.

Sometime before 1942, but still in the World War II era, Studebaker received a contract to build military vehicles for what would become our European Allies. This is a 1939 K-Series truck the company was producing for overseas shipment to France, Belgium, and Holland. Rated at 2-to-4 tons, it was quite similar to trucks being built by GMC for the same customers. Ironically, many of these trucks wound up in Nazi supply units, after Europe was overrun. At least the Germans had no trouble pronouncing the name "Studebaker."

You'd almost think the 6 x 6 was in the Sahara Desert on a special maneuver. Not so. This event was taking place in a special soft sand area of the Indiana Dunes along Lake Michigan. Studebaker had procured and prepared this area to test their trucks. This way, when some actual event did occur in far away land, the rugged vehicles would be ready. Note that dual tires have been placed on the front as well as the rear wheels, to assist in both flotation and traction.

This is the short wheelbase 2 to 5-ton cargo truck with a winch that Studebaker was famous for building. All were virtually the same, and were built under a government contract that lasted from 1942 to 1945. Studebaker trucks of this type played a large part in building the famed Alcan Highway, but otherwise were relatively rare in the armed forces.

Looking basically the same as the short wheelbase version was this long wheelbase model of the Studebaker 6x6. While the short wheelbase measured 148 inches, this model's ran 162 inches. The spare on the short model was usually carried in a vertical position, between the 108-inch body and the cab. On the long model, the 144-inch long body allowed the spare to be carried in a horizontal mode.

In 1942 to 1945, many of these heavy-duty pieces of equipment were on our highways when in convoy. This one is shown minus its roof canvas roof and cross bows, which could be installed on a minute's notice, if needed. It apparently was photographed in the parking area of the South Bend assembly plant. Although Studebaker was a prime producer of such military trucks, a high percentage of the actual production went to Russia under the Lend-Lease program, and was not used by the U.S. forces.

This later model 6x4,  2 to 5-ton cargo truck is ready to leave South Bend for duty on foreign soil. This example was produced April 10, 1943. Notice that this model still uses the sheet metal of the Studebaker commercial cab that was developed in the late 1930s. Studebaker trucks also used flat fenders, while the counterparts built by International and GMC had curved fenders.

Showing its qualities of accelerating up steep hills is this US 6-62, 6x6 long wheelbase Army transport truck. That winch may be ready for assisting someone in difficulty, or for pulling the truck itself out of a deep mud hole. Similar trucks were being built by International, GMC, and Reo, but it appears that only Studebaker used the flat-top fenders and commercial-style cab. However, some later Reo production also picked up these sheet metal parts from Studebaker, and in fact looked just like Studebaker models.

Who said they couldn't carry everything? These examples of the Studebaker 6x4, 2 to 5-ton cargo vehicles are totally loaded down with some unidentifyable types of containers, which themselves are loaded down with crates of unknown content. According to the photo caption, these vehicles are transporting military equipment to the front. However, by the looks of the background, it is more likely that they are at work on the Alcan Highway, where many of these trucks spent their life.

Nearing the end of the line, is this 1942, 2 to 5-ton cargo semi-tractor. A few last items are needed for completion, namely the bumper and winch are most noticeable. Note on the top of its 14-bar vertical grille is the name "Studebaker." Later in the war, these name plates were removed by military order. Oddly, few of these 4x6 Studebakers saw service in the U.S. Most went either to the Alcan Highway project or to Russia under the Lend-Lease program. After the war, the Russians simply copied the design for their own production, and for decades turned out virtual carbon copies of this well-designed truck under the GAZ nameplate.

Reaching the end of the line is this 1942, 6 x 6, 2 to 5-ton cargo truck, shown here receiving its general purpose body. Note the heavy duty winch, which was probably put to good service more than once in its hours of service. Although Studebaker assembled the trucks, the company did not build the engines. These were 6-cylinder units of 320 cubic inches supplied by Hercules. In addition to building wheeled vehicles and Weasels, Studebaker's other main contract called for the assembly of approximately 64,000 Wright Cyclone 9-cylinder radial engines for use in B-17 Flying Fortresses.

A very important piece of equipment was the fuel tank truck needed for refueling aircraft and larger vehicles while on maneuvers. Most of these photos have a code number for 1942 which, apparently, is when these vehicles were assembled for active duty. Despite their almost identical appearance, Studebaker 6x6 trucks had very little in common with 6x6 trucks produced by GMC and International, and very few parts were interchangeable.

This early heavy duty 6x6 tractor is pulling a 32-foot trailer of lumber which possibly will be used for the building of barracks at some army camp. The vehicle has 18 tires to carry its load, similar to today's 18-wheeler semi configuration, but a bit unusual in 1942. The "Studebaker" nameplate just below the hood edge indicates that this is a very early unit, as military restrictions did away with such nameplates later in the production period.

This strange looking thing was a 1941 prototype that Studebaker built as a possible mount for a 75mm gun. Dual controls were employed so that the vehicle could be driven equally well in either direction, and thus not have to make turn arounds during heavy combat conditions. A single driver's seat with a flip-back was employed. Placement of the engine on the side helped to keep the silhouette low. Known as Pilot No. 2, the project never went beyond this single prototype.

A view looking down upon a chassis built September 2, 1942, showing the ruggedly-built unit before body components are installed. The experimental vehicle, known as the Model LC, used an unorthodox arrangement of having the motor on the right, fuel tank on the left, and driver in the center of a relatively compact 1-1/2-ton cargo hauler. Although the design was innovative, it was just too weird for the military, and only a couple of prototypes were built.

# 1943 - 1945

Weasels were the big thing Studebaker was noted for during World War II. Created in a top secret project primarily as an attack vehicle to be used against Nazi installations in Norway, the Weasel proved to be one of the most versatile vehicles of the war. It is shown here in pre-production testing, probably in the Indiana Dunes near Lake Michigan.

Weasels could go and do almost anything asked of them. Shown here is one almost standing on its head. By being trained, the skilled drivers could either accelerate or decelerate in a fashion allowing the unit to nose down smoothly and avoid a rough crash landing. Not particularly large, Weasels were only about 10.5 feet long overall, and 5.5 feet wide.

One of the early wartime photos taken at the Studebaker Administration Building shows some of the employees who had entered military service. The amphibious Weasel will long be remember for all it did in World War II. This is the later T24 version, which has its tracks reversed so that the low end was at the front and the high end at the rear for better climbing ability. A full compliment of five passengers, including the driver, was all that a Weasel could hold, while many were designed as 4-passenger units. In all, Studebaker completed 25,124 Weasels by the time the contract was cancelled.

Demonstrating the qualities the Weasel had and all it could do is this factory photo. With these gents in suit, tie, and hat, it seems very likely that this is one of the first Weasels out of the plant, being tested by a group of factory engineers. Surely the Weasel never transported many people in this attire.

According to information supplied by the factory archives, "Weasel after Weasel is shown entering fast-moving water somewhere in the South Pacific to pick up troops who are anxiously awaiting their arrival." Actually, the Weasels were often the first motorized vehicles that many of the primitive tribes in the South Pacific had ever seen. These remote natives were introduced to the age of mechanization by the Weasels primarily because these were the only vehicles that could penetrate the dense wet jungles of the islands that were home to these tribes. Even today, Weasels continue to work in remote parts of the world, mostly in Third World countries where basic transportation still remains in a primitive state.

This amphibious Weasel came to life on December 17, 1942, according to information on the back of the original photo. The enclosed top was beneficial when the vehicle was destined for use in the Arctic, as indicated by the white paint job. The engine, a 6-cylinder Studebaker model of 170 cubic inches, was placed in the rear, with vent doors in the body deck to allow for exhaust and cooling air.

No, Studebaker did not build steam locomotives. But people tend to forget that World War II occurred in pre-diesel days, and steam locomotion was the main motive power on the nation's railroads. This engine is one of at least two good size yard or switch engines that spent their lives shuttling freight cars around the vast Studebaker complex at South Bend. Cars and trucks have come a long way since the 1940s, but railroad engines have come quite a bit further.

This 1943 Weasel is swimming deeply in an Arctic river with a small Eskimo boy alongside in his kayak. Note its light equipment on the front for possible night use. The Navy Sea Bees used many Weasels in Alaska, where they really proved themselves by their ability to cross snow, water, tundra, marsh and solid ground all in one trip, and with no time consuming modifications having to be made to go from one type of terrain to the next.

Studebaker production began in December of 1945, with the first cars rolling off a civilian production line after three years of military manufacturing. As could be expected, these 1946 models were merely a minor face-lifted version of 1942 stock.

At first, due to the minimum allotment of raw steel that the factory was given, only the Champion line was offered. Of course, all auto manufacturers were facing the same restrictions on their material, so Studebaker was no better nor any worse than anyone else in new car business.

The "new" Champion line was offered in four body styles: 3-passenger Business Coupe, 5-passenger Club Coupe, 2-door Sedan, and 4-door Sedan. These models were only built from the end of 1945 through March, 1946. The reason for the short production run was to make way for the first real postwar Studebakers, which would make their debut in June of 1946, but be classed as 1947 models.

These "true" 1946 models had a massive grille molding, larger bumper guards, and a different style hood emblem which came from the base of the hood. A wider rocker molding was also used, running from the front fenders to the rear fenders. Because of material shortages, the 1946 cars did not carry a stainless belt molding as did the 1942 cars. Among the noticeable items which called attention to the front end of the car were the chrome spears fixed to the top of the fenders. These units were used for two purposes...to add a touch of class or trim to the front end, and also to incorporate the new directional signals, if the customer ordered this accessory. Oddly, most cars came equipped with the signal light unit as a factory accessory, whether the buyers wanted it or not.

Mechanically, as expected, the 1946 cars were the same as the 1942 models. They came with the 170 cubic inch 6-cylinder engine that produced 80 hp at 4000 rpm. The compression ratio was 6.5:1, and the bore and stroke remained 3x4 inches. Again, a 15 gallon fuel tank was used. The cars gave the same economical 25 mpg as was the case with the pre-war cars. Also, the wheelbase was the same 110 inches and the overall length remained 193 inches. Tire size also remained the same 5.50x16.

Studebaker offered a good supply of accessories for the 1946 line, including its well-advertised Hill Holder, for which the make became famous in the mid-thirties. But, because of material shortages, many of these accessories were not available at the dealership level. In fact, many early Champions were seen being driven around with wooden planks for bumpers. This was a common practice throughout the entire automobile industry in 1946, due to a combination of factors, including a strike in the bumper manufacturing business and a shortage of chrome and hardened steel to produce bumpers.

A 1946 Studebaker is a very rare car today, and if one ever finds a clean, low-mileage 1946 Champion, he will have a true collector piece. Between December and March, 1946, only 16,385 Champions were produced. The calendar year story for 1946 is a different picture, as 77,567 units were produced. Most of these cars were 1947 models, however, and were sold as such from mid-June to the end of calendar-year 1946. Studebaker now ranked in 10th sales position for the year.

Studebaker's least expensive car for 1946 was this 3-passenger Coupe which sold for $1,002. It tipped the scale at 2,456 pounds. Only 2,140 were produced, making it the second lowest production style for the 1946 line. A primary feature of the car was its huge trunk space.

The first batch of 1946 Skyway Champions leave South Bend on October 5, 1945. The gentleman behind the wheel is one of the remaining members of the original Studebaker family. He is the company paymaster, Bill Studebaker, who signed all paychecks.

# 1946

This is the 1946 2-door Champion Skyway Club Sedan. This vehicle weighed 2,541 pounds and sold for $1,046. A total of 4,468 units were produced in the short model run which ended in March, 1946.

A Skyway Champion 5-passenger Sport Coupe appears exactly the same as the 3-passenger Coupe, except for the rear seat in place of a storage area. It weighed 2,491 pounds and was offered for $1,044. This model saw the lowest production run for the year, with only 1,236 units sold. Note: This example sports a tri-tone paint job which was fairly rare for this year, and is equipped with the factory accessory white plastic wheel covers.

Studebaker's most popular model for 1946 was the Skyway Champion 4-door Sedan. The car weighed 2,566 pounds and carried a price tag of $1,097. A total of 8,541 sedans were built before production ceased, making way for the truly post war 1947 models to be introduced in June, 1946.

One of the first models to be delivered to dealerships was the 1946 Champion Cruising Sedan, here being admired by the parts manager and possibly a potential customer. Note the parking lamps placed above the headlamps and the rocker molding of stainless trim. These were the tell-tale items that marked the cars as 1946 models, rather than 1942 stock. This unit also sports the rare stainless steel wheel trim rings that give it a little extra touch of class. But, due to recurring shortages of material early in the model year, many cars of all makes arrived at their respective dealerships minus bumpers, radios, ash trays, hub caps, and in extreme cases, even rear windows, all of which were considered secondary to getting the basic cars out to the public.

Here is a prototype of what the 1947 Studebaker Champion Convertible might have looked like. How about that heavy rocker molding trim? Looks like it is weighing the car down into a "Low-Rider" state. Note the "A" gas ration sticker on the windshield, showing that this car was a "driver." It was probably tested on the highway prior to 1946, while gas rationing was still in effect.

# 1946

A possibility of what the 1947 Champion Starlight Coupe might have looked like is this experimental model shown in Studebaker's design studio. This is a "near" possibility, except for the grille design, oval rear view mirror, door-shields, and forward roof area.

A very rare piece was this 1946 Model M5 half-ton express truck with a wooden body by Mifflinburg Body Company of Mifflinburg, Pennsylvania. The vehicle really never saw full production, other than possibly no more than a dozen or so. It came on the 113-inch chassis. In 1947, the Cantrell company took over production of a similar body, but it appears all of the 1947-48 Cantrell vehicles were for export, with none sold in the U.S.

A rear view of the Mifflinburg 1946 wagon shows the very large swing-down tailgate that was employed. The running boards were high, due to the fact that the chassis was that of the M-5 truck. This made it a bit less accessible when getting in or out of the vehicle. The wood body panels were maple and mahogany with a wood varnish. The spare rode truck-like under the rear section. There doesn't appear to be any provision for a rear bumper on this particular model.

The M-5 Studebaker wagon for 1946 with the Mifflinburg body is shown with the doors opened. This gives an idea of height from the running board to the actual seating capacity. The 6-passenger unit could carry a large luggage or cargo supply, especially when the rear seat was removed. Roll-up windows were used in all four doors, but the rear quarter windows were sliders. The small rear window opened in lift-gate fashion, and was provided with sliding thumb-screw latches so that it could be left open when driving.

In a totally radical departure from anything yet seen on the American automotive stage, Studebaker unveiled its 1947 models in June, 1946.

The new models offered the first of the post-war slab-sided bodies to come from any corporation other than Kaiser-Frazer, which was a new name in the automobile manufacturing business. The 1947 styles were from the design studios of an old friend of Studebaker, Raymond Loewy. It was often stated that a person either liked the car all the way, or had a total dislike for the new body style. Personally, this author always favored the radical design. The coupes were very attractive, even though many jokes were made about the style. Comedians had their jokes as to whether a 1947 Studebaker was "coming or going." At any rate, the models were different, and for those who wanted something a little out of the ordinary, Studebaker was their answer. From this design, almost all other car makers became followers, even if it took two or three years for that change to take place.

The Champion was now available in five body styles, spread out over Deluxe and Regal Deluxe sub-series to created 10 variations. The Commander made its return, the first since 1942, and offered the same five body types, again multiplied by Deluxe and Regal sub-series. The old President line was gone, but its place was taken by the one-model Land Cruiser Sedan, which was classed as a separate model within the Commander series.

Both series came with the same engine specifications as the 1942 and 1946 models offered. These were 6-cylinder engines developing 80 horses at 4000 rpm for the Champion, and 94 horses at 3600 rpm for the Commander. The Champion's cubic inch displacement was 170, with a compression ratio of 6:5:1 or an optional 7:1. The Commander and Land Cruiser cars used the 226 cubic inch Six with a bore and stroke of 3-5/16x4-3/8 inches. No 8-cylinder cars were offered immediately after the war, and the first V-8 would not appear until 1951.

For 1947, a return of a convertible showed up in both series. The convertible, the 5-passenger Coupe, and the top of the line Land Cruiser Sedan all came with a panoramic one-piece windshield. All of the other models used the familiar two-piece windshield.

The wheel size for the Champion cars was now 5.50x15 inches. The Commander and Land Cruiser Sedan used 6.50x15 tires. The Champion had a 112-inch wheelbase with an overall length of 190.75 inches; the Commander had a 119-inch wheelbase and an overall length of 204.3 inches, and the Land Cruiser came on a 123-inch wheelbase with an overall length of 208.3 inches.

New items offered for 1947 were the pull-type door handles and something everyone appreciated. . . the "black light" no-glare instrument dials, introduced on World War II aircraft. Also new were self-adjusting brakes, which re-positioned themselves after slight wear.

Prices were up substantially from pre-war days. They ranged from $1,543 for a 3-passenger Champion Coupe to $2,043 for the Land Cruiser Sedan. The model year's sales amounted to 139,299 units, while the calendar year registrations were 123,642. Studebaker remained in the 10th place sales slot.

The Studebaker DeLuxe 3-passenger Coupe looked the same as its Regal brother, except for minor trim differences. This model sold for $73 less than a Regal, priced at $1,378, and weighed an even 2,600 pounds.

This is the less expensive Champion DeLuxe Starlight Coupe for five passengers. This example weighed 2,670 pounds and was available for $1,472. Note: This model has an antenna on the front left fender which tells us it must have a radio. Two types of radios were available in 1947, the Skyway 8-tube multi-button and the 6-tube Starline.

The less expensive Studebaker Champion 2-door DeLuxe Sedan came with no extra trim, not even a hood ornament. This stripped version went out the door weighing 2,685 pounds and sold for $1,446. A total of 26,264 2-door sedans were available in both Regal and DeLuxe style. The 1947 Champions were referred to as Model 6-G.

The 1947 Studebaker Champion DeLuxe 5-passenger Sedan weighed 2,735 pounds and sold for $1,478 Champion Sedans came with a two-piece windshield. The bullet-like trim on the front fenders added a decorative touch. An interesting ventilation concept involved the dual front fender vents located behind the wheel wells. These were manually operated from inside the car, and swung outward to act as air scoops beneath the dash and into the front compartment. Remember, this was before air conditioning.

This is a "dolled up" version of the 1947 Studebaker Champion Regal DeLuxe Convertible. The vehicle is equipped with fender reflector side-markers, rear quarter panel stone deflectors, chrome trim rings, dual door-mounted rear view mirrors, whitewall tires, and rocker molding trim. It weighed 2,875 pounds and delivered for $1,902 without the added toys. Note the neat old GMC semi against the loading dock. Of about 1940 vintage, it probably spent the W.W. II years doing double duty and receiving only minimum maintenance. Considered a heavy hauler in those days, by today's standards it could be equalled by almost any of the "Big Dually" pickup/trailer combinations.

The 1947 Studebaker Champion Regal DeLuxe 3-passenger Coupe sold for $1,451. The Coupe weighed 2,620 pounds. A total of 9,947 of these 3-passenger Coupes were sold in both Champion and Commander Regal and DeLuxe styles.

This is a true example of the real 1947 Studebaker Champion Regal DeLuxe 5-passenger Coupe. This version carried the deluxe trim package not available on the DeLuxe Starlight Coupe. This model weighed 2,690 pounds and carried a price tag of $1,546. The front fender reflector, which early models didn't have, was available on later cars as an accessory.

This example is a 1947 Champion Regal DeLuxe 2-door Sedan available for $1,520. It weighed 2,710 pounds, and proved popular for families with small children.

Here is a Regal DeLuxe 5-passenger Sedan in the Champion Series. This was the most popular model of the Champion line for 1947. It sold for $1,551 and weighed in at 2,760 pounds. This example wears the not too popular window awnings which were available in a variety of colors to harmonize with the body color. This car also has the popular white plastic wheel discs.

Some happy folks will be awaiting the arrival of their new 1947 Champions that Robert H. Walker of South Bend, a Studebaker contract transporter, is preparing to deliver.

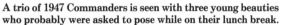

Check this parade of 1947s probably on a South Bend Street. Note the experimental Champion wagon, and the convertible with accessory mounted fog lamps. All are minus hub caps, and probably are getting ready to be transported to some distant city. But, if this is part of a drive-away program, what is the prototype wagon doing in the middle of the pack? Possibly this group is headed to the testing grounds for further evaluation.

A trio of 1947 Commanders is seen with three young beauties who probably were asked to pose while on their lunch break.

The 1947 Commander 3-passenger Coupe in the DeLuxe line weighed 3,140 pounds and sold for $1,661. It was also available in Regal DeLuxe version, weighing only 15 pounds more (3,155 pounds), and going out the door for $1,782. Three-passenger Coupes in both Champion and Commander styles saw a production run of 9,947 units.

The 1947 Studebaker Commander DeLuxe Starlight Coupe could be delivered for $1,755. The only differences from Regal models were fewer deluxe appointment. The car only weighed 15 pounds less, coming in at 3,210 pounds.

Studebaker's most expensive offering for 1947 was the Commander Regal DeLuxe Convertible. It didn't appear until late in the season. A total of 3,754 open cars in both Champion and Commander models were delivered for 1947. This example weighed 3,420 pounds. It was available for $2,236.

The fashionable 1947 Studebaker Commander Regal DeLuxe Starlight Coupe in basic form is still a very good looking car even today. This one is minus all factory approved accessories. In base form, 1947 Commanders sold for $1,877 and were technically Model 14-As.

The official car of the Pike's Peak Hill Climb, held September 1, 1947, was a rare model of the Commander series. It was this Regal DeLuxe 2-door Sedan that weighed 3,245 pounds. This car carried a price tag of $1,850. Note that this model did not come with the one-piece panoramic windshield, but shared the split windshield with the lower priced Champions. Only 26,264 two-door sedans in both Champion and Commander models were produced in 1947.

# 1947

The 1947 Commander Regal DeLuxe Sedan weighed 3,280 pounds and sold for $1,882. The Commander models all employed a 119-inch wheelbase. This is a basic model minus factory accessories. It does appear to be a two-tone model, however, which wasn't too common a Studebaker feature at that time.

Reaching the end of the assembly line is a 1947 Commander Regal DeLuxe 4-door Sedan. The car is equipped with factory Strato-Lined front bumper wing guards, white plastic wheel discs, and the Commander fender ornaments mounted on the crest of the front fenders. These ornaments blended harmoniously into the streamlined styling of the car.

The most expensive 4-door Studebaker sedan was this 1947 Land Cruiser. It sold for $2,043. Its 6-cylinder engine developed 94 horsepower. Most Land Cruisers came with the overdrive unit which cost an additional $90.

Shown, in experimental and operational form but never produced, was the 1947 Champion Station Wagon by Raymond Loewy. What a neat car to own today! Note that sliding windows would have been used in both the rear doors and the rear quarters.

# 1948

The Studebakers for 1948, as could be expected, were basically the same cars that the company had introduced as 1947 models. Only minor trim variations were used to differentiate the 1948 models from the previous year's stock.

The Champion cars now came with a horizontal bar over the four vertical bars on each side of the center grille molding. The hood ornament was of a longer configuration than on the 1947 models. The nameplate that was mounted on the front of the hood was also of a different style. The tell-tale item that most Studebaker admirers use to differentiate this year from a 1947 car is the name "Studebaker Champion" placed on either side of the hood nameplate. If it was a Commander or a Land Cruiser, the same nameplate arrangement was offered to tell the public to what series the car belonged. Overall, of course, there was no doubt that it was a Studebaker.

Commander and Land Cruiser models also offered one additional item to distinguish them from the 1947 line. That was a chrome strip at the base of the hood. Less obvious was the fact that more massive bumper guards were used on all 1948 models, while the interiors were of a much better grade of material in all lines. The Land Cruiser Sedan came with a new nylon material called "Candalon" which was supposedly washable and long wearing.

As a side note, however, the author's family had good friends who owned one of these sharp looking cars. But after three years and 33,000 miles, the front seat was thread-bare, and up by the rear package tray, the seat material had begun to separate as a result of the sun bearing in the rear window. Maybe Candalon wasn't such a wise choice as a supposed miracle fabric.

Mechanically, the 1948 models were identical to those of a year before. However, prices were up, and now ranged from $1,555 for the 3-passenger Champion Coupe to $2,431 for the Commander Regal Convertible. On a per-dollar basis, it seems that the Land Cruiser at $2,265 was by far the best buy. The public also felt this way, and its sales of 35,731 units were almost double any other single Studebaker model this year, except for the Champion Regal 4-door Sedan, which listed 30,494 units out the door.

Model year sales were a record 166,069 units, with the calendar year showing 164,753 cars built. This moved Studebaker one position closer to the top of the list, with the company now resting in 9th place.

In 1948, Studebaker offered the same units as in 1947. About the only change was the price structure which naturally went up. Seen here is a 1948 3-passenger Coupe that weighed 2,590 pounds. It was the lowest priced vehicle Studebaker offered for the year, selling for $1,535.

A 1948 Champion DeLuxe Starlight Coupe in basic form sold for $1,630 and weighed in at 2,616 pounds. The 80 horsepower cars were no race horses away from the signal, but sure did offer great economy.

This 1948 Studebaker Champion DeLuxe 5-passenger Sedan was one of 112,244 sedans that were built during the year. This unit weighed 2,720 pounds and carried a price of $1,636. Available as a Regal DeLuxe, it weighed only 5 pounds more and delivered for $1,709.

Popular with young people was this 1948 Champion Convertible that weighed 2,869 pounds. The model, technically called 7-G as were all 1948 Champions, sold for $2,086. It came with a one-piece windshield like Starlight Coupes and Land Cruiser sedans.

The 1948 Champion Regal DeLuxe 3-passenger Coupe appeared basically the same as its lower-priced brother, the DeLuxe, except for trim differences. This example had a weight of 2,615 pounds and left the dealership for $1,609.

This is the 1948 Champion Regal DeLuxe 5-passenger Starlight Coupe. This particular car is equipped with whitewalls and factory wheel trim rings which adds to its basic dolled-up looks. This style weighed 2,690 pounds and had a sticker price of $1,704.

What a sharp looking vehicle was the 1948 Commander Regal DeLuxe Convertible. The convertible models, whether Champion or Commander, only came as Regal models. This Commander weighed 3,385 pounds and carried a price of $2,431, making it the company's most expensive offering for the year.

The late Arthur Godfrey is sitting atop the rear seat of a 1948 Commander Convertible. The well-decked vehicle not only carries a speaker system, but all factory accessories, as well as the Helm front bumper guards which many other auto manufacturers also employed on their cars during the early post-war era. The photo appears to be in Minnesota, according to the license plate. Note the three trim bars that Commanders used to highlight the side vent doors.

The 1948 Studebaker Commander DeLuxe 2-door Sedan was probably the least popular body style for the model rung. It weighed 3,165 pounds and sold for $1,925. Fewer than 22,000 were built in both Champion and Commander models. The Regal Deluxe weighed ten pounds more and sold for $2,046.

Referred to as Model 15-As were the 1948 Commanders. This is an example of a 1948 Commander Regal DeLuxe Starlight Coupe. This unit weighed 3,165 pounds and left South Bend for $2,072. As a DeLuxe, it weighed 3,150 pounds and cost $1,951. There was not much difference between this model and the 1947s. Most noticeable is the chrome bar at the base of the hood and more rounded bumper guards.

Always a popular model with me was the 1948 Land Cruiser 5-passenger Sedan. We had good friends who owned a similar model back in 1948. One night while visiting us, the keys were thrown to me with the invitation, "Take the Stude out for a spin and let me know what you think of her." I just went to heaven until I got behind the wheel. I couldn't find the starter. Finally, their daughter came out to show me that you had to press on the clutch until it activated the starter. Then I proceeded to take it to visit some friends, letting them think we had just bought a new car. It was hard to later say I was just having fun. How I hated to bring it back home. The car used a 123-inch wheelbase. Only a 4-door sedan was available in the Land Cruiser line, which was classed as a sub-series within the Commander series.

The post-war half-million mark was completed with this unit, which probably intentionally turned out to be a 1948 Land Cruiser Sedan. But the factory officials don't appear to be any too happy. Maybe the car wouldn't start?

For 1949, Studebaker once again offered only face-lifting on a style that was now entering its third season. The noticeable differences over the past two years were the wrap-around bumpers used on all 1949 models, and the chrome fender markers mounted on the top of the front fenders. These markers were standard equipment on the Commander and Land Cruiser models, and were offered as optional extra-cost items on the Champion cars. Actually, so many Champions came with this accessory that many people thought it was a standard item.

A new choice of colors and even more richly appointed interiors were made available for the season. Mechanically, the cars were the same as had been offered in the past two years.

Because Studebaker was planning to come in with a big model change for the 1950 line, and wanted to get these new models on the market by mid-1949, the actual 1949 production year was cut short. Thus, model-year sales amounted to only 118,435. However, because the new 1950 models came out in August of 1949, calendar year production tallied out at 228,402 cars, with much of this being the 1950-style vehicles. This production was sufficient to once again move Studebaker upward in the national rankings, and the company now occupied the 8th sales slot.

Studebaker's least expensive vehicle for 1949 was this Champion DeLuxe 3-passenger Coupe. It sold for $1,588 and weighed 2,645 pounds. As a Regal DeLuxe it sold for $1,662 and weighed in at 2,650. A total of only 2,360 3-passenger models were sold for 1949, not making this a very popular model.

A 1949 Studebaker Champion Regal DeLuxe 2-door Sedan was available for $1,731. This model weighed 2,725 pounds. It also came in DeLuxe style for $1,657 and weighed five pounds less than a Regal, tipping the scale at 2,720 pounds.

The 1949 Champion DeLuxe Starlight Coupe for five passengers sold for $1,683 and weighed 2,705 pounds. Note this unit carries its own after market two-way radio antenna mounted on the rear quarter. The gentleman behind the wheel also is using a microphone. In this era, prior to the ubiquitous CB and today's crop of cellular telephones, two-way radios were the only way to communicate between a vehicle and a base station. However, they were seldom used except by police forces and a few municipal departments.

The well-designed Loewy Starlight Coupe for 1949 is seen here as a Champion Regal DeLuxe 5-passenger version, selling for $1,757 and weighing 2,725 pounds. Part of the year's facelift included wider bumper guard spacing which did help make the car look lower and wider. It also came as a DeLuxe Coupe for $1,683 and weighed 20 pounds less at 2,705 pounds.

Studebaker's most popular model in the Champion series was the Regal DeLuxe 4-door Sedan. This model displayed a grille revised somewhat from the 1947-48 models. It also had new wrap-around bumpers fore and aft. It sold for $1,762 and weighed 2,750 pounds. All 1949 Champions were technically called Model 8-Gs.

An airbrushed photo of a 1949 Champion Regal DeLuxe Convertible was made for catalog use. This vehicle was the most expensive Champion for the year coming in at $2,086. The convertibles came with stainless rear quarter scuff pads as standard equipment, and continued to be built on the 113-inch wheelbase chassis.

The 1949 Commander Starlight 5-passenger Coupe came both as a Regal model and a DeLuxe. They priced at $2,135 and $2,014 respectively. The weight differed only by 5 pounds, at 3,205 on the Regal and 3,200 on DeLuxe models.

On display with stanchions around it, sits this new 1949 Commander Regal Convertible. A price of $2,468 made it the most expensive 1949 Studebaker available. This unit weighed 3,415 pounds.

Only small trim changes were seen on this 1949 Land Cruiser 6-passenger Sedan. Basically, the beauty was the same car, mechanically speaking, as offered in the past two seasons. The 1949 model year was a short one with cars coming on the market in August, 1948. This model was available for $2,328. It weighed 3,325 pounds. Production amounted to 65,072 units in Champion, Commander, and Land Cruiser Sedans.

An early air brush example was submitted in 1948 of what the 1949 wagon was to look like. A more sloping roof line was used on the rendition than appeared on the actual car, and the door treatment was totally different. It appears that all-steel doors were first considered for this model, with wood being used only in the small rear quarter section above the rear fenders. It doesn't seem that this version was a Cantrell project, but may have been considered by Studebaker for in-house production.

The all-purpose Studebaker wagon with a body by Cantrell became available in the U.S. during the 1949-1953 era. It was built on the 2811 commercial chassis and had a 10-passenger seating capacity. The body weighed less than 1,000 pounds. It is not known if the bodies were shipped to South Bend for installation, or if the chassis were shipped to Cantrell's Long Island facilities for completion.

A side view of the Cantrell bodied 1949 Studebaker wagon shows many similarities to the earlier Mifflinburg design. However, the Cantrell body uses hidden running boards and has its central cross bracing positioned much lower than the earlier model. It was truly the all-purpose vehicle being put to many uses from carrying large families to being used as a builder's supply vehicle.

The rugged appearance of the Cantrell wagon was heightened by the new Studebaker chassis and cowl design. The wood framing was made from seasoned ash while the panels consisted of waterproof mahogany plywood with a Spar varnish similar to what boats of that era used. Still, with the available varnishes of the time, these bodies had to be refinished at least once every three years, and even more often if they were based in southern climates . . . for example, a Florida owner could count on an annual refinishing job.

The rear view of the 1949 Studebaker Cantrell wagon shows the tailgate opened. The rear seating could be removed. The floor was one level from tailgate to the driver's seat, making an exceptionally large area for cargo. And, additional cargo or luggage could be carried on the lowered tailgate when necessary. The Cantrell wagon was carried up to 1953, when the light Studebaker trucks went through a minor restyling. However, it does not appear that many were made during the 1950s, while none appeared on the later chassis.

With the early release of the 1950 cars, Studebaker came up with its best model year production so far, with over 320,000 units sold.

This year, there wasn't quite as radical a body change as had occurred with the "big one" of 1947. The 1950 models saw most of the change in the startling front end design, where the spinner nose took top honors for an entirely different automotive appearance. Crowning the spinner were a new coat of arms and a sail-like ornament that were placed on top of the hood. The Champion models used a chrome-based hood ornament with a lucite fixture, while the Commander and Land Cruisers used an ornament that supposedly resembled a bird in flight. Being a car of true Loewy design, the new models still held onto much of the 1947 Studebaker style.

Initially the model line followed the 1949 offerings, but late in the season the company brought out a low-priced Champion series. These cars were available as a 3-passenger Coupe, a 2-door Sedan, and a 4-door Sedan. Some information would also indicate that a "stripper" Starlight Coupe was also available in the Custom trim level. The "no-frills" models were void of any extra chrome, and had very plain interiors with a minimum of deluxe appointments. Called the Champion Custom series, the line was continued through 1955.

Mechanically, some changes were made in each series. The Champion models had an increase in horsepower, going to 85 at 4000 rpm. The engine was still a Six, with a displacement of 169.6 cubic inches, with its compression ratio raised to 7:1. An optional 7.5:1 ratio was available for high altitude driving.

The Commander and the Land Cruiser models shared the same 245.6 cubic inch 6-cylinder engine which developed 102 horsepower at 3200 rpm. This engine had the same compression choices as did the Champion block. New for the year, but not available until mid-season, was an automatic transmission, which was optional in all models. This new unit supposedly offered the smoothness of a torque converter with the economy of a standard transmission. It cost an additional $201.

Wheelbases on all Studebakers grew an inch, with the Champion now riding on 113 inches, the Commanders on 120-inch units, and the Land Cruiser having its own exclusive unit of 124 inches. Overall length also increased with the new styling, and the Champions were now 197.25 inches, the Commanders were 207-7/8 inches, and the Land Cruiser was the largest Studebaker at 211-7/8 inches. Champions used 6.40x15 tires while both the Commanders and the Land Cruisers had 7.60x15 shoes.

With the introduction of the new Champion Custom line, the price range was given more of a spread between top and bottom. The lowest price model was now the 3-passenger Champion Custom Coupe at $1,421, while the Commander Regal Convertible went for $2,328.

As mentioned, the model year sales amounted to a record 320,884 units. Calendar year production also beat all previous records, with 268,099 vehicles delivered. But other companies were also doing good, and even though Studebaker enjoyed its best year ever, it still slipped back to 9th sales position in the national rankings.

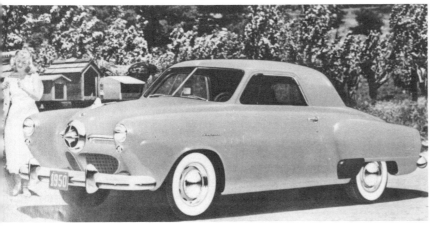

A 1950 Champion DeLuxe 3-passenger Coupe is probably the young lass' first new car. The Deluxe Coupe weighed 2,635 pounds and delivered for $1,497. As a Regal model, it was available for $1,576 and weighed 2,640 pounds. The new body style still retained the Loewy touch from cowl rearward. In sales, Studebaker placed in ninth position for 1950.

Shown in a dealership display is the 1950 Champion DeLuxe 4-door Sedan. The sign above the car says "Studebaker now gives you the Next Look." Note that this model wears painted headlamp surrounds. Many car makers this year were forced to use painted parts where chrome would normally have appeared. But, conserving on chrome was once again a must, due to the Korean conflict.

The 1950 Studebaker Champion DeLuxe 4-door Sedan weighed 2,750 pounds. The Champions saw a slight increase in horsepower for 1950. The models now developed 85 horsepower at 4000 rpm. Probably the best selling taxi cab in South Bend, in fact, in all of Indiana, was the economical Champion Sedan. This version even sports whitewall tires. This is one of the 168,307 1950 Studebaker Sedans that were sold this year.

A 1950 Champion Regal DeLuxe 5-passenger Starlight Coupe sold for $1,671. As a DeLuxe, it was available for $1,592. Mid-season, the automatic transmission became available for $201 additional on all models. As a side note, a friend of my sister had one of these cream-colored coupes. Not being a very good driver, she was often kidded about driving with her foot on the brake. Being somewhat underpowered to start with, it didn't need the automatic to add to its being sluggish. And, it certainly didn't need a driver with her foot on the brake!

Here is the 1950 Studebaker Champion Regal DeLuxe 2-door Sedan which sold for $1,644. The DeLuxe model was $79 less, going for $1,565. A total of 93,800 2-door sedans were sold, both as Regal and DeLuxe models and in both Champion and Commander series.

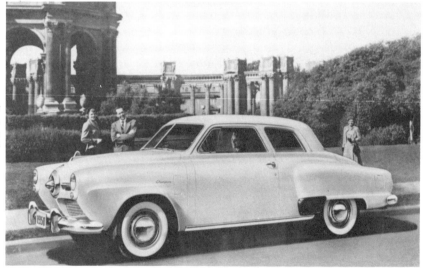

Making an early debut as a 1950 Champion Regal DeLuxe 4-door Sedan was this model selling for $1,676. The sedan weighed 2,755 pounds. This example came equipped with factory driving lights which were an extra cost item. The totally new face virtually gave the public two choices . . . like it or dislike it. It obviously took nerve to come out with a frontal design this radical.

This year Studebaker turned out its one-millionth post-war car, coming up with a half-million vehicles since the 1948 celebration. This 1950 Regal DeLuxe Champion 4-door Sedan is being admired by factory officials and assemblymen as it drives away from the South Bend factory.

The 1950 Champion Regal Convertible Coupe, being the most expensive Champion for the year, sold for $1,981. It came in at 2,900 pounds. One of the main differences on this model against the 1951 version was that the outer circle of the grille was done in chrome. Champions for 1950 were called Model 9-Gs.

The lowest priced 1950 Commander available was the Deluxe 2-door Sedan, since the 3-passenger Coupe did not appear in the Commander series for the 1950 model year. This example weighed 3,215 pounds and sold for $1,871. Notice the size of the whitewall tires of this era. These really were wide whites.

Here sits the 1950 Commander Regal Convertible with Miss Arizona helping to do the honors. The model (car, that is) sold for $2,328, being the most expensive offering for the year. The wheelbase on Commander cars was now 120 inches. Between Champion and Commander models, 11,627 Studebaker convertibles were produced.

Studebaker became involved in a lot of promotional events such as the Pikes Peak Hill Climb. Seen here is one of the official vehicles, a 1950 Commander Regal Convertible. It is getting ready to lead off the start of the climb, this year held on September 5, 1949.

An early 1950 Commander Regal DeLuxe 2-door Sedan sold for $1,992 with a curb weight of 3,220 pounds. The chrome headlight surrounds state that its an early model. After about mid-year, a shortage of chrome brought on by the Korean war mandated that these parts be painted in body color.

A nice 1950 Commander Regal Convertible is shown with the top up. The Commander and Land Cruiser models carried an ornament on the front of the hood resembling a plane in flight. As this sample displays, Commander models used the popular 7.60 x 15 tires meant for mid-priced cars of that era. The whitewall versions were at extra cost, but often ordered as long as they were available.

This is a puzzling photo. The cars in the background appear to be 1949 Chrysler products, while those in the foreground are obviously 1950 Studebakers. The picture obviously was taken at an unidentified auto show. Granted, the 1950 Studes arrived in mid-summer 1949, but why are the 1949 Chryslers being displayed in summer of 1949? In the foreground is rotating display of a new Studebaker chassis, with the electric motors to turn the display well hidden in torpedo-like pods wearing the new Studebaker nose grilles.

The 1950 Commander Regal DeLuxe Starlight Coupe was one of the company's best sellers for the year. It was available for $2,018, and weighed in at 3,220 pounds, the same as the Regal 2-door Sedan. Overall, this was a good year for Studebaker and the Starlight Coupes did their part with 64,335 examples being manufactured. The DeLuxe version sold for $1,897.

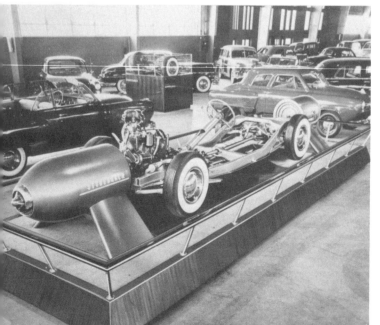

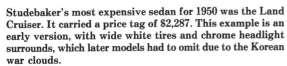

A popular model among Studebaker enthusiasts is the Commander Regal DeLuxe 4-door Sedan. It sold for $2,024. The Commander Sedans helped in the 1950 total production of 168,307 sedans manufactured. The Commander DeLuxe Sedan sold for $1,902 and weighed 3,255 pounds which was only ten less than a Regal DeLuxe. The Commander lineup were known as Model 17-As.

Studebaker's most expensive sedan for 1950 was the Land Cruiser. It carried a price tag of $2,287. This example is an early version, with wide white tires and chrome headlight surrounds, which later models had to omit due to the Korean war clouds.

This is really a 1950 Studebaker Commander. Maybe it looks a bit different . . . and it is. This is one of a fleet of sedans known as "Desert Explorers." It was owned by the Arabian American Oil Company and used in their oil drilling work in the Arabian desert. The open rear wheels and lack of the bullet nose would tell one that this is not a regular vehicle for street use, but one that was more at home in soft sand or off-road conditions. The bullet nose was removed to allow the passage of more air for cooling the greatly oversized radiator which was needed in the desert climate, while the cut-out fender wells were necessary to house the fat low-pressure sand tires.

For the brass with ARAMCO who wished a golden sun tan, an open Commander Desert Explorer was also available. How many were actually delivered is unknown. If any still exist, surely they are not low mileage "Pasadena" cars. However, it would not be surprising to find that the shells are still extant, rusting away somewhere in the vast desert sands.

For 1951, Studebaker vehicles were virtually the same cars as the 1950 offerings on the outside, but some subtle changes had taken place. Primary among these was the fact that Champions and Commanders now shared the same wheelbase of 115 inches, while the Land Cruisers used an exclusive chassis of 119-inch wheelbase. The Commanders also shared the basic body shell with the Champions. All models now came with a one-piece windshield. The front end had its central spinner redesigned with a more rounded appearance, while the side grilles became more pronounced, for both looks and to give increased ventilation to the cooling system.

But on Commander and Land Cruiser cars the similarity ended at this point. A few years earlier Studebaker had seen the hand writing on the wall . . . the V-8 engine concept was going to be norm in the near future.

This year both the Commanders and Land Cruisers became futuristic both in looks and power. Both had a new V-8 as their only power source . . . a Six was not even an option. The new block displaced 232.6 cubic inches, and developed 120 horsepower at 4000 rpm. The bore and stroke was 3-3/8x3.25 inches, while the compression ratio was 7:1 with an optional 7.5:1 ratio available for cars being sold or used in higher altitudes. Engine production was carried out at both the South Bend and Los Angeles plants, and also at the Canadian facility.

In the little car world, the Champion retained its 6-cylinder L-head engine of 169.6 cubic inches. The cars looked quite similar to the 1950 models, but as mentioned, were built on a new chassis of 115 inch wheelbase which they shared with the Commander. The overall length remained almost constant at 197.6 inches. The tire size also remained at 6.40x15. Three different lines remained available in the Champion series . . . the low-price Custom, the mid-way Deluxe, and the top of the line Regal.

In the Commander line, a name switch down-rated the Regal line to take over the old Deluxe sub-series, which had now disappeared. Replacing the Regal in name only was a return to the name "State" for the top trim level. With these cars sharing basic bodies with the Champions, the overall length dropped from 207.9 inches to the same 197.6 inches of the Champion.

Prices for 1951 ranged from the Champion Custom 3-passenger Coupe at $1,485 to $2,481 for the Commander State Convertible Coupe. The Land Cruiser continued to be the most expensive and most popular sedan, selling for $2,289 and drawing 38,055 orders.

After the record 1950 year, Studebaker sales suffered an expected slump, and thus only 246,195 units were sold in the model year. However, calendar year production of 220,000 units delivered was enough to keep the company in the 9th spot on the national sales chart.

A delivery of fresh new 1951 Studebakers is seen on this Studebaker transport, shown leaving the South Bend facility. A long hauler, this tractor displays both Mississippi and Oklahoma license plates, in addition to its home-state Indiana tag. Many of these haulers were independents, driving on a per-mile basis. The going rate for car haulers in this era was 5-cents per mile, and such drivers were enviously known as "nickel milers" at the local truck stops. Crestline/Motorbooks Editor George Dammann was hauling southern produce on a part time basis in this era, at the going rate of $1 per hour driving time . . . no pay for sleeping or eating.

Studebaker's lowest-priced car for 1951 was this Champion Custom 3-passenger Coupe. This model weighed 2,610 pounds and sold for $1,643. The 3-passenger Coupe saw its final year in 1951. Note the lack of rubber scuff shields on the quarter panel. This was an economy move on the part of the Custom line, but the shields could be ordered as an extra-cost item.

The 1951 Custom Starlight 5-passenger Coupe was the company's lowest priced Starlight Coupe for the year. It weighed 2,650 pounds and carried a price tag of $1,662. This model, considered part of the Champion line, was even devoid of a hood ornament, having instead a small emblem just above its pointed nose.

Not the most popular style with customers was the 1951 Champion Custom 2-door Sedan. This model was basically meant for a young family with small children and a budgeted income. It was available for $1,634.

Seen in all its "Plain Jane" splendor (or lack of it) is the 1951 Champion Custom 5-passenger Sedan. This model weighed in at 2,690 pounds and sold for $1,749, making it the most expensive model in the Custom line. Somehow this model even got equipped with an extra-cost factory-approved door-mounted side mirror.

The 1951 Champion DeLuxe 3-passenger Coupe resembled the Regal version at quick glance. However, it did receive less fancy trim and, with a less pretentious interior for a buyer not needing all of the frills, it sold for $1,643.

# 1951

This 1951 Studebaker Champion DeLuxe 5-passenger Sedan has already done its share of work, as indicated by the 1954 Manila license plate. The file on this photo states: "Studebakers are gluttons for punishment. This vehicle has gone over 220,000 miles in many back country villages of the Philippines."

The ideal car for the salesman who wanted lots of room for sample cases, etc., was this 1951 Champion Regal DeLuxe 3-passenger Coupe. This was the most expensive of the 3-passenger models in the Champion line. It carried a price tag of $1,727.

The top model in the Champion Starlight Coupe family for 1951 was this Regal DeLuxe 5-passenger Coupe. This version even sports the chromed headlamp surrounds not seen on too many 1951 models. This Regal DeLuxe model sold for $1,828.

A 1951 Champion Regal DeLuxe 2-door Sedan went out the door for an even $1,800. This model weighed 2,690 pounds in base form. The 1951 Champions employed the same wheelbase as the Commanders, which was 115 inches. Production figures for 2-door sedans, including both Champion and Commander models, totalled 50,148 cars for the model year.

This is a 1951 Studebaker Commander Regal 2-door Sedan. Gone were the low-priced DeLuxe series, with the Regal title now being used in its place. This 2-door Commander Regal was the lowest priced model in the Commander line for the year. It sold for $1,997. All 1951 models, as this example shows, now used a one-piece windshield.

This is a 1951 Studebaker Regal 5-passenger Sedan. The most noticeable exterior difference between this model and the more expensive Commander State model is the black rubber scuff plate mounted at the base of the rear door. This Regal Sedan carried a price of $2,143, and weighed 3,070 pounds.

Studebaker's most expensive model for the 1951 line was this Commander State Convertible. The vehicle sold for $2,481 and weighed 3,240 pounds, also making it the heaviest unit the factory produced for 1951.

The 1951 Studebaker Commander State 5-passenger Starlight Coupe was the most expensive of the Starlight models for the year. Nicely appointed with all deluxe equipment, this V-8 model sold for $2,137. A total of 46,157 coupes were manufactured in both Champion and Commander versions for the year.

# 1951

The Commander State appeared for the first time during model year 1951. This V-8 2-door sold for $2,108 and carried a weight of 3,045 pounds. The chrome spears on top of the front fenders helped to distinguish it from the Champions.

The most popular of the Commander models in 1951 was the State 4-door Sedan. This example sold for $2,143 and weighed 3,070 pounds. The 1951 V-8s came with a 7:1 compression ratio. For cars being used in high altitude, the 7.5: 1 ratio was recommended.

This 1951 Land Cruiser 4-door Sedan was the luxury liner of the sedan family. The nicely equipped model shown here may have been posed for a late season press photo, as it is equipped with 1952 wheel covers. The 1951 Land Cruiser tipped the scale at 3,105 pounds and sold for $2,289. This model was part of the sedan group, total sales of which amounted to 159,978 units. Studebaker placed ninth among car makers for the year.

A touch of both years: This unit carries the front end of a 1951 Commander, but was a hardtop from the cowl rearward. But hardtops actually were not introduced until the 1952 model year. The car also sports the 1952 wheel covers. The answer, obviously, is that it is a factory prototype, with the new body mounted on a 1951 chassis for road and track testing.

# 1952

This was the year that Studebaker celebrated its 100th anniversary, going back to the start of its horse and wagon production to select the founding year. Helping with the anniversary publicity was a healthy face-lift that took place on the front end of all Studebakers.

The bullet or spinner nose was gone, and a more conventional grille and hood were used. Just above the grille, a chrome molding ran the width of the car, and formed a curvaceous "V" as a divider in the center of the grille. On each side of this divider were mounted three vertical chrome grille bars. The entire front was protected by the use of four bumper guards mounted on the front bumper. The two larger ones were used on the outer edge of the bumper and two were placed next to the center-mounted license bracket for added protection.

The taillights were arranged so that they could be seen from both the rear and the sides. This was the beginning of making safety features a more prominent part of the car. Under the hood, everything was about the same as it was in 1951.

As in 1951, the Champions and Commanders shared the same 115-inch wheelbase chassis and used the same basic body shells, while the Land Cruiser had its own exclusive 119-inch wheelbase frame and had its own unique sheet metal.

Once again, military production got into the way of automotive production, but not nearly as bad as had happened in World War II. However, because large quantities of materials had to go into supplies needed to fight the Korean conflict, many shortages occurred. Only so much steel was allotted for the automobile manufacturing industry, and thus most companies had to conserve wherever possible. Also, the chrome that was used on all 1952 cars (not just Studebaker alone) was of a very inferior quality. In fact, it was so bad that in extreme cases, it peeled off in just a matter of months.

Studebaker again held onto its 9th spot on the sales charts with calendar year production of 161,520 vehicles built. Model year deliveries amounted to 167,662 cars, a decided downturn, but in keeping with the rest of the automotive scene.

1952 STUDEBAKER CHAMPION *Custom 2-Door Sedan*

For 1952, Studebaker's lowest priced car was the Champion Custom 2-door Sedan. This no frills unit went out the door for $1,735. It weighed 2,655 pounds and saw a combined production run of 30,357 which included the DeLuxe, Regal and Commander Regal and State models, also.

Here is the 1952 Champion DeLuxe Starlight Coupe. This model, always popular especially with young people, carried a price of $1,856. One way to distinguish this model from its "dolled-up" Regal kin, is the lack of the stainless rocker molding trim on the Deluxe.

This 1952 Champion DeLuxe 4-door Sedan was one of 159,978 vehicles sold during the year in the total grouping of 4-door models. This car weighed 2,720 pounds and sold for $1,862. As a Custom, it went for $1,769, and in the Regal category carried a tab of $1,946.

The most expensive Starlight Coupe in the Champion line was this Regal model. It sold for $1,941 and weighed 2,695 pounds. This series carried more deluxe appointments, along with the stainless rocker molding which helped make it easy to identify.

In its first year of production was the Starliner Hardtop Coupe. It came in both Champion and Commander models. This Regal Starline is a Champion, which delivered for $2,200. A total of 24,686 hardtops sold in 1952, both as Champion and Commander models. The hardtop carried the smart style of a convertible, but had the all-weather comfort of a closed car. Although hailed as one of the great post-war designs, the hardtop concept had actually been around since the early teens, but had dropped from favor during the 1930s.

The title of the most expensive 1952 Champion went to this Regal Convertible. It cost $73 more than the newly introduced Starliner Hardtop, making it $2,273. Note the stainless scuff pad or stone guard on the rear quarter panel. This came as standard equipment only on the Champion Starliner and Convertible models.

This 1952 Studebaker Champion 2-door Sedan is of the Regal variety. This car carried a price of $1,913, making it the most expensive of the Champion 2-door models.

The first car off the assembly line in Studebaker's 2nd Century was this Champion Regal DeLuxe 4-door Sedan. The event took place on February 18, 1952. The vehicle parked beside the 1952 Champion is the first Studebaker Electric, while the original Conestoga wagon is hidden in the background.

The lowest priced Commander model for 1952 was the V-8 Regal 2-door Sedan. It sold for $2,086. Inside, it was attractively styled with pleated door panels. The upholstery was of a fine quality hickory-beige broadcloth. The most expensive of the 2-door sedans for 1952 was this State Commander V-8. Quickly looking at one, it is virtually the same as the Regal. However, trim differences made these cars more costly. This car sold for $2,172. It came with rich, durable terrace weave nylon foam rubber cushions, and deep pile carpets. The Regal version delivered for $2,086.

This 1952 Commander Regal Starlight Coupe shows off the new taillights that were faired into the fenders. These lamps, clearly visible from both sides and rear, gave an extra smartness to the car. This model weighed 3,030 pounds and went out the door for $2,115.

# 1952

Again in 1952, Studebaker was well represented in Colorado Springs at the annual Labor Day Pike's Peak Hill Climb, this year held on Sept. 1. Here is the newly introduced Commander State Starliner Hardtop Coupe being used as the official pace car. The hardtop delivered for $2,488.

This is the famous "Last Vehicle of Studebaker's First Century." It was a 1952 Commander State Starliner Hardtop Couple. This unit was the company's 7,130,874th vehicle. It was produced on Friday, February 15, 1952. Harold S. Vance, Studebaker's president, right, drove the car off the assembly line with Walter C. Zientowski, the longest factory employee (50+ years) as his passenger.

This is the most expensive of 1952 Starlight Coupes. It is the Commander State Coupe which weighed 3,025 pounds and sold for $2,202. The factory turned out 20,552 of the 5-passenger Coupes in both Champion and Commander models.

The popular Commander State 4-door Sedan, like all 1952 Studebakers, offered tinted green glass for the first time. Many buyers chose this feature which was available at extra cost. This model carried a base price of $2,208. The Regal Sedan sold for $2,121.

Studebaker's most expensive vehicle for 1952 was this Commander Convertible, selling for $2,548 and carrying a weight of 3,230 pounds. One would have expected the company to put white walls on such a sporty car, but shortages created by the Korean conflict made wide whites all but impossible to find. Probably the company felt that so few cars could actually be delivered with the optional tires that there was little use to displaying them in the catalog.

The most expensive model and the one lowest in production for 1952 was the Commander V-8 State Convertible. A total of only 3,011 convertibles were manufactured between the Champion and Commander series for 1952. The convertible top was of an orlon fabric in natural color, which resisted fading and staining due to weather and traffic film.

Check the background of this 1952 photo of Ike giving his familiar wave to those who came out to greet him in South Bend before the 1952 Presidential race. The State Theater was featuring "All Quiet on the Western Front" with Lew Ayres and Louis Wolheim, while "Bombay Clipper" was listed as the second feature.

In honor of Studebaker's 100th anniversary, this car was chosen to be the pace vehicle for the 500-mile Memorial Day Race at Indianapolis, held this year on May 30, 1952. Race officials are shown giving it a good workout before the event took place.

# 1952

This well-accessorized 1952 Land Cruiser was photographed in front of the modern offices of Nordisk Diesel-Auto in Copenhagen, Denmark. It was delivered to the King of Denmark. Strangely enough, this vehicle carries the rubber scuff shield on the rear door panel, rather than the stainless shield which all Land Cruisers had as standard equipment. On the other hand, it does wear an interesting set of rear fender skirts. It weighed 3,155 pounds and sold for $2,365.

Even though Studebaker really wasn't in the wagon business at this time, here sits a 1952 creation nicely equipped with all deluxe appointments. It was built on the Commander chassis. The photo was taken in front of the home office, but there is no information as to the body builder. The license plate reads Sao Palo, and the dirt on the car makes it look as if it could have been driven to Indiana from Brazil. Very likely some Brazilian body company was the manufacturer.

In a mock-up state is the 1953 Studebaker Starlight Coupe with Raymond Loewy giving it the once-over. Maybe he's trying to decide whether it will be a Champion or a Commander. The model doesn't have any designation on the quarter panel, as to what it will be, and possibly it was not even the final selection.

The two historic 1952 Studebakers wound up traveling together. In the center rides the first body for the Studebaker 2nd Century, and at right is the last vehicle of Studebakers 1st Century, the State Starliner Hardtop. The body on the end of the trailer has neither fame nor aclaim. The truck is a company vehicle, used to haul bodies between buildings in the vast Studebaker complex.

# 1953

# 1953

The introduction of the 1953 Studebaker line was an instant success, due chiefly to one basic style. That was the beauty of the new Loewy-designed coupes, available in either pillared "Starlight Coupe" form or as the new hardtop "Starliner" design. Even if a person had not been a Studebaker fan in the past, just looking at one of these clean-cut coupes would make all but the most auto-dead person admit that the cars constituted the automotive eye-catcher of the year. In fact, the style was so terrific that the New York School of Fashion presented its Fashion Academy Gold Medal to Studebaker this year.

All models this year rode on two new chassis. The new Loewy Coupes and the Land Cruisers shared a 120.5-inch wheelbase frame. The Coupes were 201.9 inches long overall, while the Land Cruisers were slightly larger, being 202.6 inches. The regular sedans, both two and 4-door, used their own chassis of 116.5-inch wheelbase and were 198.6 inches overall. No convertibles appeared in this year's line-up, nor were there any 3-passenger coupes.

No longer was it easy to quickly distinguish a Champion from a Commander with a quick glance at the outer appearance. With both cars sharing the same bodies, the main difference now was in the rear quarter panel designation. The Champion models used a round medallion with an "S" in the center. The Commander cars came with the V-8 emblem mounted on this quarter panel. The V-8 models employed an "8" in the center of the hood and on the trunk, while the 6-cylinder Champion cars displayed the familiar "S" in these same places.

In the Commander line, the "State" name was dropped, the "Regal" name returned to its up-scale position, and the name "Deluxe" once more denoted the lower trim level.

The introduction of full-time power steering was made this year in each of the series. Other than this new option, the mechanical portions of the cars were about the same as on the 1952 vehicles. Studebaker still featured Champion economy in many of its ads, as it had in the past. This year the company entered a car in each series of the Mobilgas Economy Run, and each vehicle won its class. The top winner was a Champion 4-door Sedan with overdrive, which averaged 26.86 mpg.

Prices again were up, and ranged from $1,735 for a Champion Custom 2-door Sedan to $2,374 for the Commander Regal Starliner. Model year sales were down slightly, coming in at 151,576 vehicles. However, calendar year sales were up by over 25,000 units, peaking at 186,484 vehicles to allow Studebaker to retain its 9th sales slot.

The Studebaker dealer in Manila must have had his way with fleet sales during the early 1950s, with large quantities of sedans sold to taxi companies. Here is a Custom 4-door Sedan wearing a 1954 license plate from Manila.

The Fox-Taxi Cab Company of Manila, Philippines, ordered a fleet of these 1953 Champion Custom 4-door Sedans. The cars served the company well and gave economical transportation for several years.

The 1,912,340th post-war Studebaker came off the assembly line as a Six-cylinder Champion Regal Starlight Coupe. It was available for $1,955. Why Studebaker selected car No. 1,912,340 for honors is anyone's guess.

This economical 1953 Champion Regal 2-door Sedan sold for $1,917. Production was low on regular 2-door models with only 15,575 being sold between Champion and Commander models. Most people apparently preferred the stylish Loewy Coupes for their everyday transportation.

Another taxi company from the Philippines, this one in Pasay City, also liked the economical dependability of the 1953 Champions. This version came with chrome headlamp bezels and a stainless chrome strip on the rear quarter panel, leading one to think it probably is a Regal Sedan.

This 1953 Champion DeLuxe 2-door Sedan was the middle-priced 2-door for the year. It weighed in at an even 2,700 pounds and sold for $1,831. The 6-cylinder engine was still developing 85 horsepower. A Champion with overdrive averaged 26.86 MPG in the 1953 Mobilgas Economy Run.

1953 STUDEBAKER CHAMPION DELUXE 4-DOOR SEDAN FOR 6

The most popular model in the 1953 Champion line was still the 4-door Sedan. This DeLuxe example sold for $1,863. The dash panel on the Champions had a new bevel design which offered extra knee room. The instruments were grouped in a glare-proof recessed panel. All two and 4-door Sedans rode on a 116.5-inch wheelbase.

An introduction of the 1953 Studebaker is seen here. Probably a small town dealership has just received its allotment of coupes for a few months. Who is going to get to drive it home? Mom, Dad or the girls? Maybe the dealer would like to keep it on display for awhile.

A 1953 Champion Starliner "Hard-top" Convertible for five passengers was available for $2,116. The coupes and hard-top models all came on a 120.5-inch wheelbase. The circular medallion with the "lazy S" on the quarter panel is the best distinction to let you know it's a Champion model.

Shown here is a Commander DeLuxe Sedan being used as a police unit. Notice all the police equipment. As a regular sedan, the car sold for $2,121 and weighed 3,075 pounds. In the 1953 Mobilgas Economy Run, a Commander V-8 Sedan beat all other cars priced in the same league.

Here is a 1953 Commander Regal Sedan. Easy detection to let one know its a Commander is the small V-8 identification on the front fender vent. This example weighed 3,095 pounds and sold for $2,208. Studebaker was probably the last major car builder to use these vent doors on the sides of the front fenders.

This sharp looking V-8 Commander Regal Starlight Coupe was available with the new extra-cost power steering, as were all other Commanders in the 1953 run. This model sold for $2,213. Its tell-tale bit of distinction from a Champion version is the V-8 nameplate mounted on the rear quarter panel.

Another proud owner is shown with his Commander Regal Starlight Coupe. This model was also available as a Deluxe Starlight Coupe selling for $2,127, which was $86 less than a Regal Coupe. Check the extra-cost factory wire wheel covers! They are beauties.

This brand new 1953 Commander Regal Starlight Coupe sports a false Continental tire kit which was quite popular in the early 1950s. These units were made by a company in California called Stylecraft. It was not a factory-approved accessory, but many car dealers sold them through their accessory department. From the license frame mounted under the tire kit, it is known that this vehicle was sold by Walt Cash, a well known Studebaker dealer in Culver City, California. The paper sticker on the rear window was placed on all new cars in California while the owner waited for Department of Motor Vehicles to mail the new license plates.

The 1953 Commander V-8 DeLuxe 2-door Sedan weighed 3,055 pounds and carried a price of $2,089. It was the only 2-door sedan available in the Commander line for 1953. Studebaker this year gave substantial promotion to its new power steering unit, which it claimed was the "finest" of all such units. Power steering was available only in the Commander series, at "moderate" extra cost.

Harold Vance is shown here getting ready to take his new 1953 Starlight Coupe to the corporate office. It looks like its a cold February morning, probably shortly after the new model made its debut.

What do you suppose the young folks are talking about? Very likely, the Studebaker is being mentioned, assuming that she feels very proud that Daddy let her take the Commander Starliner to school. The vehicle weighed 3,120 pounds and sold for $2,374.

Nicely appointed is this 1953 Land Cruiser 4-door Sedan. The easiest means to identify this model against a Champion or Commander Sedan is: First off, it is four inches longer, riding on a 120.5-inch wheelbase, and secondly, it has the small rear window vent panes. It weighed 3,180 pounds and sold for $2,386.

Raymond Loewy is standing by a Special Landau Coupe that was to be his personal car. The vehicle is a variation of the Starlight Coupe, fitted with a special top consisting of a fixed rear quarter and a removable center section. It is unknown whether such a style was ever seriously considered for production, or if it was simply a custom job built for Loewy's private use.

A prototype of the special Raymond Loewy Landau Coupe gives a good look at the unique top section. Actually, this is a detailed quarter-scale model of what the real vehicle was to be. Too bad it never got to production.

This view shows the new Conestoga Wagon in clay form at Studebaker's styling studio in 1952. At this point, the wagon was intended to be introduced in 1953. However, the wagon didn't make it for a 1953 debut and thus, it had to be scheduled into 1954 production. Of interest is the small portion of grille showing behind the man in the business suit. At this stage, even the trim was in the experimental category.

# 1954

The big news from Studebaker in 1954 did not involve automobiles...it had to do strictly with financial and corporate maneuvering. This was the year when...on June 22 to be exact...Studebaker and Packard merged. The new company would be called the Studebaker-Packard Corp. of America. For the time being at least, Studebaker would maintain its headquarters and plant at South Bend, and would continue its plants at Los Angeles and in Canada. Packards would continue to roll from Detroit.

In the car line, a new model was added to the catalog. It was a station wagon, referred to as the "Conestoga." This name would help people remember that in its beginning days, Studebaker was a famous wagon maker. In retrospect, however, one wonders why this name didn't appear in 1952, when it would have provided a fitting tie-in with the 100th anniversary celebrations.

The Conestogas were available in both the Champion and Commander lines. It came only as a 2-door model, as did the two and 4-door sedans, the Conestogas rode on a 116.5-inch wheelbase.

Aside from the new wagon, the 1954 models saw only minor trim changes. Bumper guards were larger on front, offering still more protection to the hood and grille. The series and name designations were mounted on the middle grille bars.

The Champion and Commander Regal sedan and the Land Cruisers came with a body trim molding mounted rearward from the front door. To help distinguish these models in the Commander series, a small V-8 medallion was mounted next to the fender air vent. The Land Cruiser also employed this feature. Deluxe Commanders put the V-8 emblem on the side vent. Again, this was done to help distinguish the models from one another.

Mechanically, everything stayed as it had been since the 1951 introduction of the V-8 engine, except that horsepower was increased to 127 on these blocks. The Champion models continued to use their 6-cylinder L-head engines. These cars continued to sell well and were considered to be the "bread and butter" winners for the company. Economy was stressed in their sales promotion, and in line with this, the Mobilgas Economy Run played a big part in the advertising. But it was not a Champion, it was a Land Cruiser Sedan which won the Grand Sweepstakes in the 1954 run from Los Angeles to Sun Valley, Idaho. The car attained the highest mileage per gallon ever recorded to that date, on the computations which took into account such factors as weight, displacement, gearing, etc., so that all vehicles in a particular class would be equal.

Prices for the 1954 models began at $1,800 for the Champion Custom 2-door Sedan and rose to $2,556 for the top of the line Commander Regal Conestoga Wagon. This would be the last year that Studebaker would use the Land Cruiser nomenclature. Due in part to the company's merger with Packard, sales were less than the previous year. For the model run, only 68,708 cars left the plants, while calendar year production of only 85,252 units put the company down to 11th place in automotive sales.

The Champion Custom 4-door Sedan was in its next to the last year of production. Sales kept dwindling and management felt it wiser to put the eggs in larger baskets where a better return would show. This Custom sold for $1,801, making it the lowest priced 4-door sedan for the year. The interior was done in gray and gold-stripe nylon, trimmed with harmonizing vinyl. The instrument panel, steering wheel, door panels, headliner, and floor coverings were all color matched.

It's the simplicity of lines that made these coupes so popular with everyone. This version was a DeLuxe Starlight available for $1,972. In this series, these Coupes offered a ripple weave cord combined with wolfgrain vinyl to create a tasteful interior. Three-tone vinyl door panels were available in grey, green, and blue.

This is the 1954 Studebaker Champion DeLuxe 2-door Sedan that is devoid of any extra accessory trim. However, with the antenna mounted correctly on the left fender, it must have had a radio. Also, it sports a factory door-mounted side mirror. This unit sold for $1,875 without the aforementioned extras.

The first postwar wagon from Studebaker made its appearance as the Conestoga in 1954. The name, of course, was meant to bring back the fame of the early days when Studebaker built Conestoga wagons. This example was the Champion DeLuxe Conestoga, the lowest price wagon that Studebaker offered for the year. It sold for $2,187. The door windows were the traditional roll-up kind, but the center windows slid rearward to open. The rear quarter windows would not open. Of 6-passenger style, the car featured a fold-down rear seat, but no third seat in the back.

This year Studebaker had its answer to the Ford and Chevrolet Sedan Delivery models. These units were Conestogas all right, but carried blanked out window panels on the outside and full cargo area on the inside. The deluxe trim, full wheel covers, and whitewalls were all extra cost items.

A full side view shows the 1954 Champion DeLuxe Conestoga Sedan Delivery in plain form. This model rode on the same 116.5-inch wheelbase as did the sedans. The stainless trim on the rear quarter panel tells that it is classed in the lower priced series.

The Studebaker Dealers Association from Los Angeles sponsored this 1954 Champion DeLuxe 4-door Sedan in the Mobilgas Economy Run. The event began in Los Angeles and ended in Sun Valley, Idaho. As usual, the economical Studebakers placed very highly in the event.

Not much changed from the 1953 version was the 1954 Champion Regal Starlight Coupe. The larger bumper guards on the front help to distinguish it as a 1954. This model weighed 2,750 pounds and could be purchased for $2,080.

This is the top of the Champion 2-door Sedans. It's a Regal that weighed 2,780 pounds and sold for $2,026. The stainless side trim was standard on Regal models to help distinguish them from DeLuxe and Custom models.

An attractive mid-season trim change was made on the Regal Champion 2-door Sedans. Shown here is the new stainless trim on the rear quarter panel, mounted in a vertical fashion and going from the rear window sill down to the horizontal stainless trim. This car sold for $1,983. It was part of the 2-door sedan family that had a production run of 9,254 units. The model year sales of 68,708 put Studebaker in 11th place.

The 1954 Regal 4-door Sedan came with the stainless trim mounted from the front door rearward. Next to the front fender vent was a circular medallion with the "S" mounted in the center. This was done to help distinguish it as part of the Champion family.

This is the Champion Regal Conestoga carrying the full body trim molding to help distinguish it from the DeLuxe models. This one is being put to good use as a Traffic Safety Education vehicle for the City of South Bend. The full wheel covers are extra cost items available on all Champions in 1954. The Regal was the more expensive wagon version, selling for $2,298. It was also the heaviest Champion, weighing 2,950 pounds.

Here is the face lifted version of the stylish Loewy Coupe. This is a Commander DeLuxe Starlight Coupe which was available for $2,233. This model did not sell as well as the Regal version, but was part of the 18,186 total run that helped overall sales. Note the rare factory "peep" mirror that this unit has mounted on the door edge. The Regal model sold for $2,341.

In the Commander line for 1954, the 2-door Sedan was only available in the DeLuxe models. Shown here is the Commander DeLuxe 2-door Sedan with the extra cost whitewall tires and rare two-tone paint combination. Minus these extra cost items, this vehicle sold for $2,136.

This example of the Commander Conestoga Sedan Delivery is a DeLuxe version, identified by the V-8 emblem placed next to the fender air vent. The Commander designation gave this delivery unit a special luxury effect, but sales here were even poorer than with the Champion models.

Studebaker did make "mini-ambulances" available in the Conestoga line. Such a unit is seen here in Commander DeLuxe version. Sales probably were not excessive. The special unit was available in Commander series only. It is not known if Studebaker did the actual fitting, or if it farmed these units out to a specialty builder.

This 1954 Commander Regal Starliner Hardtop Coupe, oddly enough, went down in price, being $72 below its 1953 counterpart. The two-tone paint combination was used on most Coupe models at no extra charge. This view is another taken in front of the company headquarters in South Bend.

The Commander Regal 4-door Sedan in base form sold for $2,287 and weighed 3,120 pounds. This vehicle also was available in the DeLuxe line for $2,179. Most people preferred to pay the additional $108 and drove home from the dealership in the more luxurious Regal version.

The 1954 Commander Regal Conestoga was a 6-passenger wagon. This is an early version, with stainless trim appearing only on the rear quarter panel. This was Studebaker's most expensive model for 1954, selling at $2,556. As a DeLuxe Conestoga it delivered for $2,448.

The most expensive model for 1954 was this Commander Regal Conestoga. It weighed 3,265 pounds, being the heaviest vehicle for the year from Studebaker, and sold for $2,558. A total of 11,774 Conestoga's were built for the 1954 model run.

The 1954 Land Cruiser 4-door Sedan is displayed here with the regular Champion and Commander hub caps. Being the top of the line, it should have its full wheel discs. However, this picture was made in Studebaker's styling studio, and is probably of a pre-production car. Possibly the photo was for the use of artists working up the new catalog or advertising art.

An interior view of a 1954 Commander Regal Conestoga shows that the station wagon was able to be used both as a family car, or as a utility vehicle. The units were available with interiors done in two-tone blue, tan, or red vinyl for year-round durability.

A 1954 Land Cruiser 4-door Sedan is parked below the Acropolis in Athens. Note the different license plate and the small spotlight side mirror unit. This vehicle also wears its fog lights on the outer part of the bumper rather than in the customary fashion next to the license plate. The Land Cruiser was discontinued at the end of the model run.

The 2-millionth post-war Studebaker to leave the factory is seen here. With the California license plates on the car, there is reason to believe the unit was produced at the Vernon assembly plant in Los Angeles, California. As a side note, I recall in February, 1954, taking my 3-year old nephew through the Studebaker factory at Vernon. He was beside himself seeing these new cars being assembled. He kept saying, "More Stugerbuggers; I want a Stugerbugger." Needless to say, the name stuck with the family for many years to follow.

The Studebaker-Packard merger that took place on October 1, 1954, saw the beginning of two old companies planning to do business under one management team. No one was too happy, from either side. Seen here is one of the last true Packards, it's a 1954 Clipper. Actually Packard referred to this as a separate car for the years of 1954-56. This is a nice original hardtop coupe that developed 165 horsepower at 3600 rpm from its 327 cubic-inch in-line 8-cylinder engine.

The most important news from Studebaker-Packard this year came not at the season's opening, but rather at mid-year. Introduced in January, 1955, was the company's newest creation, a super sporty model called the Speedster.

Available only in the new President line, the vehicle offered a cockpit-styled instrument panel, 160 MPH speedometer, tinted glass, chrome plated garnish moldings, whitewall tires, wire wheel covers, an 8-tube radio, dual backup lights, fog lights integrated within special bumper guards, power steering, power brakes, chrome dual tip tailpipe extensions, and dual side mirrors. Since all of this came as standard equipment, there were virtually no options to buy.

Powering the Speedster was a brand new engine referred to as the "Passmaster V-8." It had a 259.2 cubic inch displacement with a bore and stroke of 3.56x3.25 inches, and developed 185 horsepower at 4500 rpm. The compression ratio was 7.5:1, with an 8:1 ratio being optional. Available transmissions were a standard 3-speed; a 3-speed with overdrive, or the automatic.

All Speedsters came with genuine leather seats and vinyl headliners and door panels. Most Speedsters were delivered with what the factory called "Tri-Level" paint combinations, which were only available on this model. The Speedster used the same 120.5-inch wheelbase as did the regular coupes and the President Sedan, and had an overall length of 204.4 inches. It was available in base price for $3,253, making it by far the most expensive Studebaker and the only one to exceed the $3,000 mark. Only 2,215 Speedsters were produced in its one year run. A similar car would appear in 1956, but would be the first of the famous Hawk models. Thus, a 1955 Speedster would be a highly collectible car today.

For the regular model run, many felt that the clean lines of the 1953/54 cars, especially the coupes, were not present on the 1955 models. Front end treatment and the side moldings did seem to be a bit overdone.

The Land Cruiser name did not appear in 1955, but in its place was the return of the President nameplate, a title not seen since the 1942 models. Initially, four styles were available in the new President series. They were the State 4-door Sedan; the Deluxe 4-door Sedan; the State Coupe with its B-pillar, and the State Hardtop. At mid-year the Speedster would join this up-scale family. As the Land Cruiser name disappeared, so too did the names "Starliner" and "Starlight" for the two coupe styles.

The Commander models were as they were for the previous two years, except that a new sub-series was added. This was a less expensive Custom line, similar to the low-buck models in the Champion series. Available in this category were either a 2-door or a 4-door Sedan, both bearing the name "Commander Custom." Neither model proved to be a big seller. They, like the Champion Customs, were discontinued at the end of the year and would not show again until the 1957 cars were introduced.

In the new President line, the same new Passmaster V-8 appeared as was used in the Speedster. The early Commander models offered a new but smaller V-8 with a 224 cubic inch displacement. This block developed 140 horses at 4500 rpm. However, later Commanders came with the 259 cubic inch V-8, down-rated to 162 horsepower. The Champion line continued with the tried and true 6-cylinder engine that developed 101 horses at 4000 rpm. It had a bore and stroke of 3x4-3/8 inches and a displacement of 185 cubic inches.

Two-tone paint combinations were available at no extra cost in all President State models and on the Commander and Champion Hardtop Coupes.

The lowest priced offering in 1955 was the Champion Custom 2-door Sedan for $1,873. Excluding the Speedster, which was the most expensive Studebaker, the next model on the high end of the scale was the President State 2-door Hardtop at $2,456, while the President State 4-door sedan sold for $2,381.

Sales were actually much higher than in 1954, but Studebaker still slipped in the sales race due to heavy competition. During the model year, a total of 116,333 cars were delivered, while for the calendar year, production amounted to 112,392 units. Still, this let Studebaker slip into the 13th spot on the national scale.

The most expensive model for 1955 was this President Speedster Hardtop. The car weighed 3,301 pounds and came equipped with all the fancy items shown as standard equipment for $3,253. Note its quilted leather pattern seat material which was available only on the Speedsters. The instrument panel was done in an engine turned pattern with white-on-black instruments, reminiscent of the 1936-37 Cords. The one-year model had a limited run of only 2,215 units. Its only engine was the Packard-sourced "Passmaster" V-8 of 185 hp.

Now in its last year of production was the Champion Custom 4-door Sedan. Sales were beginning to lag and management felt there was more money to be made in the expensive models. This unit sold for $1,783. In its Commander sister model it was delivered for $1,919. Both models looked the same until the hood was raised.

Possibly the best looking Coupe for 1955 came in the DeLuxe line, whether Champion or Commander. The lack of side panel chrome gave a more clean appearance. This unit is a Champion DeLuxe, which sold for $1,875. As a Commander the delivered price was $114 more — $1,989. The Coupes continued to ride on the 120.5 inch wheelbase.

The Champion Deluxe Coupe for 5 passengers

The 1955 Champion DeLuxe 2-door Sedan sold well to families with young children. It was the most expensive 2-door Sedan in the Champion line for 1955. It went home for $1,841. The Regal line did not offer this model for 1955. Studebaker advertising this year made much of the fact that its new Champion engine, called the "Victory Six," delivered 18% more horsepower than last year's Six, with no loss of fuel economy.

The 1955 Champion DeLuxe 4-door Sedan was virtually the same as its Commander brother as far as appearance went. It, like Commander models, rode on a 116.5-inch wheelbase. It weighed 2,805 pounds and could be purchased for $1,885.

This was Studebaker's lowest priced Conestoga Wagon for 1955. It's a Champion DeLuxe, weighing 2,980 pounds and selling for $2,141. The wagon production for 1955 amounted to 11,685 units.

The Champion Regal Hard-top for 5 passengers

For 1955, the Studebaker Champion Regal Hardtop Coupe was easily identifiable from the DeLuxe Coupe by its use of stainless trim on the side panels. The new "Victory Six" engine was increased to 185 cubic inches, developing 101 horsepower. The 1955 Champion Regal Hardtop delivered for $2,125.

Here is a 1955 Champion Regal 4-door Sedan that did honors for the company again in the Mobilgas Economy Run. Factory advertising claimed the Champions could get up to 33 MPG. However, in order to achieve this, the car required overdrive, and could not be driven over 30 MPH. Wouldn't that be a riot on a Los Angeles freeway! The Sedan weighed 2,815 pounds and could be purchased for $1,995.

Looking at this Conestoga Wagon, one would have a difficult time detecting whether it's a Champion or Commander, as both rode on a 116.5-inch wheelbase and trim differences were minor. This version, being a Regal Conestoga in the Champion line, sold for $2,312. It carries the two-tone paint-trim which gave it a little more splash.

The lowest priced Commander for 1955 was this Custom 2-door Sedan which delivered for $1,873. Its counterpart Champion, being the lowest priced Studebaker for 1955, sold for $1,741. A total of 18,714 Studebaker 2-door sedans were sold in 1955.

Studebaker's short-lived Commander Custom 4-door Sedan sold for $1,919. With the difference of merely $200, a person could own a Commander Regal Sedan with the DeLuxe appointments. So, by years end, the Custom line was history.

The massive chrome shovel-like nose on this 1955 Commander DeLuxe Coupe altered its front-end appearance greatly from the previous two-year model run. Since the merger with Packard, company officials tried to come to a mutual agreement about the sloping front end. Many did not care for it. And, since these were the chrome days, they felt if the nose were loaded up with more chrome, maybe the slant might be hidden. The vehicle brought a price tag of $1,989.

This 1955 Studebaker Commander DeLuxe 4-door Sedan was one of 58,792 Commander cars built for the year. For the first time ever, since the Champion was born in 1939, did the Commander out produce the lesser model. The Commander sales were twice what they had been in 1954. This vehicle sold for $2,614.

The Commander V-8 Deluxe Ultra Vista 4-door Sedan for 6 passengers

Studebaker continued to offer the Conestoga as a utility vehicle in 1955. Here it is seen as a "mini-ambulance," often used in small communities where a larger vehicle couldn't be afforded or wouldn't be required. As in 1954, it came only as a V-8. The DeLuxe unit sold for $2,274.

The Commander V-8 Regal Coupe for 5 passengers

This is the 1955 Commander Regal Coupe. The 3,065-pound vehicle was one of 23,234 coupes built by Studebaker in 1955. The 224 cubic-inch V-8 developed 140 horsepower at 4500 rpm. Surprisingly, management found that by using the Packard 259 cubic-inch V-8 which developed 162 horsepower, no significant advantage took place over the 224 cubic inch block. Fuel consumption was still a plus with the economy a constant feature of all Studebakers. This model sold for $2,094.

The second least expensive of the Commander Regal models was this 1955 Commander 4-door Sedan. It was available for $2,127. For the model year, the company sold 68,807 sedans among its three series of vehicles. This unit is equipped with whitewall tires and the factory wheel discs.

This is Studebaker's most expensive Conestoga for 1955. It is a Commander Regal model weighing 3,275 pounds and selling for $2,445. This model had a rear seat that would fold down to give nearly 70 cubic feet of cargo space. The upholstery was done in vinyl that harmonized with the exterior finish.

The lower priced version of the 1955 President 4-door Sedan was this DeLuxe Ultra Vista Sedan. This unit rode on the same 120.5-inch wheelbase as all President models. It weighed the least of the Presidents, tipping the scale at 3,165 pounds and was delivered for $2,311 in base form.

A rare version for the 1955 President State 4-door Sedan is this early model in a single-tone paint job. All President models came on a 120.5 inch wheelbase. The top of the line Sedan came with gold plated hardware and exquisitely tailored nylon upholstery. A folding center rear seat arm rest was standard equipment, as it was on the former Land Cruiser models.

Back after "a long winters nap" was the President series. Not seen since 1942, it came in five models for 1955. This is a late edition President State 4-door Sedan which sold for $2,381. The difference between it and early models is the wrap-around windshield and an updated dashboard. The horsepower also was increased from 175 to 185. Fender skirts were standard equipment for this model. It weighed 3,220 pounds in base form.

# 1955

The 1955 President State Coupe weighed 3,220 pounds. All President models, built after January, 1955, could be ordered with air conditioning, and power seats and windows. The tire size for the President models was 7.10x15 inches. The deluxe wheel covers came as standard equipment on this model.

The President State Hardtop Coupe sold for $2,456. The 120.5-inch wheelbase coupe weighed 3,175 pounds. It came with the 259.2 cubic-inch engine, developing 175 horsepower, if the car was built early in the year. All models, after January 1, 1955, had a horsepower increase to 185.

Packard's experimental show car for 1954 actually made its debut before the two-company merger. This example was referred to as the Panther Daytona, but originally was known as the Gray Wolf II. The car used fiberglass components. It was designed by a team under the hand of Richard Teague.

A rear view of the Panther Daytona. Information varies . . .some say only a few of this style were ever produced, while others claim the car was one-off model that underwent several minor revisions during its life on the dream car circuit. This example received a slight updating some where along the line, as it is wearing 1955 tail lights. The car was driven at Daytona Beach by Dick Rathman, a noted race driver of the time. It first clocked over 110 mph, then did an unofficial 130. Power was by a supercharged version of the big Straight Eight.

All 1956 Studebakers were given a healthy dose of re-design this year, resulting in a series of cars more in keeping with other American vehicles. The styles still said "I'm a Studebaker," but said so with less radical assertion. Also on the books were two brand new V-8s and the addition of a Carter 4-barrel carburetor to both the "standard' and "optional" equipment list. In addition, Studebaker joined the ranks of 12 volt users, having a totally new electric system geared to the higher voltage. This helped in both starting and spark performance.

New for the year, and causing a mild automotive sensation were the beautiful Studebaker Hawks. The last major project for Studebaker-Packard by the famed designer Raymond Loewy, the cars were based on the 1953 Loewy Coupe body, but with enough modifications to make them look like totally new designs. Four varieties were available: the Flight and Power Hawks, utilizing the old Starlight pillared coupe body, and the Sky and prestigious Golden Hawks, which retained the hardtop Starliner shell. The Flight Hawk was part of the Champion series, the Power Hawk belonged to the Commanders, the Sky Hawk was considered part of the President line, and the Golden Hawk formed a new one-model series of its own.

The Golden Hawk was the only Studebaker to use a Packard V-8, accepting the 352 cubic inch block of 4x3.5 inch bore and stroke, which developed 275 hp at 4600 rpm, having a compression of 9.5:1. The carburetor was a 4-barrel Carter, classed as standard equipment on both the Golden and Sky Hawks, and also on the new President Classic 4-door Sedans. However, these latter two models used a new 289 cubic inch Studebaker V-8 of 3-9/16x3-5/8 inches. This engine was also shared by the rest of the President line, but fitted with a Stromberg 2-barrel carburetor. When the 4-barrel was attached, the engine was rated at 210 hp at 4200 rpm, while the 2-barrel developed 190 horses at 4000 rpm. The compression ratio on the lower horse engine was

7.5:1, while the hot-shot used an 8:1 ratio.

The 259.2 cubic inch V-8, used in last year's President line and Speedster, now appeared in the Commanders and Power Hawks. This engine was now also available with an extra-cost Carter 4-barrel. The 4-barrel models produced 185 hp at 4000 rpm, while the 2-barrel delivered 170 hp at 4000 rpm.

Lowest level of Hawk was the Flight Hawk models, which were considered part of the Champion series. All of these cars used the L-head Six of 185 cubic inches which developed 101 hp at 3800 rpm. The bore and stroke remained 3x4-3/8 inches and the compression ratio was 7.5.

The former Conestoga wagons not only received the line's full facial treatment, but they were subject to a name change as well. The upscale wagon was now called the Pinehurst. It was part of the President series and used that line's 289 cubic inch V-8. The Parkview was part of the Commander series, and used the small V-8, while the Pelham was in the Champion family and had the Six for power.

Remaining constant was the use of two wheelbases and three transmissions. All models used the 116.5-inch wheelbase chassis except the Hawks, which used the 120.5-inch unit formerly used on the Starlight and Starliner Coupes. The transmissions were the standard 3-speed manual and the optional 3-speed manual with overdrive, or the Flightomatic automatic. Prices ranged from $1,844 for a Champion 2-door Sedan to $3,061 for the Golden Hawk. Despite the new and very attractive styling and the new Hawk models, sales were much lower than in previous years. Thus, the model year saw only 69,593 units sold. Calendar year production amounted to 82,402, which was poor but still enough to keep the company in the 13th sales position for the second year in a row. In fact, sales were down to such a point that the Los Angeles plant was shut for good. Studebakers now came only from South Bend and Canada.

The most expensive model for 1956 was this Golden Hawk hardtop. It carried a price tag of $3,061 and weighed 3,360 pounds, making it the heaviest car in the South Bend lineup. This neat example carries all the deluxe accessories even down to wire wheel covers. The basic design is still hailed as one of most beautiful ever to come from Studebaker.

An impressive looking car is this 1956 Golden Hawk done in a tri-tone paint combination. This Hawk was Studebaker's most expensive car for the year, selling at $3,061. The hardtop weighed 3,360 pounds. This model was the only one that came with Packard's Ultramatic transmission. By 1957, the excellent transmission was gone for good because of its cost, not because it lacked in performance or dependability. A total of 4,071 Golden Hawks were produced in 1956.

This nicely equipped 1956 Sky Hawk Hardtop Coupe came with all the factory approved equipment. The hardtop came on a 120.5-inch wheelbase, weighed 3,215 pounds, and delivered for $2,477. The ribbed trunk deck base was a rather unique styling exercise that proved to be quite attractive. The deck lid was enough different from the previous Loewy Coupes to let buyers know it was a new style. Dual exhausts with chrome tips add a touch of class while letting other drivers know that this model had go as well as show.

The 1956 Studebaker Power Hawk was available as a model within the Commander series. It came, as did all the Hawk Coupes, on the 120.5 inch wheelbase. Studebaker advertised these as "Budget-priced family cars with a sports car flair."

The newly designed 1956 Flight Hawk Coupe was available only in the Champion series. It used the same 6-cylinder power plant of 185 cubic inches, developing 101 horsepower at 3800 rpm, as did other Champions. This example weighed 2,770 pounds and sold for $1,996. The Flight Hawks came with small hub caps as standard equipment, but full discs could be ordered at extra cost.

# 1956

Looking quite similar to the 2-door Sedan is this example called the Champion Sedanet for 1956. The most noticeable difference between the two is the lack of full stainless trim on the entire body panels. The Sedanet example carried the trim from front fender to just beyond the door opening. It weighed 2,780 pounds and sold for a little over $100 less than the 2-door Sedan, being priced at $1,844.

Referred to as the 1956 Studebaker Champion 2-door Sedan, this model again was popular with young families who were devotees of Studebaker...sadly, there were just not enough such young people. This model carried a price of $1,946.

Dressed in its "Sunday goin-to-meetin duds" is this 1956 Champion 4-door Sedan. The car is equipped with deluxe wheel covers, whitewall tires, and full side stainless trim molding. The vehicle weighed 2,835 pounds and sold for $1,996. The Champion line saw a model year production of 28,918 vehicles, while total calendar year sales put Studebaker in the 13th sales slot.

Another car well suited for economical taxi use was this 1956 Champion 4-door Sedan. It weighed 2,835 pounds and delivered for $1,996. It came with 6.40x15-inch tires as standard equipment, but for heavy use as a taxi, the Commander tire size of 6.70x15 inches was recommended.

Studebakers lowest-priced wagon was the Pelham, which was classed as a model in the Champion line. This unit was available for $2,232. It weighed in at exactly 3,000 pounds. The Champion models for 1956 were ranked by Motor Trend as America's most economical cars. Model year sales for the Champion amounted to 28,918 units

Basically the same car as the 1956 Champion 2-door Sedan was the Commander 2-door Sedan. Only trim changes differentiated the two vehicles. Mechanically, the engine rooms were where the differences took place, with the Champions having a Six and the Commanders a V-8. This example sold for $2,076, but buyers were few.

The 1956 Commander 2-door Sedanet offered clean sculptured styling, but didn't find many buyers. It, like the Champion, came with stainless trim from the front fender to just before the door opening. It weighed 3,085 pounds and sold for $1,974.

The 1956 Commander 4-door Sedan is shown here with a special rakish "V" placed on its rear quarter panel. Obviously this was a pre-production photo as the medallion didn't appear on regular production models. The Commander Sedans sold for $2,176. Full wheel covers and whitewalls were extra cost items.

Shown here is the 1956 Studebaker 4-door Sedan in the Commander line-up. This example wears the small wheelcaps as used on the less fancy cars from 1953 through 1955. It apparently is an early production model according to information on this factory photo. This example weighed 3,140 pounds and sold in base form for $2,125.

The police version of the 1956 Commander 4-door Sedan resembled the Champion line, as far as the exterior trim of the car went. Under the hood it was a different story. It carried the 259.2 cubic-inch engine that developed 185 horsepower. It also came as a Police Special, using the President engine of 289 cubic inches. Some police departments chose these as very fast vehicles for pursuit use, as this year Studebaker made a very definite effort to break into this market. The 12-volt electrical system was first introduced on the 1956 cars. Note this vehicle does not carry the full stainless side trim as was available on deluxe examples.

The new name for the wagon in the Commander series for 1956 was the Parkview. It weighed exactly 3,300 pounds and delivered for $2,354. The total wagon production for 1956 was only 6,892 units. Studebaker used different side trim for each series of wagon, making identification relatively easy . . . if one could find a Studebaker wagon to identify in the first place.

The South Bend Police Department made good use of their locally owned automotive manufacturing firm. Studebaker also was happy to oblige. It made for good public relations both ways. This 1956 unit is the Parkview Wagon in the Commander series which carried the 259.2 cubic-inch engine. It is shown here being used as an emergency ambulance. With the rear seat down, there was room enough for a folding stretcher, loaded through the tailgate. However, the driver looks a bit scrunched, with the edge of the stretcher butting up against his shoulders.

Studebaker offered this 1956 President 2-door Sedan for the first time of what would be a two-year showing. It sold for $2,188 but found few buyers in its two-year stay. Studebaker described the car as being designed for those who liked the intimacy of a coupe coupled with the spaciousness of a sedan.

The least expensive President model for 1956 was the 4-door Sedan. It delivered without deluxe frills for $2,235. This version rode on the 116.5-inch wheelbase like its Champion and Commander brothers. The particular example shown here was part of the fleet of the Sheriff's department of St. Joseph County, Indiana.

The Pinehurst was the new name given to the station wagon in the President series for 1956. This vehicle rode on the 116.5-inch wheelbase, weighed 3,395 pounds, and sold for $2,529. The roof rack and wire wheel covers on this unit are extra cost items.

This photo shows a dealer unveiling of the 1956 Studebakers. Seen here is the 1956 President Classic 4-door Sedan. New for the season was this model with its hooded headlights and two-tone side paneling. Such festive introductions were still popular at large dealerships, during this era when buyers were actually interested in each year's new offerings.

This is the new body design that Studebaker proudly displayed in 1956. The model, shown here at a Studebaker car event, is the President Classic 4-door Sedan. It came on a 120.5-inch wheelbase, weighed 3,295 pounds and sold for $2,489. The year's production amounted to 34,019 units among the total variety of 4-door sedans sold.

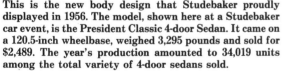

For 1957 the major change involved the Studebaker body shells, but not the Studebaker. This was the year that Packards essentially became dressed-up Studebakers, utilizing virtually all Studebaker sheet metal and chassis components, while retaining just enough cosmetic effect to differentiate between the two cars.

On the real Studebaker line, only minimal trim relocation told the 1957 from the 1956 models. Among these modifications were a new full grille that wrapped around to the leading edges of the front wheel openings and a redesigned bumper with a pronounced center dip. New for the year were the Provincial and the Broadmoor, which appeared in the Commander and President line and represented Studebaker's first post-war 4-door station wagon.

The year-old Hawk line was reduced to simply a Silver and a Golden Hawk, both considered part of the President series. The Silver Hawk could be equipped with either the Six or the 259 or 289 cubic inch V-8s, while the Golden Hawk came only with a supercharged version of the 289 V-8, which produced 275 hp at 4800 rpm. The supercharger was a McCulloch belt-driven unit. This car used the hardtop version of the coupe shell, while the Silver Hawks used the pillared version. Also added to the Golden Hawk were dual exhausts.

A performance kit, including a 4-barrel Carter carburetor and dual exhausts was available for V-8 Silver Hawks. This boosted the 259 cubic inch mill's performance to 195 hp at 4500 rpm and the 289's performance to 225 horses, also at 4500 rpm. The former Packard 352 cubic inch block was not being built at all this year, and in fact, Packards all used the same 289 cubic inch engines as found in the Studebakers, both in plain and supercharged form.

The President series also used the 289 V-8. The President Classic, available only in 4-door Sedan style, used a Carter 4-barrel V-8 that developed 225 hp at 4500 rpm, while the other Presidents used a Stromberg 2-barrel version that hit 210 horses. The Presidents also used dual exhausts.

Commanders continued to use the 259 cubic inch V-8, which was now rated at 180 horses at 4500 rpm, and the Champions continued with the 185 cubic inch Six, still rated at 101 hp at 3800 rpm.

With sales of upscale models faltering, Studebaker this year turned to the low end of the spectrum and at mid-year came out with a real "Plain Jane" series. Not since World War II had a company introduced a line with so little chrome or trim on its models. Sporting painted bumpers, hubcaps, and window surrounds, these were truly "blackout" models, more suited to late 1942 than to 1957. Regarded as a sub-series of the Champion line, this new grouping was called the Scotsman series. Models came in either two or 4-door Sedan style or as a 2-door Station Wagon. The lowest price version was the 2-door Sedan, which sold for $1,776. Also available again this year was the Custom sub-series, available in all series as a lower trim level than its parent model. Due to poor sales and the introduction of the Scotsman line, the Custom models were discontinued at the end of 1957.

In each series except the Scotsman, a buyer could order a two-tone version, with the top and rear quarter panel done in color harmonizing with the rest of the car.

Even with the new Scotsman models and the supercharged Hawks, the public wasn't buying, and sales continued to slip. Only 63,101 cars found buyers for the model run. Calendar year sales for both Studebaker and Packard were so poor this year that the two lines were combined. Their overall total was 72,889, keeping the company in 13th place for the third year in a row.

The 1957 Golden Hawk had its famous contrasting colored concave panel to help distinguish it from Silver Hawks of the same year. This beauty delivered for $3,282, making it Studebakers most costly car for the year. The factory produced 4,356 of this model in 1957. A supercharger was standard on this model, allowing the engine to develop 275 horsepower.

The 1957 Golden Hawk was basically the same rendering as the 1956 model with the exception of a more contoured flair to its rear quarter panel. The Golden Hawk came with five small chevrons on the rear quarter panel concave, which was often done in a contrasting color from the rest of the car. These features were distinguishing earmarks to help identify the Hawk models. Interestingly enough, the factory brought out a Golden Hawk 400 in April of 1957. It offered a full leather interior, carpeted trunk, and flared armrests similar to the 1956 Hawks. The interior choices were either tan or white. Unfortunately, the model did not receive much of an applause even from Studebaker enthusiasts. It is doubtful if more than its numbered title of "400" were produced. The car weighed 3,400 pounds while the regular Golden Hawk such as this came as a 3,185-pound car. This Hawk delivered for $3,182 while the luxury model delivered for approximately $3,500.

Stately looking is one good way to describe the 1957 Studebaker Silver Hawk. An easy means of identifying a Silver Hawk from the Golden Hawk is by the full-length body panel stainless trim. Silver Hawks came with bench seats in cloth and vinyl or solid vinyl. They also came with the V-8 engine or the Six, if the owner preferred a small block for some unknown reason. A total of 15,318 Silver Hawks were manufactured in 1957.

Coming on the market at mid-season was the 1957 Scotsman. This was Studebaker's lowest priced offering for the year. This 2-door Club Sedan in the Champion line sold for $1,776 and weighed 2,680 pounds. The Scotsman models were true blackout models void of any chrome except for the bumpers and minor trim. They were designed primarily for fleet use and those few buyers who wanted basic big-car transportation at the lowest possible cost.

The 1957 Custom Champion 2-door Sedan was available again for the year. It sold for $2,001 in its regular 6-cylinder form. As a Commander Custom 2-door Sedan, it was available for $294 additional ($2,295) and weighed 3,140 pounds.

A three-quarter rear view gives a good look at the taillight design of this 1957 DeLuxe 4-door Sedan. It came as a Champion with the 185 cubic inch Six for $2,171 or as a DeLuxe V-8 Commander for $2,295.

The 1957 Parkview V-8 2-door Station Wagon sold for $2,505 and tipped the scale at 3,310 pounds. The same 2-door unit came in the Champion line, again as the Pelham, selling for $2,382. A total of 5,062 2-door Wagons were delivered between the Pelham and Parkview models for 1957.

The 1957 DeLuxe 2-door Club Sedan was available either as a Champion for $2,123 or in Commander style for $2,246. Note the fender vent doors. This was a Studebaker feature from 1941 up to the last of the 1964 Hawks.

Not seen since the 1955 models was the Custom sub-series. Back for a one-year stay is this 1957 Custom available in both Champion and Commander models. This example was built as a Custom Commander 4-door Sedan as identified by the emblem on the front fender. It carried a price tag of $2,173. If the owner preferred a Custom Champion 4-door, it delivered for $2,049.

The 1957 Parkview 2-door Station Wagon was classed in the Commander line of cars. This model used the 116.5-inch wheelbase, weighed 3,310 pounds, and sold for $2,505. The 259 cubic inch V-8 developed 180 horsepower or 195 if the four-barrel carburetor setup was used. This example, with blanked in side windows, was often used as a utility vehicle for florists, funeral homes, or home tradesmen. It was sold as a separate panel delivery model, and was equipped with a full-length cargo floor rather than a rear seat.

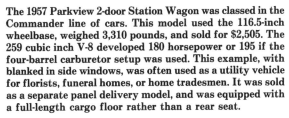

The 1957 Commander DeLuxe V-8 4-door Sedan saw little change from its 1956 counterpart. The most noticeable difference was seen in the front bumper which now lacked bumper guard equipment. Also new was a more massive grille which gave the car a wider appearance. This unit wears the white walls and full wheel covers that were extra cost items. They certainly add to its overall appearance. This model weighed 3,140 pounds and delivered for $2,295.

Offered for the first time in the Commander series was the 1957 Provincial 4-door Station Wagon. Note: This model does not carry the stainless steel ribs on the tailgate as did the Broadmoor. This unit weighed in at 3,355 pounds and carried a delivered price of $2,561.

# 1957

Totally new for 1957 was the 4-door Station Wagon. Seen here is the most expensive wagon of the year. It was referred to as the Broadmoor. It weighed 3,415 pounds and carried a price tag of $2,666. A total of only 5,142 4-door wagons were produced in 1957, which also included the Provincial, an accompanying model cataloged in the Commander series.

President Club Sedan

A rare model was the 1957 President 2-door Club Sedan. This was just a dolled up version of the Champion or Commander Club Sedan. It weighed 3,170 pounds and went home for $2,358. The Club Sedan sales, divided among the three series, amounted to 10,152 units manufactured for the year.

The 1957 President 4-door Sedan was the lower priced comparison to the President Classic. It came with a less fancy interior and some fewer pieces of bright trim on its exterior. It was available for $2,407 and weighed in at 3,205 pounds. It did not share the 120.5-inch wheelbase but came on the same 116.5-inch wheelbase used on Champion and Commander Sedans.

The 1957 Studebaker President 4-door Sedan rode on the 116.5 inch wheelbase like the Champion and Commander models. Note: This model came without the rear door quarter window as used on the President Classic. This vehicle carried a price tag of $2,407.

The 1957 Broadmoor Station Wagon was in the President series. Because of its new grille design, this example shows a wider front appearance than the 1956 cars. The lack of bumper guard clutter also adds greatly to its frontal appearance.

The top of the line 1957 President Classic rode on its own 120.5-inch wheelbase. This example weighed 3,270 pounds and sold for $2,539. The Sedan line up was Studebaker's best seller for the year with a total of 26,887 being produced.

The 1957 Packard Clipper Sedan with the V-8 engine developed 275 horsepower from its 289 cubic-inch block. A total of 3,940 of this sedan were produced for the model run.

The Packard Clipper for 1957 looked very much like the Studebaker for the same year. This example was known as the County Sedan. It used a 120.5-inch wheelbase and sold for $3,384. Only 869 were built.

The 1957 Country Sedan came with seating for six passengers. The model weighed in at 3,650 pounds. The roof rack was optional at extra cost, but most all came with this accessory. Note the fender air vent. It is very reminiscent of a Studebaker feature of prior years.

Studebaker entered 1958 with practically the same offerings that it had in 1957. The major changes on the car were quad headlights on the President and Commander models, excepting the Hawks, and canted rear fenders on all models except the Scotsman. Quad headlights were also available on Champions, but as an extra-cost option. Also, in the Champion line, the side trim continued full-length on the car, and the name "STUDEBAKER" was placed at the base of the hood, to make an easily detected difference between 1958 and 1957 stock. The new canted fenders and taillight assemblies brought the car into the same basic appearance grouping as the Hawks. Probably due to their late introduction combined with their low-buck status, the Scotsman models were unchanged this year.

New for the year was a 2-door Hardtop Sedan or Hardtop Coupe, which supposedly was available only in the Commander and President lines, although records indicate that 120 were turned out in Champion form.

Both the Silver and Golden Hawks appeared virtually unchanged this year, with only a minor grille redesign to mark the new models. This year's Hawks used a mesh covering in the side grilles which was similar to that of the main grille. A new coat of arms was now being used by the Studebaker-Packard Corp., and this was rather prominently displayed at the base of the grille center, making one think of the old crank-hole covers of the 1930s. Both the pillared Silver Hawk and hardtop Golden Hawk finished out the year, but the Golden Hawk was making its final appearance and would not return in 1959.

Mechanically the cars remained untouched from the 1957 models, except for oversized brake drums that carried 172.4 square inches of lining. Models used both 14 or 15 inch wheels, with the 14-inch variety available at extra cost for the Champion and Commander models.

Just the reverse was true on the Golden Hawk, Broadmoor Wagons, and President models. They came with 8.00x14 tires as standard equipment, with 7.10x15s offered optionally at extra cost.

Studebakers ranged in price from $1,799 for the Scotsman 2-door Sedan to $3,282 for the Golden Hawk. Model year sales continued on their downhill slide, with only 44,759 units sold. However, 1958 turned out to be a recession year for the automobile industry in general, and thus, calendar year production of 56,869 was enough to rank the company in 11 sales position. In Detroit, this was the final year for Packard, with production drawing to a close on July 13, 1958.

In its last year of manufacture was this impressive 1958 Golden Hawk Coupe. As beautiful as this car was to both drive and look at, the buyers were not buying and the company continued to slide. There were fewer than 2,500 Studebaker dealers remaining throughout the Country in 1958. Only 756 Golden Hawks were produced for the year.

The tell-tale difference on the 1958 Studebaker Hawks over the 1957 models was the relocation of the grille emblem. It was now placed at the center bottom of the grille. This example is shown with either experimental style wheel covers, which didn't go into production, or someone chose to put wheel discs other than Studebaker's on this vehicle to ready it for its factory photo. This Golden Hawk weighed 3,470 pounds, and carried a price tag of $3,282. A total of only 878 1958 Hawks were manufactured. Most Hawks came with 8.00x14-inch tires as standard equipment. However, the owner could order the vehicle with 7.10x15-inch tires as an extra cost option.

Studebaker *Scotsman 2-Door Sedan*

This 1958 Champion Scotsman 2-door sedan was the same car as in 1957, as it did not come on the market until mid-season of the previous year. The only change was in the price, which increased to $1,795, still making it the lowest priced model for the year. Advertised as "Full Size...Full Power...Maximum Economy," the car delivered just that, but at a cost of no frills and virtually no chrome trim. Studebaker claimed the Six would deliver up to 29 miles to a gallon.

One of three body styles available as Scotsman models for 1958 was the 4-door Sedan, which also was the most popular. It came available in regular family car fashion, as a taxi-cab with a heavy vinyl naugahyde interior, and as a police unit. Interestingly enough, the latter version was the only Scotsman equipped with a V-8 engine, considered necessary for the heavy duty work of a police vehicle.

The "Police Marshal" is what this Scotsman 4-door Sedan was referred to by factory officials. Police units supposedly were all equipped with the 289 cubic-inch V-8 engine. Yet this example doesn't carry the V-medallion on its grille, and has only a small "S" nameplate on the hood like those worn by regular Champion models.

Only one of two models that were available as station wagons in 1958 was this non-chromed Scotsman 2-door Station Wagon. Quad headlights were not available on Scotsman models. This example weighed 2,870 pounds and sold for $2,055.

This Three quarter rear-view of the 1958 Scotsman 2-door Wagon almost resembles a military vehicle in khaki trim. The Scotsman could only be ordered with 15-inch wheels, while regular Champions could be delivered with 14-inch wheels as an option. The sub-series was now classed as being in its second year of production, coming as a mid-year car in 1957. Management made a projection that 4,000 units would satisfy those looking for such economical transportation. Not so; the car was a success and better than 10,000 were built in its year and a half of manufacture.

This 1958 Studebaker Scotsman was designed chiefly as a utility vehicle. Actually it is basically a Station Wagon with panelled window sides. These vehicles drew a minor interest with tradesmen because their table height tailgate made for easy loading. Known as the Panel Wagon, the vehicle measured eight feet long and five feet wide, giving 93 cubic feet of carrying space.

This 1958 Studebaker Champion 4-door Sedan was equipped as a taxi-cab and referred to in the fleet trade as the "Econ-O-Miler". Studebaker's reputation for economy has been synonymous with their quality through the years. In the 1958 Champion models, the company boasted of the up to 29-miles per gallon operating economy, and claimed that the Econ-O-Miler was designed as a taxi from the ground up. This unit patiently waits for customers in front of New York's Waldorf-Astoria. This was certainly a staged scene. I can't believe there isn't more foot or car traffic in front of the famous hotel, indicating that the photo was probably made early on a Sunday morning.

This 1958 Studebaker Champion 2-door Sedan was one of a production run of 6,473 units. This figure also included the Scotsman 2-door model. This example weighed 2,795 pounds and delivered for $2,189. The Champion line used the same 6-cylinder engine developing 101 horsepower.

The 1958 Silver Hawk Coupe could be ordered as a Champion with the 6-cylinder engine, weighing 2,810 pounds and selling for $2,219, or in the President series where it was offered for $2,352 as a V-8 model.

The most noticeable change on the 1958 Studebakers was seen in the Commander and President models where quad headlights were now standard equipment. Model reduction was the order for 1958. Gone were the Commander Parkview Wagons, the DeLuxe and Custom Commander Pelham Wagons, DeLuxe Custom, and models in the Champion line. Also, the title of President Classic didn't return. However, to help fill the bill, the regular President became the President Classic and it took the 120.5-inch wheelbase for 1958. The Broadmoor Wagon was also history. So that everything wasn't a "downer" a Starlight hardtop made its debut in both the Commander and President models. This particular Provincial Station Wagon was only one of two wagons offered for 1958. This model weighed 3,420 pounds. It delivered for $2,644.

The only year for this Commander Hardtop Coupe was 1958. The V-8 engine produced 180 horsepower in regular version or 195 horsepower if the optional four-barrel carburetor was ordered. This model weighed 3,270 pounds, came on the 116.5-inch wheelbase like the President Starlight Coupe, and went home for $2,493.

The 1958 Commander 4-door Sedan was basically the same car as the Champion 4-door except for minor trim changes. The quad headlights were new for the Commander cars, but could be ordered on Champions at extra cost. The tail fins and taillight assembly are similar to the rear styling of the Hawk models. This Commander sold for $2,378 or, if ordered as a Champion, delivered for $2,253.

The 1958 President Starlight hardtop came on a 116.5-inch wheelbase. The vehicle weighed 3,355 pounds and delivered for $2,695. Note the antenna mounted in the middle of the deck lid. This new style was not a Raymond Loewy design, but was a body shared with Packard for that make's last year of life.

A front view of the 1958 Studebaker President hardtop Starlight Coupe proves that this was one highly attractive style. Approximately 4,000 were built during the model run, divided between President and the Commander Starlight versions.

This is the 1958 President 4-door Sedan which was now in its final year. This model weighed 3,365 pounds and sold for $2,639. Mechanically these were the same cars as the 1957 models.

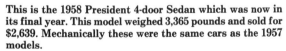

Packard had a Hawk, too. In 1958, all were pretty much the same except the 1958 Packard Hawk came with a supercharged engine developing 275 horsepower. There were only 588 of this style produced. The fake spare tire mounted on the rear deck was standard equipment for the Packard Hawk model, but did not appear on similar Studebaker styles. This was the final year of Packard production.

# 1959

A totally new car came from Studebaker this year. Called the Lark, it was the company's first compact, with the cars built on a 108.5 inch wheelbase and the station wagons using a 113-inch base. The Larks came in four body styles powered by either an L-head Six or the V-8 engine. The cars totally replaced the old Champion, Commander, and President lines of full-size cars, and except for a couple of Silver Hawks still flying around, represented Studebaker's total offerings for the year. It was hoped that the new line would be exciting, attractive, and economical enough to pull the company from its financial nose-dive of the past few years. In this respect, the Larks did help, and though the eventual end might have been in sight for the skeptics, the new little car did at least provide a few more years of life for the ailing Studebaker-Packard Corp.

Powering the Larks were the same two engines that were available in this year's Silver Hawks. the Six had a 169.6 cubic inch displacement and delivered 90 horses at 4000 rpm. Its compression ratio was 8.3:1, and it had a bore and stroke of an even 3x4 inches. The V-8 was listed at 259.2 cubic inches, and rated at 180 horsepower at 4500 rpm. Here the compression ratio was 8.8:1, while the bore and stroke was 3.56x3.25. Either engine required only regular fuel, which came from an 18-gallon tank on both the Larks and Hawks. Both cars also used 7.50x14 tires. However, Silver Hawks could be ordered with 7.10x15 tires at no extra cost.

Transmission choices for all models continued as in previous years: a 3-speed conventional; 3-speed with overdrive, and the automatic Flight-O-Matic.

Returning to the industry at this time was the use of reclining front seats, a concept that had come in and out of automotive design since the early 'teens. These seats in recent years had come to be associated primarily with Nash, which promoted them heavily in their magazines ads and brochures. Now Studebaker decided that such seats would be a smart selling feature on this year's Lark models. The split seat could either be reclined partially on the passenger side, or fully reclined in total, to produce a rather lumpy but usable bed.

Despite its attractive lines, the lowest production model for 1959 was the Silver Hawk, with sales of only 6,649. This compares to the new Lark 4-door Sedan, which recorded sales of 48,459 units to become Studebaker's most popular model of the year. Lark prices ranged from a 2-door Sedan for $1,925 to the Regal 2-door V-8 Station Wagon for $2,590. The V-8 Silver Hawk, meanwhile, listed for $2,495.

If Studebaker management was counting on the new Larks to spur the company's financial position, they were not to be disappointed. The little car gave the company a healthy sales increase for the model year, with 126,156 units delivered. This advanced Studebaker to the 10th sales position nationally. Calendar year figures showed combined Lark and Hawk production tallied at 153,823. Sales for the year amounted to $387-million, which was the best the company had seen since the big time year in 1953. Of this amount, the company recorded over $28-million in profits. With an eye on future expansion at this time, Studebaker-Packard bought the U.S. distribution rights to Mercedes Benz; DKW, and Auto Union cars. With German-sourced cars in the fold, many younger people would begin to believe that Studebaker was also a German-made vehicle.

The only Hawk manufactured in 1959 was the Silver Hawk. It was available either as a 6-cylinder model for $2,360, weighing 2,795 pounds, or as a V-8 for $2,495, with a weight of 3,140 pounds. The parking lights were removed from the top of the fenders and now were placed within the pockets of the meshed side grilles. A total of 6,647 Hawks were produced in 1959.

Caught with its pants down was this view of one of the first Larks being manufactured by the Studebaker-Packard Corporation. When put together, it will be a V-8 Lark. The publicity photo, made in a South Bend studio, uses a stage backdrop depicting a Miami Beach scene of the mid-1950s.

The 1959 Lark 2-door Sedan came only as a DeLuxe with the 6-cylinder engine. It delivered for $1,925, making it Studebaker's lowest priced offering for the year. Shown here with Alaska license plates and snowy roads, this particular example was destined to lead a very cold life. Hopefully, the heater was a strong unit.

Studebaker's lowest priced 4-door for 1959 was the DeLuxe Sedan. It weighed 2,605 pounds and carried a price tag of $1,995. All two and 4-door models rode on a 108.5-inch wheelbase.

Studebaker Lark DeLuxe Station Wagons came with the 6-cylinder engine that developed 90 horsepower. The fuel tank was of an 18-gallon capacity for all models.

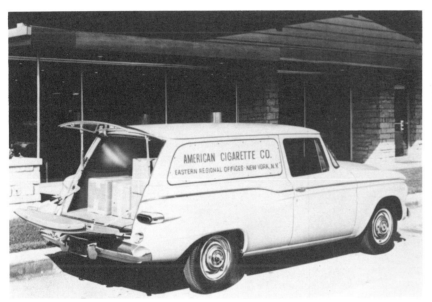

Originally this unit started out as a station wagon. But, by paneling in the side windows, it made a very compact utility vehicle. The absence of a right-side mirror had to have made for difficult lane changes. Minor alterations gave a slight price increase to the vehicle. At this point, Studebaker was the only American manufacturer still actively marketing panel delivery trucks of this type. All other companies had dropped the style years earlier, as the concept of van-type delivery units claimed wide acceptance. The wagons used a 113-inch wheelbase and gave 93-cubic feet of space when the back seat was folded down in the storage compartment. They came either as a 6-cylinder for $2,455, or as V-8, selling for $2,590.

The first of the Lark Hardtop Coupes to appear were all Regal models that were well received. They came either with a Six for $2,275, or in V-8 style delivered for $2,410. As a Six, they delivered 26 MPG at 30 MPH and as a V-8 at the same speed, the MPG decreased to 24. A total of 14,235 Hardtop Coupes were built for 1959.

This is the 1959 Regal Lark 4-door Sedan, available either as a Six for $2,175, weighing 2,600 pounds, or as a V-8 for $2,310, weighing 2,924 pounds. This unit was leaving the South Bend plant equipped with the accessory bumper guards, twin side mirrors, and whitewall tires.

Offering more trim was the 1959 Regal Station Wagon. This 2-door Wagon delivered for $2,455 if produced in 6-cylinder style. As a V-8, it was the most expensive car the company offered in 1959, selling for $2,590. It also was the heaviest vehicle for the year, weighing 3,148 pounds.

Often used in small towns for both police and emergency ambulance service were the Lark Station Wagons. This example, with a few conversions being made, carries a stretcher and the roof-mounted siren and flasher. From the tailgate emblems, the numeral VIII says that its a V-8.

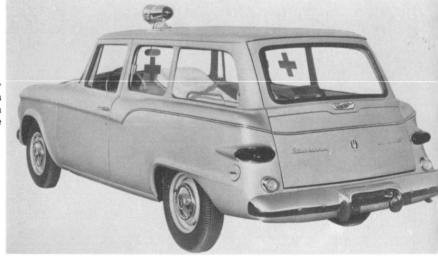

This is the 10,000 Lark to come off the assembly line at South Bend in 1959. Surely the young ladies had nothing to do with the cars manufacture. Either they are executives' secretaries, or from a South Bend modeling agency.

For 1960, the Lark did not fly alone. A wide variety of compacts were beginning to enter the market. G-M, Ford and Chrysler all had their little babies, respectively known as Corvair, Falcon, and Valiant, while Nash continued with its Rambler, which had been around since 1950. None of the Big-Three makes were perceived by Studebaker management to constitute a threat. In fact, Studebaker officials were quoted as saying that the competition would be good, as it would spur even more interest in compact-size cars. Besides, Lark had flown in a year ahead of the majors, was currently offering a wider choice of engines and models, and at least in the case of Corvair, had a much more traditional design.

As could be expected, the 1960 Studebakers were simply face-lifted versions of the 1959 models. But new for the year was the addition of a Lark Convertible and a Lark 4-door Station Wagon. The new wagon was an immediate success, outselling the 2-door version by a ratio of 18-to-5. It was instrumental in helping attain an additional 25,000 sales for the year. The convertible was a surprise move, and represented the first soft-top Studebaker since 1952. It gave the company the distinction of being the only compact line to offer a convertible in 1960.

Mechanically, only small changes were made. The V-8's combustion chamber was changed to reduce high compression rumble and allow for quieter running. The manifold and choke were altered to minimize engine warm-up and reduce the fast-idle after cold starts. The 6-cylinder engines came with a new cylinder head and carburetor to help attain better fuel milage. Both the Six and the V-8 received new air cleaners.

Behind the engine, the Flight-O-Matic automatic transmission received a new torque converter which helped reduce slippage. But overall, the cars developed the same horsepower as previously, had the same 18-gallon fuel tank, and continued to use the same Lark chassis of 108.5-inch wheelbase for the cars and 113-inch base for the wagons and the taxi-oriented Econo-Miler Sedan, while the Hawks used the old 120.5 inch wheelbase chassis.

The Hawk was continued as a single model series, but the "Silver" designation was dropped. To help distinguish it from 1959 cars, the grille emblem was changed from a black background to a red one, and the rear quarter panels contained three hash marks mounted at the leading edge of the tail fins. Although reports show that only V-8 Hawks were supposed to have been built, other Studebaker figures show that a total of 227 left the factory as 6-cylinder models, but indicate these were for export sales only.

The V-8 Hawks used a 289 cubic inch block that developed 210 horsepower in the regular version, or 225 horses when fitted with a 4-barrel carburetor and dual exhausts. Apparently the new 289 cubic inch block went only into Hawks destined for the U.S. and Canada. If the cars were shipped out of this area, the 259 cubic inch V-8 was still used. The 1960 Hawks also offered a new heavy-duty manual transmission, a larger radiator, and finned brake drums. The car sold for $2,650, ranking it fifth on Studebaker's price list, behind the new Lark Convertible and Lark Regal 4-door Wagon in both Six and V-8 forms. Hawk production lists differ, with one list showing 7,394 having been built, while another shows production of only 4,280 for the year. Overall calendar year production for Studebaker was 105,902, putting the company in 11th sales position.

Coming only as a V-8 in 1960 was the nice looking Hawk Coupe. The "Silver" designation was now history. This unit weighed 3,207 pounds and delivered for $2,650. The same 120.5-inch wheelbase was still being used. The 1960 Hawk was best distinguished by a red, rather than a black, eagle emblem mounted on its grille, and three chevron marks placed at the front edge of the tail fins. For 1960, the Hawk came again with its 289 cubic-inch V-8 developing 210 horsepower. If ordered with a 4-barrel carburetor and dual exhaust option, it developed 225 horsepower. Heavy duty 4-speed manual transmission, larger radiator, and finned brake drums were some of the available options Hawk owners could order. The 1960 models did not appear until February of that year. Some say it was to give the public an opportunity to look over the Lark and help with that model's introduction before showing the sporty Hawk in its second to last year. Only 3,719 Hawks found homes for 1960.

The lowest priced car for 1960 from South Bend was the 6-cylinder DeLuxe 2-door Sedan priced at $1,976 and weighing 2,588 pounds. Only the grille, including the side grilles, were the distinguishing differences over the 1959 cars. This model was not available in the Regal lineup. A total of 30,453 2-door models were delivered in 1960, making it the second best seller.

This 1960 taxi-cab came as DeLuxe 6-cylinder Sedan. Note the lack of basic stainless body trim. The grille emblem was mounted in the center on 1960 cars as a help in identification from 1959 models. This was actually a requirement put upon all manufacturers at this time from the Automobile Manufacturers Association which insisted on at least minor annual changes for vehicle identification.

This 1960 Studebaker 4-door DeLuxe came in both Six and Eight cylinder form. This happens to be an 8-cylinder version, weighing 2,941 pounds and selling for $2,181. If the model was ordered in 6-cylinder fashion, it went home for $2,046, weighing in at 2,592 pounds.

Fire Departments also chose Lark models as utility vehicles. This is the DeLuxe 2-door Wagon that was sold frequently as a fleet vehicle. It was available for $2,366. The unit came on a 113-inch wheelbase and weighed 2,763 pounds. Only 4,833 2-door models were sold for 1960.

A 1960 Studebaker Lark 4-door Station Wagon finds itself parked by a fashionable boat dock. This 4-door DeLuxe Station Wagon looks very much like the Regal models except for minor trim differences. This unit sold for $2,441 and weighed 2,792 pounds.

Studebaker offered this convertible in 1960, the first since 1952. It was available only as a Regal, either in six or eight cylinder form. Most everyone preferred it as an 8-cylinder, selling for $2,756, making it the most expensive car from Studebaker for the year. It weighed in base form at 3,315 pounds, also making it Studebaker's heaviest car for 1960. A total of 8,306 convertibles were produced for the year.

Available only in Regal style was the 1960 hardtop. It was produced both as a 6-cylinder such as this unit for $2,296, or as 8-cylinder for $2,431. The Six weighed 2,697 pounds while the Eight came in at 3,033 pounds. This 1960 Regal Hardtop, as a 6-cylinder, saw a little change in the engine compartment. The L-head Six received a new cylinder head and carburetor to help increase the fuel mileage. Also, the Flight-O-Matic transmission received a new torque converter to help reduce slippage. Rear seat passengers appreciated the additional leg room in all models which occurred by the redesigning of the front seat. A total of 5,867 hardtops were produced in 1960.

This 1960 Regal Lark 4-door Sedan is equipped with bumper guards, whitewalls, and deluxe wheel covers, all of which made for a neat little package. As a V-8, it delivered for $2,331 and weighed in at 2,966 pounds. A total of 48,382 sedans were built in 1960, making it the most popular model for the year.

A 1960 Regal 2-door Wagon came with all the refinements of the 4-door Regal. Being a 2-door, it was a good car for families with small children. It delivered for $2,501. Many people ordered their wagons with a roof rack to help carry additional luggage. The maximum cargo length with rear seat down was 93 inches.

Offered for the first time in the Lark series was the 4-door Station Wagon. It came in the DeLuxe and Regal models as a Six or a V-8. This model is identified as a Regal Eight by its Roman Numeral nameplate on the front fender. This wagon weighed 3,183 pounds and delivered for $2,726, making it the most expensive vehicle from South Bend for 1960. A total of 17,902 4-door wagons were built for 1960, making it one of the more popular models for the year.

Police Departments in many cities throughout the country picked the 1960 Larks. This example is equipped with all police attire, plus the accessory bumper guard equipment. Being a police unit, it was referred to as the Lark Marshal, which was a separate model engineered specifically for police duty. Size, speed, and nimbleness made these cars well fit for such a job.

The new 1961 Lark received only minor changes, but one in particular made a definite difference in its appearance. That was the addition of quad headlights, placed horizontally above new rectangular parking lamps. Also new was the elimination of the little side grilles, that space being taken up by the new quad lights. The four eyes were standard only on the Regal models. The Deluxe line continued to use single headlights, but the duals were available at extra cost, and many took this option. Also new, and available on both Six and V-8 models was power steering.

Other Lark changes included a more simple grille with the Lark emblem placed at the lower left corner, more massive bumpers, and taillight housings with small openings for side visibility.

Lark continued to offer the 259.2 cubic inch V-8 engine that delivered 180 horsepower. Also, a new 195 horse version was available, which had a 4-barrel carburetor.

But the big engine news was in the 6-cylinder line, where a totally new block appeared. Called the "Skybolt Six," this new mill featured overhead valve design. It developed 112 horsepower at 4500 rpm, and used an 8.5:1 compression ratio. However, its bore and stroke were the same even 3x4 inches and its displacement was the same 169.2 inches as found on the previous L-head models. Besides the cylinder specifications, the other main features remaining from the old block were the valve doors on the side of the blocks. The engineers felt that these doors were useful for valve lifter adjustment, which still could be done without removing the valve covers. Also new on this engine was the use of a timing gear rather than a timing chain to run the camshaft.

Despite the hopes for the new block, Studebaker officials soon realized that they should have done much more research before producing the Skybolt engine. Soon after the blocks were on the market, owners began to complain of cracked heads. Obviously, this proved to be a very costly venture which Studebaker had to cope with, as most of these cracks occurred while the cars were still under warranty.

In the Hawk's nest, things were basically the same as in 1960, probably due to the fact that a new overall body design was due for 1962 introduction. A different color strip on the rear quarter panel was the main means of year identification for 1961. Mechanically, the cars now offered a 4-speed floor shift, which helped in both performance and in giving the Hawk a flavor of a European sports car. All Hawks came with the 289 cubic inch engine, in either 210 or 255 horsepower versions.

The Larks got one new model, but it essentially was a variation of a former model. Called the Land Cruiser, it was built on the same 113-inch wheelbase chassis as the wagons, and used the same stretched body as the former taxi-oriented Econo-Miler Sedan, which was now discontinued. The Land Cruiser was available only as a V-8 in the U.S., but export models could be ordered with the Six.

Despite the company managing to show a $2.5-million profit for the year, production figures were down in each series. The 6-cylinder series had model-year sales of only 41,035 units, V-8 Larks saw the sale of 25,934 vehicles, and Hawks accounted for only 3,538, or 3,663 V-8s and 266 export Six models, depending upon which list is used. The company wound up in 12th place for the calendar year, with only 78,664 Studebakers leaving South Bend.

Studebaker held high hopes, however, as new blood entered the executives offices on Feb. 1, 1961. It was then that Sherwood H. Egbert came in as president. A human dynamo, this man arrived with great plans to help save the company and put it into the black ink once and for all. However, corporate directors, probably with stockholders in mind, thwarted many of the plans he made during his approximately three-year tenure at Studebaker. Egbert ultimately resigned, due to poor health, early in 1964. It certainly appears that his resignation helped to put the final note on Studebaker's days of production at South Bend.

Now in the final season for the Loewy coupe design was this Hawk, available only in V-8 style. The 289 cubic-inch engine developed 210 horsepower or 225 horsepower with the 4-barrel carburetor being employed. The fuel capacity stayed as an 18-gallon tank. The Loewy Coupe weighed 3,205 pounds. The factory produced 3,556 for 1961. Selling price was $2,650.

For economical transportation, the 1961 6-cylinder DeLuxe 2-door Sedan sold for $2,005. This was the company's lowest priced car for the year. A total of 14,574, 2-door models coming in either six or eight cylinder form were produced in 1961. Two-door sedans were not in the Regal series.

The 1961 DeLuxe Station Wagon is seen here as a 2-door model. With an 8-cylinder engine it weighed 3,112 pounds. The 113-inch wheelbase vehicle sold for $2,425. The 2-door wagons came only in the DeLuxe line.

In 6-cylinder style, the DeLuxe 2-door wagon for 1961 weighed 2,836 pounds and sold for $2,290. With the 4-door models now on the market, sales for 2-door wagons slipped considerably.

This 1961 DeLuxe 4-door Sedan was a 6-cylinder model. Note the single headlamps with the small parking lights mounted next to the headlight unit. At work as a taxi, this vehicle carries a two-tone paint job with hood, top, and trunk in a contrasting color from side panels. The DeLuxe sedan sold for $1,935 and weighed 2,665 pounds.

# 1961

Sharp looking is this 1961 Regal Lark Convertible in V-8 form. This model used the 180-horsepower V-8 in standard use. If the 4-barrel carburetor was ordered, it developed 195 horsepower. Most engines equipped with the 4-barrel set up were used in Hardtop and Convertible models. This vehicle weighed 3,315 pounds, being the heaviest car the company built for the year. It was also Studebaker's most expensive, selling for $2,689. A total of 1,981 open cars left the factory in 1961.

This is the 1961 Regal Hardtop Coupe. It was available as a Six or Eight. This example is a Six, selling for $2,243. A total of only 3,929 units were manufactured in 1961. As an 8-cylinder, the only difference was the VIII nameplate.

New for 1961 was the hardtop with a vinyl sunroof. Called the "Skytop," it didn't prove to be very popular. It had the same problems with leaking which are still a problem today on many other cars offered with this extra cost option. On the Lark, this item ran nearly $300 additional. If a person wanted the open air, the convertible seemed to be a more logical answer.

For 1961, the 4-door Sedan came as a DeLuxe or a Regal in either 6-cylinder or V-8 form. This model is the Regal Lark in 6-cylinder form. It delivered for $2,155. A total of 35,585 Sedans were produced for the year making the 4-door the most popular model.

Available also in 4-door style is the "Skytop" 4-door Sedan. This unit came as both a Regal Hardtop and a Regal Sedan for 1961. The top was made of a special vinyl that would slide shut on its own track. With a little body stress, and after the car put on a few miles, the tracks didn't help too much in keeping the water out. The style was not a big selling item.

The 1961 Regal 4-door V-8 Station Wagon was the most expensive wagon model offered for the year. It delivered for $2,655. Note the quad headlamps that came only on the Regal cars for this year. The bumper guards, wheel discs, and whitewall equipment were all extra cost items.

Studebaker's most impressive looking sedan for 1961 was the Lark Cruiser. It used the same 113-inch wheelbase as the Station Wagons. The vehicle had rich pleated upholstery with a rear seat armrest. Deep pile carpeting extending over the fire wall and special scuff panels, applied to the lower portion of the door panels, were standard equipment. The sedan weighed 3,001 pounds and carried a price of $2,450. It also had a rear window vent pane not seen on regular sedans. It was available only as a V-8.

The 1961 Regal V-8 4-door Marshal Sedan was designed strictly for police use. Note the special antenna mounted on the left rear quarter panel. The gentlemen in the police unit look like they are out, not for a joy ride, but mean business! Among the special items on these cars were oversized brakes, heavier suspension, a more durable interior, and special radio wiring.

The year 1962 started out with an improved looking Lark, thanks in large part to the styling directions of Brooks Stevens. All 4-door Larks were now built on the 113-inch wheelbase that formerly had been reserved for the wagons and last year's Land Cruiser. The 2-door models, including the convertible, also grew slightly, now having a 109-inch wheelbase.

Under Stevens direction, the cars now had elongated rear quarter panels and larger round taillights. The grille treatment was improved, giving the car what Studebaker hoped was a "Mercedes look." Since the corporation had purchased the rights to Mercedes Benz distributorship, apparently it felt it had the right to make the Larks look like "Baby Mercedes." Bumper extensions with larger vertical bumper guards were standard on the V-8 Cruiser, and available at extra cost on all other models. A stand-up hood ornament was now used on all Larks.

Offered for the first time was a new sub-series called the "Daytona." This grouping consisted of a Hardtop Coupe and a Convertible, and could be ordered with either the 112 horsepower Six or the 259 cubic inch V-8 of 180 or 195 horsepower. Later in the year, the 289.2 cubic inch V-8 became available for both the Daytonas and the Lark Cruisers. This engine could be ordered either as 210 or 225 horsepower vehicles. In the new Daytona series, prices ranged from $2,308 for the 6-cylinder Coupe to $2,814 for the V-8 Convertible.

Although the Lark changed somewhat, it was the Hawk line that emerged with a totally new look. Again, under the hand of Brooks Stevens, the car took on an entirely new look. Now known as the "Gran Turismo," the car had a squared-off roof line and inset rear window, not unlike that found on the Thunderbird. Despite retention of the basic body shell and the 120.5-inch wheelbase chassis, revised sheetmetal made the lower body look totally different. The sides were stripped of any bright metal trim with the exception of a stainless capping which ran the car's length, from the front fender to the end of the rear quarter panel. The grille was a stamped unit featuring a large heavy chrome band at its edges. In the rear, the deck lid came with a fake grille which was used to hide the ribbed pattern found on decks of earlier Hawks. The deck, incidentally, was of the same die as used previously, as were most of the other body parts. Still, considering the financial troubles of the company, the very pleasing facelift was the most practical and least expensive way to put a new looking car on the market.

Within the Gran Turismo was a very attractive three-plane aviation-type instrument panel with all gauges angled toward the driver. This was considered a first in automotive interior styling, and set a trend which both General Motors and Ford later incorporated into their designs. A center console option was available, and standard when the 4-speed manual was ordered. All Hawks came with the 210 horse 289 cubic inch V-8 as standard equipment, with the 225 horse version available at extra cost. A three-speed column shift was also standard. A few 6-cylinder versions were made, but these were for export sales only. Other available options included power steering; power brakes; air conditioning; power windows; the aforementioned Borg Warner 4-speed manual transmission; a 3-speed column shift with overdrive, and all of the other options such as radio, clock, mats, illumination, etc. that add that personalized touch to an already very sharp looking personal car.

Studebaker had a total of 21 models on the 1962 market, ranging from the Deluxe Lark Six 2-door Sedan for $1,935 to the Gran Turismo Hawk Hardtop Coupe for $3,095. A total of 102,387 units left the factory in 1962. Of these, 9,335 were the Gran Turismo Hawks, which were enjoying what was to be the very best year of their span.

On the corporate side, the name "Packard" was withdrawn from the company's official title of "Studebaker-Packard Corp. of America." As of April 26, 1962, the company once again reverted to the name "Studebaker." Company officials, probably rightly so, felt that the name Packard...recalling a car that was no longer being produced...was only hurting the sales picture for the current crop of Studebakers.

Sporting its Illinois plates, and parked in a driveway in rural Glen Ellyn, is this Studebaker Gran Turismo Hawk. It was owned for several years during the mid-1960s by Crestline/Motorbooks Editor George Dammann. Totally new for 1962, and with very pleasing lines, this model was void of all unnecessary chrome. In standard form, the car came equipped with the 289 cubic-inch V-8 which developed 210 HP. The Dammann car had the 225 horsepower 4-barrel carburetor, which was a very popular option. Also on this vehicle was the rare 4-speed manual floor shift. The car was beige with a red vinyl interior. As beautiful as it was to drive or to look at, two major faults became obvious...the body was very prone to rust, especially due to salt-covered Illinois winter roads, and the vinyl seat tops were very quick to rot and split open due to the hot summer sun. Also, the lack of side chrome may have been quite stylish, but it left the sides very susceptible to parking lot dents. Still, Dammann claims that this was one of his nicest cars in looks, handling, and dependability.

This is the way the car initially appeared in 1962. With the master craftsman skills of Brooks Stevens, this 1962 beauty was actually produced within a tight time frame, even though the skeptics felt it would never appear. In only a short period of time, like four months, Stevens had this car ready to be on display in dealers' showrooms by September of 1961. The car weighed 3,230 pounds and used the 120.5-inch wheelbase. It delivered for a base of $3,095, making it the most expensive South Bend offering for 1962. A total of 9,335 were built in the model year.

A good car for a family with small children or salesmen who travelled a good deal was this 2-door Sedan, only available in DeLuxe version. The 6-cylinder engine developed 112 horsepower from its 169.6 cubic-inches. Most people chose this engine with this body style even though the V-8 package was available for only $135 additional.

Even the U.S. Post Office went for Studebakers. The airbrush drawing shows a Lark DeLuxe 4-door Sedan out in rural America doing its daily chores. Note the car is right-hand drive, making mail delivery more accessible. The car is also equipped with a right-hand side mirror for safety purposes. Despite the many advantages of right-hand drive for this job, most rural mail carriers were adverse to such vehicles. The reason was because they owned their own vehicles, being paid for mileage and upkeep, but not for initial cost. And, at trade in time, no dealer wanted to take in a well-used right-hand drive Lark.

Available in 1962 in either DeLuxe or Regal form was the Station Wagon with 4-doors. After miserable 1961 sales, the 2-door version did not reappear this season. A new option that was available for the 6-passenger vehicle was the ability to turn it into an 8-passenger with the addition of a rear-facing rear seat. Not many chose the seating arrangement, as it left little room for storage, unless the family made use of the roof rack which this car carries. It was available as either a DeLuxe 6-cylinder weighing 2,845 pounds and selling for $2,405, or in DeLuxe V-8 fashion at 3,115 pounds, where it sold for $2,540.

Mr. Ed, a talking horse of television fame, appears to like the 1962 Lark, too. Looking out of his stable, he seems to be giving an approval, despite the fact that there's not room for a horse in a hardtop. Probably a top-down convertible should have been used for this scene. The Lark is either a Regal or Daytona Hardtop. With Mr. Ed's family in front of the side paneling, it's difficult to tell. Studebaker-Packard was the sponsor of this popular comedy show.

This Lark is the Regal Hardtop for 1962, available in both Six or V-8 style. It delivered for $2,218 as a Six, or $2,353 if the V-8 were purchased. A total of 8,480 hardtops were produced, divided between Regals and Daytonas.

Looking almost the same as the Daytona Convertible is the Regal convertible which moved down a step for 1962. The vehicle weighed the same as the Daytona, but cost $90 less due to the absence of a few pieces of non-expensive trim. In V-8 form, it sold for $2,714 or, if the owner preferred a Six, it was available for $2,589, in which form it weighed 3,075 pounds. The only noticeable trim difference is the lack of a model designation on the rear quarter panel, such as the Daytona models displayed.

Here sits a 1962 Lark Regal 4-door. The 1962 Sedans now were all on a 113-inch wheelbase. This model is 6-cylinder equipped, weighing 2,770 pounds and selling for $2,190. As a V-8, the Regal Sedan would weigh 3,025 pounds and deliver for $2,325. A total of 49,961 sedans were produced for 1962 making the style Studebaker's most popular model. The grille pattern certainly does exhibit a touch of Mercedes Benz.

# 1962

A 1962 Regal Station Wagon was available with the same engine choices as the DeLuxe. It did offer more deluxe appointments, which also gave it a higher price. This unit, as a Six, weighed 2,875 pounds and delivered for $2,555. If the V-8 were ordered, it weighed 3,145 pounds and had a sticker price of $2,690. A total of 10,522 wagons were delivered in 1962, making the style the third most popular model for the year.

New for 1962 was this model in the Lark series. It lived within the new family called the Daytona. The car came either as a convertible or hardtop and was available as a Six or a V-8. This example is the Lark Daytona V-8, weighing 3,305 pounds and selling for $2,814, making it the most expensive model in the Lark line.

The "Skytop" option was back again for the second year. This time it was available for the Daytona Coupe as well as the Regal Sedan, 2-door Sedan, and Regal Hardtop. This Daytona Coupe is nicely outfitted. Most all came equipped with extra cost items, such as bumper guards, antenna, and door-mounted side mirror. The DeLuxe wheel discs were standard on Daytona models. The car carried a price tag of $2,308 as a Six and $2,443 in V-8 style. The Six weighed 2,765 pounds and V-8s were 3,015 pounds.

Proudly displaying the 1962 Daytona Convertible at the 46th annual Memorial Day Indianapolis 500 Race is the new Studebaker President, Sherwood Egbert and a couple of his officials. The Lark was the first car of compact size ever to be used to pace the Memorial Day event.

For 1962, the Cruiser was in its second year of production. The sedan rode on the 113-inch wheelbase and again offered the nicely appointed interior that it started the previous season. Note the small Cruiser nameplate under the Lark badge on the front fender. This helped for easy-identification. Cruiser Sedans came only with the V-8 engine. This model weighed 3,030 pounds and sold for $2,493.

These Indiana State Police are using the 1962 Lark Marshal. This specially designed vehicle was V-8 outfitted, and had all heavy duty equipment, including the 4-barrel carburetor. The 289 cubic-inch engine developed 225 horsepower.

The 1962 Lark DeLuxe 4-door Sedan was still being specially designed for taxi service. From the looks of the vehicle, it is possible that these passengers are the first to go for a ride. This car weighed 2,040 pounds and, as a Six, sold for $2,760. The bumper guard equipment was extra cost, but was a wise choice considering the heavy duty work that a taxi generally receives.

A line of 1962 Studebaker taxi-cabs are receiving their final inspection upon leaving the South Bend factory. Note that quad headlamps are now seen on all Lark models whether DeLuxe, Regal, or Daytona.

This year the Studebaker Corp. came out with what turned out to be a win-or-die play. It introduced a brand new car, the Avanti, which was the first totally new product on its boards since the 1959 Lark hit the streets. Designed by Raymond Lowey, and in fact being Lowey's last effort for Studebaker, the car was a 5-passenger sport machine, priced at $4,445, and intended to give Corvette a run for its money. Since the Thunderbird had turned into a prestige coupe and had left the true sports car idiom, Studebaker felt that the time was ripe for an independent manufacturer to put out a low-production sports car to go up against the Corvette.

Like the Corvette, the Avanti also used a fiberglass body, and in fact, was the only other car being produced in the U.S. with such a body. The car was built on the Lark chassis of 109-inch wheelbase, but any further similarity to the Lark ended right there. Body styling, besides being of fiberglass, was also very different, with ultra-modern lines that probably turned off far more people than it attracted. It was not a Lark, it surely was not a Hawk…it was an Avanti, and it was different!

The car was obviously not intended for mass production, and this was a good thing. Right from the start, problems arose in getting the fiberglass parts to fit properly. Also disputes quickly arose among top management as to how and when the car was to be completed, how it was to be marketed, and how big a factor Avanti sales were going to be in the overall corporate financial structure, which was still in a bad state of affairs. Early sales prognosis was high among the remaining dealers, but when the cards were down, true orders just were not there. The 1963 sales picture, though not great, turned out to be the brighter of the car's two-year run, with 3,834 units being sold. In retrospect, looking at the financial condition of the company, this really was not the best time for Studebaker to be experimenting with a new sports car of limited appeal.

The engine choices for the Avanti were based on a new "Jet Thrust" overhead valve V-8. This 289 cubic inch block used the same 3.56x3.62-inch bore and stroke of other Studebaker big blocks. However, with a 4-barrel carburetor and dual exhausts, it produced 240 horsepower for the Avanti. Optional was a supercharged version, which produced 285 horsepower with the Paxton equipment described later. New for Studebaker was a 304.5 cubic inch V-8 block which would produce 280 horsepower with twin 4-barrel carburetors, or 335 horsepower with a single Paxton supercharger. In the experimental stage, and possibly never making it to street level, was another version of the 304.5 cubic inch block with a special cam, magneto ignition, fuel injection, and twin superchargers, which produced 575 horsepower at 7000 rpm. Obviously, this set-up was not intended for street use.

Avanti buyers had two transmission choices, a standard automatic, or a 4-speed manual on the floor.

In 1963 Studebaker also apparently felt a need to join the rest of the industry and add some confusion to the Lark line. It made a total of 23 models available, registering 11 in the Lark Six array and 12 as Lark V-8s.

In both series, a Regal 2-door Sedan was added to the list, as well as a Daytona 6-passenger Station Wagon. The Convertible and Hardtop Coupe now became the sole possessions of the Daytona Series. The former Deluxe Series was split into "Standard" and "Custom" models, available as both 2-door and 4-door Sedans. The two new series bracketed the remaining Regal Series, with the Standard models one step down on the luxury scale, and the Custom cars one step above the Regals. The Cruiser 4-door Sedan continued to be available only as a V-8 vehicle, and was the company's most expensive 4-door sedan, selling for $2,595.

This year's Larks went through a few more changes which really did improve the appearance. Extra-thin upper door frames were used on all sedans and wagons. These lines seemed to give a sleeker overall appearance to the vehicles. The grille design now featured more horizontal and vertical bars, while the rear deck had new circular medallions. The taillights used a radiating bar and on the more expensive models, bright trim gave an extra touch of quality.

The interior saw some improvements too, with a new vanity mounted in the glovebox. It opened like a small bar, and included a space for coins, tissues, drinking cups, and a mirror for the fair lady to use for those last minute primps. Also seen again for the first time in years were gauges with needles, and rocker-type control switches. The government was beginning to step in even back then, telling manufacturers how the car should be equipped. Along this line, as of February, 1963, front seat belts were fitted in each model. The 1963 cars also saw the first amber parking lamps in place of the previous clear lenses. This was supposedly done to add to night safety.

Mechanically, the Lark continued with the same 6-cylinder engine as in the previous year. The Lark V-8s also employed the same 259.2 cubic inch engine in all but the Cruiser, which used the 289 cubic inch version as standard equipment, as did the Hawk. The larger engine could also be ordered for the regular Larks, at extra cost.

As for the 1963 Lark wagons, another fete came along for Brooks Stevens. He brought out, at the beginning of the year, a style that was called the "Wagonaire." This vehicle had a sliding roof and was available in Standard, Regal, and Daytona trim. The vehicle was a must for those wishing to transport tall objects such as trees or bushes, and high furniture. At first it sold well, until many owners found out that it didn't fare well in inclement weather…it LEAKED! As a result, production halted early in the year, as necessary alterations were made. To keep the wagon trade rolling, a stationary-roof model was again reintroduced for $100 less than the Wagonaire.

But the cost of re-tooling at mid-season for this novel wagon was prohibitive, and Studebaker chose to limp along . . . until its final day . . . with a leaking Wagonaire, hoping that its owners would be willing to allow for some corrections when they were devised. Rust also proved to be a major factor in the edges of the roof of these vehicles, but this devastating malady did not show up in the first year.

Studebaker also experimented with a diesel engine in 1963, and actually did make a few small inroads with some taxi fleets that were willing to try this economical

The Avanti had the distinction of looking different from any angle. The models contained back-up lights right in the base of the trunk lid. The most common engine used in these cars was the 289 cubic-inch 240 horsepower V-8, with a bore and stroke of 3.56x3.62 inches. A supercharged version was available for an extra $210. The all-fiberglass body was the first totally new body design that Studebaker had produced in the past decade. The car used a modified Lark chassis of 109-inch wheelbase.

package. However, the diesel idea overall proved to be unsuccessful.

With the Gran Turismo Hawk enjoying relatively good acceptance, the company wisely made few changes, and what few changes were made seemed to constitute even more improvement in looks. The grille was revised slightly, and was now more similar to that used on the Lark. The gaping air vents alongside the grille of the 1962 models were deemed unnecessary, and were closed up. However, instead of leaving the area simply filled by new sheet metal, fake replica grilles were installed there. As on the Larks, parking lights were now done in amber. For quick identification, small tri-color bars of red, white and blue were placed on the lower left of the grille and at the top of the doors, adjacent to the Gran Turismo nameplate. The trunk deck didn't quite give the appearance of a rear grille, as in previous models, but simply had the looks of just another decoration.

Mechanically, one big item arrived in the Hawk's nest at mid-season. It was a supercharger from Paxton Products. With this unit attached to the 289 cubic inch block, the engine developed 240 horsepower, and with special tuning and a few more goodies added, could boost the horses to 300. Surprisingly, the new supercharger was not all that expensive, with the basic installation adding only $371 to the car's list. Not only did the blower find customers in the Gran Turismo market, but it also became available in big-engined Larks as well. When the device was installed, these cars immediately were termed "Super Hawk" and "Super Lark."

Sales for the year were down to 83,846 for all Larks, Gran Turismos, and Avantis combined. The company was in 12th place nationally, as calendar year production slipped to 67,918 units.

The two men responsible for the Avanti were Raymond Loewy on the left, and Sherwood Egbert on right. Egbert was then the head of the Studebaker. The vehicle delivered for a base of $4,445, going to 3,884 customers in 1963.

When Avanti changed minor features, it was just like Studebaker did in the olden days. Revisions were made not just because of a yearly change, but when it was deemed necessary. The round versus the square headlight dispute will go on forever. Some say only the round headlamps were used on early 1963s, while others say they were used throughout the 1963 model year. Who knows? Anyway, this example displays the round headlights, and thus qualifies for inclusion in the 1963 chapter only.

This is an interior view of a late 1963 to early 1964 Avanti. The dash on the Avanti included wood-paneling with a beautiful colored vinyl interior to match the cars exterior. The steering wheel was wood-grained veneer. The console offered everything, including gear selector, clock, package compartment, and radio and heater controls. Many Avantis were now air-conditioned, and these controls also were located on the console.

Now in its second year was the classic looking 1963 Gran Turismo Hawk. Minor changes were made to distinguish it from a 1962, and the result was an even better looking car with a more classic aire. The red, white and blue emblem at the lower left of the grille, and circular parking lamps mounted in the outer grilles, along with red, white and blue markers next to the gran Turismo nameplate on the doors, were the distinguishing items to tell it's a '63. Gran Turismo sales were considerably less than the previous year. A total of only 4,634 units left the factory. The elegant Hawk weighed 3,280 pounds and sold for $3,095. Surely today many people wish they had bought one of these cars when they had the chance.

Studebaker's lowest priced car for 1963 was this new Standard 2-door Sedan selling for $1,935. It used the 109-inch wheelbase. The Standard was devoid of any fancy trim. The title of Standard appeared only for a one-year stay.

Studebaker received military contracts even when regular sales were down. This 1963 example is a unit built for Navy use, and going to Japan. It was built as part of a fleet contract signed by the government on Jan. 4, 1963. Note its a right-hand drive style, referred to as model 635-42. The car is a bare bones vehicle, placing it in the Standard lineup. As a car for family use, it delivered for $2,040. As an export or government contract car, prices are not available.

The 1963 Studebaker Regal dropped one level from its top of the line status in the Lark family for this year. Also new for the year in the Regal series was the 2-door Sedan. One could order it either with a 6-cylinder engine for $2,055, or the V-8 was also available for $2,190.

The Lark Custom came in with the top model of the 2-door Sedans in 1963. This example, like Standard and Custom models, was available as a Six or V-8. The Six delivered for $2,180, weighing 2,680 pounds, and the V-8 showed for $2,315 and weighed 2,940 pounds. A total of 17,401 2-door Lark Sedans were manufactured in 1963. Note the stainless side trim on the quarter panel, making it easier to distinguish the Custom from the Regal and Standard cars.

In 1963, the Custom line took the place of the top-line Regal models. It wore the name "Custom" for only this year. It was available as a 6-cylinder for $2,285, weighing 2,800 pounds. If the V-8 was ordered, it delivered for $2,420 and weighed 3,010 pounds. Custom Sedans rode on the 113-inch wheelbase like the other sedans for 1963. A total of 40,113 sedans were produced for the model year.

The 1963 Daytona Convertible, like the hardtop, came as a 6-cylinder for $2,679, weighing 3,045 pounds, or as a V-8 for $2,814, weighing 3,265 pounds. The Daytona Convertible was Studebaker's second to the most expensive car for 1963. A total of 1,015 convertibles found homes for the year.

The 1963 Daytona Hardtop was available either as a 6-cylinder for $2,308, weighing 2,795 pounds, or as a V-8 for $2,443, and weighing 3,035 pounds A total of 3,763 1963 Daytona Hardtops were produced.

This 1963 Lark Daytona is wearing the rare "Skytop Sunroof" option. Note the console package between the front seats which was standard equipment if the bucket seat option was ordered. With these options, this would have been one rare car.

The most expensive 4-door Sedan from Studebaker in 1963 was this 4-door Cruiser. It was available only as a V-8, using the 289 cubic-inch displacement block. The vehicle weighed 3,065 pounds and delivered for $2,595. Note that the rear window vent panes were now used on all 4-door Sedans in 1963.

The Marshal was back again for 1963! This special police version basically was equipped with the same exterior trim as Regal cars. Often these vehicles were fitted with the 289 cubic-inch engine, giving them a little more power for pursuits. The interiors were done in tough vinyl. Various police options were available such as right-hand drive; loom and pull antennas; police speedometers that were specially calibrated; twin traction differential; 70 amp battery; heavy duty generators; 40-45 low cut-in transmissions, and heavy duty suspension.

One of Brooks Stevens new designs for station wagon models was this Wagonaire. The open roof was an entirely new novelty, but one that was not particularly well accepted on the market. The body style was available in Standard, Regal, and Daytona models. Prices ranged from the 6-cylinder Standard at $2,430, weighing 3,285 pounds, to a 6-cylinder Daytona for $2,700, weighing 3,245 pounds. As an 8-cylinder Standard, the price was $2,565, weighing 3,435 pounds. The top wagon and most expensive Lark that Studebaker offered for 1963 was the Daytona V-8 wagon selling for $2,835 and weighing 3,490 pounds. A total of 11,915 wagons were produced in 1963.

Available at mid-season was the fully enclosed 1963 Station Wagon. This model was brought out due to problems that the open-roofed cars had of leaking, and also to buyer resistance to the strange concept of an open-top wagon. It was available in each series at $100 less than the Wagonaire. This example is the 6-cylinder Regal 4-door Wagon weighing 3,200 pounds and selling for $2,450. In 8-cylinder fashion, it weighed 3,450 pounds and carried a price tag of $2,585.

The day of gloom was inevitable, and even though all knew it was coming, no one wished to accept the fact. The final day of manufacture at South Bend was Dec. 9, 1963. This meant, of course, that the 1964 model year was a very short one indeed. The last car off the line had a good wish for all company employees. "Merry Christmas" was scrawled on the windshield...was it a good wish or dark sarcasm! Production did continue at the Hamilton, Ontario, facility, but of course no Avanti or Gran Turismo cars had ever been built north of the border. Now Studebaker was in the same class as Toyota, Volkswagen, Mercedes, Datsun and all of the other foreign car companies...it was selling only vehicles produced outside of the U.S.

On the few 1964 cars that were produced before the South Bend closing, the name Lark was used sparingly. Studebaker was again trying to offer a fresh new start, giving the public the fairly recent names of Daytona and Cruiser, and bringing back the tried and true name of Commander, using this title to replace the Regal nomenclature. Also, the name Challenger was offered in place of the title Standard, which had been brought into the fold for the lowest price models only last year. The Wagonaire was cataloged, but it too was essentially a model within the series of Challenger and Commander and again, in the top of the line Daytona.

Mechanically, the cars were identical to the 1963 line, with the same running gear throughout. Appearance-wise, the Hawks now had an optional vinyl top for the front section of the roof. Many buyers took advantage of this attractive styling innovation. The rear section of the car now had a smoother look, but was fitted with more chrome, including larger taillight housings. An "S" in a circle was mounted at the lower left base of the grille, and a gold-brushed Hawk emblem for the grille also added to a "busy look" for the front end.

As for the Avanti, changes only occurred when the factory felt that they were necessary. The largest number of revisions occurred in August, 1963, and yet the company explained these as being only optional changes, such as the cars having square-bezel headlamp surrounds as opposed to the early round units, and of changes in the wood paneling, the solid-color vinyl trim, and a wood-grained steering wheel. The sales of 1964 Avantis amounted to only 809 cars, all with a base price of $4,445.

The Lark models introduced in late summer as 1964 issue carried a slogan of "Different by Design." A healthy face-lift was done, giving a new look from the cowl forward, with a lower hood, and fenders uplifted at the outer edges. The grille treatment gave a look of fleetness, while being uncluttered. The hood ornament was the familiar stand-up "S." The rear of the Daytonas and Cruisers seemed to offer a nice balance of trim, just enough to offer an extra touch of class. However, the less expensive versions were devoid of any glitter and looked like "cheapie" models. Prices ranged from a 6-cylinder Challenger 2-door Sedan for $1,943 to the Avanti Coupe for $4,445.

A total of 23 models were available for 1964. The Commander 2-door Special was produced only in Ontario, while all other models came from South Bend. The Daytona Hardtop Coupe came only as a V-8, while a Daytona Convertible could still be purchased with either a Six of a V-8...a strange decision.

Production for a calendar year basis is shown as 19,748 units. But since the South Bend plant closed before the start of the 1964 calendar year, this production must have all be in Canada. Model year sales were reported to have been 47,215 units sold. As far as can be ascertained, these included only 1,767 Hawks, 2,414 Daytona Hardtops, and 703 Daytona Convertibles.

The beautiful Gran Turismo Hawk appeared for the final year. The 1964 models carried a special center emblem on the grille along with another "S" emblem mounted on the lower left portion of the grille, which appeared to be a little over done. A vinyl half roof, called the Landau top, did give a touch of class. This was the only year the Gran Turismo offered this option. The vehicle weighed 3,120 pounds and sold for $2,966. A total of only 1,767 units left South bend. No Gran Turismo models were produced in Canada.

The Avanti with the square bezeled headlamps probably appeared more toward the end of the run. The total number of 1964 examples only amounted to 809 units. The minor changes consisted of small items like woodgrain steering wheel and tenite panels being discontinued in June, 1963. The hood support also moved from the left to the right side, the rear quarter window latch was redesigned, and inside the "S" emblems became standard on door panels. These were the "bigger" changes made in August, 1963, which make people feel this was the start of 1964 cars. But as I said before, Studebaker made changes only when they felt it necessary.

Representing the last Studebaker Avanti, which was built in December, 1963, as a 1964 model is this attractive example. Studebaker dropped the Avanti for 1965, but in 1966 the car was given a new life under the hands of Leo Newman and Nathan Altman, who had been partners in a large Studebaker-Packard dealership in South Bend. The pair gained all rights to the design, and also bought a portion of the abandoned Studebaker factory in South Bend. In 1965 they began producing carbon copies of the car, now called the Avanti II, on a small assembly line. The new Avanti used a 327 cubic inch Corvette engine. Production was less than 100 cars a year, but the line continued well into the 1980s. However, the Avanti II was no longer a Studebaker, and thus is outside the scope of this book.

Probably this job is one of the R-3 supercharged models out doing its thing with a 335-horsepower V-8 with a 9.6:1 compression ratio and a four-barrel carburetor. Sadly, before Studebaker phased out the Avanti, the quick little car had taken just about every speed record listed by U.S. Auto Club, including the Bonneville flying-mile mark of 170.78 mph. Performance the car had, sales it lacked, and Studebaker had to write off the experiment as just another costly failure. Happily for the fans of American-made sports-type cars, the Avanti got a new lease on life, but not as a Studebaker.

In 1964, Studebaker pulled out another trick from their box of name changes. The Challenger replaced the Standard nameplate. This 2-door Challenger Sedan weighed 2,660 pounds and went home for $1,943 as a 6-cylinder, making it the lowest priced model for the year. All models, even the least on the list, benefitted greatly from the new frontal design.

Shown at a Studebaker car show is this Challenger V-8 2-door Sedan. This basic model is equipped with deluxe wheel covers, but is truly "plain Jane" otherwise. As a V-8, it sold for $2,078. The 2-door Sedan sales for 1964 amounted to 8,315 units.

A 1964 Challenger 4-door Sedan was Studebaker's lowest priced Sedan. It was available for $2,048 as a 6-cylinder and $2,183 if a V-8 was ordered. This model was able to be delivered with right-hand drive for rural postal service as optional equipment, but as mentioned previously, right-hand drive cars were not popular because of their virtual non-existant trade in value. This vehicle sports deluxe wheel covers and the optional hood ornament, both of which were classed as accessories on Challenger models.

An interior view of this taxi shows the flat floor which made it less awkward for middle seat passengers. A basic vinyl material made for a long life of the seat and doors. Only 455 taxi units were produced, making this the last year for these vehicles.

Studebaker's lowest priced wagon for 1964 was this Challenger Wagonaire. It came as a 6-cylinder model weighing 3,230 pounds and selling for $2,438, and also as a V-8 weighing 3,480 pounds and selling for $2,573. Note that the lack of any stainless side trim for sure makes it a Challenger. A total of only 5,163 Wagonaires were produced in 1964.

This is the return of Commander models in 1964. Seen here is a 2-door Sedan, available in 6-cylinder form for $2,063, and weighing 2,695 pounds. As a V-8 version, it delivered for $2,198 with a weight of 2,945 pounds. The Commander Special 2-door Sedan was basically the same car as the regular 2-door model except for a fancier interior, which added an additional $130 to the final figure. The 1964 Commander 4-door Sedan was basically the same car as last year's Regal. It came as a 6-cylinder, weighing 2,815 pounds and selling for $2,168. In V-8 style, weighing 3,045 pounds, it cost the owner $2,303. Sedan production amounted to 27,589 units with most being built in Hamilton, Ontario, and thus technically being foreign cars.

Given a nice facelift, this 1964 Daytona Hardtop was available only as a V-8, using the 259 cubic-inch displacement block. The vehicle came on the same 109-inch wheelbase as before, weighed 3,060 pounds, and sold for $2,451. A total of only 2,414 Daytona Coupes left South Bend and Hamilton.

This is the 1964 Cruiser 4-door Sedan. As in previous years, it was available only as a V-8 using the 289 cubic-inch engine. The vehicle weighed 3,120 pounds and carried a window sticker of $2,603. The 1964 sedan sales amounted to 27,589.

Being displayed as a new product of Canada, and proudly so, the Daytona Convertible poses with this attractive young lady from the Dominion of Canada. The car is a V-8, riding on a 109-inch wheelbase. Only 703 convertibles saw production in 1964, which makes them very rare today. This was Studebaker's final year for convertible production. This unit weighed 3,320 pounds and sold for $2,805. It was not available with a Six.

The factory did not advertise the regular line of closed top Wagonaires for 1964. Studebaker still felt the open version was what would sell best, in spite of the leaking, future rust problems, and buyer resistance. This front view of the 1964 Wagonaire shows that the car is a Daytona, as the front fender carries this nameplate. Also available were Challenger and Commander models.

Here is a rear view of the 1964 Wagonaire. At this time Studebaker was trying to phase out the Lark name. These Lark models were basically referred to Challenger, Commander, and Daytona Wagonaires. This example is the top of the line Daytona weighing 3,555 pounds, and selling for $2,843, making it the most expensive vehicle in the regular models excluding Gran Turismo Hawk and Avanti vehicles.

This 1964 police special was a true screamer in sedate clothing. It was equipped with the Paxton Supercharger, used mainly for Gran Turismos. With this option, the engine developed 240 horsepower in basic structure. The car was referred to as a Super Lark.

The 1965 season was marked by the absence of Studebaker's two high styled cars, the Gran Turismo Hawk and the revolutionary Avanti. True, in the past year, Studebaker dealers had sold very few of either model, and thus on a financial scale probably didn't miss either one. But, these cars sure looked good on the showroom floor, and they were the ones that got the space in newspapers and automotive magazines. After all, few writers could or would yammer gloriously about a low-buck 2-door Lark Sedan.

The 1965 models that entered the sale market did so with a vast reduction in models. One new addition was a Cruiser Six 4-door Sedan, which sold for $2,470. Except for the Cruisers, all 6-cylinder cars were now in the Commander Series. The V-8 engines also could be put into Commanders, and were the only engines in the 2-model Daytona line. Daytonas now only appeared as a Sport Coupe and a Wagon, with the convertible leaving the scene.

The lack of annual change was explained by Studebaker as a break from planned obsolescence. Management hoped that the public would buy Studebakers with the realization that the car would not become obsolete in a couple of years, due to annual changes such as made by the Big-three for years. Sadly, the cars not only became obsolete, they became obsolete orphans after 1965.

One of the major changes that did occur this year had to do with the closing of the South Bend facility. The Canadian plant had never built its own engines, having had all of these supplied from South Bend. But with that factory in mothballs, there were no engines to be had. Thus, Studebaker turned to the McKinnon engines that were being built by General Motors Canadian operations.

Based on U.S. Chevrolet designs, the McKinnon blocks supplied to Studebaker were the 194 cubic inch Six and the 283 cubic inch V-8. The Six was rated at 120 horsepower at 4400 rpm, using a single carburetor and an 8.5:1 compression. The V-8 was rated at 195 horses at 4800 rpm. References often state that the Canadian Larks used Chevrolet engines. Technically this is not true: They used McKinnon engines, designed by Chevrolet, but built in Canada by General Motors.

Appearance-wise, the 1965 cars tendered a computer-styled instrument panel and a special-styled steering wheel. This wheel, designated as a first by Brooks Stevens, was called the "Polo Mallet" wheel. Other innovations this year included a padded vanity, accessory compass and clock, interchangeable bumpers, and recessed door handles. The 4-door cars used the 113-inch wheelbase, while the 2-door vehicles used a 109-inch wheelbase. Tire size for all models was 7.35x15.

Calendar year production amounted to 18,588 units. Model year sales were listed at 19,435 vehicles. But, even with sales dropping to less than $200-million overall, Studebaker did show a year-end profit of $10-million, giving credence to the arguments of those who had favored closing the South Bend plant.

The first 1965 model is shown leaving the Hamilton, Ontario plant, destined for a U.S. customer. The man standing beside the car is W. A. Moeser, director of the factory operation.

In 1965, the Commander 2-door Sedan was produced both as a 6-cylinder model weighing 2,695 pounds and selling for $2,125, and as a V-8 that weighed 2,895 pounds, with a price of $2,265. A total of 7,372 2-door models were produced in Hamilton, Ontario.

A photo taken in the early 1970s at a Studebaker meet at South Bend shows Crestline/Motorbooks Editor George Dammann taking notes on a well-maintained 1965 Commander 2-door Sedan. The vehicle is surely all original, right down to the proper size whitewalls and factory wheel covers. It no doubt sports either the Chevrolet 194 cubic-inch 6-cylinder engine or the famous V-8 of 283 cubic inches, since the remaining Studebakers all came with Chevrolet engines.

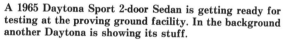

This 1965 Commander 4-door Sedan was again available both as a 6-cylinder weighing 2,815 pounds and selling for $2,230, or as a V-8 with a weight of 2,995 pounds. As a V-8, it delivered for $2,370. The Commander line was now the low-priced series, since the Challenger models had been discontinued.

A 1965 Daytona Sport 2-door Sedan is getting ready for testing at the proving ground facility. In the background another Daytona is showing its stuff.

The 1965 Daytona Sport 2-door Sedan was available only as a V-8, weighing 2,970 pounds and selling for $2,565. The vinyl top and small emblem on the roof side panel designated this as the sport model.

The 1965 Daytona Wagon still was available as the Wagonaire, with the sliding roof option. This example, however, is the more functional model with the enclosed roof. It sold for $2,790, but the open-air version could be obtained for $100 more. The Daytona wagon only came with a V-8. Studebaker no longer built its own V-8 blocks, but had them supplied by Chevrolet.

Nicely equipped for its 1965 factory press photo is this Cruiser Sedan. This year it appeared not only as a V-8, but as a 6-cylinder as well. The Six delivered for $2,470 while the V-8 sold for $2,610, an increase of only $7 over last year's model. The bumper guards, whitewalls, and full-wheel discs were standard equipment for the Cruiser in 1965.

This 1965 Taxi is truly a restored vehicle. Someone tried for a "one off" since the Studebaker ended factory production of taxi fleet sales in 1964. It has been shown at several Studebaker events. Actually, even though specially-designed taxis were not being built by Studebaker, there was nothing to prevent private owners, either fleet or individual, from converting regular 4-door sedans to cab use. And, since Studebaker sedans were still of the right size and price for this role, it seems logical to assume that minor percentage of these 4-doors did eventually enter the taxi business.

Obviously at the start of the 1966 season most people involved with Studebaker had no idea that the company was in its final year of life. Here were the new Studebakers, refreshingly redesigned by a Detroit firm, sporting a totally new look that certainly wouldn't have been applied to a car that was destined to die within six months...wrong!

The all-new front end included single headlights in place of the former quad arrangements. The grille was a full-width unit of horizontal theme, bearing no resemblance whatever to previous Lark-ala-Mercedes fronts. Body side moldings were repositioned to a much lower position. And, in a final flourish of engineering achievement, the sedans received a new ventilating system known as "Refreshaire," which had its air intakes mounted directly above the taillamps, in the place where the back-up lights were located on the 1965 models.

A split-back reclining front seat became standard on the Daytona Sport Coupes, as did transistorized ignition. Vinyl covered roofs and rear seat center armrests were standard on Daytona and Cruiser models. The factory was doing everything possible to offer safety on their cars as standard equipment. Padded dash, padded sun visors, 2-speed electric wipers with windshield washers, parking brake warning light, safety door latches, dual master cylinder, non-glare windshield wiper arms, and front and rear seat belts were all part of the "free gift" safety package that Studebaker was offering to its customers.

Probably the one big item of change came late for Studebaker. That was its new aluminized rust-proofing treatment. If this had been done on earlier cars, especially the attractive but very rust susceptible Hawks, everyone might enjoy seeing more early Studebakers at car shows today.

Mechanically, the cars were the same as the 1965 offerings. The lowest priced model was the Commander 2-door Sedan, selling for $2,060. The top honors for price went to the 4-door Wagonaire, which weighed 3,501 pounds and went out the door at a base of $2,695 to only 735 customers.

Calendar year production for 1966 showed only 2,045 units leaving the factory at Hamilton, Ontario. Model year sales were listed at 8,947 vehicles. Although the Canadian operation was at this point running in the black and turning a small profit, upper level management was not impressed with sales, and as a result car production ceased in March, 1966. At that time, Studebaker as a car became an orphan and a memory.

The Studebaker Corp. continued for several more years, but not in the automotive business. It bought the large Wagner Electric Corp. in early 1967, and then later that same year merged with the Worthington Corp. to become Studebaker-Worthington Corp. The entire company was swallowed in 1979 by the McGraw-Edison Co. of Illinois, thus making even the name Studebaker just a memory.

The first 1966 model to leave the Hamilton, Ontario, factory turned out to be a Commander 4-door Sedan in V-8 style. Carrying the Chevrolet 283 cubic-inch engine, it weighed 2,991 pounds and delivered for $2,305.

The 1966 Commander 2-door Sedan is shown here. As a 6-cylinder model, it was available for $2,060 and as a V-8 it delivered for $140 additional — $2,200. The vinyl top was an extra-cost item on all Commander models.

A 1966 Cruiser and a Commander are shown here in a suburban setting, in a neighborhood where the homeowners obviously liked Studebakers. Sadly, final year sales amounted to only 8,947 units, placing Studebaker in the 15th sales slot. In reality then, it would have been a rare sight indeed to have two 1966 Studebakers on the same street, such as seen in this posed photo.

The 1966 Daytona 2-door Sedan was built on the 109-inch wheelbase. It was available in 6-cylinder fashion for $2,405, weighing 2,755 pounds. The V-8, weighing 3,006 pounds, sold for $2,500. A total of 2,321 2-door Sedans were delivered for 1966 in both Commander and Daytona models.

The final year for Studebaker saw this 4-door Cruiser with a new grille and many safety features being offered. All models reverted to single head lamps. The Cruiser, as a 6-cylinder, weighed 2,815 pounds and delivered for $2,405. As the V-8, at 3,066 pounds, it was available for $2,545. A total of 5,686 4-door Sedans, divided between Commander and Cruiser models, were produced.

The Wagonaire in its final year did not come under the title of a special model, but was classed as a model unto itself of "Wagonaire — 4-door Wagon." It was available with a 6-cylinder engine for $2,555, weighing 3,245 pounds, or as a V-8, weighing 3,006 pounds and selling for $2,695. In V-8 form, it was Studebaker's most expensive car for the final year. A total of only 940 units were produced at Hamilton, Ontario.

# Epilogue

Management at Studebaker, whether it be South Bend or in Hamilton, Ontario, apparently felt that if a cover was placed over the problems, all the bad happenings would just go away. This "head-in-the-sand" philosophy appears to have permeated much of the latter-year thinking of Studebaker's top directors and managers. Nobody seemed willing to sit down with reality and face the fact that there were bad problems ahead.

This attitude was even occurring back in the early post-war years. Rather than trying to update the factories, management and directors just kept on going...with nice shareholder checks, fatter salaries for the executives, and good pay for hourly union workers. The overhead was terrific, considering the number of cars being produced. As an example, if Ford or Chevrolet made a $1-million change, and then spread that change over 1-million vehicles, the revision cost only $1 per car. But if Studebaker made a $1-million change, it had at best only 100,000 vehicles over which to spread the revision, and thus the change added $10 to each car.

Finally, the pot became dry, and who to turn to, or where to go for further financing was even a bigger problem. In a desparate last gasp effort, the South Bend plant was virtually abandoned and all production was moved to Canada. The Canadian workers hoped the company had revitalized enough to continue with a true Canadian-built car. But management knew differently. The company was only there long enough to use up remaining parts for assembly and, when that supply was gone, so were the cars. Hamilton didn't have an engineering or design staff, and in fact, had no plans for hiring either. Anyone could see the handwriting on the wall, if they were only willing enough to open their eyes to see and admit that the game was over.

People such as Brook Stevens and Charles Sorenson had great ideas for Studebaker's future. But to arrange for additional loans just to see the car plod along for a few more short years just didn't make sense.

Here are some photos of car ideas the designers had hoped would click. Hope you'll enjoy looking at some body styles of "What Might Have Been."

With great foresight, Brooks Stevens and Charles Sorensen thought they could still save Studebaker with this low cost fiberglass compact. The car, representing a cross between a sedan and a convertible station wagon, was to cost the purchaser about $1,100. It was estimated to be built for about $580. Innovations abounded on this vehicle, including automatic folding steps on the full-swing tailgate, a sliding roof over the rear area, and door tops cut into the roof for easy entry and exit.

Bob Bourke also had his hands in Studebaker's advanced planning, coming up with a prototype of what he felt the 1965 Hawk might have looked like. Not so, however, as the heavily chromed 1965s kept pace with all the other chromed beauties of the day.

# Epilogue

Brooks Stevens again had a "Better Idea" car and it wasn't from Ford either. This design was created in the mid-1960s and was called the Studebaker Scepter. This prototype was an earlier version than the car below, which also bore the name Scepter. The latter model today is in the Stevens Collection, but the fate of this model is not known. It was certainly typical of Studebaker to be a couple of jumps ahead of the rest of the industry, and to have come out with a car of this caliber if the financial picture had only looked brighter.

A front view of the 1966 Sceptre shows off a rather unique grille treatment. The lighting aspect of the front end is similar to what Mercury has done in recent years on its Sable. It just goes to show what was thought of some 30 years ago is just now coming on the market. If it was on sale today, it would surely be one of the best looking automobile on the block. The vehicle came with a slide rule speedometer and adjustable instrument gauges. The interior was in a special mylar upholstery. Studebaker reportedly had planned on this model to replace the Hawk line of vehicles. Today the car is still around, residing with the Brooks Stevens Collection.

Brooks Stevens got this model at least beyond the drawing board stage. It was his idea wagon for 1964, which had been conceived some while earlier, but never made it to assembly line. It featured center opening doors with no door pillar. The whole front end offered a more massive appearance. It's steering wheel, called the polo mallet, offered the tilt device which other companies had not yet marketed.

# About The Author

I was born loving cars. This pretty much sums it all up! I have remembered people by the car they own, and how long they've kept it, how well it was cared for, when it was traded in for a new one, etc. In fact, a couple of years ago, we had an eighth-grade school reunion. While we were visiting through the evening, someone asked me about a car they thought I may have forgotten about. I gave the correct answer and later said, "I remember what kind of car each of you owned in 1946, and who in the class had parents lucky enough to obtain a new one before graduating from eighth grade!" They all laughed but, when I reminisced and told one guy I remembered in the fifth grade they had come from Minnesota in a 1942 Chevy Master DeLuxe black Sedan, he looked at me and laughingly said, "He's weird." That might be true, but we all had a good laugh over it. Now, going back to my life. I taught school for 20 years, and for the past 15 years have enjoyed my avocation of selling automobile books and scale model cars through mail-order, car shows, and car-related meets throughout the country. I am married to Mary, a great person. I have two good kids and six terrific grandchildren. Jeri and Jeff are parents of Jenifer, Jaime, Jana and Jeffrey, while my son Mark and his wife, Pola, have Emily and Joe. I also have two swell sisters, Mary Therese and Rita, (who put up with all my car-noise impersonations and other car-related things throughout the years), three nieces and two nephews and their 15 offspring. There is the one still with us who helped start the whole thing, my 92-year old mother! Unfortunately, my dad, for whom I always had the highest regard, left us 15 years ago. He never owned a Studebaker either, but maybe one of these days I may choose to change that as I've looked at some of these different models I've written about and they really hold a soft spot with me. Hope you'll enjoy "Those Stupendous Studebakers" as much as I enjoyed writing it!